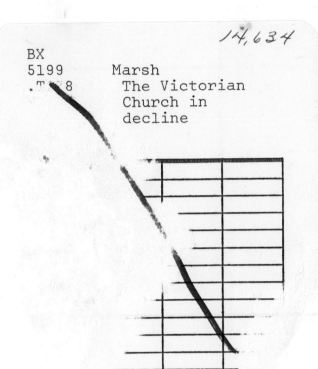

The Victorian Church in Decline

Archbishop Tait, reproduced by courtesy of Mrs E. H. Colville

The
Victorian Church
in Decline

ARCHBISHOP TAIT
AND THE CHURCH OF ENGLAND
1868–1882

P. T. Marsh

UNIVERSITY OF PITTSBURGH PRESS

First published 1969
by Routledge and Kegan Paul Ltd
Broadway House, 68–74 Carter Lane
London, E.C.4
Printed in Great Britain by
Western Printing Services Ltd, Bristol
© P. T. Marsh 1969
Published in U.S.A. by
University of Pittsburgh Press

Contents

To Margaret

List of Illustrations

Acknowledgements

PERHAPS the most valuable reward I have gained in investigating the subject matter of this book and writing it has been the counsel, assistance and friendship which teachers, librarians and colleagues too numerous to list in full have given me; and to each I wish to express my thanks. A few must be singled out by name. My supervisors at Cambridge, Dr. G. Kitson Clark and Professor Owen Chadwick, have continued to give me generous moral as well as academic support. Professor Asa Briggs and Professor Hilda Neatby helped make a year of further study in England available to me, as did the Canada Council which gave me a year's senior fellowship and in addition a summer research grant. The Warden and Fellows of All Souls College received me as the first and youngest of their visiting fellows cordially and sustained their interest in my work after I left. Mr. E. G. W. Bill and his staff at the Lambeth Palace Library did their best over several years to help me through the morass of the Tait papers even while they were being recatalogued. Mr. J. B. A. Boyle, Professor R. A. Soloway, Miss Anne Worden, Mr. J. S. G. Simmons, Dr. R. T. Shannon, Mr. Robert Blake and Dr. Clyde Binfield offered useful comments on individual chapters; Professor R. W. Greaves read through the final draft and kept me from going astray in many ways. The errors and weaknesses which remain are, of course, entirely my own. Mrs. E. H. Colville, Archbishop Tait's great-granddaughter, opened her home, family papers and photographs to me. Above all, my wife not only sustained and encouraged me even when she found the subject remote, but worked through each chapter helping to sift the wheat from the abundant chaff.

I am grateful also to Her Majesty the Queen for her gracious permission to make use of material from the Royal Archives at Windsor Castle, to the Trustees of the Broadlands Archives for permission to use the diary of the seventh Earl of Shaftesbury at the National Register of Archives, and to the National Trust for permission to quote from the Beaconsfield papers at Hughenden Manor. If by oversight I have trespassed upon anyone's copyright I sincerely apologize.

Note on References to the *Tait papers*

Because the recataloguing and indexing of the Tait papers have not been quite completed (April 1968), I have not been able to verify my references to a few of them. These references are readily distinguishable because they do not give the new volume and folio numbers and instead cite the numbering of the original letter registers (which are available), e.g. 'Penzance to Tait, 18 Dec. 1880, Tait papers, 1880 Home 144' or 'Memorandum on the representation of the clergy in Convocation, 31 Jan. 1881, by Selborne, Tait papers, 1880 separate packets'.

Introduction

FROM STRENGTH

For centuries there has not been a time of so much practical and
hearty work, so much earnest preaching, so much instruction and
consolation given, so much affectionate care for the poor and for
the young.

Gladstone to the Queen, 22 Jan. 1874

IN the first half of Queen Victoria's reign, until Gladstone's
electoral victory of 1868, the Church of England enjoyed its
last comparatively secure period of national strength. On the
negative side the Church's enemies, though newly invigorated,
were held in check. Protestant Nonconformists who were aware
that their following was approaching the size of that of the established Church and were therefore determined to end religious discrimination by the State found themselves, to their surprise, pushed
back into the political wilderness. Roman Catholicism, awakened
out of a century and a half of sleep by the conversion of Newman
and Manning, was disappointed that the subsequent flow of
defections from the Church of England never amounted to more
than a trickle. Freethought muffled its voice for fear of undermining popular morality.

Positively, the established Church displayed almost prodigious
energy. In the Oxford Movement it produced one of the two new,
wholly Anglican religious movements of major importance in the
Church of England's history.* The Church also proved most unexpectedly that it was capable of thorough administrative reform.
By spreading elementary schools over the country, the Church
sought to reassert its social and intellectual grip on the country.
Throughout the middle years of the nineteenth century to an
extent unprecedented at least since the thirteenth, members of the
Church, alive to its failures and inadequacies, dug into their

* The other was, of course, Methodism.

I

pockets, gave of their time, and devised fresh methods to make its institutions effective. There was not in the Victorian Church a great deal of the complacency which subsequent generations have claimed to see in it. Though authoritative statistical evidence of popular support is lacking except for 1851, and though indifference especially among the labouring classes and the destitute remained massive, it is probably correct to say that the Church of England made greater headway in these years than any of its religious rivals. Controversy among the parties or schools of thought within the Church became if anything more absorbing to the public and Parliament than controversy between denominations or about the relations of Church and State.

This compelling influence was a recent achievement and hard-earned. The established Church in mid-Victorian England does not fit into the general pattern of Church history from medieval power to modern obsoleteness which rationalists would like to see. Instead, as is true of most periods of vigour in a Church, its place is in a rhythm of torpidity, hostile threat, and reform. A spiritlessness overtook the Church of England after the death of Queen Anne. As early as the 1770s the Church showed signs of bestirring itself; the Evangelical revival which Methodism helped stimulate in the established Church revitalized the religion of a few; in reaction to the French Revolution the English governing classes began to take their Church much more seriously; and Evangelicals' agitation to stir the conscience of Parliament and abolish slavery produced famous results. Administratively, however, the Church of England remained perhaps the least reformed, most abuse-ridden Church in Christendom.

After Napoleon had been defeated, popular dissatisfaction in England with the institutions which upheld the existing order of society reached radical if not revolutionary proportions. The first defences to be broken by this agitation were those of the established Church. Repeal of the Test and Corporation Acts in 1828 and Roman Catholic emancipation in 1829 ended the Church of England's theoretically exclusive hold on the religious loyalties of Parliament. Once Parliament was overhauled by the 1832 Reform Act, friend and foe of the Church assumed that the Church would be dealt with quickly and in all likelihood more drastically. Thomas Arnold, the clerical headmaster of Rugby, concluded that 'The church as it now stands no human power can save.' In 1833 the Whig government of Earl Grey sought to appease discontent in Ireland by abolishing almost half the bishoprics of its established Church to which the English Church was constitutionally united. In an assize sermon at Oxford, John Keble described the implications of this measure as national apostasy.

Rather than despair, however, Arnold and Keble like so many of their fellow churchmen reacted to 'the encircling gloom'* with redoubled energy. The Romantic feeling and unwavering conviction with which Keble served the old-fashioned high and dry churchmanship of his upbringing did much to create the new and fervent high churchmanship of the Oxford Movement. Keble was quickly overshadowed by Newman whose personal magnetism and haunting power in the pulpit as vicar of St. Mary's, the university church at Oxford, impressed a decade of undergraduates indelibly. Some of them came up from Rugby where Arnold inspired a sometimes oppressive godliness not only among his own students but in other public schools reformed in keeping with his Rugby. The young men who studied at Rugby or Oxford in the 1830s carried something much more than Arnold's broad churchmanship or the precepts of the Oxford Movement into the England of the 1840s, '50s and '60s. They helped imbue its governors with a degree of moral earnestness and concern for religion unknown since the Civil War. Moreover, the Church of England became not much less effective than the Nonconformists among the middle classes. At any rate together churchmen's and Nonconformists' impact, augmented to a lesser extent by the Roman Catholics', marked mid-Victorian England out among highly civilized countries as 'one of the most religious that the world has known', to use Sir Robert Ensor's words.

Countrywide religious vitality would not, however, help to secure the Church of England's favoured constitutional position. Nearly all English communions were alert and active, and therefore denominational conflict was high. It was never higher than between 1828 and 1834 when Nonconformists thought themselves on the crest of a wave which would carry them to full religious equality with members of the established Church. To achieve that end it would be necessary not only to remove the civil penalties

---

* The hymn, 'Lead, kindly light, amid the encircling gloom'—Archbishop Tait's favourite—was written by Newman in 1833.

which had been imposed on Nonconformists such as their inability to solemnize legal marriages, but also to bring down the Church of England's overweening accumulation of privileges and wealth. The abuses which encrusted and debilitated the Church—pluralism, non-residence, and extreme variations in clerical income commonly leaving curates who did the work for absentee incumbents poverty stricken—made the demand for devastating action easy to justify.

The only way to ward off this threat to the established Church was for its sons to undertake the work of reform themselves and vigorously. The Ecclesiastical Commission incorporated in 1836 as a result of the Conservative leader, Sir Robert Peel's initiative and kept up to the mark by its dominant member Blomfield, the bishop of London, did precisely this. It worked amid cries of derision from Nonconformists and Radicals who thought it did too little, and cries of horror especially from high churchmen who thought it did too much, did the wrong things, and did them without proper ecclesiastical authority. It did enough to gain and keep the tolerant respect of the Whigs whose support was crucial in the political seesaw struggle between Church and Dissent. By 1840 most leading Churchmen recognized the wisdom of the Commission's assignment and, on the whole, of its conduct. The worst abuses in the Church had been or would soon be taken in hand, In addition, by cutting through the dense web of administrative laws which had paralysed the Church and by withdrawing funds especially from somnolent cathedral chapters, the Commission helped create and endow new parishes, many of them in the rapidly growing cities which until now the Church had largely neglected. Perhaps even more important, by making grants conditional on the collection of local voluntary contributions, the Ecclesiastical Commission stimulated a degree of personal giving unparalleled since the Reformation: a total of over £25½ million was spent on church building between 1840 and 1876.

This amalgam of administrative reform and the religious energies which the Ecclesiastical Commission could not create but released was what made the established Church strong and comparatively secure until 1868. Until then not just the constitutional union between Church and State but also many of the particular privileges of the Church such as its monopoly at the old universities survived. Indeed so did many of the civil badges of inferiority on Nonconformists including the one they resented most, their liability to pay rates voted locally for upkeep of the parish church.

The other means through which the established Church strengthened its hold on the country was elementary schooling. Members of the Church of England placed great, in fact excessive importance on all levels of educational institutions. Arnold went to Rugby and Tractarians riveted their attention on Oxford as fulcrums from which to move England. It was in providing elementary schools for the children of the labouring classes in town and country that the established Church made its highest, most costly bid to maintain something of its medieval social functions and, more important, to continue to form the mind of the nation. Elementary schooling among 'the poor' was almost virgin territory at the beginning of the century. The nondenominational British and Foreign Schools Society began work in 1808,* three years before its Anglican counterpart, the National Society. However, the National Society forged ahead so quickly that by 1833, when the government made its first grants for elementary education, Nonconformists felt abused because the grants were distributed to the rival societies in proportion to the work they were doing rather than with strict equality.

The State's entry into the field as the greatest single contributor of funds created another rivalry, much more ominous from the Church's point of view, namely between the National Society and the committee of the privy council which supervised the disposal of the government grants, over the extent to which the State should influence school policy. Stiffened by the uncompromising denominationalism of Archdeacon Denison, the National Society's will proved stronger than the State's. Government regulation was kept minimal. At the same time government grants became more generous. That this situation could develop proved the strength of the Church of England's grip at least on Parliament. The Church maintained its lead in elementary education until by 1870, of all schools receiving a government grant, Anglican schools outnumbered the total of the rest by almost three to two. The lead was not overwhelming, an indication that the Church of England's general pre-eminence in national life was marginal. Without

---

* Under a different title until 1814: the Institution for Promoting the British System for the Education of the Labouring and Manufacturing Classes of Society of Every Religious Persuasion.

continued financial support from the government, the Church's achievement in elementary schooling would be sharply deflated. Meanwhile, though, it could fairly be claimed that the established Church was England's educator.

To a lesser extent the Church was still moulding the thought of the country through other formal forums. After Newman's secession to Rome in 1845 and in reaction against the overheated theological wrangling of the early 1840s, Oxford's religious temperature fell sharply; but personable clerics there such as A. P. Stanley and H. P. Liddon exerted a winning influence. The sermon was still an effective means of persuasion not just upon the congregation which originally heard it but also in print.

On the whole the 1850s and early '60s were a period of balanced tensions for the Church of England. Its enemies were held in check but not vanquished. Parliament gave the Church the legislation it needed to be free of abuses and to build up its organization in neglected areas; but direct financial assistance such as Parliament had voted for new church building in 1818 and 1824 was politically quite impracticable now. Administrative reform through the Ecclesiastical Commission had become a permanent, continuing part of the Church's life, but particular policies of the Commission still came under heavy fire. Only momentarily stunned by Newman's apostasy, Tractarians strove on to enhance the Catholic traditions of the Church of England; however, it still remained overwhelmingly Protestant and so not repugnant to the old but strong popular prejudices of the country.

In 1851 the Church caught a glimpse of the fissures in the ground over which it was walking. A count of attendance at places of religious worship on one Sunday of that year, 30 March, was taken and analysed as a semi-official adjunct to the regular decennial census. The findings were a jolting disappointment for the established Church; and because of the subsequent denominational controversy, no such count was made under government auspices again in the nineteenth century. The census proved statistically what the repeal of the Test and Corporation Acts had implied theoretically: that the Church of England's right to continued recognition as the national Church was shaky. Of the 7,261,032 who attended one or more religious services, 3,773,474 or little more than half went to Anglican churches. Though this figure proved the Church of England to be far and away the largest single denomination, almost as large a number, 3,177,208, went to service in a chapel of one or other of the many Protestant Non-conformist denominations.* Some defenders of the Church's establishment attempted to reassure themselves by arguing that the 5,288,294 people who, according to calculations in the census report,[1] could have attended a religious service but did not were the particular responsibility of the national Church and thus were part of its constituency.

When denominational quarrelling subsided, however, this figure for more or less deliberate absentees seemed a greater cause for alarm than the 3,487,558 attendants at non-Anglican services. Perhaps England was not even a Christian let alone Anglican country. Certainly no denomination had won much support among the lower classes of the cities, which were well on their way to being the home of the majority of Englishmen. The census showed that the proportion of non-attendance was higher for urban than for rural areas.[2] Even with the aid of the Ecclesiastical Commission and Peel's enabling legislation, the Church never adequately adjusted itself to the shift of population into cities and from south to north. In the 1870s parishes in small towns or rural districts still outnumbered those in large towns or cities by more than three to one; there were five clergymen in nine of the dioceses in the south to every three clergymen in the six most northerly sees;[3] and the distribution of clerical salaries continued heavily to favour fashionable districts and the countryside against slums.

Nevertheless, in the 1850s and '60s members of the Church had responded to the revelation of their persistent failures with again redoubled energy and fresh thinking. For example, Bishop Blomfield had hoped to win over the areas to which population had spread or shifted in his diocese of London chiefly by building new churches. Many of them however, particularly those in poor areas, stood nearly empty. The man who succeeded him in 1856, the future Archbishop Tait, shifted attention to evangelism out of doors. Breaking through the dignity which encrusted his office, he preached, among other places, in Covent Garden to the costermongers and from the platform of a train to porters. In 1863 he organized a fund partly to continue building new churches to keep

* Parl. Papers, 1852–3, LXXXIX, 160. The figure for Roman Catholic attendance was 305,393.

pace with rising population but more to pay for men and women to go out into the highways and byways and draw the people in. Within nine months of the launching of his appeal, he had received almost £200,000.

The Church of England can be likened, during its quest in the middle half of the nineteenth century to reassert, extend and then maintain its national influence, to another Victorian institution, the Alpine climber. Between 1828 and 1833 part of the ground under the Church's feet fell away, but with resourceful determination it lifted itself safely up to a stretch of high terrain. The walking here was never secure; there were always crevices in sight; but for a while they served only to challenge the exhilarated walker to further efforts. However, the crevices widened. Soon after the publication of Darwin's *Origin of Species* in 1859, ideas capable of undermining commonly held Christian beliefs became popular debating topics. In 1862 the committee of the Council on Education insisted, though as yet ineffectually, that Church schools receiving a government grant must allow pupils, if their parents so wished, to withdraw from the classroom when religious instruction was given. Parliament became less reliable after the general election of 1865 and the subsequent death of the victor, Lord Palmerston. Palmerston's individual popularity in the country had helped him to hold back in Parliament the forces for change, among them militant Nonconformity, which were regaining out of doors the momentum they had lost in the 1830s. He was succeeded as prime minister by the progressive Whig, Russell. Russell, though, was seventy-three and since 1861 had been in the House of Lords. Power was moving into the hands of the new leader of the government in the Commons, Gladstone. In the recent elections Gladstone had been rejected by the clerical voters of the University of Oxford and had been returned to the Commons by the textile manufacturing constituency of South Lancashire instead. His Liberal impulses were thus unshackled.

The new Parliament was preoccupied with the subject of widening the franchise. Russell's government resigned after the failure of its Reform Bill and was replaced by a minority Conservative government led by Lord Derby and, upon his retirement, Disraeli. It was under their Ministry that the eventual Act of 1867 was passed, extending the franchise to embrace many in the working classes. Everyone sensed that the Act would soon lead to major, perhaps far-reaching changes of other sorts. However, no one knew quite what the lines of change would be, except that elementary education must be extended. To some like Robert Lowe and Carlyle the Reform Act seemed to mean almost certain disaster; others were reassured because it was produced under a Conservative government. The Church did not have to wait long for indications of what lay ahead for it. In the session after passing the Reform Act, Parliament followed Gladstone's leadership (without forcing Disraeli's resignation) in abolishing compulsory church rates and in moving to disestablish the Irish branch of the united Church of England and Ireland. The next Parliament which would be elected as soon as the 1867 Reform Act could be put into effect was unlikely to be kinder than this, if kind at all.

In fact the Church of England had come to the edge of its mid-Victorian highland. The edge did not turn out to be a cliff. In spite of dire predictions by friends and enemies, the Church was sufficiently strong and tactful to preserve its establishment, which it continued almost perversely to value. However, in spite of still energetic attempts by the Church to maintain its importance, it declined; the ground sloped away under the Church's feet to inconsequential lowland. The descent was irregular and confusing especially at first. But by the early 1880s it was unmistakable. The Church was then defensive and hesitant in intellectual controversy; religion had become almost without importance in this sphere. Furthermore the Church had been dethroned in the old universities, and its elementary schools were fighting for survival in competition with rate-financed ones. Popular opinion was both repelled by ritualism in the Church and disdainful of the bishops' attempts to crush it. Parliament usually ignored the Church, leaving its union with the State intact, but refusing to take seriously the legislation which the Church's leaders said it needed and at the same time denying it the legal power to legislate for itself.

Paradoxically between 1868 and 1882 the Church of England was led by the most powerful archbishop of Canterbury since the seventeenth century, Archibald Campbell Tait. The respect he commanded in the House of Lords was perhaps without precedent; judges and the bar honoured him for his judicial abilities;

9

he was the only archbishop whom Queen Victoria, normally quite anti-clerical, thoroughly liked. He was in large part responsible for the nineteenth century Parliament's one great attempt to govern the religious life of the established Church, the Public Worship Regulation Act of 1874. Not content to be mainly administrative overseer of the Church like all archbishops of Canterbury since Laud, he was always in the eye of the whirlwinds of internal controversy which characterized the Church during his primacy.

For he pursued a controversial policy which, though many-sided, was coherent and fairly clear: Protestant, mildly liberal, conciliatory to the Nonconformists, and Erastian, it was designed to preserve not just the establishment but the popular support and national influence of the Church which were the substantial justification for its establishment. As was inevitable in attempting to keep the Church congenial to Parliament and the public, Tait often took up spiritless, compromise positions. However, in general his leadership was vigorous, certainly vigorous enough to provoke running conflict with the most lively ecclesiastical party during his archiepiscopate, the High Church. High Churchmen were anxious to maintain and develop the Catholic traditions of the Church of England often in conscious defiance of popular and Parliamentary opinion. This opposition to Tait's policy reached the point of civil disobedience and eventually forced him to concern himself more with the unity of his Church than with its impact on the country. Never was debate within the established Church more bitter, and never, from the Church's point of view, more important. Though the debate focused often on what seems trivial and silly, at bottom the issue was how the Church ought to restore its social effectiveness. The bare truce concluded among its contradictory parties shortly before Tait's death indicated that it could not agree on an answer.

Note must be taken in this regard of the unusually great difficulties involved in labelling the Church of England's factions. In an essay in 1853 W. J. Conybeare described a basically threefold division of opinion, 'high', 'low' and 'broad'; and the names stuck. Like all Victorian party labels, political as well as ecclesiastical, these were unsatisfactory. 'Whig', to cite a political example, was used to refer both in an exclusive sense to a clique of aristocratic families and generally to those who were cautious reformers wedded to aristocratic predominance without being Conservatives. In both Church and State, mid-Victorian individualism played havoc with party lines. Ecclesiastical labels were the more confusing because most churchmen thought that commitment to party was not quite appropriate for men whose all-consuming loyalty ought to be to nothing less than the Church itself. Again and again a clergyman whose party leanings were otherwise clear would agree with his enemies against his friends on a particular issue as proof of his impartiality, a quality which, moreover, was highly regarded in a Church distinguished for its dislike of extremism. Party tags could never denote anything more precise than schools of thought or than generalizations riddled with exceptions.

Still, the label is indispensable. Across the many different controversies, certain steady and distinct bands in the spectrum of ecclesiastical opinion emerge. Furthermore, labels were important to contemporaries. Two central party organizations, the English Church Union for very high churchmen and the Church Association for the aggressively low, existed with branches throughout the country ready on any provocation to collect signatures or convene meetings. Everyone recognized party as one of the greatest facts in the affairs of the Church of England at the time.

By 1868 the distinction between one pair of tags, 'Low Church' and 'Evangelical', was becoming insignificant. The zeal of the Evangelical revival had begun to diminish even before William Wilberforce's death in 1833; but in attenuated form Evangelical piety was appropriated by the hitherto antagonistic Low Church whose roots had been formed, long before the Evangelical revival, from the Protestantism of the sixteenth century and the Puritanism of the seventeenth. To simplify matters therefore, the term 'Evangelical' which was now more common will be used for both groups. Conversely the much greater vitality of High Churchmanship in the 1870s accentuated differences between its various shades. Subdivision, though cumbersome, is necessary. The old school of High Churchmen often dubbed 'high and dry', whose characteristic toast was to Church and State, were being superseded by a younger group of moderates influenced by the Oxford Movement. Both of these High Church groups were uncomfortable about their relation to pure disciples of the Oxford Movement, the Tractarians. Young men in the 1830s when Newman's influence pervaded Oxford, Tractarians in turn felt uneasy about the new generation of pace-setters called ritualists.* Consequently the term 'Anglo-Catholic' which lumped both together will be avoided as confusing though it had begun to be used. Finally, among Broad Churchmen, heirs of the eighteenth-century latitudinarians, there was a similar division between generations but not sufficiently marked at the time to acquire separate labels.

One final word about terminology. 'The Church' and 'Churchmen' are used often in this study to denote the Church of England and its members, not out of Anglican arrogance but because these terms were so employed by contemporaries and for convenience. Simply for convenience, this study frequently uses the name 'Convocation' by itself to mean the Convocation of the province of Canterbury, never the Convocation of York.

To resume, study of the first years in the decline of the Victorian Church centres naturally on Archbishop Tait. Not only was he the pivotal figure in internal controversy, but his attempts to win ecclesiastical legislation from Parliament accentuated Parliament's increasing unwillingness to spend its time debating Church affairs. He also left behind in the form of his papers a richly detailed picture of the Church under his leadership. The Tait papers contain endless bundles of incoming letters from clergy and politicians and, especially as time went on, copies of his replies; heavy volumes of clippings from a wide range of newpapers combed by the archbishop's chaplains; and a weekly diary dictated to one of his womenfolk in which he recapitulated his week's activities and observations.

Tait has been well, a bit too well served by his official biographers, William Benham and Randall Davidson.† The dominant author was Davidson, who was chaplain to Tait from 1877 on, married his daughter and became his most trusted adviser, indeed almost his suffragan for archiepiscopal matters. Benham,

---

* That was the term contemporaries used. Its inappropriateness has since been pointed out. The men referred to were distinguished for their use of ornaments and *ceremonial*, i.e. symbolic clothes and actions, rather than for unusual *rites*, i.e. liturgical services consisting essentially of words to be read or sung.

† R. T. Davidson and William Benham, *Life of Archibald Campbell Tait, Archbishop of Canterbury* (London, Macmillan & Co., 1891), 2 vols., henceforward referred to simply as Davidson and Benham, *Tait*.

an honorary canon of Canterbury who had edited Tait's memoir of his wife and son,[4] was in this case again, one suspects, only the scribe. The *Life* of Tait reads like Foreign Office histories; it is immensely well informed and intelligent but written from the viewpoint of Lambeth Palace and calculated not to embarrass subsequent heads of the administration. For upon Tait's death Davidson was taken over as a leading counsellor both by Queen Victoria who made him dean of Windsor and by Tait's immediate successor, Archbishop Benson; and while serving in these capacities he wrote the *Life*. (In 1903 Davidson became archbishop of Canterbury himself.) Moreover Gladstone and the Queen were just two of the figures important to the story who were still alive when he wrote and therefore had to be discussed with great reticence. Davidson also admitted that he did not make use of the bulk of Tait's routine business correspondence although he recognized that it could provide an unusually good picture of the established Church in his day.[5] A new investigation of Tait's archiepiscopate has therefore been in order even apart from the advantages in perspective which later study can give.

Tait was born on 21 December 1811 in Edinburgh and of Scottish Presbyterian parents. He was to be the first Scottish archbishop of Canterbury and always thoroughly Protestant in churchmanship. The bedrock of his character hardened early: he was born with club feet. At the age of eight he was sent to a crude but able straightener of limbs at Whitworth near Rochdale who encased the boy's feet in tin boots to be worn night and day. Excruciating though this treatment was, it did the job. A few years afterward Tait was stunned by his first encounter with death;* the death of the brother who had accompanied him to Whitworth. However then for over twenty years unchecked success flowed Tait's way; at fourteen he was leading prizewinner at the Edinburgh Academy; after three years at Glasgow University he won a Snell Exhibition to Balliol College, Oxford, where he subsequently became fellow and senior tutor; in 1842 at thirty years of age he was elected to succeed Thomas Arnold as headmaster of Rugby, and it grew and prospered under Tait's management even more than before.

In spite of his Presbyterian upbringing at Edinburgh and

* His mother died when he was two, too young of course to know what had happened.

Glasgow Tait had been attracted by the Episcopal Church of
Scotland to which some of his more affluent relatives belonged;*
and on going up to Oxford he not only subscribed to the Thirty-
nine Articles of the Church of England as was necessary in order
to matriculate, but he was also confirmed at the hands of the
bishop of Oxford. In 1836 soon after accepting a Balliol tutorship
Tait was ordained. His decision to become a clergyman was
accompanied by a fervour which would have been unfamiliar in
the dry years of the mid-eighteenth century; but equally the
decision did not represent a powerful sense of religious vocation
as would be expected later in the nineteenth century. Tait took
Holy Orders as part of his responsibilities as fellow and tutor at
Balliol but chiefly as entry into the most serious of professions. He
embraced the Church of England, as other distinguished Scots
such as Brougham joined the Whig party, both through conviction and as an avenue to usefulness and power. The Calvinism
of the Church of Scotland (and of strict Evangelicals in the Church
of England) repelled him, and in 1838 he gave up the likelihood
of a Glasgow professorship rather than subscribe to the Westminster Confession of Faith. On the other hand, even before he
was confirmed a member of the Church of England, he had made
repeated half-humorous references to becoming archbishop of
Canterbury. Tait was conscious of his distinguished abilities: a
first-class mind, though it never gave him the interests of a scholar
and was not coupled with imagination; persuasiveness though not
eloquence in speech; above all tough common sense. And he was
ambitious.

Unlike most Victorian religious figures, Tait was not at all a
Romantic. He scorned emotive, mystical thinking. This characteristic coupled with the honour in which he continued to hold
Presbyterian piety made him immune to the appeal which Newman
and the Oxford Movement possessed for most of his bright contemporaries at Oxford. Tait made his debut in national ecclesiastical affairs by launching the Four Tutors' protest against Newman's
Tract XC, an act which marked the end of the rise in popularity of
the Oxford Movement. Because of Tait's temperament he could
so easily have become just another cleric whose childhood and
youthful religious feeling was dried up by self-confidence, ambi-

* Though of the gentry, Tait's father had impoverished the family in foolish
attempts to extend and improve his land.

tion and a measure of success. The danger was the greater because his theological principles coincided with prejudices popular in the country and because he thought that this popularity proved the rightness of his principles. He did not even pay lip service to the Biblical predictions of persecution and martyrdom so dear to Tractarian hearts.

He was saved from the danger of personal religious aridity, as even his enemies came to recognize, by intimacy with physical suffering and death. His life was a continual rhythm of professional success and personal disaster. In 1848 he was nearly killed by an attack of rheumatic fever. He retired from Rugby to convalesce as dean of Carlisle. Driven by desire to work hard again and released from minor cares by his devoted wife, Catharine Spooner, whom he had married in 1843, Tait recuperated enough by 1850 to take a leading part in the royal commission set up by Lord John Russell to reform Oxford. Yet Tait passed few years in the rest of his life without another stroke and few days without feeling danger signals. Friends of later days could always tell when he was about to speak in the House of Lords by a slight twitching in the arm which had been paralysed; and on horseback he had to assume an almost ludicrously bent position. However, by shepherding his strength unceasingly, he was able to do more work than most men in unblemished health.

In 1856 Tait became as familiar with death as with precarious health. Between 6 March and 8 April of that year five of his children ranging in age from ten years to eighteen months died at Carlisle in a scarlet fever epidemic. He was rescued from a state of profound shock by an abrupt summons to one of the highest ecclesiastical offices, the bishopric of London. Commemoration of the anniversaries of his girls' deaths was a nevertheless recurring feature of his weekly journal for the rest of his life. He would often note how old each would have been and how long she had been with God.

Before the tragedy, he was known to be in line for a bishopric. He had been very disappointed when passed over for the vacant bishopric of Carlisle earlier in 1856. Apart from his evident ability, he had earned the gratitude of the Whigs especially by his enthusiastic service on the Commission to Reform Oxford. Still, his nomination in September by Palmerston to London was astonishing; experience of a less important bishopric had been considered almost invariably a prerequisite for nomination to London. Lord Shaftesbury, Palmerston's usual adviser on ecclesiastical appointments, had suggested Tait as the best of the moderate Broad Churchmen, but only for a lower bishopric. Wellesley, dean of Windsor, had urged Tait's name on Prince Albert for a similar reason. The Queen in common with the higher levels of English society was moved by Tait's recent tragedy and may out of sympathy have pressed Palmerston to nominate him. Yet the final decision must have been Palmerston's. Without a moment's hesitancy Tait decided to accept the nomination upon receiving Palmerston's letter, and did his praying later. The enterprise with which he served in London fully bore out the wisdom of the appointment. In 1862 when the strain of this populous diocese seemed to be getting the better of him, Palmerston offered him the less onerous archbishopric of York. Tait was not tempted by such partial though august retirement and declined the invitation.

In spite of his proven worth, his nomination by Disraeli in November 1868 to the archbishopric of Canterbury—also deemed less exacting than London but of potentially greater power—was surprising. Unlike all eighteenth- and previous nineteenth-century archbishops of Canterbury, Tait was not a 'safe' candidate. He was a bit too energetic for politicians' comfort; as Disraeli put it to the Queen, 'though apparently of a spirit somewhat austere, there is in his idiosyncrasy a strange fund of enthusiasm, a quality which ought never to be possessed by an Archbishop of Canterbury, or', he added with obvious reference to Gladstone, 'a Prime Minister of England.'[7] More worrisome to anyone anxious not to rock the ecclesiastical boat, Tait, realizing that dogmatism in the Church would repel the educated public, was noted for his attempts to protect Broad Church writers in a time when the general sentiment in the Church was fiercely against them.* It was this which disconcerted Disraeli, not Tait's Whiggery. Disraeli, on the verge of a general election, would need all the Whig votes he could win over if he were to achieve a Conservative majority. However he placed more stock on securing support from the rank and file of the parochial clergy so strategically situated in each community. As a rule these men disliked both 'Rits and Rats', to use Disraeli's nickname for the two disturb-

---

* His record in this regard was seriously tarnished, however, by his capitulation in 1861 to the demand that the bench of bishops censure *Essays and Reviews*.

ing minorities, ritualists and rationalizing Broad Churchmen. Disraeli wanted to nominate a moderate evangelical who was also a loyal Conservative, Ellicott, bishop of Gloucester and Bristol.

It was the Queen who pushed Tait's candidacy. His inclinations were hers: schooled by Prince Albert, she was aggressively Broad Church; Tait was from her beloved Scotland; and he was united with her in the experience of tragic death. Disraeli was no match for her on this occasion because, unlike Gladstone, he was never at home in ecclesiastical matters. 'I don't know personally the Bishop of Gloucester', he moaned to Lord Derby, '—and you can't fight for a person you don't know.'[8] He gave into the Queen, but bitterly. Leaving the royal closet, he waved Lord Malmesbury off: 'Don't bring any more bothers before me; I have enough already to drive a man mad.'[9]

The new archbishop was an imposing figure: tall, initially slight but by the mid-1870s quite portly, clean shaven as befitted a clergyman, with dark wavy hair parted in the middle and reaching almost to his shoulders, but in total effect unquestionably manly. He bore himself with great but natural dignity; he looked every inch the primate. Nevertheless contemporaries recognized him to be a remarkably atypical ecclesiastic. He was soon called—with unusual respect by laymen of substance, with a sneer by his clerical critics—'the layman's archbishop'. His friends knew that to be called an 'ecclesiastic' by him was to be insulted. The part of his responsibilities he loved best was the work in Parliament. Each morning he had his chaplains read from the newspapers the foreign intelligence first, then about domestic politics, and only afterwards the ecclesiastical news—which he must often have greeted with a weary sigh.

The domestic news which came in as he tidied up his London desk and awaited consecration to the primacy was, as it would be so often during his archiepiscopate, an inextricable mixture of the political and ecclesiastical and was distressing. The returns in the general election gave a crushing majority to Gladstone, once the uncompromising champion of the union of Church and State, now the darling of the Nonconformists. The main national issue in the campaign had been Gladstone's pledge to disestablish the Irish Church forthwith.

Chapter One

THE DISESTABLISHMENT OF THE IRISH CHURCH, 1868-1869

CHEERS greeted Gladstone from all the Liberal benches when he had proposed, in March 1868, to disestablish the Irish Church. Previously divided and disheartened, the Liberals were suddenly galvanized by a clear, commanding policy and resolute leadership. Their response also indicated that, though most of them were adherents of the established Church of England and Ireland, they were willing to subordinate its interests to social and political exigencies. Furthermore, Gladstone's action showed the increasing influence of militant Nonconformists on Liberal strategy. The attack confronted the established Church and its leaders in England as well as Ireland with the need to devise a defence of its best interests, not only religious but also social, of the people of both islands.

In the Parliamentary arena, Gladstone's stroke was masterful. Lord Derby and Disraeli had driven the Russell–Gladstone government from office in 1866 by playing on the disagreements among its supporters over Russell's Parliamentary Reform Bill. Then, by the same tactics, the Conservatives not only stayed in office, but stole their opponents' thunder by passing a reform bill themselves. Their Act was all the more discouraging to the Liberals because it was more radical than even the Radicals had expected. Now no one could be sure whether the newly enfranchised working classes would conclude, as Derby and Disraeli hoped, that the Conservatives were the truest spokesmen for their interests. The vistas opened up to Liberals and Radicals by Palmerston's death clouded over.

18

Ireland cleared the view again. Fenian subversion became alarming after the release in 1865 at the end of the American Civil War of the Irish troops who had fought in it. The outrages in England reached a climax in December 1867, with the dynamiting of Clerkenwell Prison to release two Fenian prisoners. Twelve people were killed and about 120 others hurt, including children. As a result, the perennial Irish question forced its way into the vacuum left by the settling of the issue of reform. Neither the Liberals nor the Conservatives had worked out an agreed Irish policy yet; but all eyes turned to the Irish Church, the most obvious and least valuable symbol of the English yoke which Irishmen fretted under.

Disraeli, prime minister after Derby retired in February 1868, left the initiative to Gladstone, in the hope that any proposal he might make to appease and win the support of the Irish Roman Catholics would alienate the Protestants elsewhere. What Gladstone proposed was unexpectedly drastic. Nevertheless, unlike Russell's reform bill, Irish disestablishment united his supporters. Roundell Palmer, Gladstone's one time colleague in defence of Oxford and the English Church, was the only important defector. The policy which brought the Opposition together divided the Conservative leadership. Derby, Gathorne Hardy, the Home Secretary, and Cairns, the Lord Chancellor, were for uncompromising resistance; Stanley, the Foreign Secretary, and Pakington at the War Office thought this response was sure to fail and wanted only to secure the best terms for a disestablished Irish Church; Disraeli and Derby favoured concurrent endowment of the three major Irish denominations, Roman Catholic, Presbyterian and Anglican, rather than disestablishing the Anglican Church, but Cairns' Protestant churchmanship made him oppose concurrent endowment of popery almost as strongly as disestablishment.[1]

Although disestablishment was intended as an answer to the Irish question, the Liberals' case was disturbing for the English establishment as well. Liberals argued that the Irish establishment was indefensible because it lavished prestige and wealth on a denomination supported by only a small minority of Irishmen: of Ireland's 5,798,967 people in 1861, only 693,357 were members of the Church of Ireland; and though it was much the largest non-Roman denomination, there were 4,505,265 Roman Catholics.[2] English Churchmen knew that their Church, though much the largest in the country, did not enjoy the support of half the

19

population.[3] Irish hatred of their establishment arose even more from the fact that it was imposed on them by foreigners and found its greatest support in Ireland among the English and Anglo-Irish landlords. The parallel with the English Church in this case was much more distant; but in England too the established Church was identified with the landed classes, and although they were not disliked as foreigners, jealousy of the social dominance they and their Church enjoyed had long been an emotion to reckon with among the middle classes, and was spreading.

Militant Dissenters and their Radical allies made it clear that they attacked the Irish establishment as the most vulnerable outpost of the English establishment, which was their main target.[4] This was not the goal of a negligible few. Over the previous quarter century Nonconformity as a whole had moved into closer sympathy with the fight for religious equality organized by the Liberation Society. Even the Wesleyans, firmly Conservative a generation before, were now inclined to sympathize with the Liberals. The other Nonconformists offered up prayers for the success of Gladstone's proposal; and denominational assemblies of Congregationalists, Baptists and Unitarians gave it full support.[5]

The fortunes of the Church of England had been closely linked to its Irish sister. The Act of Union of 1800 joining the two countries had also united the two Churches. Since then there had been one outstanding instance of legislation tried out on the Irish Church and then applied to England: the Irish Church Temporalities Act of 1833 provided precedent for the formation of the Ecclesiastical Commission in England shortly afterwards.

The chief source of comfort for churchmen in Gladstone's assault was the assailant himself. Gladstone had been much the greatest defender of the Church in Parliament. His policy now and the fervour with which he preached it on the hustings were alarming, and he announced his willingness to apply to the English establishment the same test of popular support which condemned the Irish. However, he made it clear that he believed the English establishment could pass;[6] and, as he later told the Queen, he thought that the establishment would be stronger in England when no longer tied to its indefensible Irish counterpart.[7]

Still, even the most ardent Anglican supporters of Gladstone did not claim that his chief motive in opposing the establishment in Ireland was to strengthen it in England. Lord Shaftesbury was inclined at first to credit Gladstone with concern for the highest interests of the Irish Church in leading this attack but was disillusioned when one of Gladstone's closest friends, the duke of Argyll, explained that 'there was really no other way of getting Dizzy out of office!'[8] Gladstone was seeking his own political interests along with the welfare of Ireland. After twelve years of agitation, Edward Miall and his Liberationists had succeeded in making Irish disestablishment practical politics, and Gladstone, who as recently as 1866 had dismissed the issue, now took over the leadership of their attack. It seemed more than possible in 1868 that the Liberationists could do the same against the English establishment, and it was by no means certain that, when the time was ripe, the attack would not be led again by Mr. Gladstone.

He followed up the announcement of his opposition to the Irish establishment with a series of resolutions embodying his views. He carried them against Disraeli's government in the House of Commons by a majority of 48, and then conducted a Suspensory Bill through the Commons to prevent the Crown nominating men to offices in the Irish Church before Parliament reached a decision on its fate. In this way, despite the Lords' rejection of the Bill, Gladstone forced a general election which would be fought primarily over the issue he had raised. However, because of Parliament's desire to bring the provisions of the Reform Act into effect for this election, it had to be delayed till the end of the year. Meanwhile Disraeli was able to cling to office.

As a result, men whose primary concern was for the established Church had ample time to make their influence felt on the outcome of the election. Such men were no more than a minority of the Church's adherents. As always, Church allegiance was only one of the claims on men's loyalty and did not necessarily determine their decision. Furthermore, to criticize the Church of Ireland's establishment was not at all equivalent to criticizing the Church of Ireland as a Church. The majority of English Liberal M.P.s were members of the Church of England. They supported Irish disestablishment, not as an attack on the Irish Church, but as a means to quieten Irish discontent; and many other Churchmen agreed. Then too, the election was not a referendum on the one issue of Irish disestablishment. Each constituency had its local concerns, and other issues such as the inadequacy of elementary schooling commanded national attention. This mixture of issues and loyalties prevented the election campaign from becoming a plain denominational conflict.

In fact, only a few Churchmen responded to Gladstone's proposal by insisting, with almost total disregard of the urgent political problem in Ireland, that disestablishment must be decided on purely religious grounds. G. A. Denison, archdeacon of Taunton, pushed aside 'the false tints of social amendment, and the coarse colouring of political party' from the debate: 'Are questions of land and water', he asked, 'to make a difference of truth and fact?'[9] Denison sensed that any attempt to defend the Irish establishment on social or political grounds would be feeble. He faced up to Irish disaffection only enough to plead that disestablishment would aggravate it; he was even unwilling to support reform of the establishment,[10] the alternative to which all but the most extreme opponents of Liberal policy resorted.

This singlemindedness sharpened his insight into the religious implications of disestablishment. Denison could see that disestablishment, justified on social grounds, would increase the popular tendency to pay more attention to social pressures than to the interests of the Church; it would, he said, raise doubts about the importance of Christianity to men's welfare.[11] Moreover, because the decision would be arrived at in a general election, an adverse verdict would indicate that the loosening of popular allegiance to the Church had already gone a long way. T. R. Birks, an evangelical theologian, put it another way: 'The assault on the Irish Church is simply the crest of the immense tidewave of unbelief, which is sweeping over Christendom at the present hour.'[12]

Disregard of the problem in Ireland facing the politicians bred political ineptitude. The key in which men like J. W. Burgon (later dean of Chichester) pitched their case, stating for instance that Irish disestablishment meant no less than rejection of God by the nation,[13] was too high to do anything but repel doubtful voters. Denison stressed the inviolability of the Queen's Coronation Oath to defend the established Church,[14] a shield of straw against widespread popular agitation. In trying to uphold the Irish establishment by emphasizing its similarity to the English, he compromised himself for future battle. Denison did more than argue. He organized a Church and State Defence Society which sent to all incumbents and churchwardens copies of an address for signature to be sent to the Crown against disestablishment and disendowment. The response was poor, partly because addresses were useless when a general election was being held over the question. Undeterred, in December Denison presented his address and the signatures he had collected to the out-going Conservative Home Secretary just on his way to surrender his seals of office to the Queen.[15]

Some die-hard Churchmen opposed to Irish disestablishment argued as Tories, but in doing so, though gaining slightly in political effectiveness, they lost Denison's religious insights. The Church Institution is a case in point. Already in existence as a political pressure group to maintain the establishment in England and Ireland, it set to work on M.P.s as soon as Gladstone began his attack, and when the campaign moved to the constituencies, the the Church Institution followed with lectures and pamphlets. It also helped instigate the holding of a great rally in London of leaders in Church and State opposed to the Liberal policy. The Institution was sufficiently useful for the Conservative party to keep an agent in touch with it.[16] Its arguments, however, consisted of little more than hostility to any appeasement of Irish nationalism and unyielding determination to maintain every feature of the English supremacy.[17] The Institution's most able spokesman, the Rev. Dr. A. T. Lee, devoted much of his attention to a defence of the Irish Church's title to its property.[18]

Tait, bishop of London until late in 1868, gave a strong lead to the Anglican opposition to Irish disestablishment; but his argument[19] was an awkward combination of religious and political elements, indicative of the dilemma in which he found himself. On the one hand, establishment was almost indispensable to the well-being of the Church as he conceived it. On the other hand, his political sympathies lay with the Liberal party, and he appreciated the need to pacify Ireland.

Already Tait had distinguished himself on the bench of bishops as the leading defender of the religious worth of establishment. He was modestly Broad Church, in sympathy with the attempts of some of the clergy to liberalize the theology of the Church to bring it into harmony with the tenor of thoughtful lay opinion. By placing disputes about the Church's teaching under the dispassionate jurisdiction of the country's courts, establishment protected this unpopular minority from the attacks of the belligerently orthodox majority of the clergy. Tait also shared the Evangelicals' strong hostility to Roman Catholicism, and this fortified his opposition to disestablishment in Ireland. When presenting this point, he spoke the traditional language of English Protestantism: there could never be equality, he said, between a Protestant Church weakened by disestablishment and disendowment, and

a powerful Roman Catholic body with a foreign Prince at its head, who has the power of conferring titles of honour, and placing the chief dignitaries of his Church in a position which no clergyman of a disendowed Protestant Church can possibly assume.[20]

In politics Tait's leanings were Liberal, but the Liberal policy for Ireland was now at odds with his Broad Church and Protestant support for the Irish establishment. He solved the problem by adopting a diagnosis of Ireland's ills different from the official Liberal one. He would not deny that the Liberals were right in trying to pacify the country, but whereas they said that the cause of the discontent was Irish dislike of an alien establishment, Tait said it was internal disunity. He proceeded then to argue that establishment was an asset since it imposed national responsibilities on the Irish Church: its clergy were responsible for all the inhabitants of their parishes whether Church supporters or not.

Admittedly establishment was not enough by itself to draw Ireland together. Tait vindicated his tarnished Liberalism by recommending a national system of schools for Ireland. This would reinforce the unifying influence of establishment by bringing Irish children from all religious backgrounds to be taught together. However, he pointed out, the chief opponents of such a scheme in Ireland were the Roman Catholic clergy, and they would be able to hold it back permanently if they won as much unchecked power as disestablishment would give them. He did not point out, because he was not proud of the fact, that the chief opponents of the same scheme for England were the Anglican clergy.

The rest of Tait's argument showed the same mixture of moderate reform and fear of the consequences of disestablishment. He warned that the Irish ultramontanes would try to undermine the United Kingdom by going on, if they gained disestablishment, to agitate about Irish land and repeal of the Act of Union. Nonetheless, ever since his undergraduate days he had favoured concurrent endowment of all Churches in Ireland to reduce resentment of the privileged status of the minority Church while retaining the benefits of its establishment. This policy had never been popular in Protestant England, and he said nothing about it before the election, but afterwards he repeatedly voted for it in the House of Lords. He did not hesitate at any time to admit the need for reform of the Irish establishment, and would even have acepted some disendowment. He counselled other defenders of the Irish Church to conduct their campaign along similarly moderate lines.[21]

A small though distinguished group of Churchmen including Frederick Temple, later archbishop of Canterbury, Connop Thirlwall, the doughty scholar bishop of St. David's, and F. D. Maurice, a searching and inspiring but obscure theologian, took Tait's concern about the political problem in Ireland further, and supported Gladstone's policy. They refused to separate social welfare from religion: social justice was to them as much a religious principle as those which Archdeacon Denison so uncompromisingly maintained,[22] and its dictates on the present issue were clear. Maurice published his version of this point of view in the *Contemporary Review*[23] even before Gladstone made his move. Later, at the beginning of the election campaign, he wrote a series of eight long letters to the *Daily News*[24] on the issues before the voters, pre-eminently Irish disestablishment.

Unlike Tait, Maurice accepted the prevailing Liberal opinion that Irish discontent arose from nationalistic sentiments, and he admitted that the Irish establishment was to blame. What distinguished Maurice from other Churchmen with Liberal political sympathies was that he had worked out a more integrated religious and political viewpoint than they. Many of them, like Tait, shared in the optimism of Victorian England and were convinced by the economic and political arguments of classical Liberalism without reconciling them adequately with their religious beliefs. The Liberalism of a few churchmen, like Jowett of Balliol, was one expression of the weakening of their religious certainty. Maurice, on the other hand, had a burning religious conviction, and his social principles were the result of his theology which was his all-pervasive concern. He had tried in many ways throughout his life, which was nearly over, to convince his fellow countrymen that the kingdom of Christ was not equivalent to the Church, but equally embraced civil society; the term 'Christian socialism' he had coined as one expression of this belief. Whatever, like Irish establishment, undermined the welfare of a country was as opposed to Christ's kingdom as any heresy.

That the Irish Church should have fallen into this situation was for Maurice a travesty of its Reformation heritage. The outstanding principle of the English Reformation in his opinion had been its assertion of the proper rights of the nation: that Christ rather than the pope was the king of kings, and that Christ's lordship united both the nation, which bound together all the people of one country, and the universal Church, which transcended national and racial barriers, into one divine economy. However, establishment in Ireland meant the imposition of a Church by a foreign government, and was therefore a denial of Ireland's rightful religious distinctiveness. Roman Catholicism, which was essentially hostile to national religious rights, had flourished in Ireland by identifying itself with the justifiable hatred Irishmen felt towards an alien Church. Free the Irish Church of the harmful trappings of establishment, and its testimony to Ireland's rights could become clear and winning. Nevertheless, Maurice was no advocate of political Home Rule for Ireland; he was something of an imperialist, happy to have a son in the British army in India; and, like all English Liberals, he hoped that disestablishment of the Church in Ireland would evoke warmer acceptance of its civil government.

There was enough division and uncertainty of opinion on Irish disestablishment in the Church of England to prevent the Church from exercising decisive influence in the general election. Even though the Church Congress, an annual conference of clergymen and laymen of the Church of England and Ireland, met in the autumn of 1868 in Dublin, it felt obliged to treat Irish disestablishment in its discussions as it would most questions dividing the main political parties, and steered clear of the issue of the hour. Of all the ecclesiastical parties within the Church only the evangelicals were united in opposition to Gladstone's policy. In addition to being the most stoutly anti-papist of English churchmen, most evangelicals were Whig politically, their day in the sun had come under Palmerston, and they felt little sympathy for the new Liberalism emerging under Gladstone's leadership. Broad churchmen leant towards Liberalism in politics as in theology.

The balance lay with High Churchmen, and they were divided. Some including Bishop Wilberforce, despite his close friendship with Gladstone, fought against Irish disestablishment vigorously;[25]

but many were unenthusiastic, and a small Anglo-Catholic minority welcomed the proposal. High Churchmen influenced by the Oxford Movement were apprehensive about the impact on the Church of union with a State increasingly willing to respond to the demands of a religiously pluralist society. To vote Conservative offered no escape from their uneasiness, for this kind of liberalism tainted the Conservative party only less than the Liberal: the Conservatives' alternative to disestablishment of the Irish Church was drastic reform of it. Conservatives defended the union of Church and State more strongly than the Liberals, but it was this union which had High Churchmen worried. Furthermore, the subjection of disputes about Church doctrine and worship to the decision of civil courts, which pleased Tait, annoyed them. They regarded the Broad Churchmen and Evangelicals whom the courts had protected as little better than heretics, and the courts were going on to threaten the legality of anglo-catholic teaching and practice. Some high churchmen such as Keble, without sympathizing with the Liberal party, accepted the argument that social justice demanded Irish disestablishment[26] because Gladstone said so, and Gladstone had earned their love by fighting their ecclesiastical battles in and out of cabinets for thirty years.

The great middling body of Church opinion, the loyal rank and file and the clergy who did not belong to any Church party, were unhappy about Irish disestablishment. They did not sympathize with High Churchmen's fears about establishment or with Broad Churchmen's theological liberalism: love for the familiar, age-old order of Church and State dominated their response, and they were ready to be convinced that Irish discontent did not make disestablishment a necessity. Disraeli tried to appeal to this potential support and to confirm evangelicals in their opposition to Irish disestablishment by tailoring his ecclesiastical appointments to suit their tastes.[27] He sent Hugh McNeile, a well known Evangelical preacher against popery, to the deanery of Ripon; but that was enough for the Queen. She turned down Disraeli's nominee for the bishopric of Peterborough, another Evangelical, Canon Champneys, in favour of an eloquent Irishman of indistinct religious views, W. C. Magee.*

* Magee proved immediately to be a useful spokesman of Conservative opinion in the House of Lords, and was appointed by Disraeli's successor as Conservative leader, Lord Salisbury, to the archbishopric of York.

Then, just before voting in the general election was to begin, Disraeli found himself with a superb opportunity to make his ecclesiastical policy unmistakable: Longley, the archbishop of Canterbury, died after a brief illness. Disraeli could not, however, find a satisfactory nominee for the vacant archbishopric. The mildly Evangelical churchmanship and Conservative politics of Disraeli's nominee, Ellicott, were unexceptionable on paper, but personally the man was a busybody. 'Is he *really* such a fool as he seems to me?' Lord Granville asked of him.[28] Still, Disraeli had abundant reason for losing his usual composure when the Queen forced him to give the vacant archbishopric to Tait, a Whig though sound on the issue of the hour and a prelate whose broad church sympathies made most clergymen anxious. As it turned out, though relations between Disraeli and Tait would never be easy, each in his own field would commonly be preoccupied with the same opponent, Gladstone. Had Longley lived a few weeks longer or had the general election been a few weeks earlier, Gladstone would have been prime minister and the new archbishop of Canterbury would have been Tait's main rival, Samuel Wilberforce, the bishop of Oxford, who served for the high church the same function on the bench of bishops as Tait served for the broad.

The verdict of the general election was emphatic. The returns gave the Liberals a majority of 110.[29] What made the result particularly disturbing for the Church of England was the fact that the magnitude of the victory was due to the support Scottish Presbyterians, Irish Roman Catholics and English and Welsh Nonconformists gave the Liberals; and Gladstone knew it.[30] Furthermore, though a large majority of the elected Liberal M.P.s disliked the root and branch hostility to all establishments felt by militant Dissenters, they had won a right to greatly increased influence in Liberal councils. Liberals enjoyed the fruits of Liberationist agitation especially in Wales where, in what amounted to an electoral revolution, they won 23 of its 33 seats.[31] Generally Liberationists contributed the bulk of the independent pamphlets—825,000[32]— and speeches against the Irish establishment. The harvest of the Liberation Society's five-year campaign on its own behalf came in: 95 of the successful Liberal candidates were claimed by the Society as opponents of establishment in England,[33] one of them,

John Bright, was a leading member of the new cabinet, and another, James Stansfeld, was a rising junior minister. Britain had elected its most radical Parliament since 1832; and there could be no doubt that its first piece of business would be to disestablish the Irish Church.

Most Churchmen recognized, whether more or less reluctantly, that the dispute over the principle of disestablishment had been decided. Disraeli's Reform Act increased the authority with which the newly elected House of Commons could insist on its will. A handful refused to allow their course to be determined by these political facts; even after disestablishment had been enacted, Denison and five other members of the Lower House of Convocation questioned the Act's validity.[34] For the rest, the task after the election was to minimize any injury to the Irish Church by securing for it as favourable terms as the Ministry and Parliament would concede.

This responsibility fell to the Church's leaders in Parliament, the bishops, above all to Archbishop Tait. Early in 1869 at a party in Lambeth Palace to which Tait had invited Gladstone and the primate of the Irish Church, the Irish archbishop stumbled over Mrs. Tait's train as they were going into chapel before dinner. Recovering himself, he exclaimed that 'the best thing he could do was to hang on by the skirts of Canterbury.'[35] The archbishop of Canterbury's function as spokesman for and guardian of the Church in its relations with the State was called to the fore in the first weeks of Tait's archiepiscopate. He immediately showed his mastery as a politician. He knew exactly what he wanted. In the first place he intended to save as much of the Irish Church's endowment as possible. This was necessary in his opinion as a balance against the popular strength of Irish Roman Catholicism. A large endowment would also serve, as establishment had done, to prevent the dominance of any stratum within the Irish Church: stripped of its financial resources, the Church would be at the mercy of its wealthy supporters who would be largely laymen, and although Tait was anything but a clericalist, he was as opposed to congregational as to clerical control.[36] He also argued that the need to attract financial contributions would induce the clergy to whip up fanatical Protestant support, and thus aggravate Irish agitation rather than pacify it.[37]

Tait's other major desire was for the government to make its arrangements with the Irish Church as constituted at present rather than with a new ecclesiastical assembly. Here his concern was to prevent the domination of the currently popular ecclesiastical party. Surprisingly, in view of the determined Protestantism which quickly gained control of the Irish Church, Tait thought that the High Church was predominant there;[38] but English high churchmen were under the same illusion. Denison later confessed that, had he realized in 1868 how low the outlook of most Irish churchmen was, he would not have fought so hard in their defence.[39]

Gladstone himself drafted the necessarily very complex bill with all the competence which only he possessed; and Tait's first negotiations were with him. He did not rush to Gladstone to propose some compromise, and he cautioned the other bishops against doing so.[40] Tait left the initiative to the Queen. Through her[41] the two men met to discuss the bill before it was introduced in Parliament. The archbishop's hope of influencing the drafting of the bill was disappointed: Gladstone came with his ideas fully developed. Nevertheless, Tait's reaction was important to Gladstone, and Tait was aware of the fact. If Gladstone's self-proclaimed 'mission to pacify Ireland' by disestablishing the Irish Church was to succeed, he had to avoid turning Protestant Ulstermen and their religious leaders into angry agitators. Tait's attitude to the bill would also go a long way to decide what the House of Lords would do with it, and Tait came to his interview with Gladstone after meeting with the English and Irish bishops,[42] most of whom sat in the Lords.

No one but Gladstone yet knew how far the government's bill would go; Radicals and Liberationists had suggested terms during the election campaign which would have left the Irish Church devastated. It was a measure of Tait's apprehension that he urged Gladstone not to hand the church buildings over to the Roman Catholics. Tait was relieved, therefore, when the bill which Gladstone described did not bear out his worst fears. Disendowment was not to be overwhelming and the government would make its arrangements with the Irish Church as then constituted. Still, Tait was far from content with the bill. He took most serious exception to Gladstone's refusal to retain all post-Reformation endowments for the Irish Church.[43] He also deplored the bill's failure to earmark part of the funds from disendowment for education. His criticism did not alter Gladstone's plans. Before the bill was presented to Parliament, Tait had to keep his knowledge of its terms secret, but this did not prevent him from negotiating with those who were sure to oppose it. In particular, he and his fellow bishops tried to moderate the extreme tone of the address to the Queen against disestablishment which the Lower House of Convocation under Denison's influence put forward.[44]

The Irish Church Bill which Gladstone brought before Parliament proposed to cut almost all the special links between the Irish Church and the State as of 1 January 1871. Irish bishops were to leave the House of Lords, ecclesiastical courts were removed as part of the legal structure of Ireland, and the State withdrew its enforcement of ecclesiastical law except in regard to marriage. The only vestige of establishment which might remain came from the provision that the Crown could fill vacant bishoprics if asked by a specified number of other Irish bishops. Tait hoped that they would do so[45] but was to be disappointed. The Bill removed the restraints as well as the privileges of establishment. All the laws prohibiting the holding of a synod in the Irish Church were to be repealed, and it was empowered to appoint a body to represent it and hold property. The constitutional union between the Irish and English Churches under the Act of 1800 was also dissolved.

The most complicated and, as far as most people were concerned, now the most important clauses of the Bill dealt with disendowment. It was the disproportionate wealth of the Irish Church as much as its constitutional privileges which galled Irish sentiment, and part of the case for disestablishment had been that this revenue could be put to better use in Ireland. On the other hand, the rights of property were still reverenced little less than they had been in the eighteenth century. Disendowment of an established Church was now justified on the ground that the original donors had intended their gifts to serve the whole country; but only Radicals could contemplate depriving individual clergy of their income. The Bill accordingly ensured that no clergyman need be hurt by its operation. However, corporately the Irish Church was to lose nearly half of its sixteen million pounds worth of property. It would retain all its church buildings, burial grounds and schools, and it could sell the rent charges which it possessed in lieu of tithes back to the landowners. But it would have to buy all ecclesiastical residences it wished to keep, and, most important, it lost all other private endowments given since 1660. Since disendowment struck the Church corporately but not the clergy personally, the Bill allowed clergy more concerned for the Church's welfare than their own to give what they received to the Church. Disendowment was the Bill's alternative to concurrent endowment, and therefore the Bill treated the grants which the government had given to Irish Nonconformists and Roman Catholics, including the Regium Donum and Maynooth grants, along the same lines as the endowment of the Church of Ireland. The residue left to the State after disendowment was to be used mainly to relieve suffering in Ireland, in particular for hospitals, asylums and similar institutions, but never for any religious purpose.

The disendowment clauses shocked many Conservative churchmen such as Lord Derby.[46] Some simply could not credit that a British Parliament would confiscate property on such a sweeping scale, especially property consecrated for religious purposes. They could not believe that the electorate had this in mind when they voted for disestablishment. Disendowment was generally recognized as the corollary of disestablishment, but during the election campaign Gladstone had never made clear that he planned such drastic treatment. Outraged, Derby and Denison[47] argued that the House of Lords was quite entitled to reject the Bill, and they urged it to do so. Derby insisted that to force another election on so important an issue was entirely justifiable. Nearly all other leading Churchmen realized that another election precipitated by the House of Lords including the bishops would only worsen the subsequent treatment of the Irish Church. Still, they could see no justification for depriving the Church of its private endowments given before the Restoration of Charles II in 1660. That event had much less significance in the history of the Irish Church than the Reformation. Gladstone, however, could not have induced his supporters to treat the Irish Church much more generously, and he may have been pleased, as a high churchman, to recognize in this anomalous way that the Church of Ireland was not born with the Reformation.

Tait's strong opposition particularly to the endowment clauses of the Bill never blinded him to the need for passing it in some shape. However, he believed that it could be amended extensively and still be acceptable to the Liberal majority in the Commons.

Such amending could, he thought, be put forward with greater hope of success by the House of Lords than by the Opposition in the Commons. The Conservatives in the Commons would of course force a vote on the principle of the Bill during the debate on the second reading; but Tait feared that if they went on to propose many amendments, the Liberal majority in the Commons would be sure to reject them, thus committing the government against proposals which it might otherwise feel free to accept when put forward by the House of Lords.[48] Time too would work on behalf of these tactics, Tait hoped: before Gladstone's measure reached the House of Lords, the country would have time to realize how sweeping it was. The Church Institution was in fact at work trying to whip up the reaction Tait foresaw.[49]

Disraeli could not accept this course. His leadership of the Conservative party had been badly shaken by the failure of the 1867 Reform Act to produce a Conservative victory, and though he knew he could not resist the Irish Church Bill successfully, he could not afford to leave opposition to the Bill to the House of Lords. Moreover, amendments were certain to be proposed in the Commons, forcing him to deal with them there. Therefore Tait and he agreed on a group of proposals which the Conservatives would propose in the Commons to leave the Irish Church very comfortably endowed.[50] Tait's prediction about the result in the Commons was borne out. The Liberal majority remained firm; indeed, the government argued so resolutely in defence of its Bill that Edward Miall's hopes about future government support for religious equality in England rose.[51] The Bill swept up to the House of Lords.

Now Archbishop Tait had to deal with the Bill under circumstances which he had tried to avoid. His aims were unchanged. His tactics demanded resourcefulness and courage: he wanted the Lords to read the Bill a second time and then to amend it. Rejection of the Bill by the Lords would only harden the government against any weakening of the Bill, which would be sent right back, perhaps stiffened. In such a confrontation between the two Houses, the Lords could only lose. It would be even more unfortunate in Tait's opinion if the Bill were rejected in the Lords by a small majority to which the bishops largely contributed.[52] To win acceptance of his course of action, Tait had to negotiate on two fronts: with the majority in the Lords and with the government.

A majority in the House of Lords made up of bishops and Conservative laymen opposed the Bill, and they had to be convinced to accept unpalatable tactics. They were most unlikely to do so unless the government could be induced to indicate willingness to accept the amendments which were the object of Tait's policy.

The bishops' conduct showed a frustrating combination of political realism and contrary religious principle. Many of those who attended a meeting of English and Irish prelates at Lambeth Palace recognized the political wisdom of Tait's proposals but felt morally obliged to register their disapproval of the principle of the Bill by voting against the second reading.[53] However, at least one bishop in this group, Disraeli's Ellicott, could be swayed by the decision of the Conservative leadership.[54]

Among the Conservative peers were the most enthusiastic of the Bill's Parliamentary opponents. Of the sixty members of the Lords who signed a protest to free themselves of complicity with the measure when it finally passed their House, only four were bishops.* The Conservative lords regarded the Bill as an attack not only on a Church which they supported but also on the landlords of Ireland and the Royal Supremacy. Tait hoped to win their co-operation, relying on their political good sense. They did not seem to have much of it. At the suggestion of Disraeli, Archbishop Tait convened a meeting with nine leading Conservative and non-partisan peers, but though they recognized that some bill must pass sooner or later, only five supported Tait's course of action.† Then, in spite of his efforts four-fifths of the Conservative lords in caucus, inspired by Lord Derby, decided on rejection of the Bill. Not giving up, Tait conferred with the dissident minority and also tried to induce Disraeli to use his influence so that enough peers would abstain to allow the Bill a second reading.[55]

Meanwhile Tait was trying to evoke a conciliatory response from the government. Backed again by the Queen's initiative, he wrote to Gladstone.[56] Tait did not, however, try to win Gladstone over by minimizing the amendments he thought necessary. Gladstone replied that amendments inconsistent with the principle of

* Selwyn of Lichfield, Browne of Ely, the bishop of Tuam, and Ellicott. *Hansard*, 3rd series, CXCVII (1869), 1661–2.

† Stanhope, Grey, the Conservative rebel Salisbury, Disraeli's henchman Cairns, and the archbishop of York sided with Tait. Marlborough, Bath, Harrowby and Redesdale could not agree. Tait's memorandum, 7 May 1869, Tait papers, vol. 75, ff. 278–84.

the Bill might be worse than outright rejection, though he promised that any suggestions Tait cared to make would receive careful consideration.[57] Tait refused to weaken his amendments by letting them be drawn out prematurely, and told Gladstone that he preferred to reserve his proposals until he could assess their strength in the House of Lords.[58] Gladstone had not given the assurance Tait wanted; but Granville, the Liberal leader in the Lords, whose natural affability had been strengthened by many years in a minority there, might be more forthcoming. Together with Thomson, the archbishop of York, Tait conferred with Granville, and through him succeeded in winning a more amenable attitude from the government. Tait then tried to confirm it by enlisting the support of the Queen.[59]

The outcome of all these negotiations was unpredictable right until the vote. Tait himself was subjected to great pressure from Churchmen scandalized by rumours that he intended to acquiesce in the passage of the Bill.[60] The debate on the floor of the House of Lords could turn the balance in the voting, and Tait advocated his point of view early in a strong, straightforward speech. His was the voice of common sense; but the new bishop of Peterborough, Magee, spoke to the heart of the Lords against the Bill, winning cheer after cheer. Finally, at 3 o'clock on a Saturday morning in June, flanked by a distinguished audience, the House of Lords divided. The two English archbishops abstained by walking to the steps of the throne, technically not within the House. Of the other bishops only one, Thirlwall, voted with the government; Wilberforce joined the abstainers;[61] sixteen including waverers such as Ellicott voted against the Bill. However, political sense among the Conservative lay lords more than restored the balance, 36 of them voted with the government,[62] and the motion was carried by 179 votes to 146, a majority of 33.

Tait still had to secure his amendments, but this was easy in a friendly House of Lords. He raised the endowment from 8½ to 13 of the 16 million pounds, and helped to move the date for disestablishment on from January to May 1871. However, he failed to keep the present incumbents of Irish bishoprics in the House of Lords. At the expense of alienating the rigidly Protestant peers such as Shaftesbury, he advocated a measure of concurrent endowment, but did not obtain it in as definite a form as he desired.[63]

The real test of his amendments would come when the Bill

returned to the House of Commons. During the Lords' debates Tait tried to pave the way for their final acceptance by showing both determination to uphold them and willingness to accept conciliatory alternatives proposed by peers on the government side.[64] Once he had secured his endowment clauses, he used a letter to the Queen to point out to the government that the amended endowment of the Irish Church raised it only to the level of a moderately comfortable colonial Church, and he threatened another year's agitation if the government refused to accept the improvement.[65] Next day he made a public appeal in the House of Lords to Gladstone:

> I say I believe that the other House of Parliament will not grudge this very moderate request; but I would further say that I believe that it does not so much depend on the other House of Parliament as upon Her Majesty's Government whether this moderate endowment will be conceded. . . . But I will go further, and say that I believe it depends not so much on Her Majesty's Government as on one man, and I cannot believe that that one man, for so many years the most trusted son of the Church of England, will oppose the moderate provision of this Bill in order to gratify the monstrous and unnatural combination that has been formed against the Church of Ireland.[66]

The most trusted son of the Church was the convinced leader of that unnatural combination, and one of its most monstrous members, John Bright, had already made it quite clear that Tait's appeal would receive short shrift. In a public letter Bright had threatened the House of Lords with 'accidents not pleasant for them to think of' if they held up the Bill for long.[67] Gladstone warned the Queen that the first result of the amendments would be a strong movement to drive all the bishops out of the House of Lords. Already Victoria had cautioned her archbishop that concessions would still be necessary on both sides.[68]

Gladstone led the House of Commons in sweeping aside most of the Lords' amendments, though, almost unnoticed by his ardent supporters, he accepted two important endowment clauses. They were not enough to avert a constitutional deadlock. Victoria brought Tait and Gladstone together to work out a compromise,[69] and there appeared to be some hope of success. But on 20 July the House of Lords, with Tait's support, insisted on their least effectual and most unpopular amendment which inserted recognition of the principle of concurrent endowment in the Bill's preamble. The

THE CHANGELING.

NURSE CANTERBURY. "WHICH WE'VE TOOK THE GREATEST CARE OF 'IM, MEM, AND 'OPE YOU'LL THINK 'IM GROW'D."

MRS. PRIME MINISTER. "THAT IS NOT *MY* CHE-ILD!—NOT IN THE LEAST LIKE IT."

Gladstone and Tait, *Punch* cartoon

outlook darkened. Yet, in spite of their threats, all the key leaders wanted a solution now. Gladstone, Granville, Tait and the Conservative peacemaker Lord Cairns entered into hectic negotiations, and on 22 July produced a settlement. The clergy who commuted their income for the benefit of the Church received better terms than the Commons had stipulated, the Lords gave up concurrent endowment, and the disposal of the surplus was left to the future wisdom of Parliament.

The winner was the government. The cry of Irish disestablishment had carried them into power, Gladstone had turned the policy into a masterly bill, the Commons had given it unwavering support, and it had been enacted substantially in line with the government's intentions.* Tait was not deluded by the improved endowment he had won. He valued it greatly for the Church and for Ireland; but he confided to his diary that the Act left the country in religious circumstances which depressed him.

* Inadvertently the Act led to the repeal of the Ecclesiastical Titles Act, the ineffectual result of the Protestant panic of 1851. The Act was aimed against Roman Catholic bishops usurping the titles of the bishops of the established Church, but would now apply equally to bishops of the Irish Church retaining their accustomed titles.

Chapter Two

THEOLOGICAL PARALYSIS

Science is on the march—listen to her divine words, for what is she but the Voice of God, Deus revelatum. Mark her footsteps—and if you cannot keep pace with her, still follow her.

Charles Kingsley

THE publication of Darwin's *Origin of Species* in 1859 began a twenty-year period of some of the most intense criticism of Christianity in England's history. Few of the critics' concepts were new: evolution had been in the intellectual atmosphere for half a century. What was new was the painstaking experimentation and building up of documented proof which appropriated the name 'science'. Darwin offered it, and Huxley devoted what time he could keep free from public speaking to it; experimentation itself rather than the philosophic conclusions which might be drawn from it was becoming the religion of scientists. This kind of minute investigation was not restricted to the physical sciences. Modern historiography, inaugurated by Niebuhr and Ranke earlier in the century and soon applied to religious subjects, was based upon it. Biblical criticism, as old as the Bible itself, took on a new seriousness when fortified by the detailed scholarship of which England had its first bitter taste in 1862 and '63 in Colenso's commentary on the Pentateuch.[1] Tylor applied Darwin's methods to anthropology in his *Primitive Culture* of 1871.

New too was the publicity which the critics of Christianity gave their work. Previously English intellectuals had usually kept their religious doubts among themselves, largely through fear of the moral consequences of a popular loss of faith. Now even F. D. Maurice had publicly attacked the morality of the doctrine of everlasting punishment. Some of the mid-Victorian critics of Christianity were convinced that the beliefs of the Church were not essential to its beneficial social influence. Auguste Comte's

English disciples, particularly Richard Congreve, advocated the worship of humanity which would preserve all the appealing ceremonial and moral benefits of the Church but without its theology. Matthew Arnold wanted to keep the existing Church but reduce its theology to a humanistic level. At the same time the public had become more receptive to the writing of the critics because of improved education at all levels and the development of cheap techniques of printing. The prosperity of mid-Victorian England gave some men more leisure for reading, and emphasized the worth of scientific and technological advances on which industrialization, the source of England's economic superiority, was based. Faith also seemed more difficult in the cities where most men now lived than in the country.

This intellectual upheaval was the crucial challenge confronting the Victorian Church in the 1860s and '70s. All of its other concerns and crusades were either, like education, direct, or like ritualism, indirect means intended to strengthen religious belief. In spite of the emphasis placed by all schools of thought within the Church on personal conduct, the *raison d'être* of the Church was its religious belief. Whatever social benefits the Church conferred arose originally because of its faith, and although over the years the Church of England had become as much a social institution as a community of believers, it had rarely lost sight of the fact that acceptance of its creed was essential to its survival. The hope that the social benefits of the Church could be retained without its faith was, in churchmen's eyes, a delusion.

The responsibility to refute critics and defend the faith lay upon each minister of the Church but especially upon its theologians and only secondarily upon its assemblies and institutional leadership, with which this study is particularly concerned. Theological controversies raised between Churchmen by the wider debate against unbelief came before the authorities of the Church for decision. Here was the special function of the institutional Church in intellectual controversy, that of a commander settling disputes among his lieutenants on the front line. However, authority in the Church of England was weak and widely diffused. No person or tribunal or assembly could pronounce a decision effectively binding on the consciences of all churchmen. As a result, the voice of the Church was often the voice of internal controversy. Fear of schism within the Church paralysed its leadership. So did the increasing fear that the faith of the Church might not be able to retain its present adherents let alone make headway against the sceptical. Moreover, even vigorous attempts such as Archbishop Tait made in the second half of his primacy to speak out for his faith were almost fruitless.

The Athanasian Creed

From the very beginning of the period Churchmen replied to the critics of their faith in two diametrically opposed ways. The most famous was that of Samuel Wilberforce, till 1869 bishop of Oxford, who countered Huxley with mild derision and thumping denunciation. The other was implicit in *Essays and Reviews*, a collection of articles brought out in 1860 by a group of Churchmen united in the belief that the only hope of maintaining the faith of educated Englishmen lay in showing them that Christianity could be upheld even when the truth of some of its critics' arguments was recognized. *Essays and Reviews* was very restrained in its concessions to the critics. Its point of view was taken much farther in the work on the Pentateuch by Colenso, the Anglican bishop of Natal in South Africa.

The advocates of both approaches knew that they were incompatible, but to begin with only the determined conservatives were in a position to enforce their strategy. They were the defenders of Biblical literalism, still the popular creed; the theological reformers were advocating a new line between the Scylla of the critics and the Charybdis of the conservatives, and were subjected to abuse from both sides. Wilberforce secured a condemnation of *Essays and Reviews* and of Colenso from the bench of bishops. However, as intellectual criticism gained strength, so did the reformers. Popular delight in the confident defence of Wilberforce diminished, and the number of laymen worried by their inability to find a satisfactory answer to the critics grew. When in 1869 one of the leading contributors to *Essays and Reviews*, Frederick Temple, was nominated to the bishopric of Exeter, there was a noticeable lack of lay support for the outcry raised by his opponents.[2]

In 1870 the time had come when the reformers could take the initiative. One flagrant example of the kind of teaching alienating the educated man in the pew was the Athanasian Creed, which the Book of Common Prayer stipulated must be recited in public worship thirteen times a year.* Broad Churchmen criticized the use of this creed on three counts. First, it defined the nature of the Trinity and Christ's incarnation in impossible detail.

The Son is of the Father alone: not made, nor created, but begotten.

The Holy Ghost is of the Father and of the Son: neither made, nor created, nor begotten, but proceeding.

And so forth. Certainty on any metaphysical subject had always been difficult, and was becoming much more so. To insist upon close definitions of mysteries which transcended human understanding could be justified, the reformers argued, only if dictated by plain statements of the Bible. According to A. P. Stanley, dean of Westminster and the most outspoken of Broad Churchmen, the Athanasian Creed's definitions were only deduced from Scripture by fallible human reasoning;[3] Bishop Thirlwall concluded that further revelation would be necessary to uphold them.[4] The Nicene Creed, used in the Holy Communion service, contained a simpler but still perfectly adequate statement of the same doctrines. To force Christians farther was, to use Matthew Arnold's words, the 'insane license of affirmation'; and such over-belief would inevitably lead to a sceptical reaction.

Secondly, using the techniques of historical criticism, these Broad Churchmen questioned the credentials of the Athanasian Creed. They treated it as the product of an intellectually barbarous age rather than as the voice of the Church unaffected by time. It had not, they said, originated in the early Church but in the Dark Ages, and E. S. Ffoulkes pinned it down to the time of Charlemagne.[5]

The most offensive feature of the creed was what Broad Churchmen called the damnatory clauses at its beginning, middle and ending.

Whosoever will be saved: before all things it is necessary that he hold the Catholick Faith.

Which Faith except one do keep whole and undefiled: without doubt he shall perish everlastingly.

. . .

He therefore that will be saved: must thus think of the Trinity.

. . .

This is the Catholick Faith: which except a man believe, he cannot be saved.

* Christmas, Epiphany, Easter, Ascension Day, Whitsunday, Trinity Sunday, and the feasts of St. Matthias, St. John the Baptist, St. James, St. Bartholomew, St. Matthew, St. Simon and St. Jude, and St. Andrew.

Confronted by the advancing wave of criticism and new knowledge, thoughtful Victorians were exchanging certainty for sincerity as the chief virtue in intellectual questions. J. D. Coleridge,
later Chief Justice, put it this way:

> when a man has really done his best with his conscience I think he should
> follow its leading without hesitation, and with a firm belief that the
> Infinite God, in His mercy and wisdom, will accept all His children,
> according to their lights.[6]

To such a man the Athanasian Creed's threat of everlasting
torment for those who felt driven to unorthodox conclusions was
morally repulsive. James Fraser, bishop of Manchester after 1870,
told the Convocation of York that whenever he had stood up to
recite the Athanasian Creed in his former parish, the one educated
man in the congregation sat down, closing his prayer book with
an angry slam.[7] The 6,000 laymen who signed Lord Shaftesbury's
petition against compulsory use of the creed included 11 judges,
50 peers and 149 M.P.s.[8]

Broad Churchmen agreed that the Athanasian Creed's threat
was intolerable, not just because they sympathized with sincere
doubters, but also because they themselves were perplexed. Their
faith was not unquestioning conviction but a hope that Christianity
as a whole was right because its moral teachings were obviously
so. The core of Stanley's religion was ethical: the belief that God
was love and that men ought to conduct their lives according to
the two great commandments of love for God and for one's
neighbour.[9] This alone was sure. To condemn those who were
not convinced by the minutiae of the Athanasian Creed was to
him arrogant dogmatism at its worst.

The opportunity for remedial action had arrived. In 1867 Lord
Derby's government appointed a royal commission on the rubrics,
the instructions about the conduct of worship originally printed
in red in the Church of England's Book of Common Prayer. The
commission was set up to place in safer hands the crusade of Lord
Shaftesbury against the emergence of ritualism. However, its
terms of reference were not confined to the rubrics liable to ritualistic abuse but covered all, including the rubric governing the use
of the Athanasian Creed. The commission's discussions reached
this particular rubric early in 1870, and petitions came in for and
against change.

The only significant result of the deliberations of the ritual commission was the proof that all of its members including its one ritualist, T. W. Perry, were in favour of some relaxation either of the creed itself or of its use. However, they could not agree on any one recommendation. Several of the possible courses of action were considered, including taking the creed out of public worship and placing it with the Thirty-nine Articles as a statement of belief, making its use optional, retranslating it, cutting out its damnatory clauses, and adding an explanatory note. None commanded the support of the majority except an explanatory rubric weakening the damnatory clauses:

Note that the condemnations in this confession of Faith are to be no otherwise understood than as a solemn warning of the peril of those who wilfully reject the Catholic Faith.[10]

This recommendation carried little weight since it was approved by a vote of 11 to 7 out of a possible 29,[11] and 2 of the 11 later changed their minds. Nineteen qualified their agreement with the commission's fourth report, published in 1870, dealing with the creed, by urging more drastic treatment.[12]

The list of dissidents to the commission's recommendation was headed by Archbishop Tait, who advocated placing the creed with the Articles. His concern was not so much the teaching of the creed as its inappropriateness in congregational worship. Though this creed was not in his estimation the product of inspired authority, he valued its description of the Trinity and the incarnation; but he questioned the wisdom of imposing 'the minute logical statement of particulars' of these doctrines on untrained laymen in public services.[13] He held that the sense in which the Church accepted the damnatory clauses—which in any case he did not like—required a lot of theological training before it could be appreciated. He also regretted the fact that at least a few Nonconformists were kept out of the national Church only by the need to subscribe to this creed. Using this particular point, he had brought the question of the Athanasian Creed to public attention just when the royal commission took the question up.[14] At the end of 1870, encouraged by the unanimity of the commission in favour of some relaxation and by the comparative quietness of the debate so far, Tait suggested again publicly that some legislation should be enacted to modify the creed's use.[15]

This shocked the opposition into action so resolute that it eventually prevented the authorities of the Church from doing even the little the ritual commission proposed. The men who opposed any relaxation over the Athanasian Creed were generally High Church. They were not simply conservers of the theological status quo, but true reactionaries, repelled by what Gladstone called 'the levity of the destructive speculations so widely current',[16] and convinced by the Oxford Movement of the need to bring the Church of England back to the belief of the early, undivided Church. This was the moment when the eternal voice of the Church came through firm and clear, neither corrupted by medieval additions nor clipped by modern scepticism. High Churchmen who adopted this viewpoint were not insensitive to the intellectual confusion of their contemporaries, but could not believe that theological confusion in the Church would meet their needs; in the words of the Oxford Movement's motto, 'if the trumpet give an uncertain sound, who shall prepare himself to the battle?' And if the blast of the High Church trumpet jarred most of those who heard it into hostility, what better proof could there be that High Churchmen were walking in the footsteps of the early martyrs?

The teaching of the early Church could be found in the three creeds—the Apostles', the Nicene, and the Athanasian—the decisions of the General Councils of the Church before it divided, and the writings of the early Fathers. All the fragments of this teaching imbedded in the Church of England's prayer book including the Athanasian Creed needed to be emphasized, according to the High Church. The Athanasian Creed had come under criticism late in the seventeenth century and, in the lax and rationalistic environment of the mid-eighteenth century, had fallen into disuse. The quickening of the established Church toward the end of the century revived the controversy. The Oxford Movement helped bring the creed back into use in public worship;[17] and its unfamiliarity made it all the more striking. A few High Church laymen such as Gladstone and clergymen such as Canon Gregory were willing for the rubric on the Athanasian Creed to be relaxed or at least not enforced.[18] Nevertheless, Gladstone suspected that the attack on the Athanasian Creed was the prelude to an attack on much more in the prayer book.[19] Most High Churchmen, under the leadership of Pusey and Liddon, campaigned against any change because it would be a concession to rationalism inside as well as outside the Church. They could not discriminate between sympathetic and hostile critics. In fact their ire was aroused more by the Broad Church contributors to *Essays and Reviews* than by Huxley.

Undoubtedly it was difficult to distinguish friend from foe. Matthew Arnold was a self-touted friend whose proposals would kill supernatural religion. One extremely liberal clergyman, Charles Voysey, citing Thirlwall's and Stanley's protests about the Athanasian Creed in his defence, denied the atonement, original sin, justification by faith, the second coming, the incarnation and the Trinity; and it took the courts to drive him from his pulpit.[20] Under the mastership of Benjamin Jowett, Balliol College did not use even the Apostles' Creed in its week-day services.[21] Non-Christians found it every bit as hard as High Churchmen to comprehend how men like Jowett and Stanley could claim to be conscientious clergymen. 'There goes Stanley,' Carlyle said to James Froude one day as they passed him in a park, 'boring holes in the bottom of the Church of England!'[22] High Churchmen were determined that he should not get through. Liddon called theological liberals simply 'the unbelieving school'[23] and was not hesitant in consigning people to it. He said that he differed from Lightfoot, the able but devout Biblical critic at Cambridge, 'not merely as to some general truths of high importance, but in particular as to what is implied by a serious faith in the Eternal Godhead of Our Lord and Saviour.'[24]

The damnatory clauses—warning clauses High Churchmen preferred to call them—were the prayer book's clearest condemnation of the current tendency to place morality above true faith as the essence of Christianity, and High Churchmen upheld them stubbornly. True faith, they insisted, was the foundation of morality; the humility, purity and steadfastness with which the Christian strove to strengthen his faith lay at the heart of his moral well-being. Unbelief, so far from being excusable on the plea of sincerity, was the fruit of moral failure rather than of intellectual confusion.[25] Liddon could only account for the patent goodness of a man like Maurice whose faith he considered wrong as 'a very perplexing mystery'.[26]

The attempt to question the creed's historical credentials was irrelevant to High Churchmen. The teaching of the creed was the only vital point, and regardless of when it was written, it had been consecrated by hundreds of years of use in the western Church.[27] Therefore, though they disputed the historical criticisms, they did not take them seriously. Most High Churchmen had little sympathy with the new, exactly documented historical and Biblical scholarship. It was just another feature of the current unhealthy climate of opinion from which they were trying to remain immune: as Denison stated with his usual bluntness, 'I have always set my face as a flint against the mind of the time.'[28] High Churchmen's outlook was not as blinkered as Denison's remark implied. They knew that men were finding it hard, once they had accepted any one criticism of popular Christianity, to resist others. When J. D. Coleridge was drifting away from the High Churchmanship of his upbringing, he told his father:

a man's religion is built up of small things, and it gives one an uneasy feeling to be told that this brick is faulty, that stone must come out, and so forth.[29]

High Churchmen responded by insisting on every brick and stone.

The battle over the Athanasian Creed was between two schools of thought within the Church. The critics outside paid no attention. And the third school of churchmen, the Evangelicals, played only a subordinate role, supporting Broad Churchmen. Evangelicals had been second to none in their opposition to *Essays and Reviews* and especially to Colenso's treatment of the Pentateuch. However, their confidence and energy generally were on the wane; Shaftesbury had stood almost alone among the Evangelicals in opposing Temple's appointment to Exeter.[30] What could still arouse their ire was an attack on the integrity of the Bible, but not one on the prayer book and its rubrics; in Evangelical eyes the prayer book needed Protestant pruning. Evangelicals were also anxious for better relations with the Protestant Nonconformists, some of whom objected to the Athanasian Creed. Finally, the Evangelicals had always been more of a lay than a clerical school, and dislike of the Athanasian Creed was much stronger in the pew than the pulpit. Shaftesbury took the lead in mounting a lay protest against compulsory use of the creed in public worship, but without his accustomed enthusiasm, and he admitted privately that congregations were disturbed by it only because it was unfamiliar.[31]

Between Broad and High Churchmen the issue was crucial. To each the other was only making defence of the Church's teaching more difficult. Once they concentrated their quarrel on one particular point, tempers were bound to fray. Thirlwall called the Athanasian Creed 'a wicked forgery',[32] Burgon called Stanley 'an unscrupulous partisan',[33] and in the heat of the debate one irate High Churchman told Archbishop Tait that 'The whole controversy has been distinguished by the enormous and reckless lying of those who desire the change.'[34]

Archbishop Tait, though not quite reckless in his anxiety to remove the creed from public worship, showed less than his usual realism. He erred in interpreting the agreement of the ritual commission in favour of some relaxation and the comparative calm which greeted its report as proof that there was a consensus in favour of change. His proposal for legislation provoked the opposition into action, and as a result he had to restrain the advocates of the change he had encouraged. In June 1871 Thomas Chambers moved in the House of Commons to abolish the penalties against clergymen who substituted the Apostles' Creed for the Athanasian. Gladstone was determined to keep Parliament from embroiling itself in an internal Church controversy, and Tait felt obliged to persuade Chambers to withdraw his motion.[35]

The archbishop continued to publicize the issue as the most important one raised by the ritual commission's fourth report.[36] By the end of 1871, however, threats from Pusey and Liddon had driven him to recognize that the most that could be extracted from the opposition was an explanatory rubric.[37] Even that was in doubt since neither side thought it helpful. J. B. Mozley, the most able high church theologian, argued that no explanation was necessary since the damnatory clauses, like other injunctions such as 'Pray without ceasing', contained implicit but nonetheless clear limitations: the damnatory clauses obviously applied, he said, only to the central doctrines in the creed, not to its subordinate distinctions.[38] Denison realized that even the most cautiously worded explanation, particularly because it would be written to appease broad church discontent, would look like an apology for the creed[39] and would therefore furnish an excuse for not taking the creed seriously.

On the other side, Broad Churchmen refused to agree to any compromise which left the use of the Athanasian creed compulsory,[40] and when Tait fell back on an explanatory rubric, Thirlwall threw up the whole business in disgust. Stanley admitted, what Denison feared, that an explanatory rubric would indirectly discourage use of the creed.[41] Nonetheless, Stanley believed that any watered down explanation such as Mozley's was simply not true to the creed's obvious and historically intended meaning. Stanley made his point abundantly clear in a speech before the Lower House of Convocation:

I even admire these clauses . . . for their extreme and magnificent perspicuity of language. Whoever was the author he knew what he meant. He meant as the Emperor Charlemagne meant—that anyone who could not accept those words was everlastingly lost, and should be destroyed by sword and fire from the face of Christendom. I admire the Emperor Charlemagne; but I cannot admire those who come with these modern explanations to draw out the teeth of this old lion, who sits there in his majesty and defies any explanation to take out the fierce and savage fangs which never can be taken out.[42]

Stanley had also pointed out that an inadequate remedy such as an explanatory rubric would weaken the theological reformers' case without affording any appreciable relief.[43] Like Tait before the storm, Stanley still wanted the creed placed with the Articles, but as an expression of the charitable tolerance he prized in the Church of England, he was prepared for the use of the creed to be optional.[44] And although Tait's efforts had mobilized high church opposition, they also drew out weighty support for the reformers. 1,303 clergy including 10 deans, 9 heads of colleges, 6 professors at Oxford and Cambridge, and 15 headmasters of public schools signed a memorial objecting to the use of the creed as it then stood.[45]

Tait was not the man to be content with a debate without practical results. Early in December 1871 he secured an explanatory note from the reluctant Oxford professors of divinity including Pusey and Liddon:

That nothing in this Creed is to be understood as condemning those who, by involuntary ignorance or invincible prejudice are hindered from accepting the faith therein declared.[46]

A meeting of the bishops immediately agreed to recommend an explanatory note of some sort. Then, just before Christmas the controversy turned ugly. Fearful that Broad Church agitation would push matters farther, Liddon and Pusey renewed and stiffened their former threats: they informed Tait that if the Church either tampered with the creed itself by cutting out its damnatory clauses or modified its use in public worship in any way, they would resign from the Church of England's ministry.[47] They meant it. Liddon started to discuss arrangements for the disposal of his house.[48] They also expected that many other Churchmen would feel obliged to follow their example.[49]

It was never clear how big the secession might have been. In spite of the many setbacks they had suffered in the course of their struggle to reinforce the Catholicity of the established Church, and in spite of the beckoning arms of Rome and its converts, High Churchmen had shown great staying power. Denison, their stormy petrel, made it clear that nothing could dislodge him now.[50] Young ritualists had a cavalier disregard for adverse decisions of all existing authorities—bishops, Convocations, the Judicial Committee of the Privy Council—and later when the going got even rougher, ritualists showed no tendency to pull out of the Church. Some of them also were less concerned with doctrine than the pure disciples of the Oxford Movement, as was indicated by the proposal of their spokesman on the ritual commission, Perry, to allow the Apostles' Creed to be used instead of the Athanasian.[51]

Liddon's and Pusey's threat galvanized all degrees of High Churchmen together into adamantine opposition to any significant change;[52] no churchmen of other parties except for extreme evangelicals took the threat lightly; and it electrified Convocation. Now that Newman had left the Church of England and Keble was dead, Pusey stood alone as a leader of the original Tractarians, and his patent sanctity of life had won the respect even of those who fought his teaching; Liddon was his Elisha and a great influence both on Oxford undergraduates and on the congregations which packed St. Paul's Cathedral to hear him preach. Though Tait publicly condemned the threat,[53] his constant desire not only to maintain but extend the comprehensiveness of the national Church forced him to make very sure that the action to be taken on the creed should be acceptable to the two men.

The reformers' response to Liddon's and Pusey's threat was to delay action till a better day. An explanatory rubric would not do, and Lightfoot pointed out that in particular the Oxford professors' note, if applied to the other creeds, 'would sap the foundations of all religious profession';[54] it could always be disregarded if the plea of 'involuntary ignorance' or 'invincible prejudice' were allowed. Tait vexed the matter still more when he declared in Convocation, on the basis of the Oxford note, that nobody in the Church accepted the damnatory clauses in their plain, literal sense.[55] 315 clergy signed a statement that they did believe them in this way,[56] and once again the archbishop was forced to recognize that his fellow Churchmen were less progressive than he had hoped.

Purely without intending it, and unnoticed by the High Church opposition until it was too late, Tait secured a small measure of relief. The Act of Uniformity Amendment Act which he brought into Parliament in 1872 to provide for shortened church services[57] was altered slightly by Parliament with the result that clergymen adopting the shortened form were obliged to substitute the Apostles' Creed for the Athanasian on five of the thirteen Sundays on which its use had formerly been compulsory. Denison muttered about disestablishment,[58] but no one else objected strenuously. Tait tried for more. He attempted to convince High Churchmen that their stand logically implied condemnation of the eastern Orthodox Churches,[59] who did not accept the Athanasian Creed and with whom High Churchmen wanted to establish closer contacts. He used his casting vote to prevent the Upper House of Convocation from refusing to take any action to satisfy the complainants.[60] But if all he could get was an explanatory rubric, that he was determined to have. At least it would make public the qualifications which had long been offered in private to uneasy laymen and candidates for ordination.[61]

All he finally secured, in 1873, was an explanatory declaration by the Convocation of Canterbury, so long that it almost rivalled the Athanasian Creed itself.

For the removal of doubts, and to prevent disquietude in the use of the Creed commonly called the Creed of St. Athanasius, this Synod doth solemnly declare:

1. That the Confession of our Christian Faith, commonly called the Creed of St. Athanasius, doth not make any addition to the faith as contained in Holy Scripture, but warneth against errors which from time to time have arisen in the Church of Christ.

2. That as Holy Scripture in divers places doth promise life to them that believe and declare the condemnation of them that believe not, so

doth the Church in this confession declare the necessity for all who would be in a state of salvation of holding fast the Catholic faith, and the great peril of rejecting the same. Wherefore the warnings in this confession of faith are to be understood no otherwise than the like warnings in Holy Scripture, for we must receive God's threatenings even as His promises, in such wise as they are generally set forth in Holy Writ. Moreover, the Church doth not herein pronounce judgment on any particular person or persons, God alone being the Judge of all.[62]

Even this did not join the rubrics. It was not accepted by the Upper House of the Convocation of York; and Parliament was never asked to sanction its inclusion in the prayer book, probably for fear that broad churchmen would induce Parliament to reject it in favour of something more radical.[63]

The debate on the Athanasian Creed, the main theological controversy within the Church of England in the 1870s had been settled, temporarily, by an extremely cautious compromise which checked the hopes of every side. High Churchmen had failed to hold off an explanation which they knew would lessen the impact of the creed; Broad Churchmen's hope for a significant reform dwindled into the remote future; and the explanation did not carry the publicity of inclusion in the prayer book which Archbishop Tait, the man most responsible for it, had considered its main value. The compromise was dictated, not by fear of the critics of Christianity, but by the energetic determination with which conflicting schools of churchmen fought each other over the best way to combat the critics. The energy intended for defence of the faith against outside attack was dissipated in a fight between the defenders, leaving the enemy unaffected or amused.

The Argument from Prophecy

In 1877 and '78 it was the turn of the evangelical leader, Lord Shaftesbury, to raise the alarm against the Broad Church clergy, since one of them, Brownlow Maitland, had just published a book defending part of the Bible, *The Argument from Prophecy*, on grounds which implicitly repudiated a literal interpretation of the Bible. This incident attracted much less attention than the Athanasian Creed had done in the early '70s; Convocation ignored it. Still, the response of the bishops who were asked to pronounce judgment on Maitland's book was significant since it indicated that their concern was shifting from fear of a split between conflicting theological schools within the Church to uneasiness about the Church's ability to make headway against hostile criticism outside.

Hostile notices of Maitland's book in the evangelical newspaper, the *Record*,[64] brought it to Shaftesbury's attention in November 1877. Promptly he sent a protest to Archbishop Tait,[65] pointing out that, by accepting the conclusions of Biblical criticism, Maitland had seriously weakened the force of what was known as the argument from prophecy, the argument that the fulfilment of the Old Testament's prophecies in the New Testament proved that the Bible was a supernatural revelation. Shaftesbury said sadly that he was no longer surprised that a clergyman could write to this effect. What annoyed him was that the book had come out under the imprimatur of the Society for Promoting Christian Knowledge, the oldest and one of the most respected official agencies of the Church of England.

The Argument from Prophecy was the latest publication of the SPCK's Christian Evidence Committee set up in 1870. Dr. Hessey, one of the leading figures in the SPCK, had proposed the creation of this committee[66] while Parliament was debating the Liberal government's Elementary Education Bill. Hessey was worried about the same issue underlying most of the debate on the Bill, namely the thinking of the working classes enfranchised by the 1867 Reform Act. Infidelity was widespread among them, particularly he thought because of the activities of such popularizers of atheism as Holyoake, Charles Watts and Bradlaugh. These men propagated their creed with all the single-mindedness and confidence of evangelists. By their high standard of morality, compromised only by their advocacy of birth control, they lessened the fear that rejection of Christianity might lead to moral degradation. They understood the group to which they appealed better than most clergy did: instead of London and the highly patronized meetings of societies which clergymen found congenial, Bradlaugh headed for Wigan or the Mechanics' Institute at Leeds where he spoke to men hungry for knowledge. Speeches were followed up with cheap pamphlets and a few books such as Feuerbach's *Essence of Christianity* brought out by the Freethought Publishing Company which had been set up for the purpose. Bradlaugh also edited a weekly, *The National Reformer*, to put forward his religious and political views.

Hessey recommended that the SPCK, the Church organization he thought responsible for meeting this kind of challenge, should set up a Christian Evidence Committee to conduct a systematic study of the rationalist attack, the classes to which it appealed, and the existing anti-infidel literature which, he pointed out, was generally outdated or ineffective. In the light of this study, the committee should ask churchmen known for their concern about infidelity to write what each thought particularly desirable to combat it. The committee would pay them well, publish what manuscripts it considered suitable for its purposes, and see to their distribution. The SPCK agreed wholeheartedly with Hessey's proposals and raised the allotment which he had requested to pay the writers from £500 to £1,000.

Hessey's choice of possible writers indicated the limits of the remedy as he conceived it. None of his nominees were noted for appreciating the arguments of nineteenth-century scepticism. Some like Archbishop Thomson and Jackson, the bishop of London, were intellectual mediocrities; two, Liddon and Burgon, were distinguished for their refusal to consider for a moment that current criticisms of Christianity might have any validity. What Hessey wanted was improvement only in the presentation of the Church's teaching, not modification of the teaching itself.

The thinking behind the project underwent a shift of emphasis before the committee was set up. The SPCK asked a selected group of clergymen and laymen to come to two conferences on the subject in the summer of 1870.[67] Many of these men, reverting to their accustomed hierarchical view of English society and in all likelihood uneasy intellectually themselves, argued that infidelity among the lower classes owed its existence and continuance to more refined forms of scepticism among the upper classes rather than to the effectiveness of popular rationalist propaganda. Consequently they suggested that, in addition to light tracts, the committee should commission works at a higher literary level on such subjects as science and religion, Biblical criticism, and geological discoveries. To ensure complete intellectual honesty among the writers, the conferences proposed that manuscripts submitted to the Christian Evidence Committee be exempted from the supervision usually exercised over what the SPCK published. With these ideas and suggestions in mind, the Christian Evidence Committee was set up late in 1870 under the chairmanship of the bishop of London.

By early 1874, 28 publications, 19 of them cheap popular tracts, had been issued, dealing with subjects ranging from positivism, creation, and the date of the Pentateuch, to the moral shortcomings of Old Testament heroes.[68] The original grant of £1,000 had been exhausted, and another for the same amount was made.[69] Nevertheless, the committee had encountered a discouragingly negative response from academics in the Church; of them only Lightfoot showed any willingness to cooperate.[70] The flow of manuscripts from all sources narrowed to a trickle in 1873, only one new publication was issued in 1874, and the members of the committee resorted to writing themselves. One of the topics upon which the committee wanted a book was the argument from prophecy. After a futile attempt to find an outsider to deal with the subject, Brownlow Maitland, one of the most active members of the committee, took it up.

Maitland's book came out in 1877. Two hundred pages in length, its appeal was directed towards the middle or upper class layman who, though educated, would not plough through many pages of academic rebuttal of anti-Christian criticism. In order to avoid basing his case upon ground which rationalism had made shaky, Maitland began his book with a sweeping concession: that the argument from prophecy could convince only those who already accepted the theistic belief in a continually active God. 'To endeavour to draw out a proof of special or supernatural instances of the divine agency, before a basis was laid for them in those which are natural and ordinary, would be like attempting to build a house without a foundation'.[71] Moreover, though in the eighteenth century Christian apologists had often looked upon prophecy and its close cousin miracle as cornerstones of their argument, now, Maitland admitted, the appeal of prophecy was subordinate to the appeal of the Christian gospel as a whole:[72] no one would accept the supernatural validity of prophecies if he did not first believe in the divine worth of what they predicted.

Maitland also made wider concessions to Biblical criticism than at first apparent. His references to it were infrequent, and he accepted its results only for the sake of argument. Nevertheless, Biblical criticism had undermined confidence in so many particulars of the Old Testament[73] that he felt obliged to emphasize the broad lines of prophecy rather than its concrete details attractive and convincing to unquestioning minds. He concentrated on four general predictions of the Old Testament: the ultimate triumph of God's cause, the accomplishment of this by a person, the suffering of that person, and the establishment of a spiritual religion rather than one which placed its main stress on ceremonies.[74] Only when a person recognized the validity of these general forecasts, Maitland said, could he go on to appreciate the many more detailed ways in which the Old Testament foreshadowed and prepared the way for Christianity;[75] to the sceptic who did not believe in the great, general predictions, these lesser forecasts would be sure to appear 'fanciful and frivolous'.[76]

One group of Old Testament prophecies in particular, upon which Maitland refused to base his case, were those which dealt with the dispersion of the Jews.[77] In the eighteenth century these had been regarded as especially telling passages, predicting long before the event the dispersion of the Jews by the Romans after the death of Christ. Generally scholars now recognized that all but two of these references had been written in the kingdom of Judah when it was threatened by Assyria after Assyria had conquered Judah's northern neighbour, the kingdom of Israel. Therefore, these passages were most easily accounted for as allusions to the immediate threat of a similar fate for Judah at the hands of Assyria. As for the two exceptional passages, Maitland described them as 'rhetorical and minatory, rather than predictive', and also pointed out that most Biblical critics placed them in the same period as the others.

Important though Maitland's concessions to criticism were, the total impression which his book conveyed was decidedly and intentionally reverent and devout: 'whatever be its literary merits or demerits,' he told Archbishop Tait,

it has originated in a sincere desire to promote the cause of divine truth, and . . . from beginning to end there is not a word that is not animated by a profound reverence for Holy Scripture, and a desire to strengthen to the utmost the defences of Christianity.[78]

Shaftesbury, still true to the popular Biblical literalism of the 1860s, was not seduced by the devoutness of a writer who deviated from it. However, the support he received for his attack on Maitland's book showed a marked slump from the outcry against the work on the Pentateuch by Colenso, admittedly a much more critical author. Three evangelicals and the timid Bishop Jackson resigned from the Christian Evidence Committee, and two Evangelicals followed Shaftesbury out of the SPCK altogether. The Evangelical party did not, though, mount an all-out offensive on Maitland's book as High Churchmen had done over the Athanasian Creed, and Shaftesbury's protest created no more than a brief flurry.

He had suspected that the old popular enthusiasm for Biblical literalism had gone even before the event bore out his fear. 'I shall [be] nearly alone,' he wrote in his diary late in 1877, 'and be condemned, censured, privately, and publicly hated; and be left to myself like an Owl in the desert, a Sparrow on the housetop, or a Pelican in the wilderness.'[79] Some people even suspected that Shaftesbury might have doubts about his own position: 'this extreme jealousy about the smallest deviation . . . from the baldest theory of literal inspiration does not betoken confidence and strength', the editor of the moderate high church newspaper, the *Guardian*, wrote; 'We begin to think that Lord Shaftesbury and his friends have their misgivings.'[80] Perhaps they were right. Again in his diary Shaftesbury asked, 'Have I been over-zealous? . . . have I been blind?'[81] In any case, all the Church officials whose opinion of Maitland's book was sought formally by the SPCK repudiated Shaftesbury's stand. In less than ten years, Biblical literalism had fallen from its throne as the ruling orthodoxy of the mid-Victorian Church, and was now the creed of only a small minority at least, among articulate churchmen.

Still, the opinions which the Church officials pronounced on Maitland's book indicated that they were hesitant about what should replace Biblical literalism. It was not surprising that Archbishop Tait should defend the book, and in the letter to Maitland in which Tait gave his judgment[82] he upheld its orthodoxy and devout spirit. Nevertheless, he suggested revising the book to minimize the offence it might give to those still unaffected by Biblical criticism. With regard to the many prophecies upon which Maitland refused to base his plea to sceptical theists, Tait confessed himself unable to understand how they could confirm the faith of believers and yet be useless in discussion with doubters. He also questioned the wisdom of giving publicity to 'the doubtful conclusions of a destructive criticism'. 'It is, no doubt, wise in arguing with sceptics to meet them on their own ground,' he wrote, but 'the minds of those who take up your book without fully understanding its object, might naturally be startled and unsettled by your apparent readiness to allow that the statements of [sceptical scholars] are to be accepted as proved.' In other words, concession might be necessary to win the doubtful, but it it might also disturb the faithful.

This was the quandary in which the Church found itself. The only faith which could retain popular acceptance was an unquestioning one. To accept some criticisms and reject others required an amount of study for which few men had the time, ability or confidence. As a result many churchmen recognized the force of Shaftesbury's claim that 'the slightest concession in respect of the "Revealed Word" opens a door, which can never be shut, and through which, everything may pass.'[83] With this in mind, Bishop Ellicott recommended a more severe course than Tait's.[84] Although agreeing with Tait that the book did not go beyond the bounds of orthodoxy, Ellicott advised that it should not be reprinted. As he told Tait's chaplain, 'We have of late thought so very anxiously and tenderly of unbelievers that we have forgotten the stumbling blocks that we have placed in the pathway of average believers.'[85] Ellicott had lost confidence that more than a few outsiders could be won over by books such as Maitland's; what concerned him more was their unsettling effect on those inside the Church who, he assumed, would not otherwise be reached by the disturbing conclusions of Biblical critics. In short, the Church must give up its hopes of evangelizing those outside and concentrate its energies upon holding its own.

Only one of the bishops, the one most respected by contemporary scientists,[86] Goodwin of Carlisle, upheld Maitland's book without reserve.[87] He did not have much more confidence than Ellicott in its ability to convince the doubtful; all Goodwin claimed with certainty was that to suppress the book 'would indicate a weakness and cowardice which could not be otherwise than injurious to the cause of truth.' To concede might not work, but refusal to concede would harm. The consensus of the bishops whose opinion of Maitland's book was sought was generally favourable towards it but critical of certain passages as 'erring in excess of concession'.[88]

Meanwhile Maitland had tried to satisfy such criticisms by

preparing a second edition in which he toned down his discussion of the prophecies of the dispersion of the Jews.[89] However the SPCK insisted that he make further revisions before the book could be issued again,[90] and it clipped the wings of its Christian Evidence Committee to prevent any further controversy of this sort.[91] The Committee's statement at the beginning of its publications disclaiming responsibility for every line of argument was dropped, and a panel of bishops was empowered, upon complaint, to decide on the acceptability of works issued by the committee. The committee itself accepted the need for greater caution for fear of upsetting the assurance of unsuspecting churchmen.[92] Immediately the number of its publications tapered off even more than before, but the SPCK comforted itself with the assertion that the works already published by the committee covered nearly all the ground subject to sceptical criticism.[93]

In the autumn of 1874, satisfied that the passage of the Public Worship Regulation Act[94] during the summer had checked the rise of at least one expression of over-belief in the Church of England, Archbishop Tait concentrated his personal attention on religious scepticism. Ever since he became archbishop, his energies had been consumed either by arguments within the Church over doctrine, ritual and administrative reform, or by defending the establishment. Now he considered all such controversies 'as nothing compared with this contest between Christianity and Infidelity.'[95] He may have been impressed by a comment in a letter from his old friend recently returned from North America, Goldwyn Smith, no religious enthusiast himself: 'Nothing has struck me more in revisiting England after a long absence than the vast growth, not merely of Scepticism but of blank Materialism among the most highly educated and intellectual classes. . . .'[96] Tait was worried also by the uncertainty of the young men who came to him for ordination.

His great political opponent in ecclesiastical affairs, Gladstone, had, unbeknown to Tait, turned his attention to the same issue. In 1872, absorbed though Gladstone was in leading his vigorous cabinet, he confessed to one of his lieutenants: 'we politicians are children playing with toys in comparison to that great work of and for manhood, which has to be done, and will yet be done, in restoring belief.'[97] In 1874, out of office, he took up the pen as a religious controversialist. Both Tait and Gladstone, though usually immersed in day to day affairs, were familiar with the growing intensity of intellectual criticism; it was to reach a climax in the second half of 1877[98] when nearly every issue of the *Fortnightly Review* contained an article attacking Christianity. Tait always did a lot of serious reading between Parliamentary sessions, and knew what Mill and Arnold wrote. He also knew intellectual ability when he saw it: it was Tait who had first recognized J. R. Green's ability as a historian by giving him charge of the Lambeth Palace Library.[99] In December 1874 Tait decided to do more than arbitrate disputes between conflicting theological schools, and he published the first of a series of his own rejoinders to the sceptical attack. At first they were ineffectively old-fashioned,[100] but in 1876, after a Parliamentary session concerned with further reform of elementary and university education, his thinking crystallized. Part of his second Charge as archbishop delivered that autumn was devoted to this subject,[101] and almost attained eloquence. He followed it up, though less effectively, in his final Charge of 1880.[102]

To begin with Tait needed a clear conception of his opponents' arguments, and they were as diverse as his colleagues'. There was Huxley whose 'shallow *railings* of those who believe in the Bible and total misconception of the Belief of intelligent religious people' seemed to Tait beneath contempt.[103] Such strident opposition to Christianity was reminiscent of eighteenth-century deists such as Tom Paine. But two new ingredients had been added to the intellectual ferment. In October 1874 Tyndal, one of the foremost scientists of the day, delivered an instantly famous address at Belfast in which he advocated a careful form of materialistic atheism. Demonstrable scientific conclusions should, he insisted, be the sole foundation for philosophic speculation, and they seemed to dictate a purely materialistic conclusion. Soon afterwards Tait noted: 'When I was young we were told there was no such thing as an atheist in the world, but all that is changed. . . . A materialistic atheism is in the air.'[104] Secondly there were men like Matthew Arnold who 'tell us that they almost envy us for our hopes, and think that nothing but good to the world can follow from our acting on them'[105] so long as the theology underlying those hopes was emasculated. It was for men like Arnold and those they influenced, much the largest group of Victorian doubters, that Tait tailored his case.

Like them, Tait refused to acquiesce in the polarizing of religious thought going on particularly in continental Europe. There, he said,

Either you have atheistical philosophers or you have superstitious devotees. You have the men, except the priests, against the truth of Christ, and the women with the priests taking refuge in some debased form of Christianity which can scarcely hold its own against the growing intelligence of the age.[106]

In England too this division had occurred, though in inevitably muted form. The English counterparts of Continental ultramontanism were the Oxford Movement and the Catholic revival; indeed, there was no more fanatical ultramontane than Archbishop Manning, once a disciple of the Oxford Movement and now the most aggressive Catholic revivalist. Tait was only the most prominent of many English churchmen who were afraid that such over-belief, itself a reaction to infidelity, would only foster the development it feared. Henry Wace, the chaplain of Lincoln's Inn, warned Tait of 'robust and practical laymen, . . . who revolt from what appears to them the superstition now asserting a place within the Church, and who find it more congenial—not to a frivolous, but to a serious and manly temperament—to err with the Sceptics than to be right with modern Dogmatists.'[107] Tait did not need the warning. However he had come to the conclusion that the Church's most serious enemy was not superstition but infidelity.[108] He was worried now by the clergy who were watering down their presentation of Christianity in response to the intellectual climate.[109] Colenso's ideas had always seemed to him 'rash and arrogant',[110] and with advancing years he fell out of sympathy with the younger generation of broad churchmen.

It was from Cambridge and particularly from Lightfoot, long his chaplain for examining candidates for ordination, and soon, on his strong advice, bishop of Durham, that Tait found his answer to the intellectual assault. In Cambridge if not elsewhere there was 'a fountain-head of . . . Scriptural truth, imbuing the minds of our rising clergy with a love for the unadulterated Word of God, powerful even already, and certain, by the help of God, to become more powerful as time advances.'[111] Lightfoot and his colleagues, Westcott and Hort, were engaged in scientifically careful but at the same time patently reverent Biblical criticism designed not only to determine the authenticity of the books of the Bible and their components, but, on this secure foundation, to discover the intended meaning of the writers or, in Tait's words, 'the unadulterated Word of God'. They united this scholarly search with an active concern for the well-being of the Church of England—Lightfoot was Tait's intermediary with Liddon during the Athanasian Creed controversy—and for the welfare of their fellow citizens later expressed in the Christian Social Union of which Lightfoot was president. Tait never fully understood their scholarly work, and he did not presume to defend it in detail. He did appreciate and warmly endorsed the frame of mind from which it proceeded.

His own argument was much more crude than theirs. In an attempt to satisfy the contemporary craving for indisputable fact, he pointed to 'the two great facts' of the Bible and the Church. These grand facts ought, he argued, to carry much more weight than the paltry results of archaeologists' and geologists' digging of which the critics of Christianity made so much.

What, compared with two such facts as these, are any observed traces of primeval man in some distant cave which no one has thoroughly investigated? What, compared with these, are the traces of the feet of extinct animals impressed upon the mud here and there?[112]

Even if historical criticism proved many of the books of the Bible to be inauthentic, the few which were left, St. Paul's epistles to the Corinthians for example, were enough by themselves to vindicate the historical bases of Christianity.[113] Taking up for a moment the role of Biblical critic himself, Tait maintained that the most natural account of the origin of the books of the New Testament was that their authors honestly described and explained what they believed to be true, not that they were artful deceivers.[114] At any rate, each single book of the New Testament proclaimed the Christian gospel; therefore, proof of the authenticity of any one book led to acceptance of the teaching of the others.[115]

Nevertheless, vindication of the historical authenticity of the New Testament did not in itself prove that the Christian gospel it taught was true. To lay an epistemological foundation for his advocacy of Christian doctrine, Tait called upon the work of the greatest eighteenth-century English divine, Bishop Butler's *Analogy of Religion*. Admittedly the intellectual climate in the eighteenth century was not as radically hostile as now; admittedly too Butler had assumed belief in an intelligent and benevolent God which Christian apologists could not do now.[116] Still, Butler had shown that, except for the narrow field of mathematics, proof was always a question of probability, in the natural sciences as much as in religion. Now when so much was made of science, this old point needed reassertion; and Tait pointed out that 'there is no real difference in kind between the arguments on which the conclusions of physical science are based, and that result of all our examination of Christian evidence which pronounces the religion to be divine.'[117] Both Christianity and natural science had their 'facts'; but the philosophical or religious conclusions to be drawn either from religious or from scientific facts depended on argument, on a thoughtful weighing of the pros and cons.

Now Tait could present the conclusions which his facts induced him to draw. Christianity was not for Tait a system of thought made up of doctrines, whether High Church or Evangelical, but rather an appeal and response to the cry of conscience. There was something within man which reached out beyond the merely natural; each man possessed a soul which expressed itself from day to day as conscience, and loomed largest in the face of death. How could one, confronted by experience of death such as Tait had encountered, believe that physical nature laid down the limits of life? The heart of his religion and of his religious appeals to others was his experience of tragedy. Dry intellectual arguments might fail to convince gainsayers in the day of their health and confidence, but 'in hours of sickness and approaching death, and when friends are taken from them; then we may find their consciences awake and their hearts open, ready to return to the faith of their childhood, and to believe in the great Redeemer.'[118]

Tait believed that the spectacle of death and the voice of conscience must lead men to believe in the Christian gospel: 'That Christ died for us; that we needed that He should die for us from our weakness and continually recurring sin; that He is at the right hand of the Father, having risen from the dead, ever making intercession for us; that He will come again at the last day to own those who are faithful to Him, in the presence of His Father and the holy angels'. [119] This was more than the purely ethical religion of Dean Stanley. Tait made no attempt to minimize the miracles, particularly the resurrection, which formed a vital part of this gospel.[120] On the other hand, belief in the gospel did not mean Shaftesbury's fundamentalism. Tait placed all his emphasis on the few central gospel truths. They were, he insisted, essentially simple, and therefore their presentation could be adapted to the changing circumstances and new lights of succeeding ages.

Tait had always welcomed 'the expanding thought and stirring life of an era of freedom, enlightenment, and progress, . . . in which by God's will our lot is cast',[121] and he saw no incompatibility between the march of intellect and the Christian gospel. Repeatedly he pointed out that 'many questions connected with the form in which theology is taught may, in consequence of what we know as to language, ancient monuments, and the earth's changes, require reconsideration and readjustment';[122] and he urged his clergy to make themselves familiar with the fundamentals of physical science and the currents of philosophical thought.[123] He was anxious that the Church in his day avoid the excessive and subsequently embarrassing furore that Galileo's findings had produced in an earlier age[124] and that clerical reaction to Darwin and Biblical criticism had almost reproduced in the 1860s. Moreover, Tait expressed confidence that increasing knowledge and experience would only bear out more strongly the central gospel truths. For example, comparisons being drawn between the Old Testament and contemporary writings of Middle Eastern peoples other than the Jews seemed to Tait, far from lowering Judaism into just another ancient religion, to emphasize the validity of the concerns which the writers of the Old Testament shared with the other writers and at the same time to show up the Old Testament's superiority.[125]

Tait fortified his case for Christianity by warning that rejection of the gospel would produce moral decline, and he dismissed the sceptics' hopes to the contrary. Disbelief in God or in the immortality of the soul had always, Tait claimed, led to intellectual and moral degradation.[126] And though, as was often pointed out, other world religions might teach many high ethical principles, Christianity alone gave its adherents effective inducements to obey them. As proof Tait spoke without hesitation of the Christian as 'the best specimen of man which the world has yet seen'[127] and of the moral superiority of nineteenth-century Europe compared to the early Roman Empire, Asia and the 'regions which Moham-medanism has desolated, blasting the sacredness of family life, and treading down alike social and political liberty.'[128]

The archbishop's speeches in defence of Christianity heartened some of those who already agreed with him. Moorhouse, the vicar of Paddington, wrote to a friend; 'What a true great man is dear old Tait. . . . His words are like a battle cry, so stirring and generous, and with it *true* and *real* and *wise*. Amidst the ignorance, superstition, and *pettiness* of so many so-called leaders what a joy it is to get such a challenge as his. . . .'[129] Even Cardinal Manning told Tait of his pleasure in seeing 'how strongly and truly you had spoken of the chief peril of these days'.[130] However, upon those to whom Tait was appealing, the doubters, he had no apparent effect. One freethinker replied to Tait's Charge of 1876 with a letter full of scornful repudiation.[131] Another young man made his debut as a public speaker by scoffing at Tait's confidence in the moral superiority of Europe, and then by turning to discuss current politics.[132] No one questioned the archbishop's personal sincerity, but his message was not convincing.

In 1881 Tait was given striking evidence of the continuing loss of religious confidence. A meeting of scientists was convened under his auspices[133] to consider how best to counteract the impetus which their colleagues were giving to the decline of religious faith. The response the invitations to the meeting received was poor: of the forty-eight asked, the weightier half including sixteen pro-fessors and, not surprisingly, Darwin, declined to attend.[134] So did Canon Farrar of Westminster, who explained that he was not hopeful of the outcome of such a conference.[135] In the event those who attended failed to agree on a united manifesto. Instead they recommended that each believing scientist should be encouraged to speak out independently on the relation between his own par-ticular scientific discipline and his faith. Even this was too much for Professor Hughes, a geologist at Cambridge and the son of the bishop of St. Asaph. Hughes confessed his fear that, by de-fending their belief in public, scientists who were still Christian would only succeed in driving those of their colleagues now quietly agnostic into public opposition.[136] His alternative was friendly discussion between believing and doubtful scientists, and a hope that the current storm of scepticism would blow over.

The storm was subsiding even before Tait's death in 1882, the same year Darwin died. However, the calm was not comforting, for it stemmed, not from revived religious confidence, but from diminishing interest. The proportion of articles on religion in the *Contemporary Review*, for example, fell off from over one-half in 1866 to less than a quarter in 1884. Matthew Arnold, despite all his personal concern, admitted to a friend in 1881 that,

whoever treats religion, religious discussions, questions of churches and sects, as absorbing, is not in vital sympathy with the movement of men's minds at present. . . .[137]

Perhaps the explanation of this popular loss of interest is best left to the enigmatic comment which a minor Nonconformist Radical M.P., E. A. Leatham, had made in the debate on the Public Worship Regulation Act:

Life appears to me to be really too short for theology, such as it has become. . . .[138]

Chapter Three

NO LONGER ENGLAND'S SCHOOLMASTER

> I look forward to the time when the whole world shall have so
> improved by the blessing of Almighty God that it will be ready
> for the coming of the Lord.
>
> *From an address by Tait in 1880*

ARCHBISHOP Tait took the unsettlement in religious belief seriously, but it never destroyed his confidence that England was and in all likelihood would remain a Christian country. Above Victorian England's nagging doubts there was a thick layer of organized activity among all Christian denominations, thicker than at any time since the Civil War. Participation in religious philanthropic enterprises, concern about private and public morality, and interest in denominational and theological disputes had reached a new peak. Even anti-clericalism in England marched against the privileges of the established Church under the banner of Nonconformity.

This preoccupation with religion had not always been an English characteristic; it did not apply to Hanoverian England; and it was not to last. Archbishop Tait mistook it for proof of England's undying loyalty to the Christian religion, and he placed his faith in the country accordingly. Again and again when the interests of Church and State threatened to conflict, he sought to avert the clash by referring to public opinion. He was not reluctant to admit that this public opinion demanded the remoulding of old institutions to meet contemporary needs, a demand with which he urged the Church to cooperate even when it hurt; but equally, he believed, the public would insist that in enacting reforms the State continue to make provision for the religious requirements of its subjects. In no sphere was Tait's trust in the English public more evident than in his handling of the transformation of all levels of education during his archiepiscopate, and nowhere was both the strength and the hollowness of his confidence more clearly revealed.

The teaching of the young was the last of the major social services for which the Church had been responsible in the Middle Ages that was still largely in Church hands. Oxford and Cambridge were Anglican preserves, secondary education was given mainly by 'public' and endowed schools usually directed by clergymen, and in the last fifty years the Church had increased its hold on education by building and running three-quarters of the primary schools in the country. The Church was anxious to retain this predominance, realizing, in Archdeacon Denison's words, that 'The Religion of a People, in our time of the World, depends upon its schools'.[1] Furthermore, to serve as the country's educator was a good way for the Church to justify its privileged position as the establishment.

However, the inadequacy of English educational institutions was second only to Irish disestablishment among the questions debated in the general election of 1868, and the victorious Liberals were committed to extensive reform. The schools or colleges at every level of instruction failed to reach most of the people who needed them, and to measure up to the standard that was essential if England was to maintain its industrial superiority. A recent series of royal commission reports—the Newcastle Commission on elementary education in 1861, the Clarendon Commission on the nine most important public schools in 1864, and the Taunton Commission on the other secondary schools in 1867—had made this failure abundantly clear. Only the public schools had already been taken in hand with the passage of an Act by the dying Parliament in 1868 setting up a statutory commission to reorganize their governing bodies with or without their cooperation. Recent events both at home and abroad underlined the need to carry reform to all other schools. The victory in 1865 of the north in the American Civil War and in 1866 of Prussia over Austria had been widely interpreted as proof of the superiority of countries with extensive, efficient school systems. Above all, the Reform Act of 1867 made the education of the classes which it enfranchised imperative.

An overhaul of English education was certain to curtail the grip the Church held on it. One of the criticisms most frequently made about all levels of educational institutions from primary schools to the universities was about their more or less exclusive adherence to the established Church and the predominance of the clergy as governors and teachers. Moreover where, as in elementary education, the problem was the inadequate number of schools, the Church could not hope to make good the deficiencies on its own because already its supporters were paying as much as could reasonably be expected of them to maintain existing schools, and even so these schools also depended on government grants. Therefore, churchmen had to choose between the interests of the Church in resisting or at least restraining change and the needs of the country in demanding it. Tait tried to avoid the choice by arguing that the country wanted its schools and colleges to be religious as well as reformed. At first his point of view was widely shared, and no government ever repudiated it. However, as the reforms began to take effect, the interests of the Church and the claims of religious instruction were increasingly subordinated, and by the time of Tait's death their prospects were bleak. Public opinion had come to regard religious education not as unimportant but as less important. The pillar on which Tait had supported his case was crumbling.

Endowed Schools

W. E. Forster, the person Gladstone placed in charge of education, had served on the Taunton Commission, and he immediately introduced a bill to take the endowed schools in hand. Most of them had been founded in the sixteenth and seventeenth centuries, and they suffered from all the anomalies of outdated institutions. The charters of many forced them to admit applicants indiscriminately if they came from a locality dear to the founder's heart or were nominated by trustees.[2] A few of the schools were immensely wealthy—Christ's Hospital enjoyed an annual income of £42,000 over and above its site and buildings—but most were poor, more than half with less than £100 a year, some with less than £10. There was a 'complete absence of all organization of schools in relation to one another'[3] and to current demand. The education provided by most of them was not good, and in general they failed to prepare candidates for admission to the universities: fewer than 40 of the 800 endowed schools offering secondary education sent as many as three students per year to Oxford or Cambridge. For the most part, their only common feature was the presence of Anglican clergymen on their boards of control or as their teachers, not always popular in a country little more than half of whose church-going citizens adhered to the Church of England.

The Endowed Schools Act of 1869 called for the appointment of a statutory commission, the customary agency for reforming educational institutions, but broke from precedent by giving the initiative in reorganizing foundations to the commissioners rather than to the local trustees. The Church had reason to worry about the Act because it instructed the commissioners, in preparing new statutes for schools, to do away with any previous requirement that teachers be ordained, to insert a conscience clause excusing pupils from religious instruction and worship if their parents so wished, and to provide for the selection of school governors without regard to their religious beliefs.[4]

The commissioners appointed by the government were determined to act vigorously. One of them, Arthur Hobhouse, regarded himself and his fellow commissioners as missionaries of reform 'sent to lighten the heathen, and to be persecuted and perish at their hands'.[5] He did not have long to wait. The commissioners' schemes had to be laid before Parliament, and if neither House objected they would become law. In 1871, led by Lord Salisbury, the House of Lords delivered a blow to the commissioners' prestige by throwing out their scheme for Emanuel Hospital, Westminster. Backed by the Lord Mayor and Aldermen of the City of London, whose power to administer the foundation and nominate those who were to benefit from it was attacked by the scheme, Salisbury criticized it as contravening the will of the founder, Lady Dacre, who had stipulated that the school was for the benefit of the poor, not, as now proposed, mainly for the middle classes. Lord Lyttelton, one of the commissioners, pointed out unavailingly that the scheme would increase the number of students to be educated in the school from the present 143 to over 750.[6] In 1872, encouraged by their success against the scheme for Emanuel Hospital, the Lords rejected three more schemes.

Tait abstained from these debates and discussions until 1873. He felt no sympathy with the Conservatives' defence of vested interests and their inefficient preserves; rather, he wanted the management of Church schools to be congenial to current reformist opinion.[7] In 1871, when he had to appoint a headmaster for the Whitgift Middle-Class School, an endowed school in Croydon, he had the clause restricting the office to a clergyman rescinded, and appointed a layman, to the delight of the Liberal *Daily News*.[8] However, in 1873 the House of Lords was presented with the commissioners' scheme for King Edward's School, Birmingham, which cut its connections with the Church. The headmaster and assistant masters would no longer have to be clergymen or even churchmen, and the provision for religious instruction was weakened even though the school's statutes already contained a conscience clause. Most serious of all, control of the school was to be wrested from the bishop of the diocese, to whom Edward VI had given it, and placed in the hands of the Birmingham town council whose members, especially now that Joseph Chamberlain was mayor, were distinguished for 'their extreme and passionate dislike of religious instruction in public schools'.[9] This was too much for Tait, and he joined the Conservative peers in throwing the scheme out.

Since 1870 the Church Institution[10] and its successor, the Church Defence Institution, both reflections of politically Conservative opinion in the Church, had been campaigning against the commissioners' pinched interpretation of the Endowed Schools Act, for example their prohibition against clergymen who sat *ex officio* on a school's board of governors from continuing to do so. The Act was due to expire in 1873, and Forster gave notice that he would move for a committee of the House of Commons to inquire into the working of the Act. Immediately the Church Defence Institution organized a conference of concerned churchmen.[11] The conference appointed a committee under Salisbury's chairmanship to coordinate defence of Anglican endowed schools[12] and to bring pressure to bear in the House of Commons' committee. Subsequently it was induced to lessen the Anglican grievance about *ex officio* seats for clergymen and generally to adopt a more conservative attitude towards the reform of Church schools.[13] Still not satisfied, the Church Defence Institution mobilized its support to persuade the House of Lords to reject the new Endowed Schools Bill which the government introduced.[14] The Conservative Lords succeeded in reducing the term of the commission to be reappointed under the Bill from three years to one, thus enabling a Conservative government which, they hoped, would be in power next year, to recast the Act.

The Conservatives gained power at the beginning of 1874; and the Endowed Schools Bill of that year was Salisbury's brainchild. It was a blatant attempt to protect the interests of the established Church in secondary education. The Bill proposed to transfer the responsibilities of the endowed schools commission to the charity commission (set up in 1853 to curb some types of administative malpractice in philanthropic foundations). More pointedly, the Bill attempted to reverse the former commission's tendency toward undenominational education. Ironically, Parliament spent so much time over another ecclesiastical measure, Tait's Public Worship Regulation Bill, that the government, faced with unrelenting criticism from the Opposition to the schools Bill, reduced it to a transfer of the endowed schools commissioners' task to the charity commission, and this was all that was enacted. The change reduced the temperature of controversy surrounding reform of endowed schools, since the charity commission proved less aggressive and more tactful than the endowed schools commission. The charity commission concentrated on schools where the need for reform was most obvious and where there were no strong vested interests to be provoked.

Again Tait took no part in these Conservative manoeuvres, and his known sympathy with reform occasionally earned a reward from the charity commission. When it tried to remove his power as archbishop of Canterbury in appointing the headmaster of the Whitgift School in Croydon, he was able to preserve some of it because the commission deferred, as its secretary put it, to the archbishop's authority and experience in educational matters.[15] However, shortly afterward when he sought to maintain his position as Visitor of Dulwich College and the Anglican religious teaching and facilities for worship there,[16] he was less successful. The charity commission reinstated the office of Visitor but stripped it of power. Originally the commission had proposed to replace the reference to the Church of England in the description of the religious teaching to be given in the school with the word 'Christian'. In response to Tait's protest the commission made the dubious concession of cutting out 'Christian' without putting anything in its place.[17]

Still, in general the commission showed itself to be genuinely conciliatory. For more than ten years none of the schemes it submitted to Parliament was rejected, though some aroused protests.

When serious opposition revived, it came from Birmingham in the name of democracy[18] rather than from the House of Lords in the name of the Church.

Elementary Schools

After Parliament passed the Endowed Schools Act of 1869, Forster concentrated his attention on the base of the educational pyramid. It was at the elementary level that the Church had performed its most outstanding service to nineteenth-century England.[19] Since the formation in 1811 of the 'National Society for promoting the Education of the Poor in the Principles of the Established Church', most churchmen had come to assume that a primary school was an essential part of any parish; Blomfield, Tait's predecessor as bishop of London, had considered that, if both school and church could not be erected at the same time in new working class parishes, the school should go up first.[20] The amount of time, energy and money which churchmen, especially the clergy, had thrown into elementary education was truly impressive. One government inspector of schools reported in 1842:

I can find only nine instances out of nearly 200, where I have not reason to think that the clergyman has a deep interest in his school, not shown only by words, but by watchful care and frequent attendance. I could mention instances, where, after morning religious instruction in the day school, the clergyman teaches the school at night; . . . others again where, besides labour almost beyond his strength, pecuniary help beyond his means has been cheerfully given, poor children paid for, masters' stipends made up to a certain income, repairs done, as it were, by stealth, debts willingly taken upon himself, and contributions offered, liberal to excess, that others might be moved to contribute liberally.[21]

Proportionately churchmen and the National Society did a much larger amount for elementary schooling than the Nonconformists and the undenominational British and Foreign Schools Society; and when in 1833 the State began to subsidize the religious agencies according to the work they did, the National Society consolidated its gains and went on to increase them. Of the 8,798 schools receiving state aid in 1870, 6,724 were Anglican.

Though much had been done, it was not enough. Only half the parishes of England and Wales were served by State aided and

72

inspected schools.[22] Less than one-third of all children between the ages of six and twelve attended these schools regularly. The failure was greatest where education was most urgently needed, among the very poor, and in the industrial towns of the midlands and the north. Only a few of Shaftesbury's Ragged Schools and some Roman Catholic ones reached the destitute; and less than one-fifth of the children in Birmingham, Leeds, Liverpool and Manchester were receiving regular instruction.

The crux of the problem was finance. Voluntary religious agencies depended for the bulk of their income on personal benevolence, and even when it was given by many people generously, it was not enough to meet the country's needs. This inadequacy was bound to stand out most obviously in poor, densely populated areas. Only the State with its power to impose taxes could raise the money necessary to cover the country with schools.

Even more serious than the quantity of elementary schooling was its quality. The percentage of children in primary schools in England compared well with other countries. But only thirty-four per cent of teachers in Church day schools were adequately trained.[23] Increased financial aid from the State could help here too. However, the heart of this problem was religious as well as financial. Many Church schools were more concerned to inculcate piety and morals than to equip their pupils to compete in an industrial world; more emphasis was placed on the Bible and the catechism than on the three R's.

The very magnitude of the Church's achievement aggravated yet another problem which was purely religious. Under the influence of Archdeacon Denison, the National Society had adopted a policy of narrow denominationalism. Although as far back as 1839 the Privy Council committee on education had advised schools receiving State aid to adopt a conscience clause and since 1862 had insisted on it, the National Society had stoutly refused to agree. It had even refused to have anything to do with Lord Shaftesbury's Ragged Schools Union because it was not exclusively Anglican.[24] As a result, many parishes had only one school which, controlled by the National Society, refused to make any allowance for the children of non-churchmen in the religious instruction which permeated the curriculum. Now that compulsory church rates had been abolished, the single school parish was the chief Nonconformist grievance. Of course Nonconformists would have lessened the problem if they had thrown themselves into the work of building their own schools with as much determination as Churchmen had shown. However, to compete with much the largest and wealthiest denomination was discouraging and, in rural parishes, often impossible. During the 1860s Nonconformity was driven to the conclusion that the government must take over primary schooling completely. Most Nonconformists still wanted religious instruction to be given in the schools, but it must, they insisted, be strictly undenominational. In 1869 the National Education League was founded in Birmingham to agitate for universal, free, compulsory and unsectarian education supported by the rates and under public management.

What this amounted to in religious terms was a demand for the creation of a system of education congenial primarily to Nonconformists. Nonsectarianism in England meant Protestantism, the common denominator between Nonconformity and the Church of England. Applied to education it would be unacceptable to many Anglicans—probably a majority, certainly not just high churchmen—who considered the Church's distinctive doctrinal teaching of great if not crucial importance; and, much more so, to Roman Catholics. At present many Nonconformists who wanted their children to receive a rudimentary education had to send them to exclusively Anglican schools, undoubtedly an affront to conscientious conviction. Under the proposed system, all Englishmen would have to send their children to nonsectarian schools, an affront to the religious convictions of many more.

This religious dilemma was Forster's most difficult problem. He could not avoid it by opting for completely secular education because he knew—and this confirmed Tait's trust in English opinion—that only a small radical minority wanted it. But the Birmingham League's agitation and popular dislike of the National Society's harsh denominationalism combined to prevent Forster, even had he wanted to, from trying to make the existing network of schools complete by a great increase in government grants. On the other hand, an economy minded government such as Gladstone's could hardly contemplate the expense of creating a completely new national network of schools when a great number supported in large part by voluntary contributions already existed. And though Nonconformist support was crucial to the Liberal party, it could not afford to cast Church opinion ignominiously aside when churchmen had done so much more than any other group for primary education.

The Elementary Education Bill which Forster presented to Parliament in 1870 proposed to fill the gaps in the existing system partly by further subsidies to the voluntary schools but chiefly by creating local public authorities to build and run schools where needed and to tax the ratepayers for their support. The country was to be divided into small districts in each of which the adequacy of existing facilities would be assessed. Voluntary schools would be taken into account if their facilities were up to a certain standard and if they accepted a conscience clause. The voluntary agencies would have one year in which to remedy the deficiencies discovered. Then, wherever necessary, a local board would be elected to complete the network by levying a rate to subsidize the voluntary schools or, more probably, to establish its own. In board schools, whatever religious instruction the board desired could be given. The former denominational system of school inspection was to be replaced by a purely governmental one which would ignore religious instruction.

Militant Nonconformists and Radicals reacted to the Bill with an immediate and prolonged outcry, for denominational schools would now form a large and permanent part of the national network, fortified in some places by rate aid. And not only would the grievance of single school areas remain where existing facilities were adequate for current needs, but also board schools could give thoroughly Anglican religious instruction if the board so wished. The mandatory conscience clause for all schools was meagre consolation.

The government accepted several amendments to meet the religious objections of its left wing. Denominational schools lost their hopes of direct rate aid; the provision for building grants to them was withdrawn; the time voluntary agencies were allowed to make good the deficiencies discovered in each area was cut down from a year to six months; elections to school boards were taken out of the hands of rural vestries chaired by the local vicar and of town councils, and were placed directly in the hands of the ratepayers; the conscience clause was made more effective by stipulating that religious instruction could be given only at the beginning or end of the school day; and religious teaching in board schools was limited by a clause proposed by Cowper-Temple, a

Whig Churchman, prohibiting the use of any distinctively denominational catechism or religious formulary.

However, the government refused to abandon the main principle of the Bill, the incorporation of existing schools into the national network, and it also agreed to amendments to compensate voluntary schools to some extent for the losses they sustained through the accepted Nonconformist amendments. Voluntary schools were to be given increased grants direct from the exchequer amounting to half their maintenance costs. The rules governing possible transfers of voluntary schools to board control were stiffened: now the consent of two-thirds of the managers and the financial contributors was required rather than of one-half of the managers alone. In response to a demand from the House of Lords, provision was made for cumulative voting at school board elections: each ratepayer would be entitled to as many votes as there were seats on the board, and as a result minorities could increase their representation by plumping for their candidates. This change was designed by the Lords to protect Anglican minorities in such places as Birmingham, and for a while churchmen were able to use it to good effect.

The Bill was eventually passed by Opposition Conservative votes over the angry protests of the government's backbench supporters. The validity of their complaints seemed to be proven by the welcome with which most churchmen greeted the Act. Only thorough high churchmen berated it. Canon Gregory deplored the conscience clause, the demand for which he minimized,[25] and regarded the further time-table restriction as a refinement in horror. Still worse was the Cowper-Temple clause; as the *Church Times* put it:

'No formularies, no creed, no catechism'—truly the Church has come to a pretty pass. 'Feed my lambs'? Yes, upon the husks which a Liberal Government, egged on by political Dissenters, leaves, after sifting out all the grains of dogma. . . .[26]

Gregory also belittled the shortage of schools[27] which made State intervention necessary. And, initiating a cry which was to be heard repeatedly in the following years, Archdeacon Denison predicted that the civil servants administering the Act would insist on standards of teaching beyond voluntary schools' means.[28] Most Churchmen, however, were heartened by the Act's acceptance of their contribution to elementary education in the past. True, it had been made with the support of government subsidies, but these had been distributed to all voluntary school societies without partiality. Now all that the Church could hope for in elementary schooling was continued fair treatment, and that it had received. Of course the Act did not make them entirely happy. All its references to religious instruction were restrictive. But even an agent of the Church Institution defended the Act[29] for he knew that its concessions to Dissent were unavoidable. Moreover, with the minor exception of Gladstone's recent defence of the establishment in Wales, this Act provided the first clear evidence of the Liberal government's reluctance to deprive the Church of its pre-eminence.[30]

During the first half of 1870 Archbishop Tait was convalescing after another nearly fatal stroke which had come in the previous November, and he did not take any part in the Parliamentary debate on the Bill. His absence was not serious once the outlines of the Bill were known. If he had had strong objections to it, he could have brought his influence to bear by letter. He did write to Gladstone[31] in an attempt to persuade him to allow government inspectors to examine Church schools' religious instruction; otherwise its importance in the curriculum might well decline. With mounting Nonconformist anger to deal with, Gladstone could not agree. Except for this letter, Tait remained silent.

For, perhaps more than any other piece of legislation, the 1870 Elementary Education Act vindicated Tait's faith in English public opinion.[32] In spite of the bitter denominational conflicts which had studded the history of primary schooling in England for over sixty years and had prevented the creation of a national network of schools until now, Forster and the government had realized that the electorate would not do without some sort of Christian education. Of course the Act had its weaknesses. Tait was particularly uneasy about the Cowper-Temple clause, believing that religious teaching must be based on doctrine; but he had always thought that it was 'quite possible to give a sound Christian education and instruction, based on the great Gospel verities, which shall include the mass of English children, even those who do not belong to the Church.'[33] In any case, Church schools could continue to teach the full faith and thus complement the religious instruction in board schools.

Once the Act was passed, the Church's immediate job was to meet its requirements and make the fullest use of the six months allowed to voluntary agencies to fill the blanks. The limiting of government inspection to secular subjects created another gap for the Church to cover. The National Society accepted the time-table conscience clause for its schools. Strongly though Gregory had fought the Act, he led the National Society as its treasurer in throwing most of its resources including its reserves into a six months blitz, and when the time was up the Society had made grants to 1,411 more foundations, all but 140 of which met the standard necessary for inclusion in the national network.[34] Tait headed the effort to secure diocesan inspectors for religious instruction.

In 1871 school boards entered the fray, and Churchmen had to decide what attitude to adopt toward their financially powerful rivals who controlled the field which voluntary agencies had been unable to cover. Rivalry was inevitable, but not hostility. The elections for boards were contested largely along denominational lines, but successful Churchmen had the choice either of frustrating or assisting in the creation and improvement of schools under board control. The choice was not a simple one since, with the rates at their command and with the central education office encouraging attempts to raise standards, board schools could provide better and cheaper instruction than the voluntary schools could afford. With Olympian detachment Tait expressed the hope that the spiritual and temporal welfare of the children would be served by competition between the two sets of schools,[35] and he sympathized with the endeavour to raise standards. He was powerless, however, to prevent the more common response of men such as Gregory who ran in the second London school board elections on a platform of keeping rate charges down. Once elected, Gregory made every effort to prevent the standard of board school education from rising beyond the reach of voluntary schools.

Many Church schools soon found themselves in such financial difficulties that they transferred themselves to board control. By the end of 1873 the London board had taken over some fifty voluntary schools; Fraser, the bishop of Manchester, was so disheartened by 1875 that he was ready to hand all his schools over to the boards.[36] Other Churchmen looked for help to the recently elected Conservative government. In 1876 the new education minister, Lord Sandon, introduced a bill to extend the provisions of 1870 in the direction of compulsory attendance and also to help the voluntary schools. The help was meagre. It did improve the financial position of some voluntary schools but only the wealthier ones, and in general it did little more than lessen the pace at which board schools were outstripping their rivals.

Tait supported the bill for what little it gave, but for once he had no sympathy with the Nonconformist protest over the Church's gain.[37] The Conservatives allowed him one other improvement. The transfer of voluntary schools to board control made the question of the kind of religious instruction which board schools could give under the Cowper-Temple clause increasingly important. The clause's prohibition of the use of distinctive denominational formularies was often interpreted to rule out all credal statements, even those widely accepted among Protestant denominations. Tait induced the government to agree that board schools could use the Apostles' Creed, the ten commandments, and the Lord's Prayer.[38] Meanwhile he tried to prevent transfers within his own diocese wherever possible. When a transfer was unavoidable, he encouraged the managers of the voluntary school to bargain strongly with the local school board in order to preserve as much religious instruction and Church influence in the school as possible.[39]

The coolness of the Conservative government's response in its 1876 Education Act toward the voluntary schools' distress may have shaken Tait's confidence that the public wanted and therefore Parliament would continue to give them religious teaching as part of elementary education. At any rate, that autumn he began[40] and thereafter continued to urge his fellow Churchmen to greater efforts in order to sustain England's desire for religious education. Otherwise, he warned, the precedent which Birmingham set in prohibiting religious instruction in its board schools might be repeated elsewhere.[41] In addition to day-schools, Sunday-schools were needed, he said, to sustain the country's appetite for religious instruction. He argued on the same ground against those Churchmen who were willing to minimize religious instruction in board schools in order to accentuate their contrast with denominational schools.[42]

The return of the Liberals to power in 1880 made virtually all leaders of the Church anxious about the future of voluntary schooling. Churchmen were straining every financial nerve to sustain their schools: between 1870 and 1883 they raised £12,250,000 compared with £15 million in the previous fifty-nine years,[43] and they could not be expected to give much more. For this reason their spokesmen tended to oppose improvements in elementary schooling which might prove costly and also compulsory attendance; they realized that compulsory attendance would lead naturally to abolition of students' fees,[44] which were usually necessary to make ends meet in denominational schools. These considerations did not move the minister now in charge of education, A. J. Mundella. Though a Radical, Mundella did not contemplate throwing voluntary schools out of the national network. Most of them had proven their ability to survive in competition with a rate-financed system. Still, Mundella was quite prepared if need be to force poorer voluntary schools into the hands of school boards.[45] The new government promptly secured an Act making school attendance mandatory. In August Mundella announced his intention of bringing in a new code to regulate the distribution of government funds for elementary schooling.

While Mundella was drafting regulations for Parliament's consideration, Archbishop Tait issued cautionary remarks about the cost to the rate-payer of replacing voluntary schools with board schools.[46] The Lower House of the Convocation of Canterbury followed suit with a discussion in which Canon Hopkins, a respected moderate with particular concern for this subject, predicted that enrichment of the curriculum for elementary schools might lower the calibre of teaching in basic subjects and would push religious instruction onto the sidelines.[47] Hopkins was too proud of the Church's achievement in elementary education to adopt a purely negative stance. He stoutly asserted that voluntary schools gave as good secular instruction as board schools, with full religious instruction to boot. He went on: 'the voluntary schools are not asking for any exceptional favour. Far from it. But they claim that they are doing the work, and they ask to be allowed to do it, and to be encouraged to do it in the same way as they have been before'.[48]

The proposals which Mundella put forward in August of 1881 confirmed Anglican fears. In deciding how much each school would receive from the government, attention would be paid to what provision the school made for manual employment and play in the earliest grades, to its provision of a class to receive advanced instruction beyond what was now available, to the presence of libraries and scientific apparatus, and to the teaching of English literature, geography, and particularly science. The ratio between qualified staff and pupils was also to be improved. So concerned was Archbishop Tait by the possible financial consequences of these proposals that he took the (for him) unprecedented step of leading a deputation from the National Society to Mundella and his titular superior, the Earl Spencer.[49] Tait confronted the ministers with facts to prove the importance for primary education of the National Society and its schools: it spent £500,000 a year on its schools, money which otherwise would have to be raised by rates; Church schools were handling 2,327,000 of the 4,240,000 children now receiving elementary instruction. Then the archbishop urged reconsideration of some of the proposals which, though theoretically beneficial for elementary education, would in practice hurt even some of the best voluntary schools. Mundella, however, defended his proposals vigorously, and they took effect in the Spring of 1882.

Anglican educators could do nothing but comply. Perhaps the most telling illustration that the Church at last recognized the whip handle in primary education to lie with the State came in the form of a letter from the National Society to Archbishop Tait at the beginning of 1882.[50] Far from defying the government as it had so often done before the 1870 Act, the Society asked for Tait's help in overcoming the reluctance of impoverished Church schools to cooperate with the Society's attempt to raise their standards as was necessary for continuation of government grants. A few months later Tait was still calling his Church 'the great educational body for the benefit of the poorer classes of society',[51] but justification for the claim was slim. Rate-financed board schools had robbed the Church of some of the substance and much of the lustre of being England's schoolmaster: they had left voluntary schools dominant only in the countryside, and had made the Church an opponent of advancing standards.

Oxford

The archbishop's belief that in England educational reform would never suppress the interests of religion was nearly destroyed by the University of Oxford. This turn of events was all the more poignant because Tait was one of the fathers of university reform. As soon as he was elected to a Balliol fellowship in 1834 he began to attempt reforms in the college, and he spent the summer of 1839 in Prussia systematically studying the local system of university teaching and administration.[52] In 1850 the prime minister, Lord John Russell, arousing bitter opposition from Oxford, announced his intention of appointing a royal commission to investigate it, and he asked Tait, then dean of Carlisle, whether he would be willing to serve on the commission. Tait immediately agreed and threw himself into the work with enthusiasm.[53]

Tait, like Russell, was a reformer in the Whig tradition, anxious to preserve old but valuable institutions by tailoring them to meet present demands. Most of his fellow Churchmen were reluctant to apply this principle to Oxford and Cambridge since their inadequacy was bound up with their exclusive adherence to the established Church. No one could receive a degree from Cambridge without first subscribing to the Thirty-nine Articles, and at Oxford subscription was required even for admission to undergraduate status. Most of the fellows at both universities were or were expected to become clergymen. The subjects on which the teaching at Oxford and Cambridge was concentrated—classics in the first, mathematics in the second, and theology in both—were intended to train undergraduates for leadership in Church and State which, it was still implicitly assumed, were two sides of the same coin. In fact Oxford and Cambridge were more like theological seminaries than modern universities, the established Church relied on them for the bulk of its recruits for the ministry, and the training which young men received there was considered adequate in itself for ordination.

Nonetheless, Tait and his fellow members of the Oxford commission were moved to indignation by other restrictions which crippled the university. Only twenty-two of Oxford's 543 fellowships were filled by open competition, [54] and in any case there was a superabundance of fellowships consuming income which might otherwise have been used for the teaching of neglected subjects by the university. In an average year thirty-five fellowships fell vacant but only thirteen undergraduates secured first-class honours in the final university examinations. As for the religious restriction on admission to the University and the clerical restrictions on fellowships, they could be eased, the commissioners felt sure, without compromising the religious character of the education Oxford provided.[55] Most of the commissioners were, like Tait, clergymen, and they had no thought of secularizing Oxford. But some of them felt that the religious tests and clerical restrictions lessened the university's value as an educational institution, and also created artificial advantages for the Church not always in its best interests. As Stanley, the secretary of the Oxford commission, put it, clerical restrictions tended 'to discourage many important branches of study—to drive from the University many laymen, whose literary and scientific attainments would do it honour and service, and to offer questionable inducements for entering Holy Orders.'[56] Tait hoped that the removal of protective but sometimes debasing restrictions would incite Christian teachers at the old universities to greater efforts.

As a result of the commission's report, half of Oxford's fellowships were opened to free competition, colleges were empowered to fill one-quarter of their fellowships with laymen, and the path was cleared for introducing and developing the study of natural science and modern humanistic disciplines such as English literature and contemporary languages. A way round the religious tests was also provided. Private halls which need not demand any oath or declaration upon entrance or graduation could be founded; but the M.A., the prerequisite for office in the university, was still restricted to Churchmen. The value of these changes was borne out by the rising number of students who entered Oxford from 1862 on.

The reforms of the 1850s did not, however, satisfy the radicals in Oxford and Parliament and the militant Nonconformists. They refused to accept the retention of religious tests by the old colleges and for the M.A.; and abolition of the tests was almost certain once the Liberal party gained power. In the eyes of Oxford's High Church divines, particularly Pusey and Liddon, nothing could be more disastrous. They clung to the Oxford Movement's hope of using the university as a fulcrum upon which to move the whole Church. In order to preserve some kind of religious test, they offered to compromise. During the 1868 election campaign, Pusey came out in favour of denominational colleges for all religious communions.[57] After the election, Liddon resorted to proposing a relaxation of the religious tests to exclude total unbelievers but admit Nonconformists though only as students, not teachers.[58] Unbelief he now said was the gravest menace to the teaching of Christianity in Oxford, not defective faith.[59] Gladstone suggested that the effect of abolition of the tests might be offset by stipulating that half the fellows of each college should be Anglican clergymen.[60]

However, even High Church ranks were now divided. Some recognized the justice or at least the inevitability of ending religious discrimination at the universities.[61] More important, the pressure from Gladstone's political supporters for abolition was strong and persistent; in 1869 and 1870 the Commons passed bills doing away with tests; and though other demands on Parliament's time and opposition from the Lords prevented them from becoming law, Gladstone was forced to capitulate. In 1871 his government introduced and Parliament accepted a bill which abolished all religious tests at the universities except for divinity degrees and professorships.

Throughout the public and Parliamentary debate on abolition, Tait said little. In 1869 he joined the compromisers in suggesting the abolition of tests for some but not all fellowships.[62] Otherwise he held his peace, sorry to see the tests go but unwilling to antagonize Nonconformist and Liberal opinion on an issue which he did not think crucial. For as he told the Oxford Union on its fiftieth anniversary, he still trusted that the many Christians in England and the strong traditions of the universities would preserve their religious character.[63] And in any case it was protected by the clerical restrictions on fellowships, something the recent Act did not touch. He did not seem to be disconcerted by the fact that a Radical amendment to abolish these restrictions had been only narrowly defeated in the Commons.

Nevertheless, his old enthusiasm for reform had almost disappeared, and in 1876 when Lord Salisbury proposed further action, the archbishop responded uneasily. Salisbury wanted to place university reform in conservative hands, and the bill which he presented to the House of Lords provided for the appointment of a statutory commission but did not lay down the principles on which it should act. Some of the Oxford liberals took fright at the prospect of a commission which might only strengthen the conservative forces of the university against changes already being carried out by progressive colleges, and, playing for time, they asked for a preliminary investigation.

Tait rejected this course because he wanted an end to the period of reform so that Oxford could settle down.[64] Like reforming dons at Oxford he hoped to protect colleges against demands from the university.[65] However, his concern here was not to protect progressive colleges but to preserve the rights of Visitors many of whom were bishops and to prevent the university from forging ahead with new subjects—biology, sociology and anthropology, 'when it is certain these are sciences'—at the expense of 'those great and tried sciences [i.e. classics and theology] which the experience of ages has proved to be admirably suited for training the minds of the young.'[66] Moreover, though he favoured placing a time limit on the tenure of all fellowships, he advocated retention of non-resident fellowships[67] as a bond between the country and the university and an aid to bright young graduates trying to establish themselves professionally. The reformers considered such fellowships a waste of college income.

There was only one issue on which Tait was still an uncompromising advocate of change: the high cost to undergraduates of education at Oxford and Cambridge. He had been brought up in a family in straitened circumstances which, had it been English, might well have debarred him from receiving the higher education necessary to satisfy his ambitions. Fortunately he was born a Scot. Because the instruction in Scotland's universities was given primarily by university professors rather than in residential colleges, higher education there was much cheaper. In the 1850s Tait had urged that, without doing away with the great advantages of college life and tutoring, the English universities should provide instruction for students unattached to any college. As archbishop, Tait had further reason for advocating change in this direction: without it many of his clergy could not afford to send their sons to university.

In 1868 Oxford had opened its gates to unattached students whose number soon equalled a moderate sized college; but Tait was not satisfied by the instruction they were given. Furthermore, in remodelling scholarships and exhibitions, many of the old clauses stipulating poverty as a consideration in making the awards had been removed.[68] In the debates of 1876 the archbishop moved an amendment, supported by a petition from residents of the east London slums, to empower the proposed university commissioners to create scholarships for unattached students and to pay teachers for them.[69] The amendment was not popular among many Oxford men who often agreed with him, Jowett the master of Balliol for one. Jowett argued that the poor but bright could win college scholarships.[70] Tait was not convinced; he held that there were many young men not brilliant enough to win scholarships but quite able to benefit themselves and the country if offered a university education which they could afford;[71] and the Lords accepted his amendment.

The government did not press the bill in the House of Commons, and action was therefore delayed for a year. The bill which Salisbury introduced in 1877 and Parliament enacted incorporated Tait's amendment. Surprisingly the Act also incorporated the thorough reformers' demand that the existing clerical restrictions on fellowships could be reduced but not increased. Acting on the basis of this clause, in 1878 the secretary of the commission sent a circular to the colleges and individual fellows of Oxford asking for their views on the continuation of clerical restrictions on fellowships not specially connected with the duty of giving religious instruction or conducting chapel worship. The response was overwhelmingly hostile;[72] the Oxford radicals such as Asquith, then a fellow of Balliol, asked for the abolition of all clerical restrictions.[73]

Already the reduction of the number of fellowships held by clergymen had proceeded much farther than the Oxford commissioners of 1850 who began the change had anticipated. More and more open fellowships had been filled by laymen, fewer and fewer of them went on to take Holy Orders—no fellow of Balliol did so for at least twenty years after 1857[74]—and as a result in the 1870s clerical dons found themselves in a minority. In itself the change need not have betrayed Tait's trust that reform of the university was compatible with preservation of its religious character. Of course there was likely to be a lay reaction after centuries of clerical predominance. But what aggravated this reaction was something Tait had long feared. The excesses of the Oxford Movement and the religious wrangling it provoked had turned Oxford anti-clerical. This prejudice placed clerical candidates for open fellowships at a disadvantage, and therefore the removal of most of the clerical restrictions on fellowships would probably reduce clerical power at Oxford to a shadow.

It was only to be expected that Liddon would plead with the

new commissioners for retention of at least the existing number of clerical restrictions.[75] For the first time his opposition to reform was partially supported by some erstwhile reformers such as the Rev. G. G. Bradley,[76] Master of University College, who joined the commission in 1880 when Lord Selborne resigned to become Lord Chancellor in the newly elected Liberal government. What changed Bradley's allegiance was this anti-clericalism; it made him afraid that many of the small colleges, if allowed to do so, would exclude clergymen from all fellowships, and hire chaplains to conduct chapel services and offer instruction in divinity. The white neckwear of a clergyman would then be a badge of inferiority. Bradley also thought that collegiate education had no point unless dons were concerned for the moral as well as intellectual development of their students, a concern which he believed laymen were less likely to feel than clergy.

What particularly worried Bradley was that the clause in the Act which prohibited the creation of new clerical restrictions applied to colleges such as All Souls, New College, and Lincoln where none already existed. All Souls and New College were large and therefore would probably be willing to find room for some clerical fellows, but Lincoln College was small and, since it was markedly anti-clerical, most unlikely to do so. In a bid to relax the Act's prohibition, Bradley asked Archbishop Tait to request the publication of evidence which the commission had received but could not publish on its own initiative until its work was completed;[77] the evidence included papers which Bradley thought would strengthen his case.

Instead, Tait wrote a long letter to the commission[78] urging it to reserve some fellowships in all colleges for clergymen to conduct chapel worship and to study as well as teach divinity. Characteristically he rested his case, not like Liddon on the needs of the Church and its teaching in a hostile university, but primarily on public opinion. He recognized the 'tendency amongst those who advocate University reform in the present day, to ignore or at least to minimize the importance of Religious and Theological training.' But, he maintained, the country thought differently.

It seems to me that the feeling of the country, to say nothing of higher considerations, imperatively demands that our two great Universities shall still continue as they have hitherto been, nurseries of sound religion as well as of useful learning.

And again,

> I believe that the highest intelligence of the country, as well as an overwhelming numerical majority, is determined to adhere to the old principle that there is no better way of making good citizens than of using all legitimate means of making them good Christians.

His concern was all the greater because of his belief that

> it would be an evil day both for the National Church of England and also for the whole Christian populations of these lands if any steps were taken whereby those who are destined for the Ministry of the National Church should fail to find within our great Universities the best possible training for the work to which they have determined to devote their lives.[79]

There was, in his opinion, no better way of putting prospective clergymen in touch with the country's thinking and aspirations than to educate them in the national universities. As the universities shook loose from their former religious allegiance, many Anglicans had resorted to the creation of theological seminaries. Bishop Wilberforce founded Cuddesdon College in 1854, and when the universities' religious tests were abolished, many more seminaries sprang up.[80] Tait, however, shared the old Protestant suspicion of secluded institutions grooming young ordinands away from the public eye, and he blamed the new seminaries for fostering petty rivalry between conflicting schools of thought within the Church.[81] The only theological colleges he welcomed were those boldly placed in the university towns of Oxford and Cambridge, in particular Wycliffe and Ridley Halls, both evangelical.

His letter to the commission failed to persuade it to change its course. In fact the commission reduced the number of clerical restrictions at Magdalen College, Oxford, farther than originally proposed. Therefore, in 1882 Tait presented his case to Parliament,[82] and in particular he supported the protest by Christopher Wordsworth, the bishop of Lincoln, against the draft statutes for Lincoln College which made no provision for clerical fellowships.[83] Oxford must, said Tait, be kept in line with the nation's view of education according to which adequate provision should be made for religion, and must not be allowed to be coloured permanently by the university's current anti-clericalism.

At last Tait had found himself in the camp of the Conservatives and high churchmen resisting reform. Lord Salisbury and the

Conservative peers joined the archbishop and Wordsworth, the foremost High Church prelate, in throwing the proposed statutes for Lincoln College out,[84] and Liddon, for the first time in Tait's long career, applauded the archbishop's stand.[85] Tait still tried to dissociate himself from those who saw no hope for religion at Oxford;[86] most colleges still had one or two fellowships reserved for the clergy. But the rejection of the statutes for Lincoln College was the only success the critics of the Oxford commission achieved. Tait's trust that reform could be kept compatible with the interests of Christianity and the Church had been disappointed.

In losing its grip on education, the Church neared the end of its long history as provider of the nation's social services. This development was critical in the declining fortunes of the Church, for no other function which it might perform was likely to give it as much social power. Nevertheless, the Church still had unique means for social service at its disposal, above all the parochial system. In each of the small territorial units or parishes into which England and Wales were divided, the Church placed a man usually assisted by a wife, frequently also by daughters. He was always a person of some, often of considerable education; he might have a private income. Whatever his abilities and resources, he was expected as the local officer of the national Church to spend them in the service of the inhabitants of his territory regardless of their social standing, regardless also in theory and to some extent in practice of their religious predilections. The services he offered were not only religious. Apart from visiting the sick and bereaved, in most parishes he had helped provide elementary schooling; he usually assisted in the administration of whatever local charities there might be; and the enterprising incumbent went on to create whatever charitable agencies and services he thought were needed.

The school and the parish were the two arenas in which the clergy of the established Church sought to serve the social needs of nineteenth-century England. Contemporaries commonly appreciated this fact. Much of the Evangelicals' embarrassment in attempting to repress ritualism stemmed from the fact that some of its most notorious practioners were widely honoured for the care they took of their parishes in the worst London slums, pre-eminently A. H. Mackonochie in the alleys of Holborn and Charles Lowder near the docks. Generally the Victorian years of the estabblished Church were distinguished by a high average of performance by parochial clergy, though posterity recalls only a few, such as Keble in the village of Hursley, the evangelical incumbents of Islington, and greatest of all, W. F. Hook in Leeds.

The institutional leadership of the Church attempted to put and keep this parochial framework in good order. The reforms of Peel and the Ecclesiastical Commission had abolished pluralism, reduced non-residence, raised the lowest incomes of incumbents, and facilitated the subdivision of parishes where increased population made this necessary. Archbishop Tait was particularly concerned about the emergence in London of single class parishes caused by the flight of the middle classes to suburbs. They left unmitigated slums in their wake, and thus greatly weakened the parish church and clergy as a bridge between classes. Tait himself lived on the edge of such a slum. The chimneys of the Doulton china factory beside Lambeth Palace made the surrounding air foul, driving away those who could afford to move; and Tait strongly supported a motion in the House of Lords to set up a royal commission on contamination of the air by factories.[87] And yet, purely lower class parishes only accentuated for Tait the value of the presence in their midst of a clergyman [88] who, he assumed, would be of a higher class.

Tait pointed with pride to the parochial system in relation also to the fight against intemperance. Next to education, temperance was the social need which concerned the clergy most. The root of intemperance among the underprivileged lay deeper in the social order than all but a few churchmen dared go. Nevertheless, drunkenness was obviously and alarmingly extensive—according to an unofficial source, one out of every thirty-four houses in England was licensed[89]—and it created such degradation that it was in itself a grave cause of social disorder. In spite of the existence of other temperance societies, Tait strongly supported the separate Church of England Temperance Association[90] because it could call on the services of the established Church's unique network of officers in every locality in the country.

The proliferation of single class parishes, however, was a sign that the parochial system was anachronistic in an industrial society.

The Church needed to devise new tools, indeed a new social role for itself. An episode which indicated that this need was recognized at least dimly in the highest councils of the Church occurred toward the end of Tait's archiepiscopate. It was a time when economic depression was bringing out social antagonisms muffled for a generation by prosperity and when the Church's dominance in education was almost gone.

Sometime, probably in 1878, thirty clergymen formed a committee to consider the relation of the Church to trade unions. These clergymen were for the most part young, able, and high church, with a sprinkling of broad churchmen: they included Stewart Headlam, Henry Scott Holland, Arthur Stanton, Randall Davidson, and for the sobriety of age or position Mackonochie, Dean, Church of St. Paul's, William Walsham How, soon to be suffragan bishop of London and J. B. Lightfoot, soon to be bishop of Durham. Early in 1879 they seized on a passage[91] from one of the National Society's school textbooks which reflected precisely the kind of thinking which the Church would have to throw off if it wished to make a favourable impression on the labouring classes. The book described trade unions as opposed to the introduction of machinery, as making their members slaves of union leaders sometimes by brutal means, and as injuring 'not merely those engaged in them, but every one else also, by preventing the employment of capital in setting labourers to work, by which they might support their families.'

The committee sent the National Society a fully argued protest.[92] In it the textbook's treatment of trade unions was criticized as out of date, animated by hostility, and blind to the affinity between the principles of trade unionism and Christianity. The committee knew that the compilers of the textbook had taken its quotations covering this subject from the writings of Richard Whately who was professor of political economy at Oxford briefly before becoming archbishop of Dublin in 1831.* His words could, therefore, be upheld as true of his day if not of the 1870s. This, however, was all that could be said in defence of the quotations; the committee asserted 'resistance to the introduction of

* A spokesman for the committee later described Whately's views as reflecting 'the hard temper of a logical Protestant irritated by contact with what he thought the pure irrationality of Irish Roman Catholicism.' The Rev. John Oakley to J. Duncan, 12 March 1879, Tait papers, 1879 Home 357a.

machinery, and organized violence against Non-Unionists or Unionists who transgress the rules of the Union, have, since the Acts completely legalizing the Unions,* become things of the past.' The committee questioned indeed whether Whately's charges were ever true of trade unions as a whole; certainly the quotations conveyed a lack of sympathy 'with the position of the labouring classes under the sufferings and wrongs which they endured during the early portion of the present century.' Not content to defend trade unions against harsh accusations, the committee went on to contend that 'the sinking of individual claims for the general good is a principle which has strong Christian sanction.'

The National Society hastened to explain that it was not hostile to trade unions and that the text-book was to be superseded by one of a new series of books now in preparation.[93] The National Society stopped further sale of the book in September of 1879.[94] However, in October the National Agricultural Labourers' Union drew Archbishop Tait's attention to the offending book and asked him to have it banned in the National Society's schools.[95] The Parliamentary Committee of the Trades Union Congress quickly followed with a request that Tait receive a deputation from them on the subject.[96]

Tait's reception of the deputation could have critical importance because it would be the first official confrontation between leaders of the established Church and of the trade unions. Hitherto the general impression of the Church that organized labour had received was as yet another vehicle of upper and middle class hostility. Anxious to improve this image, the recently formed clerical committee put itself in touch with Tait,[97] stating that it too wanted an immediate ban on the book and asking to be allowed to be present when he met the deputation.

Tait did much better than that. Perhaps he was briefed for his meeting with the deputation by Davidson, his chaplain, who was a member of the clerical committee. At any rate, after the members of the deputation had spoken, Tait captivated them with a short speech.[98] Political economy like all science was, he began, progressive; many concepts which earlier political economists had

---

* Presumably the Trade Union Act and the Criminal Law Amendment Act of 1871 and the Conspiracy and Protection of Property Act and the Employers and Workmen Act of 1875.

taken as axiomatic were now open to question. Labour too had advanced in its thinking; the outrages of an earlier day were repudiated by unionists now as heartily as by anyone else. By implication the archbishop was adopting the attitude of the clerical committee. He managed, moreover, to salvage some credit for Whately, 'the author of these unfortunate statements', by pointing out to the deputation, who were staunch Liberals, that Whately had served the Liberal cause outstandingly. As for the particular matter at hand, Tait told them that the National Society had already decided not to issue any more copies of the book, and he promised to see if the Society could go further to meet the deputation's request. Then he took the deputation to meet representatives of the clerical committee who had come to support the request. Henry Broadhurst, secretary of the T.U.C.'s Parliamentary Committee and leader of the deputation, left the meeting confessing that he had been quite taken back by the breadth of Tait's thinking.[99]

The archbishop congratulated himself that the conference had 'tended to assure any who may hitherto have doubted it, that the Church of England is anxious to shew herself in every way the best friend of our working classes.'[100] However, by making no attempt to consolidate this impression, in fact by paying virtually no attention after the meeting to the Church's relations with organized labour, Tait rendered his achievement ephemeral. Without clear leadership, the voice of the Church through its clergy continued, as before the meeting, to make conflicting sounds. A growing number of clergymen, though never until the twentieth century more than a minority, spoke like the clerical committee. A dwindling though larger number were avowedly sympathetic with the employer rather than with the workman, whom they spurned as 'a selfish, drunken fellow, who wastes his money and sends his wife begging.'* Probably a majority thought either that the Church ought not to meddle with organized labour any more than with the owners of industry, or that the Church should adopt a position of strict neutrality between the two, occasionally attempting to reconcile them. There were, therefore, not even the beginnings of a consensus within the Church on the social role it should try to take up now that its medieval one as the source of the country's social services was fading away.

* The words are the Rev. Wm. Benham's in his letter to Tait, 20 Nov. 1879, Tait papers, 1879 Home 357a. Benham, interestingly, was the son of a working man.

Chapter Four

REFORMING THE CHURCH UNDER
GLADSTONE, 1869–1872

> Mr. Gladstone . . . throughout his long leadership of the Liberal
> party, has shown, on all matters of Church reform, not the spirit
> of a Liberal and a reformer, but that of a favourer of clericalist
> pretensions.
>
> *Canon W. H. Fremantle in 1888*

THE ecclesiastical side of Tait's trust in England's Christianity
was his attempt to make the Church of England think of itself
primarily as a national institution. He constantly talked about 'the
National Church'. By this he did not mean that the established
Church was the department of State for religious affairs, but he
did mean, in conscious opposition to the high church view, that
the Church should concern itself more about satisfying the religious demands of the country than about its own spiritual
autonomy.

The archbishop was far from alone in hoping to bridge the gap
between England and its Church. In fact some of the men responsible for the current religious uncertainty in England, which
might have been thought to weaken this hope, shared it. Even
Huxley believed that an established Church could exercise a
beneficial influence on the country if only it would devote itself
'not to the iteration of abstract propositions in theology, but to
the setting before men's minds of an ideal of true, just, and pure
living'.[1] In the late 1860s England was losing its earlier prosperous
confidence and Matthew Arnold, who was contributing to the
change, preached a return to the national Church, though without
most of its supernatural theology. His message was indicative of
a widespread, wistful desire that the Church of England might
strengthen the grasp on ethical and spiritual values which, it was
strongly felt, England needed.

94

However, as Huxley's and Arnold's provisos made clear, everyone saw that the Church would have to be reformed before it could be more widely effective, and they differed profoundly about what the reform should be. Huxley and Arnold believed that a more or less extreme theological revolution was required. Very high churchmen agreed, but wanted the Church's thinking and practice to be revolutionized in the opposite direction. Furthermore, they believed that the country too would have to undergo a drastic reconversion before it could be at one again with the Church. Archbishop Tait's comfortable view that England would remain a Christian country as long as a majority of its citizens adhered to one denomination or another did not satisfy, for example, the Hon. C. L. Wood,* president of the English Church Union, the organization which the very High Church had founded in 1860 to defend and promote its beliefs. Wood held that it was not enough for a person to be Christian; he must belong to the one Catholic Church properly in the country, the Church of England (the Roman Catholics were interlopers); and furthermore he must appreciate the Catholic nature of his Church. It was only by considering those without any specific religious allegiance as belonging to the established Church that a majority of the population of England could be thought Anglican; and of practising members of the Church, only a small proportion had a true conception of its nature. Accordingly Wood and high churchmen of his ilk thought of themselves as missionaries in an alien environment more than as servants of a national institution.[2]

In contrast to Huxley and Arnold on the one hand and to Wood and the E.C.U. on the other, Archbishop Tait advocated modest reform, not revolution, to make his Church more effectively national. England was Christian; much the largest single denomination was Anglican; and to many other Englishmen the established Church was an acceptable, often beneficial institution which the country would be poorer without. Yet it needed reform to do away with the remaining abuses and outmoded customs and restrictions which limited its administrative efficiency and popular attractiveness. Reform generally would appeal to the public in this 'age of improvement'.[3] And Tait shared the contemporary faith in reform; late in life he recalled the old observation that:

* Later the second Viscount Halifax.

the first thing said when any change was proposed was that it was impossible, secondly that it was contrary to the Constitution, and the third remark generally was, that nobody had ever doubted that it was fine.[4]

Changes such as Tait envisaged had already proven successful. In the wake of the Reform Act of 1832 Sir Robert Peel and Bishop Blomfield had adopted a policy of energetic Church reform which resulted not only in removing the most glaring abuses in the Church but also in making better use of its financial resources and in warding off the opponents of establishment. Further reform would continue to strengthen the establishment by refuting the two groups who attacked it: the Churchmen who criticized the restraints which union with the State imposed upon the Church, and the Radicals who attacked it as nothing but a tissue of anomalies and abuses. The archbishop hoped too that the improvements he envisaged would lessen the Church's bitter internal divisions[5] since they were caused by conflicting efforts to deal with the rot in the Church and the threats to it from outside, the very things which his reforms would minimize.

Much reforming remained to be done. Commercialism and simony coloured the exercise of some private patronage. Apart from the foundation of the bishopric of Ripon in 1835 and of Manchester in 1847, the number of dioceses had remained unchanged since the sixteenth century while population doubled, redoubled and shifted to the cities, a situation made intolerable by the legal inability of bishops incapacitated by age or sickness to resign. In 1868 four bishops who had charge of dioceses stretching from London to Land's End—Winchester, Salisbury, Bath and Wells, and Exeter—were unable to work; and they could only delegate their administrative duties to some diocesan official, and their strictly episcopal work to the already overworked bishops of neighbouring dioceses or to retired colonial bishops.

A few reforms could be carried out by the primate alone. In 1872 he changed his archiepiscopal Charge from the traditionally long treatise delivered at one assembly of all the clergymen and churchwardens of the diocese into a series of shorter speeches given throughout the diocese to small gatherings.[6] In doing so he won an enthusiastic response and good press coverage. 'Among the immense opportunities of an Archbishop', wrote *The Times*, 'there are few more valuable than that of thus putting a new life into old forms, and the Archbishop has more than once displayed a happy capacity for this task.'[7] The scope for such reforms, however, was strictly limited because, as one of the consequences of establishment, most of the organization and conduct of the Church was prescribed in the law of the land, and therefore could be changed only by Act of Parliament. Most of the changes Tait advocated involved legislation, and for this reason they aroused the suspicion and sometimes hostility of moderate high churchmen, all the more potent because the man with whom the primate would have to work to secure legislation, the prime minister, was one of them.

Gladstone wanted the Church to be reformed and modestly so, but more modestly than the archbishop. Moderate High Churchmanship was a conservative position whose advocates were willing, indeed anxious to make the Church spiritually more effective, but were equally anxious to preserve and strengthen the authority, practices and teaching of the Church as it had been in the early seventeenth century. It was the tradition of the Caroline divines, of Lancelot Andrewes and Laud, more than of the early or medieval Church, which these moderates, unlike their extreme High Church colleagues, wished to revive. This tradition had always enjoyed an honoured place in the Church of England, and they were wary of plans for change. Leader of the Liberal party though he was, Gladstone could say in 1874 that 'there is many an ancient fabric not too old or weak to stand, but too old for ambitious and organic repair.'[8]

There was one line of change, however, which Gladstone and High Churchmen of like mind wanted to follow: they wished for increased recognition of the Church's autonomy in spiritual matters. Ever since the repeal of the Test and Corporation Acts in 1828, Parliament and the Church had been drifting apart, initially because of Parliament's desire to shed the religious restrictions on its ability to represent national opinion. The drift contributed to the birth of the Oxford Movement which widened it by placing utmost emphasis on the unchangeable authority of the Church. Moderate high churchmen such as Gladstone and his clerical ally, Samuel Wilberforce, thought that the Movement went in the right direction even if too far. Gladstone was the politician most responsible for the revival of the ancient but weak clerical counterparts to Parliament, the Convocation of Canterbury in 1852, and the Convocation of York nine years later. He was pleased by the decline in Parliament's desire to interfere in Church affairs,[9] and he doubted the qualification of M.P.s and peers to deal with them. There was no inconsistency, as he saw it, between this High Churchmanship and the Liberal policy of eliminating religious restrictions in the constitution and lessening the Church's political privileges. On the contrary, some degree of disengagment between Church and State short of disestablishment would enable each to do its job better: the State could respond to the aspirations and needs of all its subjects regardless of their creed, and the Church would be less tempted to compromise its integrity in order to work with Parliament.[10]

Gladstone's political position made him even more hesitant to go along with Tait's projects requiring cooperation from the government. In view of the increasing demands on Parliament's attention, Gladstone had to allot the Parliamentary time at the disposal of the government carefully in order to push even two major controversial pieces of legislation through each year. Moreover, he was sufficiently anxious to retain the support of the Nonconformists, who were devoted to separation of Church and State more than to him, to tell John Bright towards the end of 1871 that he would 'wish to retire from public life, rather than . . . go into sharp and vital conflict with them.'[11] This sympathy of his with the Nonconformists had done much to create the alliances upon which the Liberal party was based; and while Tait liked the result, he sometimes failed to appreciate the costs involved.

Therefore, though Gladstone was willing for some changes in the Church's administration to be initiated in Parliament, he insisted that more serious or contentious measures, especially those involving the Church's teaching or worship, would have to be agreed upon within the Church before its leaders could expect legislation. Church doctrine and worship were the province of the Church alone. Moreover, by acting on questions of this sort while they were still the subject of controversy within the Church, Parliament would alienate the school of churchmen whose wishes it disappointed, and they would respond by resenting, perhaps even by defying, what Parliament had enacted, a long step toward disestablishment which Gladstone did not want.

In contrast to the prime minister, the primate deplored the widening separation between Church and State. In line with the teaching of Coleridge and Thomas Arnold, Tait believed that the welfare of the country and the Church was best served by the complementary action of State and Church. On its own the Church would become an introverted and exotic clique, and the nation would fall back rather than continue to progress. For Britain's power, according to the archbishop, stemmed from its citizens' attempt to live up to the Christian principles of reverence for God and charity towards men.[12] Consequently, he welcomed the legal necessity of working with Parliament to improve the operation of the Church. Parliament was not a necessary evil from Tait's point of view, but rather the most important expression of lay opinion. The majority of its members were Anglican; and, as the nation's representatives, they met to discuss and deal with the condition of the country including the national Church, exactly the context Tait wanted. As for the non-Churchmen in Parliament, he accepted them as a reflection of important groups within the country which the Church needed to understand.

The character of the new Liberal Government only encouraged the archbishop. As a Whig, he sympathized with many of its political principles; and the cabinet included several devoted churchmen, H. A. Bruce, the Home Secretary, Edward Cardwell, the Secretary for War, and the Lord Chancellor, Hatherley. Above all there was Gladstone, the most outstanding lay Church-man of his day and paradoxically but, Tait thought,[13] most advantageously in command of the Radical and Nonconformist elements of his party. If anyone could curb their usual antipathy to the Church and ecclesiastical legislation, Gladstone could. By securing the assistance of such a government, feared as it was in spite of Gladstone by many men whose first interest was the Church, Tait would be able to convince the Church that it could co-operate beneficially with whatever government the country elected.

The first negotiations between the new prime minister and the new archbishop boded well for Tait. It was Gladstone who took the first step, in May 1869, early in the first session of the new Parliament, by telling Tait that the problem of the disabled bishops had come up in the House of Commons. Gladstone suggested that the bishops prepare a solution.[14] Tait had been working on his own for the required legislation,[15] and he readily accepted the prime minister's proposal. They discussed a possible bill, and the cabinet empowered a lawyer to draw one up in consultation with

Tait, who in turn would consult other bishops.[16] Once the bill was prepared, Tait secured the government's support for it, and immediately presented it in the House of Lords. Entitled the Bishops Resignation Bill, it provided for the resignation of diocesan bishops and the appointment of successors, or alternatively for the appointment of coadjutor bishops not permitted to sit in the Lords, these new bishops to be paid from the sees' existing revenues. By coming before Parliament while it was debating the government's bill to disestablish the Irish Church, the Bishops Resignation Bill furnished practical testimony that the government intended to some extent to cooperate with the Church in England.

Very few peers were hostile to the Church, and the Bill ran into little difficulty in the House of Lords. The debate in the Commons turned out differently. Although Gladstone introduced the Bill there and spoke forcefully in its favour, the militant Nonconformists attacked it. They resented the fact that the State concerned itself with the constitution of one denomination. Church legislation, they complained, ate up the already none too plentiful time at the disposal of Parliament, which furthermore was not qualified to handle such questions. In short, their attitude toward ecclesiastical legislation was an extreme version of Gladstone's. Their opposition, together with the scrutiny to which some churchmen subjected the Bill, never placed it in serious danger, but induced Gladstone to conciliate critics sympathetic to the Church by making minor changes in the Bill and by restricting its operation to two years. He was careful to secure Tait's approval for these amendments,[17] and the Bill passed. However, Gladstone told Tait ominously that the measure had given more trouble than he had expected.[18]

Tait knew that this Act was not enough even for the limited problem of inadequate episcopal care. Before Gladstone had written to him about the disabled bishops, Tait supported a motion in Convocation for increasing the number of bishops.[19] In the autumn of 1869 he wrote a long letter to Gladstone[20] stressing the need to create three new sees: one to ease the burden of the bishopric of London and to include all of the diocese of Rochester north of the Thames,* Rochester then to be extended south of the Thames to relieve the other metropolitan diocese of Winchester;

---

* In 1846 Rochester had been extended north to include most of Hertford and Essex.

one to split the vast diocese of Lincoln; and one for Cornwall. Tait assured Gladstone that all the bishops and both houses of Convocation supported this proposal. He explained how the Church would finance the new sees, and suggested in regard to seats in the Lords that the system of rotation be extended. 'The thing *can* only be done by a powerful ministry', he wrote in his appeal, 'and *will* only be done by Ministers who like yourself and the Lord Chancellor have a real understanding of what is needed in such matters and a real desire to improve the machinery through which the Church acts.'

Gladstone's response was cold. The doctrine of apostolic succession which underlined the importance of episcopal care might have inclined him personally to support an enlargement in the number of bishops. But in addition to the trouble he had experienced over the Bishops Resignation Act, he was aware of the hostility toward the presence of any bishops in the House of Lords which was felt by Radicals and a few evangelical churchmen such as Shaftesbury, who disliked all clerical pretensions. Any increase in the number of bishops, even if not of their number in the House of Lords, might well bring this antipathy to the fore. The urgency of Tait's letter suggested that the archbishop too recognized this possibility but hoped that Gladstone would risk it once convinced that the goal was good. Gladstone secured the agreement of his cabinet to a conference on the subject between a committee of some of its members and Tait with two or three other bishops, but held that the bishops must take the initiative in making proposals. He also cautioned Tait that the measure's benefit to the Church would have to be clear, and insisted that the united episcopate support it.[21] The conference was held a few days later, and after full discussion the cabinet committee decided that it could not ask Parliament for legislation.[22]

As a second best, the bishops proposed that the government exercise its power under a long neglected Act of Henry VIII's reign to appoint suffragan bishops to assist diocesan bishops where necessary, and the government agreed.[23] Tait was disappointed with the failure of his original proposal since it would have met the Church's needs more effectively, and he continued to favour subdividing overlarge dioceses. Yet he urged the Church to make full use of suffragans,[24] and, together with the bishop of Lincoln who had identified himself particularly with this reform, he took the lead by asking for and receiving the government's approval of a suffragan bishop to assist him in his own diocese.

In 1870 Tait turned his attention from administrative reform to the conduct of worship. The Bible selections which the prayer book ordered to be read at Matins and Evensong were often long or of unequal length with the result, so it was thought, that they discouraged busy men working on a regular schedule from attending week-day services. People who could go to Church on Sunday only in the afternoon because they had to work in the morning always heard selections from the Epistles, never from the Gospels.[25] Evangelical churchmen thought that too many lessons came from the Apocrypha. And many Victorians found some selections from the Old Testament too earthy. At the beginning of 1870 the royal commission on ritual[26] published its third report consisting of a revised table of lessons drawn up in the light of these and other criticisms and in close contact with leading ecclesiastics and theologians.

Bishop Wilberforce asked Gladstone to lay the proposed revision before the Convocation of Canterbury, and Tait endorsed the request.[27] He was never quite happy with Convocation because it was an Anglican, not a national, assembly, because it was purely clerical, and because the Lower House had marked high church leanings. Nevertheless, as the historic and constitutional voice of the clergy of the province of Canterbury, Convocation was the most powerful expression of Church opinion; and Tait knew now that only the clearly stated consensus of recognized spokesmen for the Church could induce the government to sponsor any ecclesiastical bills.[28] The Upper House (composed of the diocesan bishops of the province) endorsed the new table of lessons or lectionary unanimously; and in the Lower House it enjoyed wide support ranging from Dean Stanley to Canon Gregory. Nevertheless, it was opposed by a determined minority of Tory High Churchmen led by Archdeacon Denison. For them, the proceedings which would lead to the bill were riddled with State interference and lay power whereas, in their opinion, the clergy were the only proper spokesmen for a Catholic Church. The lectionary had been produced by a commission which was appointed by the Crown and contained many lay members, and now the cooperation of Parliament was being sought. Furthermore, the thoroughness of the revision aroused their Tory aversion to change,[29] and they were suspicious of any measure designed to adapt the ministrations of the Church to current circumstances.

The support which these diehards were able to muster in the Lower House furnished disturbing proof of the amount of resistance the archbishop had to overcome in marshalling support within the Church for any reform. Although their own uncompromising motion was lost by 16 votes to 40, a delaying motion was defeated only by the casting vote of the Prolocutor, the presiding officer.[30] However, they spoke for no more than a small minority in the Church at large. Many High Churchmen contended that only synods could give spiritual validity to ecclesiastical legislation,[31] but they welcomed opportunities for cooperation with the government. Even though the government's initial refusal to lay the ritual commission's report containing the revision before Convocation left a rankling sense of injustice, most High Churchmen wanted Convocation to play its part in the legislative process.[32] If, as the sponsors of the measure intended, the eventual Act stated that Convocation had approved it, the role of Convocation would receive greater official recognition than at any time since its revival.

The Lower House finally endorsed the revision by a vote of 41 to 17, and Tait could convince Gladstone that it enjoyed the support of the Church. But because of the time taken to secure Convocation's approval, the Bill was not introduced in Parliament until the end of May, a little late to be sure of passing in that session. Lord Shaftesbury wanted to subject the Bill to detailed criticism, and he succeeded in changing its name from the Prayer Book (Lectionary) Bill to the Prayer Book (Table of Lessons) Bill because he saw signs of popery in the word 'lectionary'.[33] Otherwise, the House of Lords gave the Bill a smooth passage and made just a few changes in it strictly consistent with its principle. However, the prospect in the Commons of many amendments which would in all likelihood provoke a good deal of debate led the government to withdraw the Bill even before the House took it up.[34]

Archbishop Tait was annoyed, all the more because other legislation[35] upon which he claimed that the Church and in particular Convocation was agreed had not been enacted. He wrote privately to Gladstone stressing the need to pass the proposed lectionary,[36] and publicly to the bishop of London in an attempt to elicit a still

wider expression of Church opinion.[37] Now Tait contended that
the lectionary Bill would provoke the same fatal amendments in
Parliament unless it was accompanied by other legislation covering
recommendations of the recently published fourth report of the
ritual commission, recommendations which he thought—too
optimistically, as it was to prove—nearly all Churchmen supported.
They included provision for a burial service which could be used
for the unbaptized, the excommunicate and suicides, and a change
in the rubric governing the Athanasian Creed. In addition, Tait
advocated some measure to give the laity of each parish a say in
the way their public worship was conducted.

There was good reason for Tait's belief that these changes
would make the Church more popular throughout the country.
Most people were disgusted, for instance, when a clergyman
refused rites of burial to a baby just because it had not gone
through the service of baptism. However, High Churchmen
stiffened by the Oxford Movement insisted that baptism was an
absolute prerequisite to Christian burial. Tait never recognized
that the reforms which he advocated could be made only at the
expense of aspects of the Church's Catholicity as High Churchmen
understood it.

His case for extended legislation was broken by the Athanasian
Creed controversy. Some men in Parliament such as Thomas
Chambers were determined to use the introduction of any ecclesiastical bill as an opportunity to move for abolition of compulsory
use of this creed. Tait said that such a motion would be carried
whether the government supported it or not;[38] certainly he himself would vote for it. He also tried to appeal to Gladstone's
dislike of incessant ecclesiastical legislation by arguing that, in
order to prevent motions about the prayer book from coming up
each year, action should be taken on the Athanasian Creed now.

Yet even in November 1870, before the controversy over the
creed hardened, the prime minister had been cautious about
charging the government with more Church bills; the Franco-
Prussian War was dominating Parliament's attention.[39] By the
beginning of 1871 it was clear that the Church was deeply split
over the creed, and Gladstone refused to let his government take
sides. Because he agreed with Tait that it might be impossible to
avoid this subject in any Parliamentary debate on the ritual commission's fourth report,[40] Gladstone tried to transfer responsibility

for ecclesiastical legislation in Parliament to other shoulders at least temporarily. The government took hard work upon itself when it sponsored a bill;* and since private members controlled a great deal of Parliament's time, Gladstone suggested that Tait might introduce legislation through some distinguished, independent M.P.[41] Eventually the government agreed to introduce the lectionary Bill—in plenty of time to ensure its passage—but they made it clear that they would not accept any amendments carrying it beyond a table of lessons.[42] Tait felt obliged to co-operate, and he persuaded Chambers to withdraw his proposal. On other amendments Gladstone proceeded only with the approval of the leaders of the Church.[43]

Although Liberationist M.P.s opposed the Bill with a stultifying amendment, it was crushed by an adverse vote.[44] Then, late in June, the Bill was endangered by the refusal of an evangelical M.P., Locke King, to withdraw his amendment cutting down the number of lessons from the Apocrypha, a change supported by his fellow Evangelicals but opposed by High Churchmen. For fear of the debate which the amendment would provoke, Gladstone hesitated to push on.[45] Tait tried to induce Locke King to withdraw his amendment and urged Gladstone to bring his pressure to bear towards the same end or, if necessary, to strangle the amendment with an adverse vote.[46] Gladstone, however, would not presume to decide how a doctrinal issue such as Locke King raised should be settled. Alone Tait managed to persuade Locke King to drop his amendment, and the Bill passed with only minor changes.

These changes were enough to worry strict High Churchmen who believed that only Convocation's approval could make changes in the Church's doctrine or discipline valid. When the Lower House had considered the ritual commission's revision, Canon Gregory persuaded them not to introduce changes for fear that Parliament would then feel free to do the same.[47] When Parliament did so anyway, 776 clergymen petitioned Convocation, vainly, for definite authorization of the lectionary as enacted by Parliament.[48] The Act still annoyed High Churchmen[49] because Parliament had

---

* Gladstone's diary for 30 May 1872 illustrates this: 'During the evening two long conferences on Washington Treaty with Lord G[ranville]. and the lawyers, and a cabinet 10–1. Worked Uniformity bill through committee at intervals.' Morley, *Gladstone*, II, p. 410.

cut out the reference in the preamble to the approval of Convocation. Although even High Church peers, Nelson and Carnarvon, had reluctantly agreed to this amendment because it was made on the ground that Convocation had not acted in the proper form,[50] the amendment still looked like an insult to Convocation such as evangelical legislators and others who jealously guarded the supremacy of Parliament were only too ready to give.

Tait rejoiced over the passage of this Act[51] as proof of the practicability of legislative reform, all the more eloquent because three measures* reforming the administration of the Church were enacted during the same session. Yet the path for further reform looked far from smooth. Gladstone's reluctance to give the support of the government was not the only obstruction. Despite his attitude, which was never clear to the public, many churchmen feared that Parliament, especially when led by the Liberals, might use the Church's request for legislation as an opportunity to enact changes which the Church did not want. In order to meet both these difficulties, Tait concluded that further changes could be secured best if the Church discussed them still more thoroughly beforehand. Once again his desire for reform induced him to place greater reliance upon Convocation; and in doing so he could not avoid fostering the Church's sense of independence.[52]

The need for legislation had been particularly pressing since the publication of the ritual commission's fourth and final report, which covered all the rubrics in the prayer book. One division of the report consisted of recommendations for loosening the rules governing the conduct of worship. Without such a change, services could not be shortened for use on week-days. There was even some doubt whether Holy Communion could be used legitimately without being preceded by Matins. Churches could be used for preaching only if the sermon were accompanied by one of the services prescribed by the prayer book, and it made no allowance for adapting these services for special occasions such as harvest or the occurrence of a calamity. Finally, many Churchmen felt a need for a third service like Matins and Evensong. These defects could be eliminated, without making changes in the prayer book, simply by relaxing the Act of Uniformity of 1662 which enforced its use.

The section of the fourth report dealing with this subject had

* All on the law governing benefices.

received the almost unanimous approval of the ritual commissioners and had aroused very little adverse response throughout the Church. Tait himself had admired the short week-day services in Belgian churches which attracted people going to and from work, and he hoped to start something similar in England.[53] In the last few months of 1871 he sought through his public statements to consolidate and articulate Anglican support for this part of the fourth report.[54] Although he still accompanied his discussion of this subject with proposals for the Athanasian Creed and the burial service, his first concern now was for the Church rather than Parliament to reach a decision on these controversial issues.[55] Parliament might, he hoped, feel free to enact some changes upon which Convocation had not yet decided by leaving their use up to the discretion of the bishop or incumbent; but for all changes involving the wording of the rubrics he assumed that the initiative rested with the Church.[56] He had also become more cautious in his approach to Gladstone, and tried to work through Gladstone's friend and fellow high churchman, Bishop Wilberforce.[57]

The prime minister was still 'very fearful of the breaking down of the dyke which stands between us and confusion as to legislation affecting the Church.'[58] If any easier way compatible with the bond between Church and State could have been laid down to secure legislation, he would have welcomed it. He suggested to the archbishop that Parliament might leave detailed examination of measures arising from the fourth report and endorsed by Convocation to some committee. However, though both Tait and Wilberforce took up the idea,[59] nothing came of it for several years.[60]

Convocation's century of inactivity and its factiousness made it a slow legislature. In order to harness it for more effective work at the beginning of 1872, Tait secured Letters of Business from the Crown laying the fourth report before both Convocations, requiring them to consider it and to report back.[61] He then had Convocation consider the section of the report about easing the requirements of the Act of Uniformity before raising other issues. When the two houses of the Convocation of Canterbury did not reach agreement on this subject independently, he summoned a joint meeting which quickly arrived at decisions.[62] He also kept in contact with the Convocation of York so that both would speak with one voice.[63] Nonetheless, he did not ride roughshod over all opposition, but promised ample time for debate, and tried to alter as little as possible what the Lower House sent up.[64]

Only a small minority composed of ritualists and diehard Tory High Churchmen fought the proposed amendments to the Act of Uniformity. The second group were simply hostile to change, but the first had more reasonable grounds for their stand. Like Tait's campaign for this reform, ritualism sprang from a desire to make public worship responsive to contemporary needs. However, the changes which ritualists advocated were much more radical than Tait's, and they derided his proposals: '. . . with some word of congratulation upon our freedom from superstition, and our excellent moderation,' said C. L. Wood, 'we suggest an additional hymn, or some abridgement of the prayers, or, possibly, some more stirring preaching, as the only remedies that are required.'[65] Revelling in their hostility to the pragmatic liberalism dominant in Parliament and hostile to its power over the Church, ritualists did not want the Church to ask for any legislation. Finally, the proposal to amend the Act of Uniformity was part of the ritual commission's general revision of the rubrics; and revision in the current state of Church opinion could be nothing but harmful to the ritualists.

This opposition was numerically small. Moderate High Churchmen were pleased by the place which the Letters of Business gave Convocation in the legislative process. They also welcomed a reform which could make public worship more adaptable without changing its substance.[66] Tait was therefore able to present the necessary bill to the government endorsed unanimously by the bishops of both provinces[67] and by thumping majorities in the Lower House of Canterbury. Gladstone gave the government's support to the Act of Uniformity Amendment Bill as it was called, but he requested assurance that the Bill's sponsors would resist any important additions to it, and he asked the archbishop to introduce it first in the Lords.[68] There the only notable critic was Shaftesbury who pointed out how little it did.[69] A number of amendments were proposed in the Commons, but each was vetoed either by Gladstone or by the archbishop without whose approval Gladstone would not act.[70] By now even Tait did not want alterations in the Bill since they might disturb the consensus of the Church.

The path of ecclesiastical legislation was still thorny. The House of Commons divided twice over the Bill's mention of Convocation, and showed signs of annoyance at the amount of attention devoted to Church measures. When Parliament was permitted to make minor changes in what Convocation had endorsed, the doctrinaire defenders of the authority of Convocation objected immediately. Denison supported an attempt to protest to the prime minister over the changes and to have Convocation's original report on the Bill appended as a schedule to it. 'Parliament has no right', he declared, 'to alter the resolutions of Convocation unless with the consent of Convocation.'[71] His fear of legislation was confirmed especially by the amendment which had the effect of reducing the number of times on which the Athanasian Creed had to be used.[72]

The Bill passed into law, and even before doing so won for the Church some public admiration as Tait hoped.[73] In the long run, however, it was a disappointment. The clergy did not take advantage of its provisions to anything like the extent Tait expected;[74] in general where the Act was used, lay attendance at daily services did not increase.[75]

Most of the fourth report's recommendations, many of greater importance than those to relax the Act of Uniformity, had yet to be acted on. However, proposals which touched the prayer book itself rather than just the Act of Uniformity were a much more serious business to high churchmen: the Act of Uniformity was only an Act of Parliament, whereas the Book of Common Prayer was the fullest expression of the teaching and practice of the Church of England and its chief claim to Catholicity. Few high churchmen welcomed the prospect of a general revision of the rubrics,[76] partly because they valued these rules, no matter how unpopular and impracticable, as expressions of the authority of the Church to which it behoved Christians humbly to submit. The ritual commission's proposals to water down the rubric ordering daily use of Matins and Evensong and to permit the words of administration in the Holy Communion to be said for a number of communicants at a time rather than for each separately found little favour in high church eyes.[77]

With such powerful opposition to contend with, Tait could not hope to command anything like the overwhelming support necessary to secure Gladstone's cooperation. Furthermore,

Parliament had had its fill of ecclesiastical legislation. In 1872, in addition to the Act of Uniformity Amendment Bill, Parliament enacted bills altering diocesan boundaries, abolishing baptismal fees, providing for the resignation of deans and canons, and perpetuating the term of the Bishops Resignation Act beyond its original two years; it debated a bill to allow Anglican and Nonconformist ministers occasionally to exchange pulpits, a Union of Benefices Bill, and a Public Worship Facilities Bill; all this in addition to debates on Nonconformist attempts to open up the Church's cemeteries and to secure an inquiry into parochial revenues. Tactfully Tait did not plan any more legislation for 1873.

On the one major proposal affecting the Church which Parliament dealt with in 1873, a High Church amendment to the Supreme Court of Judicature Bill, Gladstone departed slightly from his general policy toward ecclesiastical legislation, to the anger of Archbishop Tait. To understand this reversal of positions, it is necessary first to investigate the controversy which the growth of ritualism provoked.

Chapter Five

RITUALISM AND THE COURTS

Again shall long processions sweep
through Lincoln's minster pile:
Again shall banner, cross and cope
gleam thro' the incensed aisle;
. . .
England of Saints! the peace will dawn,
—but not without the fight;
So, come the contest when it may,
And God defend the right!
John Mason Neale

With the cry sounding in our ears, 'Arise, shine,' how can we
waste time by disputing about the shape of our lanterns?
Mandell Creighton

HOWEVER insecurely rooted its religion may have been, England was still Protestant. As W. E. Forster (who was Matthew Arnold's brother-in-law) put it: 'There is enough earnestness, as it seems to me, just now in the English mind to refuse assent to a belief not felt, and yet the only belief much felt is that we are not and will not be papists.'[1] Hatred of popery and suspicion of anything redolent of it had been burned into the country's soul by the double threat, alive from the Reformation into the eighteenth century, of external attack by foreign Roman Catholic powers and internal subversion by British Roman Catholics. Protestantism had been the religious counterpart of nationalism in England and was coupled with the victory of Parliament over the Stuarts. It was also, as the Oxford Movement was not slow to point out, the intellectual parent of the political liberalism on which Victorian England prided itself. By the nineteenth century this Protestantism was less a religious conviction than an instinctive national sentiment. However, any thought that it had died was proved wrong by the popular reaction against the Oxford Movement and against the creation of a Roman Catholic hierarchy in England—'Catholic aggression', it was called—in 1850. England had become more tolerant, again in line with the Protestant belief that every man must judge for himself; at least among the well educated, Newman and Pusey were treated with personal respect. Yet the attempts they and their disciples made to remodel the national Church in accordance with what they understood to be Catholic doctrine and practice provoked determined resistance.

On 1 December 1868, the day Gladstone was asked to form a government, Tait wrote to Wilberforce, his most powerful rival for the archbishopric to which he had just been nominated, saying that 'the heads of the Church are so substantially agreed on all important matters, that we may well present one united front in coming before the country.'[2] Whatever truth there may have been in this eirenical claim, before Gladstone's Ministry was over the Church of England was in the grips of its hottest internal controversy of the century, which later led to the imprisonment of five clergymen and, by its bitterness, contributed to the deaths of two others, A. H. Mackonochie and Mandell Creighton.[3] The point at issue was ritualism, and it was this problem which dominated Tait's archiepiscopate.

Ritualism was an aesthetic expression, the tangible poetry, of the Oxford Movement, though it originated primarily from Cambridge with the founding of the Camden Society in 1839 to guide church building and restoration along medieval Gothic lines. The Oxford Movement was primarily concerned to reassert the Catholic doctrine and dignity of the Church; but a bare assertion of these tenets could not win widespread acceptance particularly, it was thought, among Englishmen with their characteristic disregard for theories not translated into practice. Moreover, as the Oxford Movement developed, its adherents placed more and more emphasis on the doctrine of the Real Presence, the belief that Christ was pre-eminently and in actual fact present in the consecrated elements of the Holy Communion. There, right before one's eyes, was God drawing men to Himself, a reality to cherish with special fervour in a period of uncertainty. This doctrine, however, was incredible to many so long as the clergyman who consecrated the elements did not make it obvious in his behaviour. Newman had realized this well before he became a Roman Catholic: 'you must make the Church . . . more suitable to the needs of the heart', he had said. 'Give us more services, more vestments and decora-

The Holy Communion

Drawing of a Clergyman in Eucharistic vestments,
om John Purchas, ed., *Directorium Anglicanum* (London 1858)

tions in worship; ... give us the signs of an apostle, the pledges that the Spouse of Christ is among us.'[4]

To begin with the ritualists, particularly John Mason Neale, the leader of the Camden Society, responded to this need by tearing down the three-tier pulpits and high box pews erected in the seventeenth and eighteenth centuries when church buildings were thought of as preaching houses. In contrast, Neale and his followers wanted churches to be treated as shrines for prayer and sacraments. Accordingly, they focused attention on chancels and altars, and introduced surpliced choirs, bowing to the altar, flowers, candles and coloured altar cloths. Ritualism developed quickly beyond this. From the outset Neale hoped to reintroduce eucharistic vestments, and those who searched for authentic precedents in restoring church buildings soon found themselves in a world of high ceremony. Vestments began to be used in St. Thomas's, Oxford, in the 1840s, and together with the burning of incense their use spread to a few other churches in the '50s and '60s. Neale revived the practice of perpetual reservation of the consecrated elements of the Holy Communion in 1857, and Benediction in 1859. With the publication of the Rev. John Purchas's *Directorium Anglicanum* in 1858, the most advanced ritualists began to advocate and adopt explicitly Roman Catholic practices: Purchas's book provided instructions for a 'Solemn Service in the Presence of a Bishop assisting Pontifically'.

The movement was still small, but it was not purely clerical. Some clergy foisted ornate practices on astonished parishes, but others, who preached the underlying doctrine and personally liked these innovations but intended to proceed discretely, were surprised when their congregations asked for their introduction. Unlike the Oxford Movement, ritualism did not owe much to towering leaders but seemed to spread in response to an already existing desire, which the Oxford Movement undoubtedly fostered.

For a while, embarrassed by the tide of anti-popery which had swept through Parliament in 1851 over 'Catholic aggression', and disgusted by the riots which comparatively mild ceremonial in the London parish of St. George's in the East had provoked in 1859, educated public opinion treated both ritualism and its tumultuous opponents with disdain. In the early 1870s the problem began to be taken more seriously. For ritualism was spreading.

Its seed had not fallen on shallow ground, with the hard rock of Protestantism just below the surface, and withered. More and more pockets of English soil were proving to be surprisingly fertile. The most notable were in the London slums. Rich worship offered a solitary source of beauty amid desolation. Furthermore, although until the late 1870s the leading ritualist clergy in the slums, men such as Mackonochie and Lowder, were not socialists, they were peculiarly attracted by ministry in the slums, which stood as a judgment on the inadequacy of English social action, akin to the inadequacy ritualists saw in English Church life. At the other end of the social spectrum some aristocrats found ritualism attractive. The dowager marchioness of Bath presented W. J. E. Bennett to the benefice of Frome in Somerset where he was soon behaving, so the wags said, as if he had forgotten the first letter in the village's name. Purchas settled successfully in Brighton. Ritualism seemed able to flourish wherever it had advocates. To those who found the land of religious doubt, political strife and factories parched and repellent, ritualistic worship was one kind of oasis particularly attractive because so distinct from the world outside.

It was the very vitality of ritualism in some areas and among some people which brought the Protestantism which still prevailed over most of the country angrily to the surface. Furthermore, ritualists' concern about clergymen's clothes and the paraphernalia of public worship jarred against the stern virtues in which most Victorians took pride: manliness, sober seriousness, and hard-headed practicality. In its own way ritualism was characteristically Victorian; it was an effort to 'improve' public worship. Some of its advocates also pointed out that they were decorating worship just as other Victorians were decorating their houses.[5] Such arguments were unavailing. What was suitable in the relaxed comfort of home seemed out of place in the most serious of all concerns, religion.

Ritualism even threatened the continued existence of the national Church. For if ritualists succeeded in impressing their stamp on public worship in the established Church, it would be repugnant to the dominant religious sentiments in England, and Parliament might very well cut it adrift. Edward Miall and the Liberation Society began to capitalize on this possibility. In 1873 he said that one of the strongest arguments for disestablishment was the fact that 'the influence of legal authority, the prestige, the honours, the pecuniary resources, and the social patronage of the state were almost ostentatiously made available to the clergy of the Church which enjoyed them, for decoying the people of England back to the depository of ecclesiastical rubbish which their forefathers had sturdily quitted.'[6]

Disestablishment might also be the result of another situation which ritualism was aggravating. The Church of England was a coalition, never firmly cemented, between two traditions, one emphasizing and one minimizing the Church's links with its pre-Reformation past. One of the most effective bonds holding the Church together was the common form of worship prescribed in its prayer book. By transforming public worship in their churches, ritualists therefore strained the coalition more severely than at any time since the days of Laud, and by 1874 talk about a split in the Church or about forcing the ritualists out was rife. Those who seceded or were ejected would be sure to join militant Nonconformists in demanding disestablishment. The bishops often concentrated on this aspect of the problem and attempted to deal with ritualism as a threat to the unity of the Church, with the result that the controversy looked like yet another internal Church affair. Yet many of the bishops, and above all Archbishop Tait, realized that they were also fighting to keep the Church congenial to the country. 'I do not think there is the slightest danger of this country ever becoming Roman Catholic,' Tait was to say. 'I do not think there is the slightest danger of this country ever adopting a semi-Romanism. But,' he went on, referring to the years before 1874, 'I think . . . that there was a danger lest the foolish conduct of a few might so shake the confidence of the people in their National Established Church, that they would consider it no longer worth preserving.'[7]

Tait knew that he was partly responsible for the foothold which ritualism had acquired.[8] As bishop of London, the diocese in which all extremes seemed to flourish, he had held the reins over his clergy loosely in the belief that 'each man will best serve God by acting as in God's sight on his own strong convictions'.[9] It was hard to draw the line when, as he realized, the Church's comprehensiveness rested on a practical more than a theoretical foundation: a purely logical application of Tractarians' and ritualists' Catholicism might lead them out of the Church of England.[10] And the loss of any group would diminish the spiritual resources of the Church which it so urgently needed, confronted by the overwhelming religious destitution of the world's greatest city.

His perspective altered when he moved from Fulham Palace to Lambeth Palace. Now his task was to keep a watchful eye, undeflected by the peculiar needs of any one place no matter how important, on the lines along which the whole Church was moving. He still tried to calm the exasperation of the majority of churchmen at the ritualists. He held up for admiration the contributions which each school had made: High Churchmen had raised the quality of public worship throughout the Church (he could not see much else of value in their activities); and how much the Church would have lost if the Evangelicals of the eighteenth century had been driven out! He also pointed to the developments akin to ritualism which were taking place among Nonconformists and in the Roman Catholic Church:[11] Rome was in the grip of rabid ultramontanes, and Nonconformists were, as Gladstone observed, using 'Crosses on the outside of chapels, organs within them, rich painted architecture, that flagrant piece of symbolism, the steeple, windows filled with subjects in stained glass, elaborate chanting,'[12] and so forth.

Nevertheless, the time had come to draw the line. Tait had always made it clear that he disliked and feared over-belief and its embodiment in ceremonial. He had also questioned extreme high churchmen's right to revolutionize the character of the Church. Above and beyond belief in the Gospel it demanded, he said, acceptance of the tenets which distinguished it from Rome.[13] As soon as he became archbishop, his opposition toward ritualism hardened. 'I have great sympathy with earnestness, and I have great sympathy with liberty,' he declared in 1869, 'but I have no sympathy with persons who make the Church of England something quite different from that which it was made at the Reformation, and', he went on, 'something totally different from that which the great and overwhelming majority of the people of England regard their national Church'.[14] Independently of its significance for the survival of the establishment, popular English Protestantism weighed heavily with him, for though it might be an uninstructed sentiment, it was 'the echo of great truths which have been proclaimed in the history of the country.'[15] The Church of England, he said, tolerated, only tolerated, Catholic doctrines like the Real Presence; but any ceremonial which savoured of 'an uneasy hankering after a foreign and less pure system of religion' was beyond the pale.[16] He also accused the ritualists of diverting Churchmen's attention from what ought to have been their chief concern, ungodliness and ignorance.[17]

Archbishop Tait was sure that, in trying to bring ritualism to heel, he was not narrowing the comprehensiveness of the Church. He was happy that it provided for considerable variation, all the way from the simplicity of country churches to the rich dignity of the cathedrals;[18] but ritualism stretched this tolerance beyond the limit. His confidence that it did so seemed to be proved by the fact that, outside the ranks of its devotees, ritualism found few sympathizers and many determined opponents among the well established schools of thought within the Church. Evangelicals of course were vehemently opposed. Ritualism to them was a harbinger of the reign of the Beast about which the Book of Revelation (the same book from which the ritualists derived a lot of their imagery) had warned,[19] and the ritualists were 'ferry-men to the Pope'.[20] Tractarian theology was bad enough, but so long as its advocates conducted public worship as, in evangelical opinion, the prayer book stipulated, then their teaching would be corrected or condemned by their sound practice.[21] Ritualism ended this hope. It made the Tractarians' point intolerably obvious and insidiously attractive.

High Churchmen too denounced ritualism. Christopher Wordsworth led the first great deputation against it, and J. W. Burgon, rarely fond of moderation, inveighed against it as strongly as against Biblical criticism.[23] For, much as High Churchmen disliked unmitigated Protestantism, they had always taught that the Church of England had been rightly reformed. Wilberforce also seconded Tait in deploring the attention which ritualism diverted from more urgent problems.[23]

Keble agreed.[24] Even the Tractarians were uneasy about ritualism. Ceremonial was, in their opinion, only a means of expression and therefore never more than a matter of variable expediency. Once men embraced Catholic doctrine, they would want to express it in the forms hallowed by use in the Catholic Church over the ages; but to impose them on unwilling congregations would only alienate them.[25] The passionate determination with which ritualists upheld their practices made Pusey suspect that they were motivated by ideals different from the Oxford Movement's.[26] Like the poetry of Tennyson, ritualism could be embraced as a substitute for the definite theology with which Tractarians were greatly concerned. And whereas Tractarians made much of the need to obey the consecrated leaders of the Church, ritualists defied all constituted authority in the Church of England and adopted whatever rites appealed to them in a way which looked very like an expression of the Protestant belief that the final authority in religious matters was the individual.[27]

Furthermore, extreme ceremonial did not appeal aesthetically to most Tractarians. By and large they were a generation older than the ritualists and had spent the formative years of their youth in the turbulent and hungry 1830s and '40s, not the prosperous and confident '50s and '60s. Consequently the religious expression they found congenial was austere; the garment which Pusey valued most was a hair shirt. Even judging by a much less severe standard, ritualism could go to ridiculous lengths. Purchas suspended a stuffed dove above the altar of his church on Whitsunday, and Hawker of Morwenstow went about his parish dressed in a claret coloured suit, a blue jersey and a brimless pink hat.

However, as Keble explained, Tractarians were afraid that, if the less idiosyncratic ritualistic customs were suppressed, 'the Truth itself which they symbolize will be openly persecuted, and probably forbidden to be taught in the Established Church'.[28] As a result, most Tractarians felt obliged to stand by the ritualists especially when the rest of the Church bore down upon them. The ritualists received even more reluctant and less reliable support from broad churchmen such as Dean Stanley.[29] Proscription of ritualism would circumscribe the Church's comprehensiveness which he valued in principle and which in practice protected him as a member of another unpopular minority. These considerations did not, however, prevent Broad Churchmen from being caught up in the wave of hostility toward ritualism which arose in 1873. Except for these two groups, the ritualists stood alone, attacked not only by Evangelical and moderate High Churchmen but also by the many unaffiliated to a particular party, the man in the pew resentful of any flagrant departure from custom, baffled by the ardour with which the ritualists defended their ceremonies, and unable to see how they could be reconciled with honest membership in the Reformed Church of England. As one lawyer told Tait,

I can understand going out at 'Stonehenge' and seeing *the Sun Rise*— and worshipping, (under the miseltoe) with all my heart and soul,—one '*great Being*',—but I cannot follow *this movement*, or *revival*.[30]

Tait therefore had good cause for believing that, by straining the comprehensiveness of the Church and the willingness of the country to perpetuate the establishment, ritualism was a threat to the national Church which he so dearly wished to strengthen. The policy which he adopted to remove the threat, however, aggravated another source of tension between Church and State, the role of the courts. The simplest way to deal with ritualism would have been for Parliament to pass a law making its characteristic features such as eucharistic vestments and incense illegal. This was what Lord Shaftesbury advocated in 1867, with Tait's support. High Church opposition prevented action. For over thirty years most High Church clergy, however moderate, had been raising the standards of worship in their churches by adopting the simplest ritualistic innovations, wearing a surplice while they were preaching for example, and they had often disturbed local custom and provoked Protestant feeling in doing so. Extreme ritualism was the van of this movement; to eliminate it with an evangelical, legislative axe would frighten High Churchmen generally.

Tait fell back upon the courts. Although his support for legislation seemed to imply that he was aware of some ambiguity in the Book of Common Prayer's regulations governing ceremonial, Tait regarded the legislation as declaratory, an elucidation of the existing law. He had no doubt that extreme ceremonial transgressed the law as it stood; and he depended now upon the courts to enforce it. In two judgements handed down in 1869 and 1871 the Judicial Committee of the Privy Council construed the law more or less as he expected, and he tried to secure general obedience to its decisions. He failed.

There were two general reasons for his failure: the position of the Judicial Committee as the supreme court for ecclesiastical appeals, and the powerlessness of the law generally when it came into conflict with men's religious convictions. Obviously the second point was the fundamental one. As Denison put it,

when [law] comes into collision with the faith by which men live here, and hope to live hereafter, [it] has always been, and always will be, a poor, weak, unworthy thing—no longer respectable; powerless for all, save only for the purposes of a persecuting tyranny, and for promoting the very things it proposes to 'put down.'[31]

Nevertheless, a clear repudiation of the law as interpreted by the courts would have drastic consequences; and since the requirements of the law as well as the authority of the courts which enforced it were disputed, there was no need to go so far. Therefore, the second issue took the form of a quest for a supreme court whose authority would be accepted as religiously binding. The Judicial Committee was the focus of the debate.

The courts' jurisdiction over the Church of England was an integral part of its establishment. Any religious denomination—and not the Church of England only—which possessed property was subject to the courts, and since the terms regulating the use of its property would probably include adherence to its particular doctrines or discipline, the courts could and occasionally were obliged to clarify these religious stipulations.* The position of the established Church was different in several ways. Its courts such as the Court of Arches, the court of the province of Canterbury, were among the courts of the realm. As a result, they could impose temporal punishments such as fines, deprivation from a benefice, and even imprisonment. These were powers properly belonging to the State which it had conferred upon the ecclesiastical courts, but subject to appeal.

In 1832 and '33, while Convocation was dormant but with the consent of the bishops in the Lords, Parliament had abolished the old supreme court for ecclesiastical appeals, the High Court of Delegates, and transferred its powers to the Judicial Committee of the Privy Council in an attempt to make the procedure in such cases more economical and efficient. Strictly speaking, the Judicial

---

* On one occasion Chancery had to decide whether baptism was necessary in order to be a communicant in a Baptist church. On another, the Queen in Council upheld the right of a deceased Canadian Roman Catholic to burial in consecrated ground denied him by the highest authorities within his Church because of offences he was alleged to have committed against it. Sir Roundell Palmer's speech, *Hansard*, 3rd series, CCVI (1871), 517 and Tait, *The Church and Law* (London, 1877), p. 43.

Committee was not a court but a group of advisers to the Crown which, however, invariably followed their recommendation. The question whether the Judicial Committee was an ecclesiastical or secular tribunal when it dealt with ecclesiastical appeals did not admit of a clear answer. Aside from the fact that the monarch was supreme governor of the Church, the three prelates who were members of the privy council—the two archbishops and the bishop of London—could sit on the Judicial Committee when it dealt with ecclesiastical cases, and at least one of them had to do so for any appeal under the Church Discipline Act of 1840.

To begin with, these enactments did not provoke much comment since the affected cases were generally of minor importance: odd instances of clerical immorality, suits against churchwardens, and such like. Of all the 177 cases which the High Court of Delegates had heard, only seven were even remotely involved with questions of doctrine.[32] Consequently the transfer of its powers to the Judicial Committee had been made without doctrinal litigation in mind. Then in the 1850's the Judicial Committee was confronted with the first of many suits arising from controversies within the Church about its doctrine and the conduct of its worship. Whatever its decision, the Judicial Committee was likely to alienate the school of thought it disappointed. In doctrinal cases the Judicial Committee made every effort to interpret the Church's formularies as broadly as possible, but as a result the evangelical Gorham and the prosecuted contributors to *Essays and Reviews* escaped censure for opinions which most high churchmen considered heretical. A handful of High Churchmen, preeminently Manning, took these decisions as proof that the Church of England was not a reliable defender of the true faith but rather putty in the State's hands, and seceded to Rome.

Those who remained behind began to argue that the Judicial Committee's jurisdiction over ecclesiastical appeals violated the Reformation settlement upon which Church and State had agreed in the sixteenth century, and that as a result the Church need not be implicated in the decisions of the Judicial Committee. After plunging into the muddy waters of Tudor legislation and the records of Convocation and the High Court of Delegates, high church spokesmen emerged with the discovery that the supreme ecclesiastical appeal court had to be a distinctly ecclesiastical tribunal, recognizable as such, if not by its composition, at least because Convocation had sanctioned it. The only tolerable alternative was for the supreme court to be a distinctly secular body whose jurisdiction extended only, as it would with any non-established denomination, to the Church's temporalities. Though in dealing with cases within these limits the court might still have to elucidate the Church's doctrinal and disciplinary formularies, the court's interpretation of them would not necessarily be regarded as the view of the Church. The Judicial Committee fell between these two stools. It was indeed a secular court, so the argument went, but the presence of bishops on it obscured this fact and gave grounds for believing that its decisions on doctrinal and liturgical questions bound the Church.

Even before he became archbishop, Tait had tried to refute this argument by denying the distinction, on which it was based, between secular and ecclesiastical courts for the established Church.[33] He also maintained that since the doctrine and discipline of any denomination could come before the Judicial Committee for clarification, the presence of bishops on the Judicial Committee in cases involving the Church of England was a unique advantage not to be surrendered lightly.[34] Tait's fundamental reason for defending the Judicial Committee had been that it buttressed the Church's comprehensiveness against temporary swings of popular opinion; and though it was the tolerance of the Judicial Committee which had angered High Churchmen, Tait trusted that they would come to see the benefits of its policy. Between 1870 and 1872 he gained the evidence he needed. The fear that the Judicial Committee would never declare any teaching, however wild, as beyond the limits of the Church's formularies was dispelled by the condemnation of the extreme liberal, Voysey, in 1870.[35] In 1872, in the Bennett case, the Judicial Committee upheld the legality of the doctrine of the Real Presence. Now the right of the three main parties within the Church to maintain their distinctive viewpoints had been secured without committing the Church to any one of them.

It was too late. The centre of attention had swung from doctrinal to ritual cases; again the High Church was the alarmed party; and this time what Tait expected from the courts was not tolerance but repression. Neither he nor the courts saw any illogicality in combining latitude about doctrine with rigidity about ceremonial. The Judicial Committee explained in its Bennett judgment that, 'If the Minister be allowed to introduce at his own will variations in the rites and ceremonies that seem to him to interpret the doctrine of the service in a particular direction. the service ceases to be what it was meant to be, common ground on which all Church people may meet, though they differ about some doctrines.'[36] As for Tait, his underlying concern in both doctrinal and ceremonial disputes was for the Church's national popularity. He had been happy to defend Broad Church clergy because, however unpopular in the Church, they were attempting to bring it into line with the 'march of intellect' in the country. Ritualism on the contrary was, so far as he could see, the froth of ecclesiastical reaction to liberal, Protestant progress and therefore, quite rightly, offended national sentiment.

The widespread dislike felt also among Churchmen toward ritualism was not enough to enable Tait's policy of reliance upon the courts' censures to succeed. He needed an equally large consensus within the Church in favour of obedience to the courts. There were many reasons to expect that it would be forthcoming, and he drew attention to them repeatedly. English respect for law and the courts would be doubly influential among the clergy of the Church particularly responsible for the moral welfare of the country. The very real possibility that defiance of the courts would bring on disestablishment would give all but a very few of the clergy second thoughts. Finally, the possession of a benefice gave a clergyman in the Church of England an unusually advantageous legal status, much stronger than that of a Nonconformist minister dependent on the good will of his congregation or a Roman Catholic priest subject to the dictates of his bishop. A benefice was freehold property limited only by the obligation to conform to the liturgy, discipline and formularies of the established Church as they applied to a cure of souls. Otherwise the beneficed clergyman could do what he liked, regardless of his parishioners' protests and his bishop's remonstrances. For him to use his highly protected legal position to make enforcement of these minimal legal requirements as difficult as possible, and then, faced with judicial condemnation, to defy the courts and carry on as before, seemed indefensible.

Tait's archiepiscopate had scarcely begun when such considerations were thrown to the winds by the ritualists. Until now they had drawn strength from the Judicial Committee. For in 1857, in the first ritual case to come before it, Westerton v. Liddell, the Judicial Committee upheld the legality of some moderate ritualistic accoutrements such as coloured altar cloths, credence tables, crosses behind the altar, and candles though, with a refinement which caught Disraeli's sense of humour, the candles were to be lit only when necessary for purposes of light. The Judicial Committee in this judgment seemed to accept the ritualists' interpretation of the ornaments rubric. Read without reference to the tangle of legal and historical detail which might be involved in discovering its requirements, the ornaments rubric appeared to give the ritualists all they wanted and even to make their practices mandatory: the rubric stated that the ceremonial of the Church should be as it was in the second year of the reign of Edward VI, when the conduct of public worship had been much more ornate than was later customary.

However, early in 1869 in its judgment in the fisrt of the many Mackonochie cases, the Judicial Committee apparently changed its mind by deciding that whatever ceremonial the rubrics did not explicitly specify they prohibited. All of the practices for which Mackonochie was arraigned—the use of incense and altar lights, mixing water with the wine, elevation of the vessels containing the consecrated elements, and 'excessive kneeling'—were condemned either by the Court of Arches or, on appeal, by the Judicial Committee. The treatment which Mackonochie received from the Judicial Committee increased the ritualists' sense of outrage. The costs which he had to pay included what the Church Association had spent on hired informers.[37] Litigation between the parties within the Church had become embittered by the formation of rival organizations with large war chests to pay legal expenses. 'Prosecution in these days', said Bishop Magee, 'is reduced to a science, and is carried on, like many other enterprises, by joint-stock companies with limited liability.'[38] It was the extreme High Churchmen who had taken the lead by creating the English Church Union in 1860. The E.C.U. had tried to use the courts to prevent Evangelicals from conducting mission services in unconsecrated buildings such as theatres, and to secure a condemnation of Waldegrave, the evangelical bishop of Carlisle, for heresy. Their failure, coupled with the Judicial Committee's decision in the *Essays and Reviews* cases in 1864, led High Churchmen farther towards a denial of the Judicial Committee's jurisdiction; and the initiative passed to the evangelical Church Association, formed in 1865. From then on most of the great cases began with prosecution financed by the Church Association, the E.C.U. paying for the defence.

There was worse in store for Mackonochie than paying the Church Association. He submitted to the Judicial Committee's judgment about the ceremonial at issue, but interpreted it as narrowly as possible in order to salvage some symbol of the Real Presence: he genuflected where he had formerly knelt. The Judicial Committee then forbade him to genuflect, and he resorted to bowing. Exasperated, the Judicial Committee prohibited this too, and suspended him from his benefice for three months. With all the holes plugged, Mackonochie did not attempt to act in conformity with the judgment when he resumed his duties.[39]

The rest of the ritualists were amazed only that Mackonochie had tried to obey the Judicial Committee in the first place. They did not hesitate to continue the practices for which Mackonochie had been condemned. What made their disobedience more alarming was that it was virtually impossible to stamp out, revealing another weakness of Tait's reliance upon the courts. Strictly, the Judicial Committee's decision applied only to the one defendant though it would serve as a precedent governing similar cases in future. Both Tait and the Church Association had expected that, once the law had been clarified by the courts, it would be generally obeyed. This hope was now shown to be illusory. The only way to enforce obedience was to prosecute each deviant. To do so would not only create a distressing spectacle and take time, but would also place a heavy financial strain on the prosecutors. The Mackonochie case had lasted more than three years and cost well over £6,000.[40] Throughout Gladstone's first Ministry Tait tried to speed up the particularly tortuous procedure in ecclesiastical cases and to reduce its cost. Again high churchmen,[41] unwilling to facilitate litigation, frustrated the attempt.

Disobedience of the Mackonochie judgment was restricted to the few determined ritualists. Denison was emphatic in his demand that the law must be obeyed though under protest.[42] The bishop of Ely claimed some success in securing conformity with the ruling in his diocese.[43] However, already in 1869 the Church Association had instigated the suit which, 'like ambition, o'erleapt itself', Elphinstone, later Hebbert, v. Purchas. Purchas, arraigned on thirty-five counts including his stuffed dove, pleaded poverty and did not appear before the courts either personally or by counsel, with the result that the decision would be open to the accusation of one-sidedness. The dean of the Court of Arches who first heard the case ruled against Purchas on most of the charges, but on the two key ones, eucharistic vestments and the eastward position of the celebrant during the prayer of consecration in the Holy Communion, the dean upheld the defendant. The wearing of eucharistic vestments was the quintessence of extreme ritualism, and its condemnation was necessary if the courts were to live up to Tait's hope. As yet eucharistic vestments were a rarity, and judicial condemnation of them might have met with sufficiently widespread approval to succeed.

The eastward position, on the other hand, was a sign of historic high churchmanship. It had been used by some high church clergy every since the Reformation and had become common among them during the nineteenth century as symbolic of a high doctrine of the Holy Communion and as an aid to sacramental devotion. Furthermore, like the ritualists' interpretation of the ornaments rubric, High Churchmen's reading of the rubric governing the position of the celebrant was the obvious one. The rubric required the celebrant to stand 'before the Table'; the clergyman who adopted the eastward position stood in front of the table facing eastward away from the congregation; the alternative was to stand at the north end, the short side, of the table; and if this had been the rubric's intention, surely it would have said 'beside the Table'. Although the eastward position had not been at issue in the Mackonochie case, the Judicial Committee had seemed to uphold it then in presenting the reasons for its other conclusions. As a result several clergymen, pre-eminently Bishop Wilberforce, changed their previous practice, and the dean of Arches cited the Mackonochie judgment when pronouncing the eastward position legal in his Purchas judgment. If on appeal the Judicial Committee condemned the eastward position, it would greatly increase the doubts about its consistency already aroused by its shifting treatment of the ornaments rubric. Much more serious, it would alienate the whole High Church party. If that should occur, Tait's policy would be in ruins.

On the appeal of the complainant, the Purchas case went up to the Judicial Committee of the Privy Council. It pronounced a sweeping condemnation of Purchas's practices including both eucharistic vestments and the eastward position. Amid the subsequent storm, Purchas furnished light relief. He was ordered to conform and also to pay the entire costs of the original suit and the appeal. Blandly he ignored the judgment, and as for the bill he explained that he could not pay since he had made all his property over to his wife. Thereupon the Judicial Committee suspended him from his benefice, but he ignored this too. He died quietly in 1872, and his wife and five sons did not find themselves in straitened circumstances.[44]

Meanwhile, within a week of the Judicial Committee's judgment, the Church Association announced that it would harry the bishops until they enforced the decision throughout the Church.[45] The main consequences of the judgment were very different. The English Church Union declared it spiritually null and void, and advised men to disregard it.[46] The Church Association's action destroyed Liddon's hope that time and abstinence from extreme language would provide an opportunity to work out a compromise, and as a canon of St. Paul's he informed the bishop of London publicly that he would continue to use the eastward position.[47] A meeting of High Church laymen and clergymen persuaded Canon Gregory to join Liddon.[48] And five thousand clergymen, not all High Churchmen, F. D. Maurice for example, signed a solemn remonstrance to the bishops against enforcement of the judgment throughout the Church.

The ritualists were utterly uncompromising in their defiance. Mackonochie declined to sign the remonstrance as too mild. Within a few months another ritualist, Arthur Tooth, later to become famous as the first to go to jail for his actions, refused even to discuss the practices in his parish with his bishop.[49] But Liddon disobeyed the Purchas judgment, as his first hopes indicated, without relish. In a similar spirit, Pusey disobeyed only as a recognized way of challenging the Purchas judgment's legality and thus of obtaining a fresh hearing, this time with the defendant represented.[50] Furthermore, he circulated the remonstrance against general enforcement of the judgment as a way to minimize the amount of blatant disobedience.

Most of those who signed the remonstrance had no wish to defy the courts, but they were repelled by the Church Association's aggressiveness and afraid of the threat the judgment contained to historic High Churchmanship. The judgement seemed so unfair. Why did the Judicial Committee confine ceremonial so rigorously when it was indulgent in the more important sphere of doctrine? What justice was there in condemning excessive ceremonial when the deficiencies of the evangelicals went unrebuked? The English Church Union's abandonment of its early attempts to prosecute its opponents was bearing fruit, for without prosecutions of the evangelicals to deal with, the courts were deprived of opportunities to show themselves ready to enforce the law on both sides, and the ritualists could wrap themselves in the mantle of martyrdom.

Tait had no choice but to make the best of a bad job. If as archbishop of Canterbury he had publicly agreed with the remonstrance, thus implicitly criticizing the supreme court's decision, he would have shaken the establishment as no one else could. He replied to the remonstrators by pointing out that they were in effect asking the bishops to connive in violations of the law.[51] Nevertheless, he set out a policy for applying the Purchas judgment as though it had condemned extreme ritualism but left high churchmanship unscathed. Eucharistic vestments must, he insisted, be abandoned, and he came close to advising that, where this did not happen voluntarily, prosecutions should be initiated. On the other hand, he tried to soften the blow to the eastward position by giving the assurance that, though the bishops must enforce the law where it was invoked, they would not seek out offenders, and that, as sympathetic Fathers in God, they would take the particular character of each parish into account.[52]

Nevertheless, by relying upon the bishops' discretionary power, Tait weakened the authority of the courts' decisions. Like all the other interested parties, Tait was treating the law as if it coincided with his own wishes. Ritualists held up the ornaments rubric as proof that they were right and that only tolerant charity restrained them from trying to enforce its requirements throughout the Church. Evangelicals were equally confident that the law was a bulwark of Protestant practice. As Gilbert and Sullivan's Lord Chancellor in *Iolanthe* sang,

> The Law is the true embodiment
> Of everything that's excellent,
> It has no kind of fault or flaw,
> And I, my lords, embody the Law.

Every Churchman had become his own lord chancellor.

The Supreme Court of Judicature Act

The legal situation took another turn for the worse from Tait's point of view in 1873. The presence of bishops on the Judicial Committee when it heard ecclesiastical appeals provided grounds for doubting its impartiality. None of the three member bishops at the time—Tait, Thomson of York, and Jackson of London— were High Church, and therefore they did not provide a fair reflection of Church opinion. It could also be argued that the duty of a bishop on the Judicial Committee was not compatible with his duty to his diocese.[53] He ought to offer his flock firm guidance on the issues which tormented the Church. But these were the very issues which tended to reach the courts, and if he had spoken out on them, he could not be an impartial judge. Consequently, it was reasonable to contend that the removal of the bishops from the Judicial Committee would increase Churchmen's willingness to obey its decisions by raising its impartiality. Moderate High Churchmen who strongly denied that they wanted to provide an excuse for disobedience adopted this line of argument.

Archbishop Tait had good reason for being suspicious of it. The removal of the bishops would seem to bear out the more extreme high church contention that the Judicial Committee was a purely secular tribunal and therefore did not possess any rightful jurisdiction over religious matters. Disobedience would then be easier to justify. At present the contrary impression that the Judicial Committee was at least partially ecclesiastical was strong; Archbishop Thomson pronounced its decision in the Bennett case. Furthermore, both the critics and the defenders of a the Judicial Committee's inclusion of bishops admitted that their opinion carried great weight within the Judicial Committee.[54] This was especially true of Tait who was highly esteemed by lawyers for his judicial abilities: when one eminent lawyer was asked who the best judge he had known was, without a moment's hesitation he named Tait.[55] As for the supposed incompatibility between the bishops' responsibilities to their dioceses and on the Judicial Committee, Tait pointed out that all the bishops were entitled to preside as judges over their diocesan courts[56]—which, inconsistently, High Churchmen wished they would do more often.

The government provided High Churchmen with a golden opportunity to get rid of the bishops in 1873. Lord Selborne, the Lord Chancellor, introduced the Supreme Court of Judicature Bill under which the whole structure of the judiciary was to be recast. A new supreme court composed solely of lawyers was proposed, exactly what High Churchmen wanted for ecclesiastical appeals. However, the Bill excluded ecclesiastical appeals from the new court's jurisdiction, leaving them under the otherwise defunct Judicial Committee. Lord Salisbury moved that the Bill be extended to include them. For the new supreme court would not only be free of bishops. It would also meet other High Church criticisms of the Judicial Committee: that its composition fluctuated from case to case, and that, regardless of whether its decision reflected the opinion of a bare majority of the judges, no dissenting opinion could be expressed.[57] Pusey hoped that a new supreme court would feel free to disregard previous disputed decisions of the Judicial Committee.

Salisbury received strong support, not just from High Churchmen. The Church Association realized that the presence of bishops made disobedience of the Judicial Committee less justifiable in High Church eyes and therefore increased its ability to curb ritualism.[58] But this consideration was overridden in some Evangelicals by their suspicion of bishops generally. The English veneration for the impartiality of the law also worked on Salisbury's behalf.[59]

Tait's opposition, however, defeated the amendment in the House of Lords. His influence there had become immense. He attended the Lords' debates with extraordinary regularity, spoke only when necessary and only on ecclesiastical issues, but then was heard with the respect which only constant, alert attendance could earn. He spoke as the Lords liked, not with the ephemeral brilliance of the orator but with strong practicality. And his prejudices were theirs: the epithet, 'the layman's archbishop', uttered with contempt by his clerical critics, was a compliment in this company. Salisbury withdrew his amendment without pressing it to a vote.

When the Bill went down to the House of Commons, another frontbench Conservative High Churchman, Gathorne Hardy, proposed a similar amendment. It commanded impressive support: the moderate Churchman and Conservative Spencer Walpole, the low church Liberal Vernon Harcourt, and even the Radical Osborne Morgan spoke on its behalf. In fact, no one rose to oppose it.

Gladstone delayed expressing the government's attitude to the amendment and waited for more M.P.s to speak until the motion was on the verge of being put to the vote. However, departing from his previous policy of careful Ministerial neutrality on ecclesiastical issues which divided Churchmen, he had already found out that the cabinet approved of the change. He would have preferred, he claimed, to have discussed the amendment with leading bishops before speaking. But the course of the debate in the Commons led him to act now.[60] As a High Churchman, he had been among the foremost advocates of similar proposals after the Judicial Committee pronounced its decision in the Gorham case.[61] As prime minister, however, he would not present his religious predilections as the determining element in his political decisions.

He addressed the Commons from an entirely political point of view, indeed his argument must have delighted Radicals unfriendly toward the established Church:

it would appear rather hard upon the public [he said], when they had long ago come to the conclusion not to vote one shilling for purposes purely denominational, unless there were something very important beyond that mere consideration, that the paraphernalia of a Court and the charges for its officers should be kept up by funds from the Exchequer, simply on the chance that from time to time some ecclesiastical suit might crop up, with which this semi-animate Court might be called upon to deal.[62]

The government, he informed the House, had no objection to the passing of the amendment, for the Lords could still do what they liked with it. He gave it his personal support, and the Commons agreed to it without further discussion.

Tait was furious at the speed with which this took place. He may not have acted beforehand with his accustomed vigour, assuming that Gladstone would adhere to his usual policy toward ecclesiastical legislation. Now he wrote to Gladstone threatening to oppose the Bill when it returned to the Lords unless the mixed composition of the supreme court was preserved; he expostulated with Gathorne Hardy, who took pride in being the staunchest of the establishment's defenders, for supporting the removal of what Tait considered an important feature of the establishment; he tried to enlist Disraeli's support; and he pressed his views upon the Liberal leaders in the Lords,

Granville and Selborne.[63] With Selborne's assistance he secured a compromise whereby bishops could sit with the new court when it heard ecclesiastical appeals, but only as assessors to advise the lay judges. The bishops eligible so to serve would not be restricted any longer to the three who were privy councillors. Tait supported the compromise reluctantly, and it was enacted.

This was the last legislative struggle which High Churchmen were to win for many years. While it was taking place, a Protestant storm brewed. The Church Association was angry about the bishops' failure to demand general conformity to the full requirements of the Purchas judgment. Evangelicals also thought that the Judicial Committee had virtually condemned Bennett's doctrine of the Real Presence by calling it 'rash and ill judged, and perilously near a violation of the law' and had acquitted him only because the case was a criminal one in which the defendant had to receive every benefit of the doubt. Accordingly, at the beginning of May 1873 the Church Association presented a memorial to the two archbishops, protesting against Romish teaching in the Church of England and appealing to the bishops to refuse to ordain, licence or present to benefices any clergymen whose views or practices were infected by it.[64] The memorial bore the signatures of 60,000 laymen.

It was in these circumstances that extreme High Churchmen's ambition o'erleapt itself. On 9 May Convocation received a petition from 483 clergymen asking it to 'consider the advisability of providing for the education, selection, and licensing of duly qualified confessors'. Formal, 'auricular' confession to a clergyman was the one practice which, more than any other, made extreme High Churchmanship odious in popular estimation. To ask for official approval of it was sure to provoke a popular reaction. Even to mention it without condemning it was enough to arouse dark suspicion. Tait and most of his fellow bishops would have liked to condemn auricular confession outright, and in the debate when the petition was presented to the Upper House of Convocation they did not mince words. Tait spoke of 'this evil'.[65] However, in formulating their joint, official response, they had to be wary not to impede the seeking and giving of spiritual counsel between parishioner and parson and not to run counter to the teaching of the prayer book which encouraged auricular confession in time of sickness. Therefore, the Upper House referred the petition to a committee. This restraint elicited a roar of disapproval from Lord Shaftesbury.[66]

Tait and Archbishop Thomson replied to the Church Association memorial with similar caution. The earlier clerical remonstrance about the Purchas judgment had made Tait realize that rigorous application of the judgment throughout the Church would only have increased dissension and disobedience. With this in mind, he misread the country's religious temperature. He urged Evangelicals to rely not so much upon legal compulsion, which after all was not consonant with the free ethos of Protestantism, but rather upon personal influence and sound argument. In their answer to the Church Association memorial, the two archbishops deplored the prospect of 'an unlimited number of judicial investigations founded upon charges and countercharges made by contending theological parties against their opponents. . . . Episcopal government exists among us,' they said, 'charged with the grave responsibility of seeing that the undoubted law of the Church is observed, and, at the same time, of saving the Church, by the exercise of a wise discretion, from being plunged into endless unseemly contests.'[67]

The primates' response only stiffened the demands of militant evangelicals. If bishops would not make the courts' decisions effective, the courts must be enabled to do the job themselves; and the Church Association pressed for immediate legislation.[68] Another evangelical body, the Church of England Laymen's Defence Association, urged that the lower ecclesiastical courts be completely abolished and their work transferred to expeditious civil ones.[69] Nor was insistence on drastic action confined to a strident minority. *The Times* rebuked the archbishops for the feebleness of their reply: 'What is admitted is the existence of a great danger in the Church, and was asked, and will no doubt be expected of the Bishops, is that they should adopt exceptional measures to repress an exceptional abuse.'[70] Fear that the national Church was slipping back into medieval superstition and mummery, lay hostility toward clerical claims about their sacramental power, and legal anger at defiance of the courts, gathered force. Tait prepared to modify his course. Fortune favoured stiff action to repress ritualism, for Wilberforce, the one bishop powerful enough to hold his colleagues back, was thrown from his horse in July and instantly killed. The Public Worship Regulation Act was on its way.

Chapter Six

THE TENACITY OF THE ESTABLISHMENT

> Now, with advancing years, not usually more sanguine, [Mr.
> Gladstone] is even more deeply struck with the tenacious vitality
> of the Church of England . . . than with its serious dangers, and
> its unquestionably great and grievous scandals . . . .
> *Gladstone to the Queen, 22 January 1874*

THE first session of Parliament after Disraeli's victory in the
general election of 1874 was to be dominated, not by any of the
imperialistic adventures or social legislation for which his Ministry became famous, but by a bill to regulate the public worship
of the established Church. Establishment, the word used to denote
the complex of legal ties between the Church of England and the
State, imposed obligations which still weighed heavily in the
counsels of both. This weight was created partly by the very fact
that the establishment aroused discontent in the country and the
Church. Disestablishment could have eased these tensions. The
treatment of the Irish Church seemed to point to such a solution,
and it was advocated by two of the most dynamic minorities
concerned, ritualists and militant Nonconformists. Both argued
that the union of Church and State in England was a harmful
constitutional lie, at odds with the actual circumstances and best
interests of each.

However, if the fortunes of the English establishment during
Gladstone's first Ministry provided a true indication, Englishmen
and Anglicans on the whole regarded the lie as a white one and
beneficial. In almost every other way these years witnessed a
deterioration in the position of the Church of England. The establishment, on the other hand, seemed stronger at the end of the
Ministry than at its beginning. This strength was the product of
apathy as well as of firm belief; it owed perhaps even more to fear
about the possible consequences of disestablishment. Certainly the

political or religious arguments by which men upheld it were often among their weaker convictions. The arguments of its opponents were frequently more incisive and consistent than those of its defenders. Nevertheless the fact remained, important because anomalous: the establishment had become more secure. The prospects for its survival seemed good even if its correspondence to the realities of English life were to become still more tenuous.

The establishment was the constitutional embodiment of Archbishop Tait's desires. On the one hand, England's religiousness was not measuring up to his hopes; on the other, many Churchmen were clinging to old concepts and forms and even reviving archaic ones which set the Church increasingly at variance with opinion in the country. Yet over all the establishment stood as a symbol of the ideal of a national Church in a Christian country. It also imposed responsibilities and provided machinery which could help in the pursuit of this goal.

Tait's speeches were thickly interlarded with arguments in defence of the union between Church and State and refutation of its critics. He described the claim that religion was no rightful concern of the State as a 'degradation of the civil power . . . dethroning it from its position as an institution of God'.[1] He argued that those who thought that the tide of history was running against the union of Church and State were deluded. Among the countries of Europe only Ireland and Italy had abandoned any sort of religious establishment, and—not to speak of Ireland—the bitter feud between the papacy and the Italian government now was scarcely an inducement to follow that precedent.[2] The rights of the individual conscience and the existence of an established Church were quite compatible with each other: where could one find greater freedom of opinion than in England?[3] As for the social prestige which those who attended the parish church enjoyed over those at a Nonconformist chapel, the establishment could not be held accountable since Roman Catholics often enjoyed as much if not more respect than Anglicans. Finally Tait warned Nonconformist advocates of disestablishment to take heed of the fact that they were supported by secularists. The secularists were the ones who knew what they were about: severance of the union between Church and State would weaken not just the established Church but Christianity generally in England.[4]

These arguments were unlikely to have any effect on those who were already determined to break the union. However, the fate of the establishment did not rest with its convinced opponents or defenders. Both were trying to catch the ear of the two large groups whose willingness to preserve the union was uncertain, the Liberal party and the High Church.

Within the Liberal Party

In 1870 Thomas Salt, a Conservative M.P. staunch for the establishment, said bleakly at a Church Institution meeting that he could not recall 'a single question that has been discussed in Parliament, during the last ten years, which we have endeavoured to meet, upon which we have not been utterly defeated.'[5] Certainly the events of the previous two years had given him good reason for pessimism. Compulsory church rates had been abolished, under a Conservative government though on Gladstone's initiative, in 1868. In 1869 the Liberals had weakened the Church's hold on endowed schools. Above all, the Irish Church had been disestablished and disendowed, casting a dark shadow over its English counterpart. Lord Salisbury and others were led to question the wisdom of building up the endowments of the Church of England since they seemed likely to be confiscated in turn.[6]

Edward Miall and his Society for the Liberation of Religion from State Patronage and Control, commonly known as the Liberation Society, were in high spirits. Founded by Miall in 1844,* the Society had since been built up by him till it was the best organized and most powerful political lobby in the country. Its influence was all the greater because British political party organization was as yet in its infancy. Miall's personal power was enchanced by his election as a Liberal M.P. for Bradford in 1869.† The Elementary Education Act of 1870 shook his confidence in the Liberal party's willingness to move further toward complete religious equality in England. In order to regain momentum by setting men's sights on this goal, he decided to propose the disestablishment of the State Churches of England and Scotland immediately. He gave notice of his resolution at the end of the Parliamentary session of 1870 and used the recess to build up his

---

* Under a different name, the British Anti-State Church Society.
† He had served as M.P. for Rochdale from 1852 to 1857.

popular following through public meetings. In May 1871, he presented his resolution:

> That it is expedient, at the earliest practicable period to apply the policy initiated by the disestablishment of the Irish Church by the Act of 1869 to the other Churches established by law in the united Kingdom.[7]

Miall did not expect the resolution to pass, and it was defeated by 376 votes to 91. However, 144 Liberals were absent from the division without pairs. The Liberation Society called them Miall's reserve and with some justice, for had they been strongly opposed to his motion, they would have taken the trouble to vote. Miall intended to present Parliament with motions toward the same end every year until the next general election, and then to present his case to the electorate. No one dismissed his threat lightly. In 1869 Archbishop Tait had spoken of a grim struggle within at least ten to twelve years;[8] *The Times* said that disestablishment would occur before the century was out.[9]

To the militant Dissenters whom Miall led, the establishment of the Church of England was the source from which all their disabilities had flowed. Most of the particular Nonconformist grievances had, like the inability of Dissenting ministers to solemnize legal marriages, been abolished already or, like the religious tests at Oxford and Cambridge, were about to be. This fact did not lessen the militants' desire for disestablishment. They had attacked each disability in the belief that, once stripped of its outworks, the establishment itself would be unable to resist its foes.

Furthermore, as long as the State paid special respect to the Church of England, invidious inequalities would be perpetuated. And even though the respectability and political influence which Nonconformity had now attained lessened its social inferiority, the legacy of past maltreatment still rankled. In 1862 with loud fanfare Nonconformists celebrated the two-hundredth anniversary of the ejection of nearly two thousand Puritan clergymen from their benefices under the Act of Uniformity of 1662. In the debate on Miall's motion one of his supporters reminded the members of the House of Commons whose memory might have been dulled by time that the Dissenters' forbears had been 'falsely imprisoned, whipped through the town, and placed in the pillory'.[10] Soon, he trusted, it would be the Nonconformists' turn to eject the Church of England from its privileged and richly endowed position.

Miall's argument for disestablishment was, however, more than a demand from a once persecuted minority for justice or revenge. It was also an attempt to bring down one of the arches which sustained the old but still strong aristocratic order in England. The leading offices in the Church were no longer engrossed by the aristocracy and wealthy gentry as they had been a century before. The Church of England was almost as much a middle class institution as its Nonconformist rivals. Yet few benefices were given to clergymen who were not considered gentlemen. Moreover, the privileges and emoluments of the established Church worked as a bribe fortifying its members' conservatism. Disestablishment was therefore an important plank in the Radical platform, akin to the attack on the purchase of army commissions which Gladstone's War minister, Cardwell, abolished in 1871.

It meant still more to Miall. He was a Congregationalist minister whose (self-appointed) ministry for thirty years had been to lead the assault on that work of Mammon, the State Church. Somewhat like the Tractarians and ritualists but in contrast to Tait, he looked upon the Churches as islands of light set in a sea of darkness. The establishment blurred this contrast by spreading a a veneer of ecclesiastical institutions and formal observance over the country. Whereas Tait made much of the civilizing effect which Christianity had had on Europe in contrast to heathen countries, Miall argued that the Churches were much more vigorous among the heathen than at home.[11] To treat England as a Christian country as Tait did was, in Miall's opinion, to disguise the true state of affairs. If only it were appreciated, Christians would be moved to greater effort:

were our whole population left to downright, positive, palpable ignorance—were its wants and woes left in their own naked deformity to meet the eye of compassion—were spiritual destitution not concealed behind the screen of baptized nominalism—and were human depravity suffered to harden into its own natural forms, instead of being made to run into artificial forms wearing the semblance of a Christian Church— surely, the earnest Christianity of the country could not, as now, consent to let it be, or look upon it only with cold emotions of regret.[12]

Miall argued that establishment also debilitated the Church it was supposed to strengthen. By binding the Church to the existing social order, establishment laid it open to particularly rough shaking during upheavals. Moreover, in welcoming the temporal assistance of the State, the Church of England seemed to say that the unaided spiritual resources of Christianity were inadequate for its mission.[13] The parochial clergy's concern about church rates, tithes and fees led men to equate Christianity with externals.[14] Here again Miall was akin to high churchmen such as Archdeacon Denison who had deplored the concentration in the House of Lords' debates about increasing the number of bishops on episcopal income and seats in the Lords.[15] However, Miall lumped the Church of England's forms and rules, cherished by high churchmen, with endowments as peripheral externals which the soullessness of establishment made unduly important.[16]

Though probably few members of the Liberation Society fully appreciated Miall's religious arguments, he succeeded in inspiring them 'with the zeal of the crusader and the fanaticism of a covenanter'.[17] He told them that controversy about the union of Church and State was 'exciting thought and . . . stirring action in every country in Europe', and had assured them that they were 'engaged in a work to which Omnipotence itself is pledged'.[18] Repeatedly in the previous half century the Radical demands of one day became Whig orthodoxy on the next. In 1871 Miall's Liberationists were hopeful that before they were many years, perhaps even months older, disestablishment would become the test question of Liberal opinion throughout the country.[19]

The future of the establishment politically depended on the Liberals since only they would give the proposal to dissolve it patient consideration. Though on occasion the Conservative party had been lukewarm in defending particular features of the establishment such as church rates, its reaction to the idea of complete severance between the Church of England and the State had always been one of horrified hostility. Moreover, attempting to capitalize on reaction to Irish disestablishment and to the religious provisions of such measures as the Endowed Schools Act, Disraeli placed support for the established Church among the main planks in his platform when in 1872 he began to campaign in preparation for the next general election. This confirmation of the Conservative position made Liberals' attitude more important. Polarized by the duel between Gladstone and Disraeli, politics were becoming increasingly partisan. Liberals might in turn react to Conservative policy by looking at the establishment still more critically; and they were certain to form the government again, if not after the next general election, then after some other not too far distant.

Despite the support which the Celtic fringe and Nonconformity gave the Liberal party, an overwhelming majority of Liberal M.P.s were Anglican. According to Dr. J. F. Glaser's calculations, among the 384 Liberal candidates successful in the general election of 1868 there were 53 English, 7 or 8 Scottish and 3 Irish Nonconformists, and 6 Jews. 23 Roman Catholics were elected, chiefly Irish Home Rulers; 2 members of the established Church of Scotland were elected, but as Conservatives.* Presumably all the other M.P.s who supported Gladstone's government adhered, whether strongly or loosely, to the Church of England. They would accept the Liberation Society's demand only if it met with extensive sympathy throughout the country. Widespread discontent over the establishment would indicate that its supposedly beneficial influences were no longer adequate to justify its preservation. But at present, though not much more than half the population of England could be considered Anglican, over 70 per cent of English marriages took place in Anglican churches. Apparently many Dissenters were willing to make use of some of the ministrations of the established Church. If so, they were unlikely to be determined opponents of the establishment. Furthermore, a minority of prominent Dissenters like Samuel Morley who were determined to abolish every concrete Nonconformist grievance made it clear that, unlike the Liberationists, they felt much less hostility towards the establishment itself. It was, Morley thought, an insubstantial though valid grievance, and he had no desire to force its abolition upon an unwilling Church. Instead he wanted to wait for the Church of England to realize how beneficial disestablishment would be for all concerned.[20] W. E. Forster, though an erstwhile Quaker and never a full member of the Church of England, thought of himself as among its friends, sometimes attended its services, and supported its union with the State.[21]

Judging by such evidence, the demand for disestablishment did not seem popular. This conclusion allowed Liberal Churchmen to give full weight to the reasons which convinced them personally

* Glaser, *Nonconformity and Liberalism, 1868–1885* (Harvard University doctoral dissertation, 1949), pp. 484–5. Glaser breaks the English Nonconformists into 18 Unitarians, 13 Congregationalists, 7 Quakers, 6 Baptists, 5 Wesleyan Methodists, 2 Presbyterians, 1 Calvinistic Methodist, and 2 of unspecified denomination, a total of 54. One was a Conservative.

that the union of Church and State should be preserved, particularly now that most Nonconformist disabilities had been removed. They felt all the more confident of the wisdom of their case because of the support which the opponents of Christianity gave to the Liberationist campaign.

Some of the right wing Liberals, pre-eminently Sir Roundell Palmer, defended establishment ardently. In 1868 Palmer had given up otherwise certain prospects of high cabinet office because he could not agree to disendowment of the Irish Church. His elevation as Lord Selborne to the Lord Chancellorship in 1872 increased the Liberationists' uneasiness about the government. Palmer argued[22] that disestablishment was not the logical outcome of Liberal policy. Its aim had been to abolish what curbed the liberty and rights of a minority, whereas disestablishment would impose the ecclesiastical wishes of a minority upon the whole country. Turning to positive arguments which revealed the traditionary framework of his mind, Palmer said that establishment helped to make the Church one of the State's most valuable allies in pursuit of the nation's well-being. The Church's assured income from endowments enabled it, he claimed, to do more in the slums than the Dissenters could. By strengthening the bond of a common profession of faith embracing a large proportion of the population, establishment was a safeguard against social upheaval. Disestablishment on the other hand, by abolishing the special national responsibilities of the Church and its protected position, would confront the Church with the need to pay more attention to its own interests, and might induce it to show less charity than previously towards other denominations. Finally, the legal enforceability of the doctrinal formularies of the Church did not make it an impediment to intellectual progress in the country, but rather, by giving clergymen alleged to have gone beyond these bounds the benefit of judicial trial, opened the Church, if anything too widely, to the growth of liberality and freedom of thought.

Most moderate Liberal Churchmen did not defend the establishment as fully and ardently as Palmer. Perhaps they were afraid that national opinion might yet resolve itself in favour of the Liberationists' demand. The Home Secretary, H. A. Bruce, contented himself with praising the work the established Church was doing and the freedom within it.[23] However one Liberal backbencher, Thomas Hughes, a disciple of F. D. Maurice and famous as the author of *Tom Brown's Schooldays*, but interesting in the context of party politics because he was a Radical, spoke out in support of the theory which still made many men on both sides of the House averse to disestablishment. Though purely religious issues rarely dominated the attention of Parliament, many of its members took a high view of their responsibilities. They welcomed the establishment for, in Hughes' words, imposing 'on the Legislature, on the Government, on statesmen, on all men engaged in public affairs—in short, upon the national conscience—the fact that the nation, in its corporate capacity, has a spiritual as well as a material life, that it cannot confine itself to the preservation of material things, of body and goods.'[24]

The key man in determining the stand which the Liberal party would take was, of course, Gladstone. It was his decision in favour of Irish disestablishment which precipitated action on that issue. During the passage of the 1870 Education Act his repeated assurance that the government would carefully avoid involving itself in denominational education partially revived Liberationists' blighted hopes. And as his speech against the perpetuation of the Judicial Committee solely for ecclesiastical appeals indicated, he was strongly averse to the use of State funds for the purely religious purposes of any denomination.[25] On the other hand, his support for the Bishops Resignation Bill in the midst of the debate on the disestablishment of the Irish Church showed that he was prepared to work as prime minister in cooperation with the leaders of the English Church. He also stepped firmly on Watkin Williams' attempt in 1870 to disendow the Church in Wales to pay for the creation of a network of undenominational schools there.[26]

Gladstone opposed Miall's motions, in 1873 even more firmly than in 1871.[27] The core of his argument was that English opinion was opposed to disestablishment; and the strength of his speech in 1873, with a general election around the corner, seemed to indicate that he was surer than ever that he had read public opinion aright. His dismissal of the issue as far from a pressing political reality could give only cold comfort to the defenders of the English establishment who remembered that he had brushed Irish disestablishment aside as remote and impracticable in 1865, barely three years before he embraced that proposal. However, he contended that the English and Irish establishments 'were distinguished broadly, vitally, and essentially upon every point without exception upon which they could be brought into comparison.'[28] In England disestablishment was 'at variance with the practical wishes and desires, the intelligent opinions, and the religious convictions of a large majority of the people'.[29] Even in Wales, he claimed, a considerable majority were attached to the Church by some tie or other. He belittled the significance of Miall's support in the House of Commons by saying that only temporary causes, presumably the importance of Irish disestablishment in the 1868 election campaign, had enabled it to rise to its existing size, and he predicted that another election would thin it out. Concluding his reply to Miall's first motion, Gladstone told him that he should convert a majority throughout the country before demanding a favourable reply from Parliament.

Gladstone also threw a cold light upon the legislative practicability of disestablishing the Church of England. He estimated that it would be left with £90 millions in contrast to the less than £3 millions the Irish Church retained, alarming wealth for a body to be set free from State control. Furthermore he, the most capable legislator of his day, quailed before the immensity of the matter which would be involved in English disestablishment.

Yet more than head counting and bill drafting moved Gladstone to the ringing eloquence of his speech of 1873. Disestablishment and disendowment would cause incalculable harm to the Church which he loved both as its devoted adherent and as an Englishman. He would acquiesce in delivering the blow, if ever, only under the greatest pressure. This was the only conclusion to be drawn about a man who could say that:

the Church of England has not only been a part of the history of this country, but a part so vital, entering so profoundly into the entire life and action of the country, that the severing of the two would leave nothing behind but a bleeding and lacerated mass. Take the Church of England out of the history of England, and the history of England becomes a chaos, without order, without life, and without meaning.[30]

1873 marked a turning of the tide away from the Liberationists, perhaps a temporary fluctuation or perhaps of critical importance. In 1872, Miall's support in the House of Commons rose by ten votes over the previous year and the number against him dropped by ninety-one, though he was still soundly defeated. The Liberals split roughly into thirds, one for, one against, and one abstaining. The significance of this vote was confused by the decline of interest in the issue after the apparently decisive vote of the year before and by the more moderate form of the motion Miall now presented. But there could be no doubt about the implications of the vote in 1873. Three hundred and ninety-six M.P.s voted against him, 20 more than ever before, and, much more significant, only 61 voted with him, a loss of 40.

This swing was partially attributable to a campaign by ardent supporters of the establishment, particularly the Church Defence Institution.* Shocked by Miall's attack in 1871, Bishop Ellicott had taken the lead in reviving the torpid Church Instituion and, under the new name, concentrating its energies on defending the establishment. The Church Defence Institution was given official blessing when Archbishop Tait agreed to be its honorary president and all but five of the other bishops, honorary vice-presidents. The five dissidents, Fraser, Temple, Mackarness, Moberly and Hughes, were all Gladstone nominees. Few men upheld establishment more whole-heartedly than Fraser, a Broad Churchman. But he was a staunch Liberal politically and feared that the Church Defence Institution would work to the benefit of the Conservatives. Therefore, he contented himself with the belief that the establishment would remain secure so long as the Church did its job well.[31] Gladstone's four other episcopal appointments, Lord Arthur Hervey, Goodwin, Durnford, and Wilberforce whom Gladstone elevated from Oxford to Winchester, joined the Institution.

It proceeded to build up a network of local associations until by the beginning of 1874 there were nearly 450 covering most of the country. The monthly newspaper which the Church Institution had founded in 1870, the *National Church*, was put to good use, and its circulation raised from 4,000 in 1872 to 20,000 in 1873. In addition, the Church Defence Institution issued over half a million other publications: handbills, copies of speeches by national leaders, pamphlets, and statistical analyses of the Church's membership and work. A few of the publications were hysterical, for example *How Our Church Became a Drinking Saloon: A vision of disestablishment*,[32] but most were sane and some thoughtful.

* The following information on this society is drawn mainly from its newspaper, the *National Church*, and from the collection of its pamphlets in the British Museum.

The Institution opened offices near the Houses of Parliament. It selected a committee to maintain constant scrutiny over all relevant measures arising in Parliament. The case which sympathetic M.P.s could present was strengthened by circulating petitions and by collecting statistical information to refute the Liberationists who drew comparisons to the detriment of the established Church between Anglican and Nonconformist Church attendance and between the number of new churches each side built. To do all this the Institution needed money, and through subscriptions and fund-raising campaigns it trebled its annual income to £3,000 in 1873, still not half the Liberation Society's.

Disraeli welcomed this campaign as one aspect of the reaction to Liberal legislation and of uneasiness about Liberal leanings which he hoped would bring him to power. 'My name', he wrote, 'is entirely at the service of the "Church Defence Institution," and all the aid that I can ever afford to the best and most sacred of causes.'[33] He accepted an invitation to become a vice-president of the Institution's branch in his constituency of Buckinghamshire. Though expressing agreement with the branch's motto, 'Church above Party', he said that of course the sympathies of churchmen were likely to rest with the defenders of order and the constitution.[34] And indeed the Church Defence Institution became almost a tool of the Conservative party by treating the attempt to permit Nonconformist services in parish churchyards, virtually Liberal party policy by 1873, as a direct attack on the establishment.

With this one exception, however, the Institution made a determined attempt to be non-partisan. Some of its most distinguished supporters, Tait for one, would have disassociated themselves from any organization which allowed its weight to fall entirely into Conservative hands. More to the point, the establishment would never be secure unless the Liberal party was prepared at least to tolerate it. Accordingly, the course which the Institution pursued was one of building up popular support for the establishment in the knowledge that, though this would probably work to the Conservatives' benefit, it would also strengthen the moderate majority within the Liberal party in resisting Miall.

Events seemed to justify this strategy. In Devon, where Nonconformity was widespread and the local branch of the Church Defence Institution correspondingly militant, it enjoyed notable success. Lord Arthur Russell, the M.P. for Tavistock who had voted with Miall in 1872, publicly repudiated Miall's policy at the beginning of 1873.[35] Later that year the Liberal candidate in a by-election in Exeter, Sir Edward Watkin, opposed disestablishment which in 1869 he had considered permissible if circumstances should so dictate.[36]

Many signs indicated that in the political arena the union of Church and State in England was much more secure as Gladstone's first Ministry neared its close than at its beginning. Archbishop Tait's confidence increased correspondingly: 'nothing will shake our position', he said, 'unless we unfortunately should be unfaithful to ourselves or unfaithful to the great duties which God has laid upon us.'[37]

Among High Churchmen

Tait's proviso was echoed by other commentators. 'If the connection between [Church and State] is ever dissolved,' Sir Stafford Northcote told the Church Congress of 1873, 'it will not be so much by the blows from without as by those from within the Church that its destruction will be brought about.'[38] Discontent with the establishment was if anything more widespread within the Church than in the country at large. To the State, union with the Church was only one of many concerns and never the most important. To the Church, union with the State was the most powerful temporal fact in its life. Difficulties with the Church were irritants to the State; difficulties with the State were crises for the Church. Since 1828 Parliament had seen to the removal of most of the sources of popular antagonism towards the establishment: the specific Nonconformist disabilities, compulsory church rates, and the worst abuses in the Church's use of its income. But this very appeasement of popular discontent aroused high church suspicions of State intervention in Church affairs. It was the Irish Church Temporalities Act of 1833 abolishing ten superfluous bishoprics which moved Keble to preach his Assize Sermon, the event which according to Newman marked the beginning of the Oxford Movement. The uneasiness in High Church circles was aggravated by a series of episodes—especially the nomination of Hampden in 1836 to the regius professorship of divinity at Oxford and later to the bishopric of Hereford, and the Judicial Committee's decisions in the Gorham and *Essays and*

Reviews cases—in which the Crown's power over the Church was exercised in a way High Churchmen considered offensive. If similar episodes should continue or worse ones occur, High Churchmen might throw their support behind Miall's campaign. Then he would be irresistible.

Another such event happened in 1869. That August, Gladstone was confronted, as a result of the Bishops Resignation Act just passed, with the need to fill several bishoprics. Those who hoped that he would use his power of nomination to benefit the Church party which personally he favoured were more than disappointed. His religious convictions did make him uniquely conscientious in filling ecclesiastical vacancies. When an important office was at stake, all other business was driven from his mind, to his secretaries' despair.[39] But he believed that his position as head of the government obliged him to act in the interests of the Church of England as a whole. Liberal political sympathies were an asset to a potential bishop in Gladstone's eyes, but not High Churchmanship.[40]

In the present situation, he thought immediately of Frederick Temple because a volume of his sermons and his work first as an inspector of schools and now as headmaster of Rugby had impressed him, because Temple was one of the best representatives of the Broad Church school, and because he had been prominent among the few clergymen who defended the Liberals' Irish Church policy. Gladstone discussed the possibility of nominating Temple with Archbishop Tait who probably warmly approved.[41] Temple was then named to succeed Phillpotts, famed for his irascible High Churchmanship, as bishop of Exeter.

As soon as the nomination was made public, there were loud protests. For Temple was the author of one of the articles, the introductory one in fact, in *Essays and Reviews* which Convocation had solemnly condemned 'as containing teaching contrary to the doctrine received by the United Church of England and Ireland, in common with the whole Catholic Church of Christ.'[42] This censure had no legal force. Furthermore, Temple's essay had differed from most of the others in its moderation; many people thought that Convocation's condemnation did not apply to it. However, he had not attempted to secure his position by withdrawing his essay from the book's many subsequent editions. Instead he published a volume of his sermons to let the alarmed see his essay in the context of his whole teaching.

148

This action had by no means entirely dispelled the cloud over Temple's head. His nomination to the bishopric of Exeter re-united the Evangelical–High Church alliance led by Shaftesbury and Pusey* which had been formed against *Essays and Reviews*. However, to Shaftesbury's chagrin, his fellow Evangelicals gave him much less support now than on the previous occasion. More-over, the laity by and large were less upset by Temple's nomination than they had been by the book in which he collaborated.† The protest came mainly from the clergy, especially High Churchmen.

This did not deprive it of seriousness. For Pusey was so indignant that he turned against the establishment.[43] Who could Catholic churchmen rely upon to exercise the Crown's power of nomina-tion if not upon their hitherto trusted friend and sympathizer, Gladstone? And Gladstone had not only proposed this disastrous appointment; he refused to withdraw it in spite of the protests of devout churchmen. Pusey's anguish soon affected less extreme men. At first Wilberforce, who had instigated the attack on *Essays and Reviews*, even welcomed the nomination of the least objec-tionable and most respected Broad Church clergyman to the bench of bishops. As the controversy became more inflamed, however, Wilberforce wavered.[44]

The nomination was sent to the dean and chapter of Exeter cathedral in whose hands election to the bishopric rested. Their action was supposed to represent the will of the diocesan clergy. But the chapter were obliged, under threat of imprisonment and confiscation of lands and goods (in other words, under threat of 'praemunire'), to elect the Crown's nominee. These rough shackles, imposed in the turbulent days of Henry VIII, provoked resent-ment because of the increased sensitivity which the clergy had acquired about their spiritual responsibilities. Temple's oppo-nents put great pressure on the chapter to reject the nomination. If they had done so, the Crown could and certainly would have appointed Temple through Letters Patent. But such a clash be-tween Church and State would have strained their union severely.

Archbishop Tait drafted a letter[45] to the chapter to convince them that the existing safeguards against the Crown's nomination

---

* Although poles apart on all other ecclesiastical issues, they were cousins and preserved a cordial personal relationship.

† The bishop of Ely estimated that 19 out of every 20 laymen approved of the nomi-nation. G. W. Kitchin, *Edward Harold Browne, D.D., Lord Bishop of Winchester*, 331.

of an unfaithful person to a bishopric were effectual. However, the safeguards he listed were not legally binding checks on the Crown but merely expressions of its own good will. Tait argued that the prime minister spoke for a country which still loved its national Church. He was also in constant communication with the leading bishops whose advice, especially when expressing the consensus within the Church, would carry great weight. In addition, the Queen herself could always refuse to accept any nomination she thought intolerable. The prime minister might well feel obliged to nominate someone representative of an unpopular minority within the Church, but never, said Tait, someone who was unworthy. Tait never sent the letter. In the event the chapter elected Temple by thirteen votes to six with four abstentions. Even so the number of malcontents was not reassuring.

The appointment still had to receive confirmation from the archbishop through his vicar-general's court, to which the opposition now resorted. Temple's elder sister had to be summoned at short notice to testify that he had been born in lawful wedlock. The vicar-general would not examine the other charges brought against Temple, insisting that the royal mandate must be carried out. This ruling seemed to deprive the Church of one of the few possibly real checks upon the Crown's power.*

The controversy continued to grow, all the more so because Temple would not elucidate his views to clear himself of Convocation's censure. At first most moderates respected his silence. No self-respecting man loyal to his friends, they conceded, should bow before clamour. Once he had been elected by the chapter and his election legally confirmed, however, uneasiness at his continued silence mounted. Some extremists insisted that they could not remain happily in a Church one of whose leaders was a condemned heretic; and the *Guardian* did not dismiss this implied threat lightly.[46]

Temple would not make any statement beyond those required of him in the course of the legal and religious ceremonies preliminary to becoming a bishop. Nor would he promise that, once he had been consecrated, he would clarify his views. He placed

---

* This 'loss' had been revealed before over Hampden's nomination to the bishopric of Hereford in 1848. The vicar-general acted in the same way then as now. Indeed, the story of Hampden's nomination and appointment is similar in many respects to Temple's. See Owen Chadwick, *The Victorian Church*, part I, 237–49.

great value upon the freedom of thought which the legal establishment of the Church ensured for its members. Under this consitution, enforcement of the Church's rules and formularies lay with the courts. It was up to them to decide how far these rules were legally binding and when a member of the Church had transgressed them. Any statement of belief which Temple's opponents succeeded, because of Convocation's censure, in extracting from him beyond what the law required would reduce this freedom. To admit that he did not share some of the more extreme views expressed in other contributions to *Essays and Reviews* would imply that they could not properly be held by members of the Church. Moreover, if he made a statement, it would create a precedent which might be insisted upon in future unpopular nominations—perhaps, ironically, of a Tractarian—to the episcopate. And in any case, the only statement which Temple might have felt able to make would not have allayed the fears of his Tractarian opponents, for it would have explicitly upheld the right of private judgment which they denied in theory if not in practice.

The persistence of his silence eventually puzzled even the prime minister. Some of Temple's personal friends and Church leaders whom he trusted urged him to make some declaration. After serious reconsideration, he refused. Tait tried to lessen the uneasiness in Church circles by writing a public letter[47] in which he pronounced his considered judgment that Temple did not fall under Convocation's censure of *Essays and Reviews*. The archbishop made reference to his personal admiration for Temple and to the public confidence in him which the swelling student enrolment at Rugby indicated. On the other hand, Tait voiced his regret that Temple had not withdrawn his essay from the condemned volume long ago, and he concluded that at least as soon as Temple took up his duties in Exeter he ought to make his viewpoint clear. Then, exhausted by the hectic negotiations over the Irish Church Bill and deprived of any time to recuperate because of this second controversy, the archbishop had another stroke, leaving him unable to do any more to restrain the mounting unrest. (Immediately Gladstone began to consider possible successors.[48])

Temple's silence jeopardized his consecration for which the presence of at least three bishops was necessary. Even some of the bishops who thought Temple's appointment unexceptionable felt obliged to refuse to join in consecrating him so long as he remained under the shadow of a synodical condemnation. Of the seventeen bishops of the province of Canterbury, nine eventually objected to consecrating him, five unofficially and four formally,* some just when the service was about to begin. Four of the dissidents appealed to the fourth canon of the Council of Nice which required the consent of all comprovincial bishops to a consecration. This canon was not, however, a recognized part of the Church of England's law, whose requirements were fully met in Temple's consecration.[49] A small minority led by Denison kept up the fight by asking Convocation to object to the appointment.[50] When Convocation was informed through a friend of Temple—but without Temple's approval—of his intention to withdraw his essay from any further issues of *Essays and Reviews*, most of these dissidents were satisfied.

Otherwise, once the consecration had taken place, the storm immediately subsided. Twenty-six years later Temple was to become archbishop of Canterbury, a promotion which provoked no more than smiling incredulity at men's behaviour a generation before. Yet his initial appointment left the union between Church and State strained. By objecting to his consecration, nine bishops had set themselves in opposition to the will of the Crown, a long step, so Jackson of London feared, toward disestablishment.[51]

In the wake of the agitation, attempts were made by both high and evangelical churchmen to modify the way vacant bishoprics were filled, and they secured the support even of the Church Institution.[52] In spite of Tait's reluctance to throw this important aspect of the connection between Church and State open for debate in Convocation,[53] a joint committee of the two houses was selected to consider the subject. In its report[54] it made no objection to nomination by the Crown, but recommended that the nominee's election and confirmation and the consent of the comprovincial bishops to his consecration should become effectual expressions of the will of the clergy. Nothing came of the report; its importance lay in the feeling which dictated it.

The more significant consequence of Temple's nomination was its alienation of Pusey from the union between Church and State.

---

* Informally Ollivant of Llandaff, Campbell of Bangor, Magee of Peterborough, Claughton of Rochester, and Wilberforce; formally Ellicott, Selwyn of Lichfield, Atlay of Hereford, and Wordsworth of Lincoln. E. M. Goulburn, *John William Burgon*, II, p. 38.

Ecclesiastically the future of the establishment rested with high churchmen just as, in politics, it rested with the Liberals. Each was the party least attached in its respective sphere to the union, and if either decided to break it, it would be broken.

Ripples of dissatisfaction with the establishment ran across the surface of Evangelical opinion over Temple's appointment, Bennett's acquittal by the Judicial Committee, and the ineffectiveness of the courts in repressing ritualism. 'We cannot be surprised', the Claughton branch of the Church Association told Tait, 'that the conviction has spread far and wide amongst Churchmen that in the presence of . . . deliberate treachery, those who are loyal to the Reformation can no longer continue their active support to the permanence of the establishment!'[55] Generally, however, Parliament could be counted upon, when required, to exercise its influence over the Church in a firmly Protestant direction. Moreover, the State's power in Church affairs was deemed to express the voice of the laity, and since it was among the laity that evangelicals found much their strongest support, they would never opt for disestablishment without great provocation. Ecclesiastically they were the counterparts of the Conservatives in regard to establishment; and whenever in office Disraeli tried to consolidate their support through his ecclesiastical appointments.

Broad Churchmen too were stalwart supporters of establishment in spite of their Liberal predilections in politics. For it provided the legal guarantees of the Church's comprehensiveness. Furthermore, union with the State forced the Church to take heed of national opinion as broad churchmen wished. Tractarians branded this pressure as secularizing. In Dean Stanley's eyes, however, it not only prevented the Church from turning in upon itself but was ennobling.[56] To those who maintained that the bishops' proper assembly was the Upper House of Convocation rather than the House of Lords, Stanley replied,

I regard the Bishops of this realm as much more Fathers in God when they are sitting in the supreme council of the nation, addressing the peers of England, than when they are talking to half a dozen reporters in a private drawing-room in Dean's-yard.[57]

But High Church opinion was in turmoil. Bennett had advocated disestablishment soon after the Gorham judgment in 1850.[58] The first years of Gladstone's Ministry were marked by a rapid succession of blows like the Gorham judgment to high church susceptibilities: the Mackonochie judgment and Temple's nomination in 1869, the Education Act of 1870 which Denison took particularly hard, the Purchas judgment in 1871. Little wonder that extreme High Churchmen were profoundly discontented with the way the union of Church and State was working. What was surprising was their failure resolutely to seek its severance.

After Mackonochie's condemnation, enthusiastic ritualists like his curate, Stanton, too young to have been tempered by the experience of warriors such as Pusey, called impatiently for an end to the Church's bondage. 'Nothing is so fatal to us as this Establishment;' Stanton exclaimed, 'and if by the blessing of Almighty God the suspension of Mr. Mackonochie overturns that rooks' nest so much the better.'[59] Mackonochie himself, though an older man, also lacked Pusey's respect for the inherited traditions of the Church of England, for his background was Scottish. The Oxford Movement had appealed to him because of its quest for sanctity resisting the earthward pull of fleshly desires. If only the Church of England could divest itself of its establishment, Mackonochie trusted that its members would begin

to feel as a body, and not merely as individuals, that we belong to a 'kingdom which is not of this world.' Our bishops will know that their power is that of servants of *Christ*, not Lords of Parliament; we of the clergy shall be free from the temptations to worldly gain and ambition with which an Establishment surrounds men; and our people will receive or reject us for *Christ's* sake, not as ministers appointed by the State.[60]

The choice was not so simple to the older men. Denison wavered back and forth, furious when the State assailed the Church but hesitant to pledge himself irrevocably to disestablishment. By the time of the Purchas judgment Pusey had had second thoughts and confessed himself unable to favour disestablishment until the situation should deteriorate still further.[61] On the other hand, for over thirty years he had tried to parry the blows of the State to what he considered the well-being of the Church. Liddon, Pusey's second self, was equally fearful of the influence of churchmen who, in order to maintain the establishment by making the Church more widely acceptable, were trying to lessen the dogmatic quality of its teaching.[62] The establishment often seemed in his eyes, as in Miall's, to debilitate the Church in addition to depriving it of defence against hostile acts of State.

On the other hand, according to traditional High Church teaching, never treated lightly by these apostles of dogma, establishment was the providential imposition upon the Church of heightened responsibility for the English State and people.[63] The Church might suffer hardships as a result; establishment, they often said, was more beneficial to the State and country than to the Church. But rough and overbearing though the beneficiary was, the Church could not escape from this divine commission unless the State treated the Church in a way which made the Church's overriding duty to teach the faith and preserve the ecclesiastical order of the early Church impossible. After each affront by the State to Tractarians' teaching, they asked themselves whether this moment had arrived. So far most of them had been unable to answer with an unqualified 'yes'. The minority who disagreed went over to Rome. Those who remained behind wrote long explanatory pamphlets.[64]

The most trying time was not the early 1870s but the five years from Newman's secession in 1845 to the Gorham judgment. For most of that time royal patronage was in the hands of Lord John Russell and Prince Albert, both hearty opponents of dogmatism.[65] It was Russell who appointed Hampden to the bishopric of Hereford in 1847. The Tractarians had emerged from these years with a determination, hardened by adversity, to stand by the Church of England. They were heartened in 1852 when the government agreed to a resuscitation of Convocation. Convocation was all the more useful to high churchmen because for twenty years the stiffly Evangelical clergy who were entitled to seats in it stayed away, refusing to fraternize with their enemies. The 1850s also saw the beginning of what proved to be a steady increase in Tractarians' support and influence within the Church, giving them greater confidence in their position and a brighter hope of inducing the whole Church to reaffirm its Catholic heritage. This was no time for counsels of despair.

Furthermore, disestablishment had its liabilities. It would involve a measure of disendowment, which Liddon realized would be particularly hard on a Church unaccustomed to reliance upon the collection plate.[66] Disestablishment might also make life even more difficult for extreme High Churchmen. They were still a small minority within the Church and would probably fare badly in a free Church governed by a popular assembly. The militant

Protestantism which disestablishment released in the Irish Church gave the English high church fair warning.

Among the less extreme and especially among High Church laymen, support for the establishment was markedly stronger. Some were Liberals politically and hoped, somewhat like Gladstone, that perhaps by surrendering some of its temporal assets, the Church could ease the tensions in its union with the State.[67] Many staunch High Churchmen such as Canon Gregory were equally staunch Conservatives. High Churchmanship and Conservatism were in their minds kindred positions, defending the old order in Church as in State. To them disestablishment was a Radical and militant Nonconformist policy; and they resisted it in the same spirit with which they sought to counteract the theologically liberal and evangelical forces inside the Church. High Church laymen, less involved in this theological warfare, accepted the Church's comprehensiveness which establishment undergirded more calmly than their clerical leaders. Thus Gathorne Hardy, the most eloquent right-winger on the Conservative front bench and an equally ardent High Churchman, disapproved of the outcry against Temple's appointment.[68]

Therefore, in spite of the fact that there was more anxiety in Church than in State over the working of their union, it was in fact even more secure ecclesiastically than politically. On no subject was the essential conservatism of the Church more apparent than on preservation of the establishment; almost all churchmen clung to it even when it worked to the detriment of their religious or political convictions. Some would continue to talk of disestablishment.* But it was idle speech, little more than a cudgel which one school would use to threaten another into submission. Each time the threat was employed, its hollowness would become that much more obvious.

The general election of February 1874 removed disestablishment from the political arena at least temporarily. Disraeli rode triumphantly into power with a majority of 50, the first clear mandate Conservatives had enjoyed in more than a quarter-century. Changes in denominational voting helped determine the result, though it is impossible to know to what extent. Alienated by the Elementary Education Act, some Nonconformists such as R. W.

* *Infra,* 212.

Dale, the leading Congregationalist minister in Birmingham, turned against the Liberals; others, as advised by the Liberation Society's journal the *Liberator*, took no part in the campaign except where Liberal candidates sympathized with their political aims.[69] It is also likely that Churchmen who were embarrassed into voting Liberal or abstaining in 1868 because of the glaring injustice of the Irish Church's establishment slipped back into the Conservative fold, pushed—if they needed to be pushed—by fear of the anti-establishment tendencies of Gladstone's government and, much stronger, of its supporters.

No one believed that disestablishment had disappeared as an electoral issue. Yet the setback it suffered may have been more decisive than even those who had worked for the setback realized: the results of the election reinforced Joseph Chamberlain's conclusion that Nonconformity was not powerful enough in itself to impose its will on the country.[70] At any rate, the new Parliament was to waste no time on debates devoted to the question of disestablishment. On the contrary, it began by taking up its responsibilities toward the Church of England with disruptive seriousness.

Chapter Seven

THE PUBLIC WORSHIP REGULATION ACT, 1874

1874 was the last year of English history in which for a whole session Parliament was preoccupied with the condition of the established Church. The excitement engendered by passing the Public Worship Regulation Bill was spectacular. Queen Victoria spoke of exiling herself, for five months Tait enjoyed an influence no archbishop had possessed since Laud, and the front benches of both political parties split.

When the new Conservative cabinet met in February, it found itself with little important legislation to propose to Parliament other than the budget.[1] They had not expected so unquestionable a victory in the general election. Furthermore they had won it, not because of the measures they promised, but because of the electors' fatigue and annoyance at the legislative diet Gladstone had forced them to swallow. Consequently, though the cabinet contained men such as R. A. Cross at the Home Office who would prove to be distinguished legislators, they did not have ready-made proposals. They turned to Disraeli. However, he was an old man now; he had inspiring ideas, but not such as could be easily translated into bills; he lacked Gladstone's gifts of legislative draftsmanship.

Archbishop Tait moved into the vacuum. During the last half of 1873 a Protestant storm had been gathering, bred of anger and frustration: anger at the ritualists' assimilation of their churches' conduct to the practices of Rome, in particular the Mass and the confessional; frustration at the courts' inability and the bishops' seeming refusal to stop this seduction. To many of those whose religious reactions were not so strong, the ritualists' defiance of the courts seemed anarchic and, especially in view of the privileged position of the clergy of the Church of England, indefensible. The demand for disestablishment might be on the wane, but to a corresponding degree the demand for strict maintenance of the Protestantism of the national Church increased.

On January 13 and 14, ten days before Gladstone's sudden and unexpected dissolution of Parliament, the English bishops met for their customary new year's council, and it was from the resolutions of this meeting that the Public Worship Regulation Bill grew. The parentage of the idea of the bill is not, however, quite as certain. In the previous July, Tait had suggested to Parliament that it attempt to curb extreme High Church practices by increasing bishops' power over their dioceses;[2] and at the top of the agenda which he drew up in November for the forthcoming bishops' council he placed Church discipline, by which he meant the problem of defiance of the courts by high churchmen over ceremonial. Still, it is improbable that he planned to propose major legislation under this heading since he listed seven other items for discussion. Tait may have been induced to propose something ambitious by the Church Association, which petitioned the bishops to introduce legislation against 'changes which tend to obscure the work of the Reformation'.[3] Read against the background of mounting Protestant unrest, this petition may have been taken by Tait as warning that, unless the bishops took action, the Church Association and Lord Shaftesbury would bring something more drastic before Parliament which it might accept.

More probably, it was Queen Victoria who propelled the archbishop into motion. The Queen was almost as militant a Protestant as Shaftesbury, though disagreeing sharply with his fundamentalism, a theological stance from which Prince Albert had weaned her. Her relationship with Tait enabled her to exert unusually strong influence in his deliberations. Though again like Shaftesbury she disliked bishops as a breed, Tait was an exception. She personally had made him archbishop, and her admiration for him only increased with the years. When he died, she bestowed upon him the supreme honour not even given to Disraeli: she asked for a lock of his hair. Tait had responded to the Queen's regard with veneration of her, quite in keeping with his idea of the proper relations between Church and State. In August 1882, although in the exhausted condition which led to his death three months later, he forced himself to make the trip to Osborne to confirm two of the Prince of Wales' children as a last service to their grandmother.

Tait was at Osborne early in January 1874 for the confirmation of Princess Beatrice. Queen Victoria used the opportunity to urge him to see that legislation was introduced in Parliament for the purpose of strengthening the bishops' ability to stop the corrosion of the Church's Protestant character. The specific proposals she outlined were remarkably like the measure Tait drafted after the bishops' meeting. She told Tait to let the bishops know what she thought; and she followed up the interview with a letter. 'It is clear', she wrote, 'that . . . the liberties taken and the defiance shown by the Clergy of the High Church and Ritualist party, is so great that something *must be done* to check it, and prevent its continuation.'[4]

Tait opened the bishops' meeting by proposing that the matter of Church discipline be taken up in Parliament as speedily as possible.[5] The High Church bishops reacted with immediate caution. Mackarness of Oxford opposed the suggestion, but did not explain why; Wordsworth of Lincoln* wanted Convocation to be consulted. But they were sheep without a shepherd, for Wilberforce was gone. Tait's pre-eminence was, for the first time, unrivalled. Even if Wilberforce had been alive and present, the High Church bishops would have been at a loss. For they too disliked ritualism heartily, and as bishops were concerned about the anarchy in the Church. Furthermore, Tait was presenting the policy recommended by the Queen. Though she was not their spiritual guide, the personal reverence which she commanded made her constitutional position as supreme governor of the Church no idle fiction in their eyes.

Eventually all the bishops but Mackarness agreed that they should introduce legislation to regulate the services of the Church. They discussed its provisions in a tentative manner, and asked the two archbishops, Thomson and Tait, to draft a bill for consideration at a subsequent meeting of the episcopate. Wordsworth secured agreement to submit the bill to the two Convocations at the same time as to Parliament. He also proposed that an address should be issued by the bishops to prepare Churchmen for the introduction of the bill. In this he encountered opposition not only

* Nephew of the poet.

from the two primates and the evangelical bishops but also from Mackarness. He was fobbed off with a committee to try to devise some statement to which all the bishops would agree.

As soon as the meeting was over, Tait put his legal adjutant, J. Brunel,* to work. From then on Tait was the prime mover, and the bill came to be considered as his. The bishops were his chorus, occasionally discordant, Thomson his second fiddle. Whether before or after the meeting, Tait had made up his mind to see a bill passed that year. And there was nothing he liked more than securing Parliamentary legislation. The thornier the path, the more he enjoyed negotiating his way through it. When in the midst of the struggle the excitement became too intense, he found relief in novels.

The Queen continued to push the enterprise on. Tait reported the outcome of the meeting to her, and she conveyed the bishops' decision to Gladstone.[6] She informed Gladstone that she had urged them to make it. 'Protestant to the very *heart's core* as the Queen is, she is shocked and grieved to see England forgetting her Position and the Higher Classes and so many of the young Clergy tainted with this leaning towards Rome! for it is nothing else.' Parliament, she hoped, would co-operate with the bishops. And such co-operation was 'especially necessary on the part of Mr. Gladstone, who is *supposed* to have *rather* a bias towards High Church views himself, but the danger of which she feels sure he cannot fail to recognize.'

Before replying, Gladstone asked for a dissolution of Parliament.[7] He did so because of a threatened split within his cabinet over financial policy. Yet the proposed legislation can only have increased his desire to obtain a fresh mandate from the electorate before dealing with it in Parliament which was certain to retain strong Protestant sympathies. Two days later he answered the Queen's letter.[8] He did not rule the legislation out. However he cautioned her that, 'if the violent internal controversies, which so greatly strain the framework of the Church, when carried on within, were transferred to the floors of the two Houses, the probable, indeed the almost certain, end would be the total banishment of the subject from the Parliamentary arena, by the disestablishment of the Church itself.' On the day he wrote this reply, the Queen agreed to the dissolution.[9]

* Chancellor of the diocese of Ely.

A general election was something the bishops had not considered. It prevented the simultaneous introduction of the bill into Convocation and Parliament. For the two Convocations were dissolved automatically with Parliament. Although they could be re-elected promptly, they would not be able to meet as soon as the new Parliament. Parliament's first meeting would fall during Lent, and by invariable custom no Convocations were held in Lent since many of the members who were parochial clergy would be unable to attend then. Yet to delay the introduction of the bill till Convocation had considered it would deny it enough time to pass through both Houses of Parliament that year. And if the bishops did not introduce their bill early in the session, Evangelical members of Parliament who wanted more extreme legislation would go ahead.

The outcome of the general election confirmed Tait's desire to proceed quickly. The Liberals were driven from power by the party which prided itself on being the friend of the established Church. Gladstone, Tait's chief Parliamentary obstacle, was so disheartened that he prepared to resign the leadership of the Liberal party and in the meantime announced his intention of attending the first session of Parliament only occasionally. The electoral returns also fortified Tait's belief that national opinion was opposed to anything which compromised the Church's Protestantism: not a single Roman Catholic was elected by any constituency outside Ireland.[10]

Within Disraeli's first week after taking office, Archbishop Tait sent him a memorandum outlining his proposals.[11] They were moderate. Essentially they amounted to a request for legislation to create a simple, summary and inexpensive process for securing obedience to the law governing public worship. The memorandum did not propose any change in the substance of the law. Queen Victoria wanted the bill to include a revision of the rubrics capable of a High Church interpretation, but Tait had restrained her.[12] She was also worried about sacramental confession[13] but this too was ignored.

Both in its moderation and in the specific process for enforcing the law which was suggested, the memorandum was calculated to undercut high church lawlessness. High Churchmen made much of their willingness to defer to episcopal authority rather than to civil courts. Very well, to the bishops they would go. All the relevant formularies of the Church pointed to the diocesan bishop as the person to whom disputes about ceremonial should be referred. The bishops' authority had, however, proven ineffective because they did not wield coercive power. Tait's proposal was that the bishops should be given such power by the only authority which could do so, the State; hence the need for legislation. He suggested that the diocesan bishop's decision in a dispute over ceremonial should be capable of being enforced immediately. If the incumbent did not obey, his benefice could be sequestrated. Since to invest each bishop with such arbitrary power would not be popular to say the least, Tait proposed the creation of diocesan boards composed of equal proportions of clergy and laymen to advise the bishop in exercising his new power. The lay members were to be elected by the churchwardens of the diocese.

Tait did not, however, spell out the relationship between this enforcing authority and the law. For the memorandum said that 'while a general uniformity ought to be the rule, still, where there is a loyal acceptance of the Prayer Book, certain minute diversities which have grown up by custom, or from the varying circumstances of different communities, need not be interfered with.' This provision was intended to protect the moderate majority of clergymen whose practice, like that of their predecessors for generations, fell somewhat short of the rubrics' requirements. Tait may also have intended it to leave the eastward position undisturbed in parishes where it did not create offence. To secure such protection, the bishops and their advisory boards would have to be given discretionary power to decide when to enforce the law and when to overlook infractions, a need which the memorandum ignored.

The memorandum had another characteristic which deceived no one. All of its proposals were presented as coming from the bishops when in fact they had only discussed the possible provisions of a bill without reaching any conclusions. Tait's assessment of the consensus was fairly accurate since most of the bishops supported the eventual bill at least until near the end of the Parliamentary session. But in any case, everyone who read the memorandum assumed that its detailed provisions were Tait's.

He accompanied the memorandum with a letter to Disraeli[14] appealing for the government's advice and support. He came, he pointed out, with powerful backing not only from the episcopate. 'Her Majesty is much interested in [the measure], thinking I believe rightly, that, unless something of the kind indicated is done, the Church of England will go on the breakers.' He admitted that his proposals would arouse fears which would have to be allayed, and some opposition. 'Lords Salisbury and Carnarvon B[eresford], Hope and Hubbard must be persuaded that we do not mean to persecute their friends, only to make them act reasonably. Lord Shaftesbury and his following must be convinced that there is no danger of weapons intended for other purposes rebounding against themselves, unless in such cases as are obvious violations of the law. . . . certain influential Lawyers make a milch-cow of the Church's present difficulties, and their opposition must be if possible neutralized.' The great body of moderate persons however would, he said, approve.

The archbishop's proposal was exquisitely calculated to distress Disraeli. It was, Disraeli later said, 'the hardest nut to crack that ever was the lot of a Minister.'[15] Salisbury and Carnarvon were members of his cabinet. Since they had been foremost among his opponents within the Conservative party over the second Reform Bill and thereafter, he had had to employ careful diplomacy in bringing them into the cabinet. They had particular misgivings about the cabinet's religious divisions.[16] Though all of its members were Churchmen, Cairns, Disraeli's closest lieutenant and now Lord Chancellor, was an Irish Orangeman, and Derby, the son of Disraeli's former chief and now Foreign Secretary, was a firm Protestant. As a result the cabinet had been formed on the understanding that, if any ecclesiastical legislation particularly on ritualism was proposed from an independent quarter, members of the government could treat it as an open question.[17] The archbishop was asking Disraeli to confront the cabinet, before its members had learned to work together, with the one issue on which they were deeply divided.

Furthermore, Disraeli's relations with the Queen were already strained over this religious issue. Two of the influential Conservative peers whom he nominated to offices in the royal household, Beauchamp and Bath, were sympathetic towards ritualism. The Queen protested, and then accepted them only on condition that they agree not to take any prominent part in Church politics.[18] The introduction of the archbishop's bill into Parliament would probably induce them to depart from this agreement or, if the government supported the bill, to resign.

As soon as Disraeli received Tait's letter, he sounded his colleagues out. The results confirmed his fears. Derby expressed his full agreement with the archbishop's proposal;[19] but Salisbury, who had already received word of the bishops' resolution through the garrulous Bishop Ellicott, was even more emphatically opposed.[20] 'The Archbishop', he said, 'is asking for an impossibility: that it shall be as easy to apply a much-disputed law, as if it were undisputed.' He also put his finger on the memorandum's ambiguity about what the proposed tribunals could forbid. If they could prohibit whatever they wished, they would be at variance with the whole tenor of English law and would break up the establishment. For, as he explained to Ellicott,[21] the elections to the bishops' advisory boards would lead to 'a battle royal between Church parties—in which sequestrations will be the penalty of the defeated.' Instead he suggested allowing the public worship in each parish to be conducted as it was at present, changes to be subject to the jurisdiction of the bishop and his advisory board.

Disraeli's own reaction was one of cautious neutrality inclined only slightly in favour of legislation. A converted Jew, he was, so he is reported to have said, the blank page between the Old and the New Testaments. He was of course a member of the established Church, but of no particular school within it. Whatever his real religious inclinations and convictions, he never let them obtrude upon his political calculations in this instance. His sole concern was to preserve his political position: the unity of the cabinet, the esteem of the Queen, the confidence of Parliament. The archbishop to him was peripheral, he had never wanted to appoint him in the first place, and he treated him now with scant respect. Perhaps it was inevitable that Tait, a strong primate, should have had strained relations with both prime ministers in office during his archiepiscopate.

Controversy spread beyond the cabinet into the public arena early in March. Bishop Wordsworth had drafted an address for the episcopate to issue to prepare the public for the coming bill. Instead, to Wordsworth's annoyance and before the bishops had seen the archbishop's memorandum, Tait asked *The Times* to publish an obviously authoritative report of the intended bill. This would serve better than a formal address for gauging public reaction, as he was anxious to do particularly now that he knew of Salisbury's objections. It would also give Tait an opening for personal negotiations with leaders of Church opinion, Shaftesbury for example, without committing the archbishop as irrevocably as the suggested episcopal address. Accordingly, he sent a memorandum on the bill to Delane, the editor of *The Times*, with a request for his co-operation.[22]

The Times broke the news[23] in a way certain to alarm all high churchmen. For, as illustration of defiance of the courts by clergymen, *The Times* alluded to the continued use of the eastward position, particularly by the 'two or three Clergymen of distinction' (viz. Liddon and Gregory) who had publicly announced their intention of doing so. Furthermore, by making no mention of the fact that evangelical worship often fell far short of the rubrics' demands, *The Times* made the proposed legislation seem more one-sided than many bishops intended.

Pusey reacted immediately with three long letters to *The Times*[24] in which he resisted the proposal and pleaded for delay. He pointed out that five of the points on which the Judicial Committee had pronounced its judgment in the past were at present the subjects of fresh litigation. Legislation to enforce existing decisions while this was true was, he said, absurd. In particular, the eastward position was treasured by too many people to be effectively eradicated; punishment of those who insisted on using it would only endanger the establishment. Pusey also pointed out the apparent one-sidedness of the whole proposal.

Yet he admitted, though vaguely, that ritualism was out of hand; and for the sake of peace he tried to conciliate those whom ritualism offended. Instead of *The Times*' remedy, he suggested that the bishops be guided, regardless of the Judicial Committee's rulings, by the joint wishes of the congregation and the clergyman in each parish vexed by a ritual dispute—an alternative which no law-abiding Parliament would tolerate. In addition he held out the hope that, if the new supreme court pronounced the eastward position legal, the ritualists would abandon their extreme practices. As soon as he had written his first letter to *The Times*, he joined Liddon in urging Mackonochie, as a leader of the ritualists, to disarm their opponents by giving up these practices now.[25]

Mackonochie's reply[26] proved the impossibility of conciliation. Even on a tactical level, Mackonochie said, his experience had shown him that compromise was unlikely to avert attack. And tactics were out of place on this subject, for ritualist congregations had been taught by their clergy to regard 'each act and each object as a sermon preaching Christ to them'. The clergy could not with consistency, therefore, sweep these practices away. The low standards of religious ceremonial in other parishes were, Mackonochie continued, at least as great a scandal to ritualists as ritualists' behaviour was to their opponents. All that he would advocate was mutual forbearance.

Tait spoke through *The Times* again,[27] still anonymously, in reply to Pusey's criticisms. The very fact, *The Times* said, that the Judicial Committee's decisions could be challenged by fresh litigation deprived Pusey and his friends of any excuse for disobeying the existing decisions. Only one clergyman should have acted contrary to the particular ruling with which he disagreed in order to provoke a new trial. All the rest should have conformed to the existing ruling until it was reversed. Under pressure from Bishop Magee, Tait also induced *The Times* to weaken the claim that the proposed measure was one-sided by pointing out that it was intended only to enforce the law impartially.[28]

Moderate High Church reaction was not discouraging. W. C. Lake, dean of Durham and Tait's closest High Church friend, approved of his intentions and raised doubts only about the diversities which might arise between dioceses governed by dissimilar bishops.[29] Carnarvon agreed that some stiffer regulation to public worship was necessary though he was anxious about the loss of freedom involved and the consequent need for discretionary power.[30]

If Shaftesbury's reaction was any indication, Evangelicals were almost as apprehensive as the more extreme High Churchmen. On the day of *The Times*'s first announcement, Archbishop Tait sent him a copy of his memorandum with a request for suggestions.[31] Shaftesbury replied[32] with his usual hostility to anything emanating from the bishops. The memorandum, he said, proposed nothing to clean up the existing ecclesiastical courts as he had repeatedly tried to do. He was uneasy about giving the bishops increased power. The advisory board only aggravated his fears since, as far as he could see, it would make each bishop irresponsible. 'He will shelter himself . . . under the opinions of his Advisers; who, in nine cases out of ten—such is the supineness of the Laity—will be the Clerical Half of the Body.' The memorandum also provided for appeal to the archbishop and no farther. What, then, was to become of the royal supremacy?

Tait's reply, another memorandum,[33] went some way for the first time towards clarifying the relation between the proposed episcopal tribunals and the law. He tried to win Shaftesbury over by offering to co-operate with him in seeking a reform of the ecclesiastical courts from Parliament at the same time as it was asked to do as the first memorandum advised. Tait argued that the two measures were not mutually exclusive alternatives but complementary. The bill he had outlined was not intended, he said, to set up a new court or to decide disputed points of law. It was only meant to make the power which the formularies of the Church already vested in the diocesan bishop for settlement of parochial disputes over ceremonial effective. In other words, the 'forum domesticum' of the bishop was to be strengthened. Hence the appeal to the archbishop rather than to the superior courts. The determination of what the law governing the Church's ceremonial required would still rest with the existing courts. A reduction of the costs of litigation in them was, of course, desirable. However, such litigation would always remain costly because of the fees necessary to secure the services of eminent counsel. Court reform would not, therefore, secure what the bishops thought necessary: a simple, inexpensive process for settling those disputes which no one wished to subject to court action.

The distinction Tait drew between the proposed episcopal tribunal and a new court was still far from clear, and it was not surprising that Shaftesbury failed to recognize it. Though slightly appeased by Tait's explanations, he turned down the proffered co-operation.[34] In his perversity, Shaftesbury disparaged the alarm over ritualism which in years gone by he had done so much to arouse. Sacramental confession, he said, was now the abuse in most urgent need of eradication: 'unless the Church can cleanse herself of the foul thing, she and all her Children will sink into the dark.'

The extension of the debate to the public increased the pressures on Disraeli. Provoked, he wrote to the archbishop sharply. 'I conclude, by the article in the "Times" today, that you have a bill prepared. Is there any objection to my seeing it?'[35] Tait explained that the article was based on the memorandum the prime minister had already seen.[36] During the next week, the first rough draft of the bill was completed, and Tait sent it to Disraeli immediately. Tait asked for suggestions, if possible before the bill was submitted to the bishops.

Under the terms of the bill,[37] a complaint about the conduct of worship in a parish could be laid by the local archdeacon or rural dean, or by any parishioner resident or non-resident who declared himself a member of the Church of England. The bill did not specify whether every such complaint no matter how frivolous or vexatious would have to be heard. Those which did proceed would go before the bishop who would be advised by a board composed of the dean, an archdeacon, two elected incumbents and four laymen elected by the churchwardens of the diocese. They would hear the dispute and decide whether the bishop should issue a monition, in other words a command. Nothing, not even the judicially established illegality of the practices complained of, would force the board to recommend action. If it did not do so, that was the end of the matter. If they did recommend action, the terms of the monition would be determined by the bishop alone. The clergyman could appeal against it to the archbishop. The archbishop would then hear the appeal, assisted by the vicar-general or a superior court judge (assistance designed to placate Shaftesbury). If the clergyman did not make this appeal or if the archbishop rejected it, the clergyman would be obliged to obey the monition. Unless he did so, he could be inhibited from ministering in his parish for up to three months, and during the inhibition, he would not receive his official income which would be used largely if not entirely to pay his replacement.

Disraeli sounded out the most interested members of his cabinet. 'Cardinal Hardy and Monsignor Salisbury', as Shaftesbury called them, were hostile, especially Gathorne Hardy, the War minister.* Salisbury was less rigid in his opposition because he

---

* Edwin Hodder, *Life of Shaftesbury*, III, p. 347; Salisbury to Disraeli, undated, in Monypenny and Buckle, *Disraeli*, V, pp. 318–19. Gathorne Hardy said, 'It would be difficult to draw a worse Bill than that proposed by the Archbishop.' Gathorne Hardy to Disraeli, 20 March 1874, in A. E. Gathorne-Hardy, *Gathorne Hardy, first Earl of Cranbrook*, I, pp. 338–40.

knew that many of the bishops—eleven in fact*—were concerned to restrict the bill to illegalities. If that was done, he and perhaps Gathorne Hardy would co-operate. Cairns too was critical of the archbishop's bill.[38] His first consideration was political: if the government supported it, several members of the cabinet would probably resign. He also doubted whether his fellow Evangelicals would be willing to give so much power to the bishops. However, he began to explore the possibility of making the bill more practical, and Disraeli joined him.

Tait asked Queen Victoria to bring pressure to bear upon the prime minister;[39] but much as she wished for vigorous action, she had no desire to contribute to a split in her new government. Consequently she too urged the archbishop to be content with the repression of illegalities. 'Get as much as you can,' she told him, 'but don't risk the loss of the Bill.'[40] She counselled Disraeli in a similar fashion.[41] He should, she said, have little difficulty in supporting a bill to repress illegalities. But, true to herself and her archbishop, she pressed for more. In particular she expressed her hope that the government would support any dispensing powers in the bill to protect those who wanted to see public worship carried on according to long established (i.e. Protestant) usage even when it fell short of the law. 'Her earnest wish is that Mr. Disraeli should go *as far* as he *can* without embarrassment to the Government in satisfying the Protestant feelings of the Country in relation to this measure.' Disraeli replied that, though he entirely sympathized with the Queen, the question was very difficult. He had, therefore, not brought the bill formally before the cabinet; but he was conferring with its individual members in order to bring them, if possible, to some concurrent action.[42]

When Tait sent yet another memorandum to the prime minister, this time justifying the provisions of the bill, Disraeli replied without gratitude. 'I have taken a box full of your papers, and remarks upon them, into the country with me, not entirely without hope, that my meditation may end in some fruit; but that is all I can say.'[43] Undeterred, Tait sent him two more letters in rapid succession. By now he was equipped with Cairns' suggestions, which he was prepared to go a long way to meet.[44] For

---

* Peterborough, Winchester, Rochester, Norwich, Carlisle, Lichfield, Oxford, St. Asaph, Ely, London and Exeter.

example, Cairns preferred the composition of the bishop's advisory board under the Church Discipline Act of 1840—the dean or an archdeacon or the diocesan chancellor, a barrister of seven years standing, and a nominee of the bishop—to the board Tait had suggested; and Tait did not object. More important, he was willing to consider limiting the bill to violations of the law. However, he insisted on three points. The first was that the process should be summary and inexpensive. Secondly, if the government stipulated that appeals go not to the archbishop but to the Judicial Committee or the new supreme court, with the inevitable result of delay, then the bishop's monition should take effect as soon as it was issued until reversed on appeal. Tait's last demand was for prompt action by the government. He was determined to present some bill in the Lords on 20 April, the first Monday on which the House would meet after the Easter recess.

By the middle of April Tait, Cairns and Disraeli seemed near agreement on a measure which would treat the episcopal tribunal as much more like a regular court than the archbishop had originally planned. But Disraeli still refused to commit the cabinet to it: 'all the Lord Chancellor, and myself, have done in this matter, is as two sincere Churchmen and personal friends of your Grace,' he told Tait; '. . . nor can Her Majesty's Government, in any way, undertake, so far as at present advised, to support any measure which your Grace may introduce.'[45]

The bishops met on the seventeenth. By now the High Churchmen, especially Moberly and Mackarness, doubted the need for legislation. Nevertheless, they all agreed to accept the bill as revised in line with Cairns' suggestions.[46] Next day, two days before Tait was to present the bill to the Lords, both archbishops went to see Disraeli. He did not pledge himself any further, and he exaggerated his difficulties in a light-hearted sketch of the theological opinions of the members of his cabinet. Salisbury, Gathorne Hardy and Northcote were high he said, Ward Hunt rather high, Derby only neutral. 'As to myself I am a decided Anglican—but with no extreme views.' He dealt with the Queen's strong support for the bill by saying that she took 'a female view' of the question.[47] However, immediately afterwards he promised her to place the bill before the cabinet soon after Tait had introduced it in Parliament.[48]

After all the animated discussion which had gone on within the cabinet for two months and among the public for one, Archbishop Tait's presentation of the Public Worship Regulation Bill to Parliament was an anti-climax. The Bill[49] had lost its most contentious feature: only illegalities were to be dealt with. Appeals by beneficed clergymen would go directly to the Queen in Council unless the archbishop wanted an intermediate hearing by the provincial court. Consequently, as Tait had insisted, the bishop's monition was to be in force pending appeal unless the bishop directed otherwise. Enforcement was stiffened by the provision that the inhibition of a clergyman who disregarded a monition would continue indefinitely beyond the maximum term of three months unless he promised to obey. But this rigorous procedure for enforcing the law was to be eased by giving the bishop unfettered discretion in deciding whether any complaint, even if about illegalities, should be taken up by his tribunal.

At face value, the Bill scarcely merited an excited reception. It would do no more than enforce the law more effectively, largely because the bishop's monition would take force immediately. Otherwise, there could still be two hearings as had been customary in previous ecclesiastical litigation. Since this Bill, unlike the earlier draft, allowed the parties to be represented by counsel, lawyers' fees would continue to make enforcement of the law expensive. In one respect the new state of affairs would be easier on the ritualists than the old. Until now any clergyman found guilty of disobeying the rubrics was automatically punishable by the courts. Under the new measure he could be punished only if he repeated the offence after the bishop's monition had been sent him.

The bite of the Bill came less from its clauses than from the speech with which Tait introduced it.[50] His speech had been awaited as the first official statement of the intentions of the Bill's promoters.* Tait said that the Bill was not directed primarily against deficiencies arising from slovenliness but was meant to suppress ritualism, which he described by recalling Purchas' practices though he did not mention the eastward position.

Since the Bill was being presented only for its formal first

* The exact source of the *Times'* announcement was not generally known.

reading, there was little debate. Lord Nelson and Bishop Wordsworth took the opportunity to plead for a postponement of the second reading to give the Convocation of Canterbury time to consider the issue.[51] As things stood, the House of Lords was to read the Bill a second time on 28 April, the very day on which Convocation was to begin its meetings.

Tait did not want a delay, for every day lost would reduce the possibility of securing legislation during this session of Parliament. Moreover, the Lower House of Convocation was certain to dislike a measure which would restrict the clergy's freedom of action at the behest of their ecclesiastical superiors to placate the laity. Since the law defining the worship of the Church was not at stake, only its enforcement, Convocation had no established constitutional right to be consulted. And in a sense Convocation had already been consulted since in drafting the Bill Tait had used some of the recommendations which the Lower House had made about clergy discipline and ecclesiastical courts in 1869. Wordsworth, however, had good reason for warning of the possible consequences of alienating the clergy by ignoring their one assembly over a measure which so affected their legal position. He induced Tait to postpone the second reading so that Convocation would have three days for debate. The government then turned the three days into three weeks to put off the time when it might have to commit itself. Tait was obliged to accept the delay since without the government's co-operation he had little hope of success.

However, it was he and not the government who directed the procedure of Convocation; and he used his power to prevent the Lower House from making its undoubted opposition to the Bill clear. Instead of asking the Lower House for its opinion of the whole subject raised by the Bill, he sent it two detailed questions.[52] In the first he singled out those recommendations of the Lower House in 1869 on clergy discipline which he had incorporated in the Bill. Did the house, he asked, still adhere to these resolutions? Secondly, could it suggest any way, without unduly interfering with the liberty of the clergy, to stop a clergyman, pending appeal, from continuing the practices in his church which a court of first instance had ordered him to abandon?

The archbishop's questions complicated the dilemma in which the High Church majority in the Lower House found themselves.

Like the High Church bishops, they did not like ritualism. Nor did they like the lack of discipline which ritualism aggravated within the Church. In addition, for years they had been preoccupied with schemes for reform of the ecclesiastical courts. But what they wanted was a revival of all diocesan and provincial Church courts, a cumbrous network whose sole asset was its supposedly greater command on churchmen's allegiance.

After two days of passionate debate which often spilled beyond the archbishop's questions, the Lower House sent back an answer.[53] It was almost valueless to the Bill's opponents, though it certainly did not strengthen the archbishop's case for legislation. The house stood by its former resolutions, a decision which Tait interpreted as a declaration of adherence to the principles embodied in the Bill.[54] In doing so he ignored the fact that the Lower House's answer also contained a protest against the Bill's application of the earlier resolutions to one class of ecclesiastical offences, those involving ceremonial, rather than to all classes as the house had intended. Tait's second question they met with a simple 'no'. Taking the initiative, they asked the archbishop to permit them to appoint a committee on clergy discipline in general and the Bill in particular. Tait agreed but directed the committee to concentrate its attention on offences involving public worship and to report on that subject within six days before going on to deal with doctrinal and moral cases.[55]

Once again the committee's report,[56] which the Lower House accepted, fell between the stools of support for and opposition to the Bill though, of the two, the report was very much closer to opposition. It began by stating the committee's preference for action by canon through Convocation rather than by statute through Parliament, and it denied the need for a new tribunal devoted to ritual offences. It ended by refusing to recommend legislation in the manner proposed by the Bill.

However, the bulk of the report consisted of detailed recommendations to improve the Bill, taking it as it stood. If all the recommendations had been met, little would have been left of the Bill. Nearly all of them were designed to restrict its operation or to protect the clergy. The most important were for the release of cathedrals and college chapels from the Bill's provisions, for at least three parishioners who were residents and communicants to join in laying each complaint, for the replacement of the advisory board by the diocesan chancellor, for intermediate appeal in all cases to the provincial court, for the restriction of the Act to a one year trial period, and against enforcement of the bishop's monition pending appeal.

Nevertheless, the recommendations gave Tait an opportunity, by meeting some of them, to maintain that the Bill had been revised to help satisfy the declared wishes of the clergy in Convocation. He adopted all he could without vitiating his primary objective, a summary and inexpensive method of curbing ritualism. In particular he was prepared for the number of parishioners eligible to make a complaint to be raised from one to three, and for the bishop's advisory board, already altered to please Cairns, to be replaced by the diocesan chancellor.

To allow the incorporation of these changes in the Bill, the Lords agreed to read it a second time 'pro forma'. As a result the second reading, which was agreed to without a division, meant no more than that the Lords recognized the necessity of action and accepted the Bill as a workable basis for legislation. Decisive action was deferred to the committee stage when the altered Bill plus the many and sweeping amendments which other peers proposed could be dealt with. The government was quite ready to concur in this procedure.[57] But Salisbury left no doubt that at least one member of the cabinet was very doubtful about the wisdom of taking action of any sort. He implied that it might alienate the whole High Church party.[58] In that event the establishment, the undermining of which the Bill was supposed to check, would be weakened perhaps fatally.

However slow the pace in Parliament, outside an ecclesiastical hurricane raged round Archbishop Tait. The extreme high church press hurled abuse at him. His mail was flooded by letters conveying threats, doubts or pledges of support. One High Church clergyman told him that if the Bill was enacted, he would use it against Low Churchmen who fell short of the rubrics' commands.[59] From the Evangelical camp Dean Close expressed his fear that this would indeed happen.[60] Only his great personal regard for Tait prevented him, he said, from publicly agitating against the Bill; 'I tremble for the Ark—I can only *Pray*!!' Many other Evangelicals, however, assured Tait that they were prepared to bring their practice up to the rubrics' standard so long as ritualists were brought down to it.[61] There were rumours of hostile agitation from ecclesiastical lawyers. But another clergyman urged Tait on with well calculated praise: 'no previous Bishop since the time of William the 3rd has had the wisdom and the moral courage to attempt to bring the Church more up to what the age requires it to be.'[62]

Broad Churchmen's devotion to tolerant liberty had all but disappeared. Dean Stanley and the Hon. and Rev. E. V. Bligh still feared a rigid enforcement of the rubrics which would tie them to what they considered obsolete or intellectually offensive rites.[63] They wanted provision for discretionary power in the application of the machinery to be created by the Bill. Nonetheless, both men were in favour of 'fortifying and strengthening and encouraging the Protestant element in the Church.'[64] And Bligh strongly protested against any toleration of the eastward position.[65]

Wordsworth broke the public unanimity of the bishops first in Convocation, then in a pamphlet.[66] He argued that as long as the rubrics' requirements were disputed, rigorous enforcement of the existing judicial decisions would produce a great deal of acrimony if not schism. He asked instead that the two Convocations be permitted to decide what practices they regarded as obligatory and what as indifferent. Even a distinctive eucharistic dress ought to be permitted. Only after the Church itself had been empowered to define the limits of toleration in regard to ceremonial afresh should Parliament be asked for the necessary legislation to enforce them.

Quiet in the eye of the hurricane, Tait usually refused to engage in argument with his correspondents, reserving himself for the debate in Parliament. He did agree to confer with deputations from the English Church Union and the Church Association. There was no hope of agreement with the first. One of its spokesmen, Canon Carter, longing for a settlement, told the archbishop that all his fellow high churchmen wanted was toleration for its doctrines about the Holy Communion and confession and for the corresponding ceremonial, the eastward position, vestments, candles and so forth.[67] This was no compromise; it was a polite request for complete surrender. Tait's conference with the Church Association was much more congenial since the Association wanted only amendments in the Bill plus parallel legislation to tighten the rest of ecclesiastical discipline.[68]

Until the end of May most of the agitation and negotiations over the Public Worship Regulation Bill went on outside Parliament, producing only the occasional rumble within. At the beginning of June the Lords tackled the Bill in earnest; and from then on it consumed more and more of Parliament's attention until almost everything else was abandoned. First the enchantment which had held the Lords in passive unanimity broke. The High Church peers, Bath, Beauchamp, Devon and Nelson, supported by one bishop, Moberly, divided the House against proceeding with the Bill. They were crushed by 137 votes to 29, a result which pledged the House to action but did not ensure the Bill an easy passage. Salisbury, for example, voted with the majority though he was sure to subject the Bill to critical investigation during its ensuing stages. On the other hand, Cairns replaced Salisbury as the chief spokesman of the government in regard to the Bill, and he left little doubt that he now wanted action.[69]

The Lords moved into committee to deal with the mountain of amendments with which they were confronted from every angle: from the high church earls designed to stultify the Bill, from the Irish Protestant Lord Oranmore and Browne to include confession among its maledictions, but above all from Selborne, Shaftesbury and Bishop Magee.

Selborne's amendments were intended to minimize litigation by vesting immense powers of initiative and discretion in the bishop.[70] He would be empowered, without receiving a complaint, without a hearing, and without raising the question of whether the present practice of a clergyman was legal or not, to issue orders to him about the conduct of worship in his parish. If the clergyman did not challenge the order, he would be obliged to obey it until the courts declared the practice enjoined to be illegal. Similarly, if the clergyman did challenge the order, he would not be obliged to obey it until the courts declared the practice to be legally binding. The bishop or any parishioner or, indeed, the clergyman himself could apply in a summary way to the archbishop for a ruling on the legality of the bishop's order. The archbishop would then refer the appeal directly to the supreme court which would deal with it as a matter of urgency. The supreme court's hearing would be regulated by a very simple procedure. Support for this scheme came from Archbishop Thomson and

Bishops Moberly, Temple and Jackson, but from few more even among Selborne's fellow Liberals in the Lords.[71] Cairns criticized it on legal grounds. Selborne withdrew it without pressing it to a vote.

Shaftesbury proposed to alter the Bill equally radically but in an opposite direction. There was an ambivalence within the archbishop's Bill between strengthening each bishop's discretionary power and a more stringent enforcement of the law. Selborne's amendments would have accentuated the first. Shaftesbury concentrated on the second. Instead of the bishops' tribunals, he moved for the appointment of a single, well paid judge for the two ecclesiastical provinces of York and Canterbury to whom all complaints would automatically be sent for hearing. Vexatious litigation would be impeded, not by allowing the bishop to decide whether a complaint should be heard, but by obliging the complainant to give security for costs. Yet proceedings would be less expensive than at present since the judge would be empowered to hear cases on the spot and since the procedure for hearing appeals would be greatly simplified.

Though Archbishop Tait had been at pains to meet Shaftesbury's earlier suggestions in a conciliatory spirit, he did not like the substitution of judicial for episcopal authority. For the extreme high churchmen had long made it clear that they would not obey what they deemed civil courts in religious matters. Tait's proposals were intended to deal with ritualism by strengthening ecclesiastical authority: the bishop with appeal to the archbishop. However, just before Shaftesbury's amendments came up for debate he learned that Cairns stood behind them with the consent of the government.[72] Now the only way for Tait to beat Shaftesbury's amendments was to abandon the Bill. That resort might be worse than what it was meant to stop. J. M. Holt, a member of the Church Association, had presented a more drastic alternative bill to Tait's in the Commons, providing for prompt suspension by the diocesan chancellor of any clergyman refusing to give up illegal practices.[73] If Tait withdrew his Bill, Holt's might be swept through Parliament by the Protestant storm which Tait's Bill had intensified.

The archbishop therefore, without any display of enthusiasm, accepted the amendment to institute a judge[74] and voted for it. He carried most of the bishops with him. The amendment was passed by the wide margin of 112 votes to 13 since the High Churchmen split. Lord Bath for instance voted in favour of the amendment in the belief that somehow it would minimize the harm which could otherwise be done to the clergy under Tait's Bill.[75] As consolation Archbishop Thomson, acting on behalf of the Bill's promoters, persuaded the Lords to maximize the ecclesiastical authority of the new judge. It was agreed that, as soon as the chief offices in the existing ecclesiastical courts—the offices of dean of Arches, official principal of the Chancery Court of York, and Master of the Faculties—were vacated, the new judge would assume them. Thereafter he would act in their name.[76]

Once the Lords had accepted Shaftesbury's proposal for a judge, his subordinate amendments were passed with little opposition. He preserved the concord by abandoning his attempt to deprive the diocesan bishop of a veto over the commencement of suits. Instead he proposed an acceptable compromise by which the bishop would be required to state his reasons for exercising the veto.[77] One of Shaftesbury's amendments, out of keeping with his normally rigorous insistence on the law, was welcomed by the bishops, and they succeeded, though against strong opposition, in having it passed. It provided that, if both parties to a dispute agreed, the diocesan bishop could adjudicate it and pronounce a final sentence from which there would be no appeal. His decision would not, however, be regarded as a judicial clarification of the law.[78]

One big stumbling block remained. Again working in league with Cairns,[79] Bishop Magee had moved an amendment to exempt from the operation of the Bill seven common deviations from strict rubrical observance.* Some, such as evening celebrations of the Holy Communion, were evangelical practice; some, pre-eminently the use of hymns, for which the prayer book made no provision, were universal; only one was a High Church custom but it was critical, the eastward position. The intent of the amendment was to prevent internecine litigation between the major parties in the Church. This however was also the function of the bishops' veto which had the additional advantage that the Bill did not specify the situations in which it could be exercised. Partisans on either side might only grumble if a bishop acting in a particular

* The illegality of some of them was far from certain.

case used his veto to do what the amendment proposed. But die-hard Evangelicals roared their disapproval of Magee's attempt to tolerate the eastward position officially and generally. One retired colonial bishop informed Tait that if this were done, he would feel compromised in his fidelity to Christ.[80] Cairns himself dealt the death blow to the amendment by proposing to extend it to embrace the rubric enforcing use of the Athanasian Creed.[81] What might otherwise have worked to appease High Church devotees of the eastward position would only make them angry if it made the use of the Athanasian Creed optional. With Cairns' consent,[82] Magee withdrew his amendment before the House could vote on it.

The government contrived to offer High Churchmen some satisfaction by slight but gratuitous public criticism of Archbishop Tait. The discussion about Magee's amendment brought to a head the pressure which High Churchmen had been exerting to secure permission for Convocation to reconsider and revise the rubrics in view of their impending stiff enforcement. The cabal of High Church peers hostile to the Bill promised to withdraw their opposition if this permission was granted.[83] Under Letters of Business which were issued by the late Liberal Ministry* and lapsed with the dissolution of Parliament, Convocation had been examining the rubrics in the light of the ritual commission's reports; but only paltry alterations had been agreed to, certainly not enough to warrant the importance High Churchmen placed on a renewal of the Letters. Nevertheless, Tait had announced early in June that he would be pleased if the government reissued them.[84] After a delay of two weeks, Cairns stated the government's willingness to do so, and chided the archbishop for not acting more promptly.[85]

A few days before, the English Church Union convened a rally in London for its supporters to protest against the Bill.[86] Determined high churchmen such as Canon Gregory and Tractarians led by Pusey closed ranks with Mackonochie and the ritualists. In a hall packed to overflowing, they denounced the Public Worship Regulation Bill while claiming it as a tribute to the growth of their influence, and they recharged their spirits in preparation for the onslaught. How could the bishops propose such a measure and in such a place as Parliament? Only Wordsworth, Liddon said,

* *Supra*, 107.

'felt the heart of an Apostle beating within him'; and he held Tait up to ridicule as the villain of the piece.

Nevertheless, the Bill left the House of Lords in a strong situation. For the Lords' debates on the third reading indicated that they supported it with unusual earnestness and unanimity,[87] thus discounting the impression that ritualism held influential sway among the aristocracy. The High Church lords regarded the Bill as no more than a small piece of legal reform. Salisbury suggested dubbing it 'A Bill to give £3,000 a-year to the Dean of Arches, and to reprint certain minor portions of the Clergy Discipline Act.'[88] They were only surprised that it should be creating such a fuss outside.[89] Nelson pointed out that some of the amendments proposed by Convocation had been accepted.[90] The only peer still to express doubts about the wisdom of enacting the Bill was Salisbury. He feared the excitement but blamed it, not on the present Bill, but on the speech in which Tait had presented his original one.[91] Otherwise the debate was marked by warm endorsement of the measure even from those such as Selborne who had wanted it amended differently. And out of doors there was important evidence that moderate High Church opinion recognized the need for legislation to curb ritualist excesses: the *Guardian* supported the amended Bill against the attacks of the E.C.U. rally.[92]

The prospects for enactment of the Bill were, however, far from clear partly because of the still non-committal stance of the government, more especially because of the advanced date. Little more than a month remained of the current session of Parliament; and the Commons had just begun to consider two other contentious pieces of legislation, both brought forward by the government, the Endowed Schools Acts Amendment Bill and the Church Patronage (Scotland) Bill. Both aroused denominational opposition, the first from the English Nonconformists, the second from the Scottish Free Church and the United Presbyterians. 1874 was marked out for religious notoriety.

So far as could be seen, the only consideration which might induce the government to take on the Public Worship Regulation Bill was the fear that otherwise the cry for and against leglisation to crush ritualism would intensify, forcing the government's hand to an even more unpalatable not to say dangerous extent next year. Archbishop Tait played on this fear in a letter to the Queen intended for Disraeli's eyes.[93]

Then, just when the Commons was to debate the second reading, Convocation met again; and the hitherto surprisingly high degree of unanimity among the bishops fell steeply.[94] As soon as the Upper House was convened, Wordsworth proposed a new ornaments rubric which would allow anything from a surplice, which was more than many Evangelical clergy used when preaching, to the very rich ceremonial of Edward VI's reign, but always subject to each bishop's discretion. Tait replied by asking Wordsworth to admit that originally he had agreed with the other bishops in proposing legislation to curb excessive ritualism. The request backfired. Wordsworth took the archbishop to task for the leak to *The Times.* Then he launched into a defence of his proposal to tolerate eucharistic vestments. He won the support of the four other High Church bishops* and of Magee, the apostle of toleration.

The archbishop countered them by questioning the need for and wisdom of a revision of the ornaments rubric to passify high churchmen. The clergy who asked for acceptance of eucharistic vestments, he said, were the very ones who were trying, without the consent of the nation, to alter the spirit of the established Church. He went on:

the best way of allaying the excitement is not for us to use honeyed words which may be misunderstood, but boldly and clearly to pronounce those convictions of our hearts by which we are deeply attached to the existing constitution of our Church, deeply attached to its Prayer-book, conscious of the many blessings which for centuries it has conferred upon the country; and anxious to prevent any thoughtlessness even in the best men from leading themselves or their people or us astray from the plain principles which have guided the Church of England since the Reformation.[96]

Cowed by this unusually candid and uncompromising speech, the House agreed to refer the question of the ornaments rubric back to a committee of the whole, and Convocation was immediately prorogued for the summer. Tait tried to turn this debate to political advantage by telling Disraeli that it proved the need to stop agitation by enacting the Bill; otherwise even the bishops could be intimidated into proposing concessions to High Church extremists which the Protestant people of England would indig-

---

* Oxford (Mackarness), Salisbury (Moberly), Lichfield (Selwyn) and to a lesser extent Winchester (Browne).

nantly reject; thus another year's clamour might bring on disestablishment.[96] Disraeli was not convinced.

On 9 July the Bill was presented to the House of Commons on behalf of the archbishops, still without any pledge of government support, by Russell Gurney, an eminent legal figure on the Conservative backbenches respected on both sides of the House.* He was followed almost immediately, to general surprise, by Gladstone. Since the election Gladstone, true to his word, had been coming down from his home in Wales to the House of Commons infrequently. Almost no one had expected his descent on this occasion. Tait had not even bothered to make sure of his acquiescence. Granville and Hartington who led the Liberals in Parliament during his absences were forewarned of his intentions, and had tried to dissuade him.[97] For, as Gladstone himself had recognized,[98] the one subject on which he was most out of touch with his party was religion. He insisted however that especially in view of the government's neutrality, the question at hand was non-partisan, and that since he had studied it deeply and had strong feelings upon it, he would have his say.[99] He thought Tait had acted with little insight and much partisan feeling, and he was full of foreboding.[100] The Bill would strike near at home: one of Gladstone's sons who was ordained and in charge of Gladstone's parish church belonged to an extreme high church society, the Confraternity of the Blessed Sacrament.

Gladstone's speech,[101] while it lasted, had the effect of an enchanter's wand over the Commons except when he showed signs of smarting under the recent ingratitude of the electorate. The pith of his argument was twofold. In the first place, the Bill did not measure up to the requirements which during his Ministry he had regarded as necessary before ecclesiastical legislation could expect enactment by a modern Parliament: the Bill was not supported either by a consensus within the Church or by the government. His second point went deeper. The Public Worship Regulation Bill was founded on the assumption that uniformity in public worship was both the Church's bond of unity and the

---

* He had been appointed by Liberal governments to two important commissions, in 1865 to the one on the Jamaican uprising, in 1871 to the one on the Alabama claims.

State's guarantee that, as it had intended since the Reformation and as the country still wished, the Church would remain Protestant. Gladstone questioned the wisdom of a more or less rigid enforcement of uniformity. It would, he said, compromise the existing if not strictly legal toleration of diversities in local custom which had grown up, some over a long time, between parishes within the Church.

He concluded his speech by presenting six resolutions. Even apart from their great length, they defied passage because of the futile debate they would provoke and the vagueness of the alternative they presented. In one the House was asked to acknowledge 'the great and exemplary devotion of the Clergy in general to their sacred calling'. The fourth resolution, Gladstone's main response to the present discontent, expressed willingness to assist any measure recommended by adequate authority to provide more effectual securities against neglect of or departure from strict law which might give evidence of an intention to change the established religion without the nation's consent. The fifth promised protection for the laity against arbitrary changes introduced by an incumbent in the teeth of local opposition. Yet the Bill before the House purported to do exactly what these two resolutions suggested, and Gladstone failed to show just how his alternative was different.

Nevertheless, he had challenged the basis of the Bill, and he made the House pause. Even if the members rejected his resolutions, the amount of debate involved would kill the Bill for this session. However, the latent Protestantism of the House was brought to the surface as quickly as it had been checked. Another frontbench Liberal, Sir William Harcourt, previously Gladstone's solicitor-general, opposed his leader in a clear and hard-hitting speech.[102]

In ecclesiastical matters, Harcourt was the very reverse of Gladstone: a self-confessed erastian dedicated to the subjection of Church to State, a champion of the laity against the clergy, and a backwoods Protestant steeped in the stories of the Reformation.*

---

* Later that month, in a letter to *The Times*, he defined a Protestant by referring to the boast of the Spanish confessor to the King, 'I hold your God in my hand, and I have your wife at my feet.' Harcourt continued, 'It is to lead the way up to a similar pretension that all the paraphernalia of Ritualistic practice and doctrine are devised. It was in order to subdue such domination that the English Reformation was accomplished.' *The Times*, 30 July 1874.

He assured the House 'as a lawyer, as a politician, and as a Church-man, that every man who was a member of the National Church, even though he stood alone in the congregation, had a right to have the observances of the Church practised according to law.'

The Commons had the lead it wanted. When Gathorne Hardy, often the eloquent darling of the Conservative backbenches, seemed to support Gladstone's case,[103] he was met by noisy demonstrations of disapproval. Harcourt's speech had also shown that the Bill divided the Liberals' front bench as deeply as the Conservatives'. The political risk for Disraeli in cooperating with the Bill's promoters was, therefore, lessened. Nevertheless, Gladstone's speech had frightened Disraeli into even more wary neutrality towards the Bill. Before the debate was adjourned, in the early hours of the morning, he cast doubt upon whether time could be found to resume it.[104]

Everything hung on Disraeli. It was his responsibility to decide how the time at the government's disposal still remaining in the session would be apportioned. If he made room for the Public Worship Regulation Bill, there was little doubt, barring a high church filibuster, that the Bill would pass even without the government's support. The Conservatives' chief whip reported that many of their backbenchers were very anxious to see the Bill enacted.[105]

Once again the Queen may have been the deciding force. She informed Disraeli of her disapproval of the government in no uncertain terms. She was, she said, 'deeply grieved to see the want of *Protestant* feeling in the Cabinet.'[106] Whatever the reason, at their meeting two days after the Commons' debate Disraeli and the cabinet but Salisbury agreed to give 'every facility . . . to the Archbishop's Bill, consistent with the general interests of the country';[107] and when Disraeli expressed unwillingness to proceed without unanimity among his colleagues, to his surprise Salisbury gave in. Disraeli afterward wrote the Queen a letter which, though undoubtedly worded to flatter her, indicated that it was her pressure which had tipped the balance in the cabinet's deliberations. 'If this blow is dealt against the Sacerdotal school,' he said, 'it will be entirely through the personal will of the Sovereign. The Lords were not well-disposed at first to the measure; the Cabinet has always been averse to it; and the House of Commons hesitating and ambiguous. Mr. Gladstone's speech brought affairs to a focus. It is a more trying and anxious business, than even the Reform Act of 1867: because the movements are, necessarily, to a great degree, subterranean.'[108]

The speech in which the prime minister announced the cabinet's decision to the Commons[109] did not explain what he thought of the Bill; in making up its mind on the Bill, the Commons would make up his. However, he left no doubt of his opposition to Gladstone's resolutions. They pointed, he said, 'to the abolition of that religious settlement which has prevailed in this country for more than two centuries, and on which depends much of our civil liberty.'

The second day of debate underlined the Bill's popularity and Gladstone's comparative isolation. Two of his chief lieutenants, Goschen and, though he was not strictly a churchman, Forster, spoke in favour of the Bill.[110] Even Miall's successor as the Liberationist leader in Parliament, Henry Richard, abjured Gladstone's proposals to apply what Richard called the congregational principle to the established Church, though Richard's remedy for its troubles was, of course, disestablishment.[111] Gathorne Hardy bemoaned the fact that Conservative back-benchers cheered expressions such as 'a Parliamentary Church' and assertions that the Queen was its head.[112]

When the debate drew towards a close, Disraeli cast his die. With calm assurance he pledged personal support for the Bill in a speech instantly famous for two epigrams.[113] The Bill's purpose, he said, adopting a phrase currently in circulation which he now made his own, was 'to put down ritualism'. And he damned ritualism as 'Mass in masquerade'. Once he had spoken, the House was impatient for the vote. But Hussey Vivian, a Liberal who had voted against Gladstone only once in twenty-two years, rose to implore his leader to drop his resolutions. Never before, Vivian said, had he seen more unanimity in the Commons on any measure. Not as many as twenty Liberals would vote with Gladstone, an admission which was greeted with jeers at Gladstone to Vivian's anger. Then a High Church Conservative announced his capitulation in view of the evident determination of those surrounding him. Gladstone had been brought slips of paper apparently confirming Vivian's prediction, and left the House. The Bill passed the second reading without a division.

That night Archbishop Tait attended a party at the German embassy where everyone was agog with the day's events. He saw

Gladstone standing alone and out of spirits.[114] Two days later Gladstone withdrew his resolutions in order, he said, to avoid impairing the chances of some amendments he intended to propose.[115] Meanwhile Tait was flooded with congratulations. Bishop Thirlwall, long the Broad Church champion, now old and retired, hailed the unopposed passage of the second reading as proof of 'the continued attachment of the great mass of the intelligent Laity to the Church, as a Reformed Church, and the deep interest they feel in its welfare.'[116] 'You are as triumphant as Laud in his worst times', Lord Houghton remarked to Tait; to which he replied, 'I hope it will not end in the same way.'[117] Still more extravagantly, the Queen said, 'If my faithful Commons had not supported me, I should have been fain to give up my heavy crown to some of my Italian Cousins—the representatives of the Stuarts.'[118]

The House moved into committee to amend the Bill, Gurney had the date on which it was to come into effect deferred from January to July 1875 to give Convocation time to recommend clarifications or relaxations of the rubrics if it should see fit. The Commons insisted that the parishioners who laid a complaint must be residents, not simply property owners. Most of the other changes the Commons agreed to stiffened the Bill. The contrary amendments which Gladstone and his fellow high churchmen proposed with some Radical Nonconformist support were usually swamped by votes of nearly three to one.[119] The Bill's application to cathedrals was stiffened even more severely than to parish churches.* The High Church dean and canons of St. Paul's had brought this on themselves. Canon Liddon and Canon Gregory were notorious for their public defiance of the Purchas judgment on the eastward position. Liddon's public abuse of Archbishop Tait was inexcusable in Protestant laymen's eyes. And the dean, R. W. Church, defended the eastward position and the earnestness though not the extravagance of the ritualists in a letter to *The Times*[120] while the House of Commons was in committee on the Bill.

Three snags developed. As July neared its end, the House was still deep in the Bill. Their work could not be completed in time unless the government abandoned much of its own legislation still before the House. The most important, the Endowed Schools Bill,

---

* Any three churchmen resident in the diocese could lay a complaint about the practice in the local cathedral.

Salisbury's revenge for the 'depredations' of the previous commission appointed by the Liberals,* was provoking a lot of partisan debate. After a week of uncertainty in Parliament, the cabinet abandoned most of the government's proposals including the most controversial clauses of the Endowed Schools Bill in favour of the Public Worship Regulation Bill. The PWR Bill must have fallen even farther in Salisbury's estimation as a result. Still, Disraeli took this moment to give it the government's support.[121]

The second problem was the salary of the judge. The Lords had provided for him to be paid out of the funds of the Ecclesiastical Commission which would gradually be reimbursed by receiving the fees and other emoluments he was given in the course of his duties. In the meantime, however, the Ecclesiastical Commission would be deprived of funds which could otherwise be used to increase the endowment of poor benefices. Gladstone objected, and Gurney agreed to withdraw the clause. In its place Disraeli proposed the same arrangement but with the Consolidated Fund in place of the funds of the Ecclesiastical Commission. This too was unacceptable since it violated the now customary rule that State money should not be spent for purely denominational purposes. Disraeli thought he had discovered a solution when he announced that a retired judge, as yet unnamed, was willing to accept the new post without any remuneration beyond his existing pension.

He was wrong. The man who had agreed to the archbishops' invitation to serve was Lord Penzance. They quickly wrote to inform Disraeli that Penzance had accepted the appointment 'subject to the provisions as to salary and emoluments which may be embodied in the Bill, or which may hereafter be made by Parliament.'[122] The two archbishops went on to say that they would be able to submit a plan for payment of the judge by rearranging ecclesiastical fees. Parliament could deal with the matter next session, since the Public Worship Regulation Bill would not come into effect for a year. This gap in the Bill was therefore left unfilled.

Penzance's appointment created another difficulty which Parliament did not notice. Though a staunch Churchman, he had been a judge of the divorce court under the Act of 1857 which legalized the dissolution of marriages on the grounds of adultery. High Churchmen considered this a flagrant violation of the Church's

* *Supra*, 69–70.

teaching about the indissolubility of marriage. A radical paper, the *Examiner*, commented on Penzance's previous career from another angle. Recalling John Bright's words about the 'adulterous connection between the Church and the State', it predicted that Penzance would dissolve yet another adulterous union.[123]

Just when Tait thought the Bill was secure, a third obstacle emerged in its course and threatened to prove insurmountable. The bishop's power of veto over the commencement of a suit was unpopular in the Commons. It seemed to compromise the sovereignty of the law which the Commons valued as a bulwark both of the Protestantism of the established Church and of the laity's rights against arbitrary innovations by the clergy. The bishops' behaviour at the last meeting of Convocation can only have increased suspicion of the way the veto might be exercised. The veto might be conceded as necessary to prevent all round and unreasonable persecution. But its use could still be subjected to a check beyond the requirement already in the Bill that the bishop must state his reasons for each exercise of the veto. Holt, the Church Association's spokesman, proposed an amendment to allow for an appeal to the archbishop whenever the veto was used. Gurney accepted the proposal. High Churchmen backed by Gladstone protested against it strongly. They were beaten by a vote of nearly three to one;[124] and the Bill with the Commons' amendments went back to the Lords.

Holt's amendment suddenly became the straw which seemed sure to break one or other camel's back. In their present temper, the Commons were unlikely to brook any opposition. Disraeli warned Archbishop Tait that if Holt's amendment were rejected, the Commons would throw the whole Bill out no matter how much the government tried to dissuade them.[125] Tait had no strong feeling about the amendment though he did not favour it, but he was frightened by the prospect of another year's agitation and the great lift to High Church spirits which the last minute failure of the Bill would produce.[126] Thomson and he decided to vote for the amendment, informed by the Conservative whip in the Lords that they would carry a majority with them.[127]

However, when Tait went to the House of Lords for the debate, he found that nine bishops led by the bishop of Winchester had come to town to vote against Holt's amendment. Winchester brought word from Gladstone that if the amendment were not

rejected, he would hold himself 'altogether discharged from maintaining any longer the Establishment of the Church.'[128] In the
dissident bishops' minds, this warning outweighed Disraeli's
which, in any case, they did not take at face value.[129] Furthermore,
Gladstone's fight in the Commons to relax the Bill had won their
sympathy and aroused their spirits hitherto checked by Tait, while
Harcourt's erastianism worried them.[130] Winchester regarded the
amendment as a violation of a bishop's jurisdiction over his diocese.[131] His feelings ran so high that he was inclined to follow
Gladstone's lead in regard to the establishment.[132] Tait, on the
other hand, may have discounted Gladstone's threat because of
his impending retirement from the Liberal leadership. Still assured
of a majority by the Conservative whip, the archbishops held
to their course. But Holt's amendment was rejected by 44 votes
to 32.

Tait turned on the dissident bishops bitterly.[133] Disraeli too was
annoyed with Salisbury and the High Church lords-in-waiting who
had helped to give the amendment's opponents a majority.[134] He
was as afraid as the archbishop of another year and another session
bedevilled by ecclesiastical agitation. Both men did what they
could in the few hours at their disposal to prevent the apparently
inevitable. Disraeli prepared to bring on discussion of the Lords'
amendments* in the Commons first thing next morning to fore-
stall the emergence of a hostile combination between high churchmen and militant Protestants to defeat the Bill.[135] Tait spent his
day trying to persuade leading M.P.s including Gurney to accept
the loss of Holt's amendment, but without apparent success.

The faithful *Times* came out in the morning with similar advice.
At the suggestion of Richmond, the Conservative leader in the
Lords, Tait tracked Harcourt, the leader of the irreconcilables, to
his club and drove him around in his carriage, plying him with
arguments. Then Tait went to the lobby of the Commons to try
his luck with others. At 12 o'clock, when the House reconvened,
all seemed hopeless. The M.P.s were particularly angry at Salisbury
for describing the argument that the Lords should always defer to
the wishes of a majority in the Commons as 'bluster'.[136]

However, Gurney began the debate by asking the House, reluctantly, to accept the defeat of Holt's amendment. He was fol-

---

* The Lords also rejected the Commons' inclusion of collegiate churches under
the Bill. *Hansard*, 3rd series, CCXXI (1874), 1255–6.

lowed by Harcourt who agreed with this advice but consoled himself by pouring out his wrath on the majority in the Lords, on Gladstone and on Salisbury for an hour and a half.[137] Aroused particularly by Salisbury's language about relations between the two Houses, Harcourt appealed to Disraeli to vindicate the honour of their House 'against the ill-advised railing of a rash and rancorous tongue, even though it be the tongue of a Cabinet Minister, a Secretary of State, and a Colleague.' To general astonishment, Disraeli not only complied but in doing so called Salisbury 'a great master of gibes, and flouts, and jeers;'[138] surely the pot calling the kettle black. Gladstone eliminated the threat of continued opposition from the high church side by supporting the request for passage of the Bill now that the Lords had amended it.[139] Yet he too was affected by the religious acid which had dissolved political party ties; and he flailed Harcourt for displaying a lack of 'good taste, good feeling, and courtesy'. One M.P. walked out of the House rather than yield to the Lords. Its amendments were, nevertheless, accepted without a division, and the Bill was duly enacted. Word reached Tait in the House of Lords, and he was warmly congratulated.

Normal political loyalties immediately reasserted themselves. Before Salisbury had time to hear of Disraeli's remarks, Disraeli wrote to excuse himself. Salisbury, equally anxious to preserve the unity of the cabinet, responded cordially.[140] On the Liberal side, A. J. Mundella, a rising backbencher, had already expressed uneasiness about the Protestant militancy which had gripped the House of Commons.[141]

Mundella's reaction was ominous. If it was shared by many other M.P.s, it would indicate that Parliament's Protestantism and its concern for the national Church were not deeply rooted. In that case, Parliament might recoil from further entanglement in Church affairs. Yet the Public Worship Regulation Act was not the end of a road. Parliament had yet to provide a salary for the new judge. If Convocation decided on a revision of the rubrics, Parliament's consent would have to be secured to give the revision legal effect. If the way the Act worked in practice did not measure up to expectations and it needed amendment, again Parliament's cooperation would be necessary.

Tait hoped that, with judicious management,[142] the Public Worship Regulation Act would serve to keep the Church within the bounds necessary to preserve both its internal cohesion and its union with the State. This hope rested on two uncertain assumptions, first that ritualism was a movement without extensive, well imbedded popular support or sympathy.[143] This assumption was valid only if the Commons' behaviour in the last six weeks was in line with the sustained convictions of the Church and the country as a whole. Many of those who knew and loved the seats of power —Delane of *The Times*, Jowett of Balliol, even Wellesley the moderately high church dean of Windsor, and of course Tait— thought this was so.[144] Salisbury, whose eyes above his thick black beard were often farseeing, doubted it.

The second assumption was that civil laws and Acts of Parliament could control a religious movement. Disraeli referred in his speech on the second reading to the great conflict between temporal and spiritual power which was going on in Europe.[145] During the week in which the Public Worship Regulation Bill was finally enacted, the Prussian government took steps to imprison a fourth bishop in line with Bismarck's 'kulturkampf' against the Roman Catholic Church. Similar struggles were being conducted as far away as Brazil. The principle on which the Roman Catholic bishops in these two countries based their defiance of their States was the same one which high churchmen proclaimed in England: the invalidity of civil law and courts in matters they considered purely spiritual and ecclesiastical.[146] Even with the full energies of the State on one side, the outcome in Germany was far from clear. There were certainly no grounds for having greater confidence in the civil power in England.

Chapter Eight

REFORMING THE CHURCH UNDER DISRAELI, 1875–1879

Can you suggest a good High Church Dean, who is not a damned fool, and won't make himself ridiculous?

> *Disraeli to Salisbury, 15 Oct. 1875*

— a formidable restriction!

> *Salisbury to Disraeli, 31 Oct. 1875*

The Quest for Legislation

NEARLY everyone expected that the Conservative government would do more than its Liberal predecessor for the Church. Defence of the Church had been linked with a spirited imperial and foreign policy and social reform in the forefront of Disraeli's campaign before the recent election. Shortly afterward the *Quarterly Review*[1] urged the Church to make good use of the impending five years of Conservative rule, since otherwise the Church would find itself in worse shape than five years before, in 1869, when Parliament's chief concern had been Irish disestablishment.

By the Church Disraeli had meant the establishment. He was prepared to resist Nonconformists' demand for their ministers to conduct burials in parish churchyards. He wished to keep the established Church as one of the cluster of great national institutions headed by the Crown to be upheld and cherished. Just as he encouraged the Queen to play her full role in the country's affairs, so he wanted the Church for example to issue a national acknowledgement of God's mercy in giving English arms the victory over the slave-trading Ashanti tribes of west Africa in 1874.[2]

He was not, however, interested in helping the leaders of the Church enact ecclesiastical legislation, especially after he burnt his fingers over the Public Worship Regulation Act. Even during Parliament's excitement over that bill, Gorst, the principal agent of the Conservative party, had warned him not to underestimate the potential electoral strength of the High Churchmen whom the bill upset.[3] At the end of the year Gorst repeated his message. Relations between High Churchmen and the Conservatives were, he said, strained though not yet ruptured. But if 'the Archbishop of Canterbury pursues his career of ecclesiastical legislation, there seems to me great danger of our Government being broken up by the High Church Party, as Gladstone's was by the Dissenters.'[4] The point had already been driven home by letters Disraeli received from High Church clergymen renouncing their Conservative allegiance. In addition, nearly 1,500 clergymen had sent him a declaration against rigid enforcement of uniformity in public worship and for liberty to use the eastward position and a distinctive eucharistic dress.[5]

It was inadequate compensation for Disraeli to be hailed as a trusted leader of 'the orthodox Protestant church men of England'.[6] The Conservatives relied on the support they gained as defenders of the established Church against Nonconformist attack. They stood to lose by alienating any part of this Anglican constituency except at moments when such a move was overwhelmingly popular. When in 1876 High Church leaders, especially Liddon, threw themselves into the agitation over the Bulgarian atrocities and against Disraeli's Middle Eastern policy, he seemed to be paying the price of the Public Worship Regulation Act.

Furthermore, as Gladstone feared, ecclesiastical legislation which was disliked by any one school within the Church might break the school's loyalty to the establishment. Its members might then join forces with the militant Nonconformists, whose dislike of the union of Church and State deepened whenever Parliament gave much attention to Church affairs. After the 1874 session, the Liberation Society issued a special circular on the amount of time thus spent by Parliament.[7] Gladstone was convinced that another one or two sessions like the last would bring on disestablishment.[8] Disraeli might not be as pessimistic as his rival, but he had no wish to try the experiment since politically he stood to lose more if it went wrong. Consequently his policy towards ecclesiastical legislation became as cautious as Gladstone's—even more so because Disraeli lacked Gladstone's legislative energy and personal concern for the welfare of the Church. Had Disraeli been on his own, his policy would have amounted in practice to inactivity.

He was checked, however, by two men, Cross, his Home Secretary, and Archbishop Tait. From 1874 until the death of his son in May 1878, Tait was at the height of his powers. For the first and last time he played a prominent part in London society. The esteem in which he was held by the Queen and her children rose still further. Even her grandson Prince William of Prussia, the future Kaiser, while visiting England was taken to see him. Tait's influence in the House of Lords also increased. Earl Russell, the former prime minister now very old, told him, 'I do not know when I shall attend Parliament but if you ever want me, you have only to write a word, and I shall attend to vote or pair as you desire.'[9]

Liberal though Tait's political predilections were, he probably welcomed the result of the general election. For a few years he would not have to deal with a High Church prime minister reliant upon Nonconformist support. Even Disraeli's ignorance of the clergy and his lower degree of interest than Gladstone's in ecclesiastical appointments gave Tait an advantage. Nothing, Disraeli told Lady Bradford, gave him more trouble than bishoprics: 'There are so many parties, so many "schools of thought" in the Church.'[10] The archbishop's advice accordingly became more influential. For his part, Tait was prepared to work with the new government loyally: he left no doubt in 1876 of his support for Disraeli's controversial Middle Eastern policy.[11] Nevertheless, without support inside the cabinet, Tait could not break down Disraeli's passivity.

The 1875 session of Parliament could have been almost as ecclesiastical as the preceding one. For the Public Worship Regulation Act dealt only with ritual offences, leaving judicial procedure for moral and doctrinal ones untouched. Such lop-sided emphasis on the least important though most urgent cases provoked comment, and Russell Gurney had promised to introduce legislation in 1875 to deal with the others. If Convocation made use of the time allowed for revision of the rubrics before the Public Worship Act came into effect in July 1875, Parliament would be expected to give the revision legal effect.

By the end of 1874, however, it was clear that to press for such legislation would not be wise. Tait sensed that Parliament would not stomach an extended ecclesiastical diet. He also discovered from his rural deans that the desire for calm after the last year's storm was as widespread among the clergy as among politicians.[12] Shaftesbury raised difficulties about the details of further reform of ecclesiastical judicature.[13] Gurney went into mourning over the death of his daughter. The Evangelicals and High Churchmen were as far apart as ever about how to alter the rubrics. And Tait was quite happy to defer their revision until the way in which the Public Worship Regulation Act would work in practice had been tested.

Provision for Lord Penzance's salary as judge under the Act, however, needed to be made quickly. One obvious source for the salary was the fees received at present by the host of officials who served the bishops' legal requirements and the existing ecclesiastical courts. Much of their work would devolve upon the new judge. The number of officials and the income they received was excessive, and related to the day when ecclesiastical courts and bishops handled a lot of legal business now in civil hands. Anomalously the office which dealt with the most work, the deanery of Arches, soon to be taken over by Penzance, had been deprived of nearly all its income in mid-century when the ecclesiastical courts lost their probate and divorce jurisdiction. Many of the other offices—apparitors, sealers, seal keepers, cryers and so forth—were sinecures, gravy for the bishops' servants. To turn this income to better use did not seem too difficult because since 1847 most officers of the ecclesiastical courts held their positions subject to the future determination of Parliament and could not acquire any claim to compensation if Parliament abolished them.

The problem was that it would take time to create enough capital from these fees to provide a reliable income for the judge. Parliament had been unable to decide on an interim arrangement in 1874 and had put the matter off to the next session. Since then Archbishop Tait had discovered a sum of £1,112 8s. 1d. in ecclesiastical hands waiting for appropriation by Parliament. He proposed to give this, plus a portion of the fees received by men subsequently appointed to offices in the ecclesiastical courts or as the bishops' legal assistants, to the Ecclesiatical Commission. From the fund so created the Ecclesiastical Commission would pay the new judge and his clerk an amount not to exceed £1,000 a year.[14] Thus no call need be made on the income of the Ecclesiastical Commission intended for other purposes; or so Tait hoped. But there was considerable doubt whether, once the nugget of £1,200 was used up, the income from fees could meet this continuing expenditure.

Tait showed the bill in which he embodied his proposal to Disraeli in April. Disraeli promised to give it his best consideration, but then turned it down.[15] Tait went ahead and introduced it in the Lords. They emasculated it by cutting out the section on fees, by refusing to specify the amount the judge and his clerk should receive, and by implying that a further way of providing him with an adequate salary should be found.[16] In this form the Bill passed the Lords but did not move beyond a first reading in the Commons. Meanwhile, Tait came up with a supplementary measure to pay the judge out of other officers' fees as they accrued. And although he was disenchanted with the government, he urged Disraeli to co-operate before the session expired.[17] Again he was unsuccessful.

Tait brought the subject before the bishops, and with their cooperation he had a new and comprehensive bill drawn up by 1876.[18] It proposed to abolish unnecessary offices, to consolidate others, and thus to provide the needed salary. Penzance was to receive £1,500 a year as from 1 July 1875. Until the income from fees was adequate to pay him and the other remaining officers, a portion of marriage licence fees was to be used to make up the difference. The bill was intended to be modified as the government might wish.[19]

The very thoroughness and exactitude of the measure provoked a multitude of interest and so made government support less likely than ever. Or, as Tait preferred to see it, the bill revealed some of the dense underbrush which ecclesiastical legislation often encountered, impenetrable except with a government axe. The bishops' secretaries, who were their chief legal advisers, and the diocesan registrars met to present their criticisms.[20] Archdeacons objected to the proposed abolition of registrars for their obsolete courts.[21] A committee of the Lower House of Convocation, fearful as ever of central management, wanted diocesan fee funds instead of one national one.[22] Some officers of the Inland Revenue did not want to make and sell the stamps which the bill would require.[23] High Churchmen did not want to do anything to pay Lord Penzance. There was a distinct possibility that marriage licence fees, upon which the proposal would rely in its early stages, would be abolished shortly. One clergyman, quite carried away by surrogates' role, which the bill tampered with, in issuing marriage licences, told Tait that a surrogate was 'not only dealing with a matter of the highest moment, affecting the happiness of families, and the purity of the National life, but he is also entrusted with the privilege of using the name of your Grace'.[24]

The bishops made some small alterations in the bill to appease its critics. It was introduced in the Lords which amended and passed it. However, lacking government support it did not reach a second reading in the Commons. Early the following December, in preparation for the next Parliamentary session, Tait urged the government to cooperate.[25] Word came back from Disraeli[26] that the government could not see its way to include the bill among the measures it intended to introduce.*

Still determined, Tait had the Bill introduced in the Commons by backbenchers, Cowper-Temple and Gurney. It was read a second time and referred to a select committee. By now the registrars and episcopal secretaries were reconciled to the principle of the Bill.[27] But another hitch developed. Among the few changes the committee proposed, one would have reduced Penzance's salary from £1,500 to £1,000 and would have started it as of July 1877 rather than 1875.[28] Penzance was already irritated over the failure of the previous bills and had muttered about resigning.[29] When word of the select committee's proposal leaked out before the committee reported, he came near to carrying out his threat.[30] It was hard enough to establish his court's jurisdiction in the teeth of ritualist denial. To be humiliated by the very Parliament which had created the jurisdiction was intolerable.

The situation was eased, providentially, in June by the death of Viscount Canterbury who held the lucrative post of registrar of the Faculties Court. Tait, acting on his own authority, was able to transfer the lion's share of the fees of which the registrar's income had been composed to Penzance as Master of the Faculties, so that at last he had an income of appropriate size. The urgency to amalgamate offices and reduce fees disappeared, and the Parlia-

---

* Disraeli had become earl of Beaconsfield in August, but will generally be referred to by his family name as the one by which he remained famous.

mentary Bill was abandoned. Penzance was not entirely mollified by this makeshift.[31] Tait continued to seek the Bill's object, but through existing means without fresh legislation.[32]

The fortunes of the fees bill were particularly discouraging because of its connection with the Public Worship Act. The failure of the one proved the other to have been a flash in the Parliamentary pan.

Disraeli's cabinet was redeemed from Tait's point of view by one member, the Home Secretary Richard Assheton Cross, who turned out to be second only to Sir Robert Peel among nineteenth-century English ministers in his determination to cooperate in reforming the administration of the Church. Peel and Cross had much in common. Both had middle class backgrounds: Peel's father was a textile manufacturer, Cross had for a time been a banker. Both were distinguished for their practicality and lack of colour. Cross's speeches on his ecclesiastical legislation were brief, factual and self-effacing. Both were earnest but undemonstrative Churchmen.

In each of the three Ministries during Tait's archiepiscopate, ecclesiastical legislation gravitated toward one member of the cabinet: first Gladstone, now Cross, later Selborne. Of the three Cross did the most both in taking the initiative and in what he accomplished, though Gladstone was a close second. However, none of them came close to matching Peel's achievement, and none satisfied Tait's hopes. The failure of the fees bills, though, was not Cross's responsibility since they fell within Cairns' province as Lord Chancellor.

Disraeli's contribution in Church affairs as in social reform was merely memorable phrases. It was Cross who brought in the bills. After the Conservatives' defeat in 1880, Lord Randolph Churchill embraced Disraeli as the prophet of Tory social concern. The bishops, with more discernment though less inspiration, recognized Cross as their benefactor in ecclesiastical matters. In him Tait had found a Home Secretary close to his own heart. Benson, Tait's successor as primate, held Cross's advice in higher esteem than that of any other politician.[33]

1875 was, thanks to Cross, the most productive year for social and labour legislation in the nineteenth century. It was also the year in which he began to divide and increase the number of English bishoprics; 'spiritual sanitation,' Buckle called it,[34] thus coupling it with Cross's Public Health Act. Ever since the Reformation, schemes to increase the episcopate had been put forward intermittently. However, 'the world does not love Bishops over much';[35] and nothing came of the proposals until the nineteenth century when the growth and shift of population made the need pressing. In 1836 and 1847 two new sees were created, Ripon for the West Riding of Yorkshire, and Manchester. Their success, particularly Manchester's, in stimulating local activity promised well if others were created. Simultaneously Samuel Wilberforce showed as bishop of Oxford* what a resourceful and energetic diocesan could do for his flock. His example was quickly imitated elsewhere: the very zeal of the bishops and the high standards they now set themselves made their vast dioceses too much for them.

In 1869 Gladstone had resuscitated the Tudor statute for appointment of suffragans to assist the most hard pressed diocesan bishops.† But his government's rejection of Tait's request for more dioceses did not dampen the desire for them. During the debates on the Public Worship Regulation Bill, Wordsworth argued that the remedy for ritualism lay partly in an increase of the episcopate so that bishops and clergy could be brought into closer filial contact.[36] The *Quarterly Review* appealed to Conservatives by saying that an extension of the Church's administrative agencies, specifically bishoprics, was the best means of Church defence.[37]

In one important respect, to add to the number of bishoprics was more difficult now than in Peel's day. In 1850 the funds which the Ecclesiastical Commission received from episcopal endowments were merged with its common fund. Once that was done, to use Commission money for new bishoprics seemed to deprive poor clergymen of what they might otherwise receive from the Commission. Those who wanted a subdivision of dioceses were obliged to look elsewhere for funds. And since the bishops were the ones most anxious for this reform, they would have to dig further into their financial resources. Those who thought that the bishops' income was more than adequate would welcome what amounted to its diffusion. At the beginning of the century episcopal

* His position from 1845 to 1869.   † *Supra,* 101.

salaries had varied widely, from Canterbury's £19,182 to Llandaff's £924. In 1836, as a result of Peel's initiative, most of the salaries were equalized to between £4,200 and £5,000 a year, though six were allowed more: Ely £5,500, Winchester £7,000, Durham £8,000, London and York £10,000, and Canterbury £15,000. These were still handsome sums, intended to keep up the bishops' position as colleagues of the aristocracy in the House of Lords. Yet as the bishops devoted themselves more conscientiously to their dioceses and less to Parliament, local calls upon their purse increased without any compensating reduction in the cost of maintaining their official residences in London which could amount to £3,000 a year.*

In the autumn of 1874 Harold Browne, the bishop of Winchester, proposed to cut these knots by selling Winchester House, one of the largest houses in St. James's Square, worth at least £70,000.[38] He thought he could find an adequate replacement for between £15 and 20,000. He stipulated that the balance was to be used to endow a new bishopric for south London. 'South London makes my heart ache,' he told Tait; 'When I find thousands of human beings under one often half educated and inefficient pastor, with no one in the parish richer than a clerk on £200 a year, and where the mass of the people, operatives engaged in East London, only wish to be let alone to live a mere criminal life. A Bishop, who could give all his energies to them might do much to quicken work among them.' The main drawback he saw was that in such a diocese the 'operatives' would not have any opportunity for civilizing, uplifting intercourse with other classes. To deal with this, Browne proposed to include a rural part of Surrey in the new diocese.

He put himself in touch with Cross. Gladstone warned Browne against asking either for an income for the new bishop on a par with the others or for a seat in the Lords:[39] a Radical attack on the wealth and privileges of the existing bishoprics might result. Cross, on the other hand, favoured both the income and the seat, though he wanted the bishopric to be set up with an initial income of £2,000 rather than wait until it could reach the larger sum. And, recognizing the futility of attempting to increase the number of bishops in the Lords, he proposed to extend the episcopal rota

---

*Bishops had responsibilities besides attendance at Parliament taking them to London: attendance at Convocation for those in the province of Canterbury, and supervision of Church societies and administrative agencies.

of seniority, begun with the formation of the bishopric of Manchester, for seats in the Lords.

Cross, the three bishops whose sees were affected,* and representatives of the Ecclesiastical Commission which would administer the funds for the bishopric, met to hammer out the details of the necessary bill. They agreed on a new diocese of St. Albans to include Essex and Hertforshire which had been within the diocese of Rochester. Rochester would take east and mid-Surrey, which included south London, from Winchester and one parish from the diocese of London. As soon as £2,000 a year was forthcoming, the see of St. Albans would be created. The bishop of Rochester proposed to sell his country residence, Danbury, to pay for the erection of cheaper homes for himself and the bishop of St. Albans. [40]

The Bill which Cross presented to Parliament in March 1875 authorized the Ecclesiastical Commission to put the scheme into effect. It encountered opposition from the Liberationists, loath to see Parliament's time spent on such a subject. They were defeated by 273 votes to 61, and the Bill was quickly enacted. The apparent ease with which this took place was deceptive. Any opposition could be enough, particularly in such a hard working session as this one was, to choke a bill out unless the government firmly supported it. Furthermore, the care with which Cross had worked out the Bill's details weakened the opposition by depriving it of all but abstract ground for attack.

In 1876 the story was repeated, this time over the creation of a see for Cornwall at present combined with Devon under the bishop of Exeter. The part which the sale of Winchester House had played was filled by a gift of capital to yield £1,200 a year from Lady Rolle, an elderly Cornish widow who lacked heirs. She insisted, however, that the offer would hold good only if the see were founded during her lifetime.

Financial problems began to accumulate. The creation of the St. Albans bishopric hung fire, waiting for gifts from private sources to augment the proceeds of the sale of Winchester House to a level which would yield £2,000 a year. Until contributions came forward to this extent as an earnest of lay support, the bishops of Rochester and Winchester would not give an additional £1,000 per year as they had jointly promised from their salaries. [41]

* London and Rochester as well as Winchester.

In regard to the Cornish see, Exeter cathedral possessed five canonries instead of the usual four, each worth £1,000 a year, all in the patronage of the bishop; and he was prepared to surrender one for the new bishopric.[42] Cross knew, however, that High Churchmen such as the Conservative backbencher Beresford Hope would strongly dislike robbing cathedrals for new bishoprics,[43] much though they favoured their creation. The bishop of Exeter offered £800 a year from his salary for the see. Cross had Tait and him explore the prospects of receiving more from interested laymen.[44] Cross's function was as a midwife. Adequate financial support had to come from members of the Church. He urged the baby bishoprics on: 'I think I could undertake to introduce a Bill the first night of the session', he told Tait, 'if I could see my way clear to the money up to £3,000 a year without the Canonry. . . . But I am *very* anxious that the matter should be carried through.'[45]

Tait issued an appeal for funds to bring the St. Albans bishopric into being, and to make sure that Lady Rolle's offer for Cornwall was taken up.[46] Till private contributions indicated that men really wanted to increase the episcopate, he wrote, nothing more could be done. By early June support was sufficiently forthcoming for Cross to introduce the Cornish Bill. This was comparatively late in the session, and the Bill encountered protracted resistance in the Commons particularly from the Liberationists. However it passed the third reading on 1 August, moved rapidly through the Lords, and so was enacted. Cross followed through by seeing that the funds required to put the Act into operation were assembled quickly.[47] Both of the new sees were set up in 1877.

Even before the Cornish Bill was introduced, Cross had secured the government's agreement to another bill to provide for the eventual creation of three or four more bishoprics without approaching Parliament over each.[48] This was ambitious since the opposition to comprehensive legislation for more bishoprics was already mobilized. For many years Lord Lyttelton, Gladstone's irritable brother-in-law, had been bringing in bills which would empower the Ecclesiastical Commission to draw up schemes for the creation of new bishoprics, how many he did not specify. Each new bishop would receive at least £2,500 a year and would join the rota for seats in the Lords. Each scheme would be presented to the government and would become law if the privy council approved and neither House of Parliament objected.[49]

Perhaps because he acted before the time was ripe and so looked like a crank, Lyttelton received at best faint-hearted moral support from the leaders of Church and State, and provoked insurmountable resistance. Cross deliberately ignored him over the St. Albans Bill in 1875[50] although earlier during the session Lyttelton had again brought in his bill. The Lords passed it; but this was merely a patronizing gesture since without government cooperation the bill was bound to fail in the Commons.

Harcourt, an old fashioned radical with no love for episcopacy, led the opposition there, heartily backed by Liberationists. Presuming that Lyttelton's bishoprics would have to be financed by local contributions, Harcourt had already warned Tait that 'cheap subscription Bishops by the side of the existing Bench in all their panoply of purple and gold' would raise the whole question of episcopal salaries and so shake the establishment.[51] Harcourt's alternative was drastic redistribution of all episcopal revenues. Speaking in the Commons,[52] he tickled the layman's sense of humour. 'In London', he said, 'this deficiency of Bishops was not so observable, because if you went by the Atheneaum Club, every other Gentleman you met wore a shovel hat and an apron.' He based his case, however, not on a denial of the need for the proposed increase but on the vagueness of the way it was to be brought about: 'It was as if Parliament were asked to pass a Railway Bill which proposed to sanction a line from anywhere to anywhere, and where there was no capital, no subscribers, and no directors.' Lyttelton's bill was eventually talked out. Clearly Cross's comprehensive bill would have to be precise. He set the two archbishops to work negotiating with the bishops whose sees might be divided and the representatives of the Ecclesiastical Commission on boundaries for new dioceses, emoluments, and other details.[53]

This was no easy assignment. Since local contributions would provide the bulk of the sees' income, local susceptibilities about boundaries and the towns in which the new cathedrals would be placed had to be taken into account. The number of bishoprics to be created would have to be modest to disarm opposition. Yet more places were put forward for new dioceses than could be satisfied; Liverpool, Bradford, Newcastle, Birmingham, Coventry, Sheffield, Bristol, south Wales and another diocese for south London, all came into the reckoning. The two neighbouring High

Church bishops, Wordsworth of Lincoln and Selwyn of Lichfield, wanted their dioceses divided as it was generally agreed that they should be, Lincoln to lose Nottinghamshire, Lichfield to lose part of Derbyshire. But they wanted separate dioceses for each of the two counties rather than their amalgamation into one. Wordsworth was particularly unyielding, and Cross thought he imperilled the whole project.[54] Wordsworth was also unwilling to follow the example of the three bishops who had sacrificed some of their income to assist in the creation of new sees. He explained that the cost of maintaining his country palace, Riseholme, would make this difficult.[55] Then, when Selwyn died early in 1878, Wordsworth had the temerity to plead with Cross for the bishoprics bill, holding Selwyn up as a martyr to overwork.[56]

The negotiations did not proceed quickly. Cross brought repeated pressure to bear upon Tait so that a bill could be presented in 1877. Though Tait was fully cooperative, the initiative in this matter certainly lay with Cross. The archbishop was wrapped up in his fees bill. Moreover, he was not entirely happy about extending the rota for seats in the Lords. The longer it grew, the longer each new bishop would have to wait before entering the Lords and the deeper he would fall into what Tait described as 'the Stereotyped habits of routine Diocesan work inconsistent with any active part in the more public work of the Church.'[57] On the other difficult point, salaries, both men agreed that bishops of the new sees should receive around £4,000. The St. Albans and Cornish Bills had specified less in order for them to come into effect quickly. The need for prompt action under the comprehensive bill would not be quite so urgent since the bill was intended as enabling legislation to give the Church room for expansion over several years.

Cross presented his Bishoprics Bill at the beginning of May 1877,[58] later in the session than he had hoped. It provided for four sees: Liverpool including the West Derby Hundred of Lancashire (Cross's constituency of South-west Lancashire would fall within its limits), the southern part of the comparatively new diocese of Ripon, part of Northumberland, and Derbyshire plus Nottinghamshire. The new bishops were to receive £3,500 a piece. The funds were to come partly from the revenues of the existing sees out of which the new four were to be carved. The Evangelical bishop of Durham made a handsome contribution for Northumberland;

the desire for subdivision of dioceses was not restricted to any Church party. But most of the endowment was to be raised by private contributions.

After very brief debate, the Bill was squeezed out and withdrawn. Again the problem was popular support, not financial this time but moral. Demand for the Bill did not appear to be strong enough for it to make its way among the great issues pressed upon Parliament such as Disraeli's controversial foreign policy and the first signs of economic depression. Lord Beauchamp, the Lord Steward, agreed to introduce the Bill in the upper chamber early in the next session. Just before he did so a meeting of clergymen and laymen was convened to strengthen his hand.[59] Beresford Hope who disagreed with some of the Bill's provisions submerged his criticisms in the general effort to act before the present government's term of office expired. Even *The Times* spoke out on the Bill's behalf but for a distinctive reason; that it would create more police to keep an eye on the clergy.[60]

This time the opposition was led, not by a Radical or a Liberationist, but by a maverick peer, Lord Houghton. Houghton had given near classical expression of his reasons for opposition in a public letter a year before.[61] He harked back wistfully to the day when a bishop was

a man of sufficient wealth to raise him above anxiety and suspicion of private motives, and of sufficient dignity to stand in social parity with the highest in the realm . . . hospitable and accessible without the continual invasion of his time and intellectual life. . . .

Then a clergyman

no more expected an autograph letter from [his bishop] than from the Lord Lieutenant, or thought of interviewing him any more than the Prime Minister.

Episcopacy in Houghton's eyes ought to have remained a well-earned repose providing opportunities for scholarship. He had a case when he recalled the intellectual contributions which in earlier centuries prelates like Bossuet and Tillotson had made, without parallel in Victorian times. When distinguished scholars such as Stubbs and Creighton accepted bishoprics, they all but abandoned their scholarly pursuits* for a life of often hectic episcopal activity. Tait sympathized with Houghton when he pointed out that the

* Lightfoot did not.

extension of the episcopal waiting list for admission to the Lords would give rise to a bench of 'aged men, unused to Parliametary life and unable to cope with an aggressive laity.'

Nevertheless, Houghton's attempt to roll the clock back was not very effective. The Lords passed the Bill, though after considerable debate. The Bill still had to run the gauntlet of Liberationist opposition in the Commons. But in July, under pressure from the bench of bishops, Sir Stafford Northcote, Conservative leader in the Commons now that Disraeli was Lord Beaconsfield, promised the Bill firm support.[62] The Bill encountered renewed resistance dangerously near the end of the session. Cross then induced Beaconsfield to agree that the Commons must reach a clear decision before Parliament was prorogued, and the opposition quickly subsided.[63]

Cross followed through by urging the bishops to see that money was found to make full use of the Bill.[64] Otherwise, he said, the advocates of legislation would look ridiculous. The deepening depression in agriculture and trade made exclusive reliance on local contributions impossible. The bishops and the Additional Home Bishoprics Endowment Fund issued appeals to the public at large. As a result, the Liverpool see was set up early in 1880; and in one of his last acts as prime minister, Disraeli was able to appoint as its first bishop a partisan Evangelical, J. C. Ryle. The three other new dioceses had to wait, one until 1888. In old age Cross was able to claim, in a light moment of self-congratulation, that no one save Henry VIII and he had been concerned in the formation of six new sees.[65]

Virtually all other attempts which the bishops made to secure ecclesiastical legislation fell outside Cross's department as Home Secretary and were abortive. For example Magee, bishop of Peterborough, with general support from his colleagues, sought reform in the use of lay patronage.[66] Around half of the livings in England and Wales were in the gift of lay patrons,[67] a fact which most clergymen welcomed because it diversified the composition of the parochial clergy more than would have been the case had nomination rested largely with the bishops and the Crown. Bishops and cabinet ministers tended to appoint safe men and moderates; the beneficed extremists usually owed their appointments to laymen. Lay patronage was also an important way in which laymen were involved in the conduct of the Church.

Patronage was a form of property, and was treated as such. It was bought and sold, and the newspapers often contained advertisements extolling the trout stream and salubrious climate of a particular benefice the nomination to which was up for auction. This behaviour degenerated into virtual simony over what was termed the sale of a next presentation: the sale of the right to nominate to a benefice when the current incumbent left or died. Though it was illegal for a clergyman to buy such a right for himself, he could easily act through a middleman, a father, brother, friend or discrete agent. All this was grist to the Liberation Society's mill.

Every attempt at patronage reform foundered in the House of Lords which was sensitive to all infringements on the rights of property, especially of a form of property which many peers possessed. Any limitation on the rights of sale would lessen the property's value. Even if the sale of next presentations was legally prohibited, it would be almost impossible to stop in practice so long as outright sale was permitted. Furthermore, the bishops' hands were not entirely clean. Tait in particular, devoted as he was to his kin and his unusually able chaplains, appointed many of them to the livings of which he was patron, passing over men who had served long years in his diocese. He gave Magee determined support in the attempt to stop the sale of next presentations.[68] All they achieved was the appointment of bootless boards of enquiry.

Disraeli gave Tait another enquiry, a royal commission on cathedrals. From the 1820s to the '60s, cathedral offices—deaneries, canonries and prebends—had been under heavy fire as the most useless of ecclesiastical sinecures. Some were abolished and others received a reduced income under an Act of 1840, part of the redistribution of Church endowments which was entrusted to the Ecclesiastical Commission. In the early 1850s a royal commission investigated the cathedrals but Parliament took no further action. However, following the example set by the new generation of parochial clergy and bishops, some deans and canons began to dust themselves off. Tait gave a lead as dean of Carlisle from 1849 to 1856. In the *Edinburgh Review* in 1853 he pleaded against further decimation of cathedral offices and instead for their mobilization as centres of diocesan life in education, concern for the towns or cities in which they were situated, charity, worship, preaching and scholarship. But enterprising individuals found themselves limited by their cathedrals' statutory regulations and by the need of corporate authorization from their colleagues for most improvements.

Tait asked Disraeli in 1876 for a royal commission to investigate the cathedrals and recommend ways of facilitating reform. Disraeli put him off;[69] but in 1879, likely to be the last year of the Ministry before a general election, he accepted the archbishop's repeated request.[70] The commission would not have the power to make statutes as had been given to the contemporary university commissions. Furthermore, its mandate would expire with the present Parliament, leaving the subsequent Ministry free to decide whether to reconstitute it. If such an innocuous gesture would appease the bishops, Disraeli was willing to cooperate.

Apart from Cross, nothing but gestures. The Conservative government had produced little more ecclesiastical legislation than its Liberal forerunner. Severe cabinet caution and Parliamentary absorption in other matters seemed to be inevitable, whichever party was in power. Parliament was still the most attractive forum for Tait personally; but he was now prepared to look elsewhere for action.

The Quest for Autonomy

Convocation's energy was absorbed in revising the rubrics, the task assigned to it by the royal Letters of Business in 1872 and '74 as a result of the fourth report of the ritual commission in 1870.* It had been decided not to speed action on the most contentious rubrics before the Public Worship Regulation Act went into effect in July 1875. Tait hoped that litigation under the Act would settle the points at issue. However in 1877 the Act began to break down in practice.† Convocation could continue to defer making final recommendations only at its own expense; to produce nothing would seem to prove the case of Convocation's denigraters, that it was utterly incapable of leading the Church to a settlement of the problems distressing it. 'As for "the Letters of business," ' Shaftesbury told Disraeli's private secretary, 'those gossips [of Convocation] will put them into a pot, and make tea of them.'[71] Moreover, there would be pressure upon Parliament to move into the vacuum. Harcourt had already asked the government to bring

* *Supra*, 42, 106–7 and 180.   † See chapter 9.

in a bill reforming the rubrics,[72] presumably without wishing the government to seek the advice of Convocation which Harcourt despised; and he was not without sympathizers.[73]

The treatment which the rubrics received from the Convocations of Canterbury and York showed that ecclesiastical legislation was impeded as much by the stammering of the Church as by the caution of the State. Action within the Church was held up by its administrative division into two provinces, by its religious divisions, and by High Churchmen's fear of Parliament confirmed by the Public Worship Act.

The Convocation of Canterbury's debates on the rubrics concentrated heavily on three topics: the Athanasian Creed, the burial service, and the dress of the clergy. The first two are dealt with elsewhere.* The ornaments rubric was the crucial one. It was the centre of the controversy which vexed the Church most and had goaded Parliament into unwonted action. Yet the ornaments rubric was also the pivot on which the balance between high and low within the Church currently rested. Its beauty in this regard lay in the eye of each beholder. To ritualists it made vestments mandatory, to Wordsworth it made them permissible, to Evangelicals, most judges, and the archbishops it made them illegal. To adjust this delicate rubric without disaster would require a fine hand. Even the ritual commission, behind closed doors and unencumbered with backwoods canons, had left it untouched although it lay at the heart of the commission's assignment.

In 1875 Convocation put its toes into this water, and for the next four years dabbled them around, out and in again, those of the Upper House usually at odds with the Lower. At length nearly all the members of Convocation concluded that, apart from other historical documents perhaps involved in the legal interpretation of the existing ornaments rubric, it called for the use of vestments. The practical question still remained, whether and to what extent their use, so far confined to a small minority of parishes, should be permitted. The need for action became urgent in 1879. A general election could not be far off. That might bring a Liberal government which most Churchmen assumed would be less friendly than the Conservatives toward the Church: even the very moderate Liberal leader, Lord Hartington, had uttered disturbing words about establishment recently.[74] In any event, the

* Chapters 2 and 10.

dissolution of Parliament would create the necessity of applying for yet another renewal of the Letters of Business which would be tantamount to an admission of failure.

After a great deal of confusion, the Lower House proposed to keep the existing ornaments rubric in its integrity but to qualify its requirements by an addition.[75] The addition stipulated that in all services the priest or deacon was to wear a surplice and stole or scarf plus the hood of his academic degree; in preaching the same or a black gown, scarf and hood; and the other vestments specified in the first prayer book of Edward VI were not to be brought into use in any church, except for cathedrals and collegiate churches, without the prior consent of the bishop. The thrust of this suggestion lay in the words 'brought into use': they implied that churches which already used Edwardine vestments could continue to do so. The Upper House whittled this concession down by proposing that these vestments should not be worn contrary to the monition of the bishop.[76] What this would mean in practice was not clear since some bishops might allow the vestments in parishes which strongly desired to retain them. Perhaps this uncertainty was what induced the Lower House to accept the amendment.

The other changes the two houses desired in the rubrics had already been agreed to. Most of them were peripheral in the extreme:* the Easter anthem, for instance, was to be permissible in place of the Venite at Matins throughout Easter week. Regardless of what was recommended, however, the assignment under which Convocation had been labouring for seven years had been brought to a conclusion, and in the nick of time. At Wordsworth's prompting, the Upper House rose and united in reciting the 'Gloria in Excelsis'. Their jubilation was premature.

Fear clogged the pipeline for ecclesiastical legislation at both ends: fear in the cabinet of exacerbating its own religious divisions and those within the established Church; fear in the Lower House of Convocation that Parliament, if asked to pass a bill touching spiritual matters, would remould it intolerably. There were two routes of escape from this near paralysis. The most obvious was

---

* For a summary of them, see R. C. D. Jasper, *Prayer Book Revision in England 1800–1900* (London, 1954), pp. 125–6.

disestablishment, but it still found surprisingly few advocates within the Church. Early in 1877 a Church League for the Separation of Church and State was set up by extreme high churchmen under the presidency of Mackonochie. It was a measure of the discontent that such an old-fashioned Tory as Denison joined. However, the League was primarily concerned about the Church's subordination to the courts rather than about Parliament, though of course the Public Worship Regulation Act was the focus of the League's agitation. Even so, the League failed to convert the bulk of the ritualists let alone of more restrained high churchmen to their cause. In 1876 and '77 the most important of the ritualist fraternities, the Society of the Holy Cross, voted down disestablishment though by small majorities.[77] Wood, the aristocratic president of the English Church Union, worked steadily against the League's policy. Pusey dismissed its supporters as 'very short-sighted or blinded by self-contemplation, if they do not see that Disestablishment would leave them a small minority'.[78]

The alternative was to relax without breaking the bond between Church and Parliament. Modest administrative reforms such as the Bishops Resignation Act and the creation of new dioceses would probably have to continue to go through Parliament in the regular way since they affected property and political privileges. Such measures were not the main problem. What the Lower House of Convocation repeatedly shied away from was legislation on the rubrics. This was a purely religious subject; Parliament's spiritual right to deal with it was at least dubious. In any case, the prospect of Parliament going through Convocation's recommendations one by one, accepting, rejecting and altering them, perhaps even adding to them, was enough to daunt even the most sanguine bishop or most co-operative cabinet minister. Parliament simply lacked the expertise needed to avoid falling into the shell holes created by generations of inter-party warfare within the Church; and Parliament could not afford the time.

In the wake of the ritual commission's fourth report Tait, Wilberforce and Gladstone had examined the possibility of leaving detailed examination of the commission's proposals which Convocation might endorse to some committee, but nothing came of it.[79] Jackson, the bishop of London, took the question a step farther by introducing a Bill[80] in 1874. Under its terms the two Convocations acting under licence from the Crown could propose amendments in the rubrics to the Queen in council. Each proposal would also be laid before Parliament. If the privy council approved and if within forty days of receiving the proposal neither House of Parliament petitioned the Crown to withhold its consent, the proposal would become law.

The Bill was never pressed to the point of debate in Parliament. But Convocation took it up. After over twenty years of revived activity, Convocation felt sure of itself; indeed, the Lower House had never doubted its own competence. Furthermore, schemes like the bishop of London's were in the air. The *Quarterly Review* proposed a central planning agency for the Church to be composed of representatives of Convocation and a committee of the privy council.[81] Even Dean Stanley suggested a continual version of the royal commission on ritual.[82] Parliament had deputized commissions to deal with charities, endowed schools and the universities. The Ecclesiastical Commission administered much of the Church's property. Why could not a similar agency be devised to deal with the rubrics? The established Church of Scotland enjoyed a much greater degree of autonomy than the Church of England; autonomy and establishment were not therefore incompatible.

However, the circumstances of the two Churches were different in another crucial respect. There was widespread suspicion among the laity of the English Church toward its clergy, much more than in Scotland. This feeling was aggravated by an institutional division. Unlike the General Assembly of the Church of Scotland, Convocation was a purely clerical body. Parliament provided the English laity with their one forum capable of supervising the conduct of the Church. Many proposals were put forward to bridge this institutional division by adding a house of laymen to Convocation. But the advocates of such a reform could not succeed in overcoming some High Churchmen's veneration for the historic constitution of Convocation or the Tractarian claim that only the clergy were entitled to a voice in purely religious matters. Moreover to associate laymen with Convocation would probably require Parliamentary approval; and to request this approval might weaken what little autonomy Convocation now possessed.[83]

Archbishop Tait sympathized with the objections to increasing the power of Convocation, and he opposed the bishop of London's Bill in 1874.[84] Tait knew that to bring both Convocations into agreement before requesting legislation, as the bishop of London's Bill would necessitate, could be a very slow and often unproductive business. Yet taught by Gladstone's insistence that only the clearly expressed request of a united Church would induce him to facilitate ecclesiastical legislation, the archbishop had already increased the legislative role of Convocation over the Table of Lessons and Act of Uniformity Amendment Acts.[85] His love for the establishment and Parliament and his patent uneasiness about Convocation blinded many of his contemporaries to his really distinguishing quality: willingness to alter his tactics if circumstances so required. When it became clear to him that to work bills through Parliament in the usual way was as difficult as the bishop of London's proposed procedure would be and more dangerous, he threw his weight in favour of the change.

1877 was a critical year for the Church. Penzance convicted his first ritualist under the Public Worship Act in February. Thereupon R. W. Church, dean of St. Paul's, drew up a memorial to the bench of bishops[86] and circulated it among a distinguished few for signature. Despite the event which gave rise to the memorial, it was concerned not so much with the courts as with relations between Church and Parliament over ceremonial. It provided an incisive statement of the reasons for clerical uneasiness:

no peace can be secured for the Church, nor can her existing relations with the State be long continued, unless laws for the regulation of divine service, and for other spiritual matters of primary importance, are made by an authority which both clergy and laity would feel to be binding upon conscience; and we are equally satisfied that no authority will be considered thus binding which does not proceed from the synods of the Church as well as from Parliament.

In saying this we must add that the legislative action of the Church is now paralyzed by the apprehension that when her synodical acts are submitted to Parliament in the constitutional manner material alterations may be made in them, and that the final result may be seriously at variance with the intentions of the synods, and may become law without their consent.

The memorial was eventually signed by 77 clergymen including 4 deans, 8 archdeacons, 13 canons, mostly high churchmen but not all. One, F. G. Blomfield, was a chaplain of Tait's. Blomfield explained his concern in a letter to *The Times*: 'How to give the Church greater freedom in regulating its own spiritual affairs without weakening the bonds which unite it to the nation is a problem of the greatest difficulty, but it is a problem which must be solved if we are to continue to have a National Church.'[87]

The memorial provoked of course a good deal of opposition. In the eyes of the *Pall Mall Gazette*, the memorial was tantamount to a request 'for the abolition of the Royal Supremacy and for putting Convocation in the place of the Pope.'[88] Another group of clergymen got up an address against any hasty alteration in the relations between Church and State.[89] Its signatories were equally impressive, including another four deans, Lightfoot, and as a symptom of the uncertainty within the Church, Archdeacon Purey-Cust who had signed Dean Church's memorial too.

Archbishop Tait was thus given plenty of ammunition with which to shoot the first memorial down. Instead he studied its argument carefully and had a meeting with its signatories. When they came to practical detail, they were fuzzy. One canon seemed 'disposed to die on the floor of the room rather than submit to something, which he could not quite explain.'* Yet Tait did not dismiss them all lightly. In the following October he took a significant opportunity to comment on the issue they raised. He had agreed to preside then over the Church Congress for that year, the first archbishop of Canterbury to do so. Church Congresses and diocesan conferences were symptoms of the increasing demand for corporate distinctiveness among churchmen. Tait had not welcomed this development originally, nor had Evangelicals. He feared anything which tended to separate the Church from the country as a whole; evangelicals feared dilution of their distinctive principles in mixed company. But once the development was widespread and well rooted, both joined in though warily. The Congress of 1877 furnished startling evidence of the extent to which the desire for more Church autonomy had grown. Even the secretary of the Church Defence Institution maintained that if the union of Church and State was to be preserved and the Church enabled to satisfy the expectations of the country, a measure of internal self-government must be conceded to the Church.[90] Ryle, one of the most influential Evangelicals, asked for the addition of laymen to Convocation to strengthen the Church's ability to make its wishes heard in Parliament.[91]

In his closing address, Tait spoke on the side of caution.[92] If

* Tait's diary, 22 April 1877.

England were an infidel land such as Turkey, he said, he could understand those who claimed that the national legislature exerted an injurious influence over the Church. In pooh-poohing such a parallel, he held up the representatives of his own county of Kent, Nelson in the Lords and Beresford Hope in the Commons, as fair specimens of the membership of Parliament. He implied that there was no urgent need to transform the relations between Church and Parliament. Nevertheless, he advised the discontented to propose a concrete alternative for securing legislative changes so that it could be examined and, if it recommended itself, acted upon. Liberationist reaction to the Congress's discussion vindicated Tait's caution. The *Nonconformist* interpreted the question as whether the Church of England could be 'so transmogrified as to be placed in the position of an unestablished sect, while continuing to possess the privileges of an Establishment.'[93] *The Times* thoroughly agreed.[94]

The day was passing when the Church could be run as from the editorial offices of *The Times*. *The Times* was an often faithful reflection of what the country thought. Parliament represented a much broader spectrum of national opinion; the Church a much narrower one. That was the crux of the problem. Parliament's concerns were much more widespread than and different to the Church's. The clogging of the legislative pipeline between Convocation and Parliament revealed this general fact in the concrete. Archbishop Tait continued loyal to his goal of a more truly national Church in partnership with the State. However, faced with yearly increasing evidence of the divergence between Parliament's interests and the Church's requirements, he fell back upon Convocation as the assembly which could act on the Church's behalf most effectively.

In 1878 the Lower House of Convocation passed a resolution in favour of a procedure like the bishop of London's to enable the Church to adapt public worship to the changing requirements of the times.[95] The Upper House agreed in principle and advised the Lower House to draw up a bill.[96] The result, which came to be known simply as the 'Draft Bill'[97] and was modelled upon the bishop of London's, reached the Upper House in July 1879 when final negotiations on revision of the rubrics were taking place. Tait still had his doubts.[98] Although the Bill would not prevent Parliament from proceeding with ecclesiastical legislation in the present way, the new procedure would become the expected one. Tait realized that Parliament might therefore resent it as an infringement of its rights. He also pointed out the inflexibility of the new procedure. If the privy council suggested an alteration in what the two Convocations proposed, the suggestion would have to go back for approval by both Houses of both Convocations. On the other hand, the archbishop had come to believe that the laity and therefore Parliament were tired of disputes about ceremonial and would be glad to delegate responsibility for detailed examination of relevant legislation to other hands, subject of course, as the Draft Bill provided, to royal assent.[99] Without further ado he and the rest of the bishops substantially accepted the Bill.[100]

Both the need for the Bill and the probable fruitlessness of the procedure it would set up were demonstrated almost immediately. When Tait proposed the formal address in which the Convocation of Canterbury would present the Crown with the changes in the rubrics to which it had finally agreed, the Lower House baulked. It was afraid that to address the Crown would be tantamount to asking the dreaded Parliament for legislation under existing procedure. The Lower House gave its consent to the address only after it was amended to say that, in forwarding the recommendations, Convocation did not wish to be understood as inviting Parliamentary legislation before the Draft Bill was enacted.[101] Meanwhile, hopes that the Draft Bill would facilitate legislation were dimmed by the Convocation of York. It failed to reach agreement within itself on revision of the ornaments rubric[102] and so did not endorse its southern counterpart's proposal. Under the Draft Bill, no request for action by the Queen in council could be made until both Convocations spoke with one voice.

The fate of the Bill rested with Parliament; and Archbishop Tait's prediction that it would be relieved to see detailed examination of rubrical changes in other hands might well prove wrong. He had underestimated laymen's concern about ritual on a previous occasion, in 1873. Probably Parliament would not indulge in another ecclesiastical session like 1874. However if there was one subject more than any other on which the laity were determined not to permit the clergy to go their own way, it was public worship. Parliament might reflect this feeling by deciding that it was better to be a dog in the legislative manger than to let Convocation in.

Chapter Nine

THE FAILURE TO PUT DOWN RITUALISM

Like some disorders Ritualism will go on until the elements on which it feeds are exhausted, or the Patient dies.
Jowett to Tait, 23 June 1874

Put down Ritualism? Why, you could no nothing more to encourage Ritualism than by making martyrs of Ritualists.
The Rt. Hon. E. H. Knatchbull-Hugessen, 3 August 1874

THE Church of England in the wake of the Public Worship Regulation Act was rather like the English body politic after the Lords' rejection of the 1909 budget. Both measures broke the compromise on which their respective institutions rested, and inaugurated a period of bitter strife with touches of lunacy. Then the Church and later the country drew back from the brink of domestic catastrophe, the country under the impact of war, the Church for fear of schism.

The Public Worship Act was to take effect on 1 July 1875; and it behoved the bishops to see that it was put into operation well. For the issues at stake were crucial. The Act was intended to preserve the unity of the Church and of Church and State against a movement which threatened to pull them apart. Moreover, it had been proposed originally by Archbishop Tait in the name of his colleagues. And it was a bid to strengthen control over the clergy from the top, from the courts and, through use of the episcopal power of veto over attempted prosecutions, from the bishops. The *Quarterly Review* saw the Act as a step toward more effective central guidance for a Church whose troops at present often fought at cross purposes.[1] The success or failure of the Act's machinery was not the resonsibility solely of the bishops. It also depended on the way Lord Penzance conducted his court and on the practicability of the procedure laid down in the Act and further defined in the rules and orders drawn up by the Lord Chancellor, Tait and Penzance. Still, the bishops could try to instruct the public about how the Act should be viewed and what to expect from it.

Tait took the first opportunity after the passage of the Act to plead for mutual understanding within the Church.[2] To the clergy he said that public worship existed primarily for the benefit, not of themselves, but of the laity; to the laity, that they should not be suspicious of clergymen elevating the tone of public worship, for only thus had it been improved so greatly in the last twenty-five years. He tried to remove unnecessary alarm by declaring publicly that the Act was directed only against the tiny minority who acted in disregard of the spirit of the Church of England.[3] But against those few he was firm: 'no amount of good intentions, no amount of self-sacrifice,' he told Convocation, 'can justify a man in doing his best to overthrow this great and venerable institution upon which we all agree the safety of this kingdom so depends.'[4]

Exhausted by the excitement of the Bill's enactment, the Church quietened down, preparing for the first trials under the new order. Strident voices were few though bitter. Tait was accused of not being baptized, falsely of course. Yet how else could ritualists explain his unregenerate churchmanship? More serious, the English Church Union's membership rose twenty per cent from 10,517 in 1874 to 12,602 in 1875.[5] However Pusey, its apostolic father, wrote about the Act in moderate terms.[6] He also expressed impatience over the ritualists' insistence on each bit of ceremonial, the use of incense for example, even when they could not agree on its significance.[7]

The bench of bishops echoed and amplified Tait's statements in a public address which they issued in March 1875.[8] It was highly desirable for them to agree on principles to govern their role in administration of the Act. Otherwise the standard of uniformity in public worship which the Act sought to strengthen might vary widely from diocese to diocese. Furthermore, the decision not to revise the rubrics before July increased the importance of each bishop's power to decide which suits for enforcement of particular rubrics should proceed. The bishops' address to the public implied that they would not oppress those who used the eastward position, at least until the courts had reconsidered its legality. On the other hand, the episcopate's lack of sympathy with higher ritual was made clear; and they insisted upon loyal obedience to the law as soon as the courts reached a decision on points now doubtful.

All but two of the bishops signed the address. Since the two who did not, Baring of Durham and Moberly of Salisbury, were at opposite ends in churchmanship, their protests neutralized each other. Baring, reputed to be an oppressor of the High Church in his diocese, thought the address insufficiently rigorous in its opposition to illegal ritualism; Moberly, a diffident disciple of the Oxford Movement, thought the address too censorious. [9] But the other bishops were less united than the address indicated. Baring's objections won the sympathy of the archbishop of York[10] who, however, lacked spine enough to refuse to sign. Ellicott signed with the idea that the address might goad ritualists into secession.[11] Selwyn, Wordsworth's alter ego, signed with enthusiasm,[12] presumably because he thought the address would allay the fears of moderate high churchmen. Many other bishops, fearful of doing anything to rock the boat, signed only on condition that they were joined by the great majority of their colleagues. Response to the address was mixed. *The Times*, the *Guardian* and, more guardedly, the *Record* welcomed it though interpreting it according to their own lights. R. W. Church, of like mind to Moberly, thought the address so unjust that momentarily he thought of resigning the deanery of St. Paul's in protest.[13] Extreme Evangelicals' suspicion of the bishops was not abated.

The Act rumbled into motion like a large, untested threshing machine. Many expected it to cut a wide swath. Pusey had heard that a society was being formed to use the Act to eliminate all ritualistic practices including the eastward position from churches in London;[14] and the Church Association did not intend to stimulate prosecutions diffidently. Nevertheless, the existence of the bishops' power of veto dissuaded all but determined complainants from initiating proceedings. The Act was fed one blade of clerical wheat at a time.

The Ridsdale Case

As it happened, the first blade came from Tait's own diocese of Canterbury. Two weeks after the Act came into effect, three parishioners of St. Peter's, Folkestone, encouraged by the Church

Association, submitted a complaint about the manner in which their incumbent, the Rev. C. J. Ridsdale, conducted public worship. They specified twelve of his practices including the two crucial ones, eucharistic vestments and the eastward position. Tait did not exercise his veto to stop proceedings. He had had trouble before with Ridsdale whose ritualism was particularly conspicuous because of the strong Nonconformist element in Folkestone. On the other hand, Tait wanted to employ all means for conciliation: personal discussion with Ridsdale and, if both parties consented, settlement of the case, as the Act allowed, by Tait as diocesan bishop without appeal to the courts. Discussion between the archbishop and Ridsdale was delayed because the complaint reached Tait on holiday in Switzerland and Ridsdale on his wedding trip. When the two men eventually met, the interview was fruitless.

Ridsdale refused to submit to Tait's arbitration since Tait, he was sure, would feel bound by the existing judicial pronouncements, the Judicial Committee's Mackonochie and Purchas judgments. The Public Worship Act had not swept these precedents away; it was only a procedural measure. Many men wanted a judicial review of these decisions, and by refusing arbitration Ridsdale could bring this about. Though justifying his course on these grounds, he implied that he would not in any case obey a civil court on a religious matter.[15] He presented himself before Lord Penzance's court thereby recognizing its validity as a civil court, but he denied that it had any spiritual jurisdiction.[16] The most extreme ritualists, however, would not have subjected themselves to the courts at all. Ridsdale's stance was not unpromising from the archbishop's point of view.

Penzance condemned Ridsdale on all twelve accusations brought against him. Consequently, Ridsdale was issued with a monition to conduct public worship accordingly. However, the object of Ridsdale's stand was a fresh consideration of the law governing ceremonial by the supreme court, to which he was entitled to appeal under the Public Worship Act. Penzance's judgment was of little importance to Ridsdale because Penzance had felt obliged to abide by the precedents set by the Judicial Committee. Ridsdale appealed on four of the twelve points: the crucifix and candles on top of the screen dividing the nave from the chancel in St. Peter's, the use of wafer bread, vestments, and the eastward position. For the interim he announced his intention of disregarding the monition. He escaped the legal consequences of his disobedience by suspending his services in St. Peter's pending the appeal, another indication that he was not prepared to take things to the extreme.

For some time all eyes in the Church had been directed toward the supreme court which would deal with this crucial appeal. Some Conservatives had not been happy about the abolition of the appellate jurisdiction of the House of Lords by Selborne's Supreme Court of Judicature Act of 1873. Soon after the Conservatives gained office, the Act's appellate clauses were suspended. This allowed the debate about the composition of the supreme court for ecclesiastical appeals to revive. Tait investigated the possibility of restoring the bishops to full membership.[17] High Churchmen and the Lower House of Convocation argued for a purely lay court whose title to bind the Church to the court's decisions on purely spiritual issues would thus be impaired.[18] Clearly there was still no consensus in the church; and in 1876 when Parliament passed the Appellate Jurisdiction Act, the compromise of 1873 for ecclesiastical appeals was preserved though they were transferred back to the Judicial Committee: when it dealt with these cases, bishops would sit with it but as assessors, not as full judges.

The number and selection of episcopal assessors was left to be settled by order-in-council. This matter was urgent and delicate because the first ecclesiastical appeal to be handled by the Judicial Committee as soon as it was reconstituted would be Ridsdale's. His case was deferred precisely so that it could be considered by the revised court. Tait wanted the assessors to be the five bishops holding the most august sees: Canterbury, York, London, Durham, and Winchester. Four of these five were currently occupied by Low Churchmen; Durham was aggressively so. Wordsworth mobilized the other bishops to insist on a meeting of interested bishops to consider the question. He threatened to air his views in public unless Tait agreed.[19] The archbishop capitulated, and the consequent meeting agreed to add four junior bishops selected by rotation to the five Tait had proposed.[20]

This proposal did not satisfy High Churchmen of Pusey's stamp. Ever since the Purchas judgment, he had placed his hopes for peace on a fresh hearing of the points it dealt with. If the two archbishops served as assessors for the Ridsdale appeal, the necessary freshness would, Pusey told Tait, be imperilled.[21] Archbishop Thomson had sat on the Judicial Committee for the Purchas case and after judgment was delivered both archbishops had insisted on obedience to the courts. Moreover Ridsdale was appealing in a case which Tait had allowed to proceed and against a decision handed down by Penzance as the judge of Tait's provincial court.

Tait defended his impartiality in reply.[22] All he had insisted upon, he said, was obedience to judicial rulings until reversed; and an archbishop was quite entitled to hear an appeal from his provincial court since it did not express his opinion any more than Queen's Bench did for the Queen. Tait was determined to hear the Ridsdale appeal. He did not want to leave such an important case to inexperienced, junior bishops. Furthermore, they might allow the law lords on the Judicial Committee to subordinate the assessors' position unduly, thereby creating a precedent to govern more senior bishops in future cases. And if the Judicial Committee should decide to relax the Purchas judgment, Evangelicals would find the new ruling more palatable if they knew that Archbishop Tait had approved it.[23]

After further negotiations with the Lord Chancellor, the order-in-council about episcopal assessors was issued. There were to be five: one of the three bishops who were privy councillors—Canterbury, York, and London—and four others, all to be chosen by rotation and to serve for one year. To begin with, for the Ridsdale appeal, Tait and the bishops of Chichester, St. Asaph, Ely and St. David's were selected.

Up to this point, the English Church Union had been paying Ridsdale's legal expenses, and as a result he had been defended by an eminent lawyer, Sir James Fitzjames Stephen. When the composition of the board of assessors was settled, the Union told Ridsdale that if he did not object to Tait's inclusion, the Union would withdraw its support. Stephen on the other hand threatened to withdraw from the case if Ridsdale did as the Union demanded. The Union was shaken but felt unable to back down since it had already told Tait of its intentions in an attempt to induce him to keep out of the case.[24] Ridsdale went ahead with the appeal, assured of Stephen's continued assistance without charges beyond his means.

The appeal gathered an impressive battery of legal talent together. Ten law lords led by the Lord Chancellor sat to hear Sir

James Stephen on Ridsdale's behalf and A. J. Stephens, the foremost Evangelical lawyer, against him. The seating of the judges occasioned surprise and gave Tait satisfaction. It was expected that the episcopal assessors would sit behind the judges. Then it was realized that Tait would be the senior privy councillor present, and he was placed at the head of the judges' table on an elevated chair. When counsel had finished their arguments, the judges and assessors retired, each to consider his verdict separately.

Disregarding his earlier plea for judicial impartiality, Pusey wrote to tell the archbishop how the case should be decided.[25] Pusey sensed that the eastward position and wafer bread might be allowed. He insisted on vestments as well. They could be declared illegal, he said, only by subordinating the clear requirements of the ornaments rubric to political convenience. To do so would lead eventually to imprisonment of the supposed offenders and as a result to disestablishment. Tait maintained judicial silence.

The final judgment was delivered in May 1877. It went against Ridsdale on the crucifix and vestments. Wafer bread too was found to be illegal, but the Judicial Committee held that the complainants had not proven Ridsdale to have actually used it. The eastward position was declared permissible though barely so and only if the manual acts of the clergyman in breaking the bread and taking the cup could be seen by the congregation. Since the complainants had also failed to establish that Ridsdale violated this requirement, he was acquitted on this particular charge.

If at the time of the Purchas case the Judicial Committee had permitted the eastward position but proscribed vestments, it might have succeeded in curbing ritualism. By now it was too late. The Ridsdale judgment seemed too obviously an expedient compromise to be respected as a detached interpretation of the law. This impression was confirmed when the public later heard that at least one of the judges had disagreed with the majority verdict and thought that it was influenced by policy as much as by law. In fact three of the judges had dissented but had been prevented from pronouncing their opinion in court by the Lord Chancellor.[26] Determined ritualists felt no hesitation in ignoring the verdict.

Ridsdale wavered. For two weeks he continued to wear eucharistic vestments.[27] Then he intimated that he would comply with the judgment if Tait as his spiritual superior gave him a dispensation from the obligation he felt to obey the rubrics as he still interpreted them. Free of such sentimental foibles and without asserting a claim to extra-legal spiritual prerogatives, Tait complied. 'I gather,' he wrote, 'that, while you consider yourself as being under a sacred obligation to act upon what you conceive to be the literal meaning of the Ornaments Rubric in the Prayer Book, you yet acknowledge a general dispensing power in this matter to reside in me as your Bishop. . . . I am quite ready to satisfy your conscience and do hereby grant you a complete dispensation from the obligation under which you believe yourself to lie.'[28] Dean Burgon called this 'the most quiet piece of wit and gentle humour I have ever seen in my life.'[29] But it did the trick. Ridsdale conformed. With oiling from the archbishop, the Public Worship Act's machinery had produced one satisfactory result.

The Tooth Case

Already a less tractable ritualist lay under censure from Penzance's court, the Rev. Arthur Tooth, vicar of St. James's, Hatcham, in the diocese of Rochester. Ominously he had been born on the feast day of St. Alban, the first English martyr, and his church was named after the first apostolic martyr. Unwilling to recognize any authority whatsoever in Penzance's court, he had refused to appear when cited before it. This only complicated matters legally by increasing the onus on the prosecution and the judge to see that their proceedings did not violate the rights of the defendant. The English Church Union's lawyers stood by to pounce on the first error. 'The siege of Troy was nothing to an undefended ecclesiastical suit', *The Times* remarked. 'It transcends in indomitable vitality every form of legal proceeding that has survived to the present generation.'[30] For his part, Tooth treated the successive ruling of Penzance with single-minded disregard. The combination of this form of civil disobedience and the English Church Union lawyers' acumen was explosive.

Penzance's first difficulty was to find a room in which to try the case. He applied to the Admiralty Court, which had been linked with the ecclesiastical courts, but the judge in charge, having no sympathy with attempted judicial suppression of ritualism, turned him down. Then the Treasury officials refused to pay for the rent of any room at all—the failure of the fees bills to provide revenue for Penzance's court was taking its toll. Thereupon Tait offered him the use of the library in Lambeth Palace. It was not suited for a court. Those who attended the hearing turned blue with cold, and Penzance heard the case with a railway rug over his knees.[31] Yet it would do, or so Tait and Penzance thought.

Tooth had been charged with a number of ritual offences some of which were *sub judice* in the Ridsdale case when the Tooth case came before Penzance. Carefully excluding those, Penzance condemned Tooth for the other practices which had previously been condemned by the Judicial Committee. Tooth was issued with a monition to conform. However, he would not bow to the command of any existing court. When he continued to conduct worship heedless of the monition, he was inhibited from serving in his church for three months as the Public Worship Act provided. If he continued his defiance for three years, he would be deprived of his benefice.

Tooth did not take Penzance's sentence seriously enough even to appeal to the Judicial Committee against it. The bishop of Rochester sent a curate to take over. Tooth prevented him from entering the church. The police were called upon to assist the curate but refused on the ground that, since the case was one of disputed right of possession, they had no right to interfere. The curate resigned. He was followed by other nominees of the bishop, all equally unsuccessful. The bishop was in despair. 'Tooth will continue Master of the situation—', he moaned to Tait, 'even if an actual riot is fomented—'[32] To avoid a riot the bishop ordered closure of the Church,[33] but Tooth and his churchwardens ignored this too.

So far Tooth had elicited little sympathy. Clergymen who defied the courts, said Wordsworth, 'are not martyrs but persecutors. They are persecuting the church of which they are ministers by disturbing its peace, and by stirring up strife, and by spreading confusion and anarchy, and by marring its efficacy and imperilling its safety.'[34]

Then, in mid-January 1877, the complainants applied to Penzance to cite Tooth for contempt of court. The designers of the Public Worship Act had assumed that a sentence of inhibition would be obeyed, and therefore they had not provided for its enforcement. The omission was fatal. The complainants invoked a forgotten statute of 1813[35] which had changed the penalty for contempt of an ecclesiastical court from excommunication, for

The Rev. Arthur Tooth in jail

many years an ineffective punishment, to imprisonment. Not even the critics of the Public Worship Act had recalled this in 1874. Now Tait and Penzance were thrown into dismay. Though Penzance wanted to refuse the complainants' petition, he believed that he lacked discretionary power to do so.[36] The machinery of justice had been set in motion, and no one but the complainants could stop it. Tooth was arrested and locked up in Horsemonger Lane jail.

His new setting transformed him from a violator of the law into a martyr. Imprisonment was a penalty distressingly inconsistent with his original offence; and public opinion recoiled at the spectacle. The English Church Union convened meetings which capitalized on the reaction. Its president, Wood, heir to the viscountcy of Halifax, resigned his post as groom of the bedchamber in the Prince of Wales's household rather than fail to announce his sympathy for the imprisoned law-breaker publicly.[37] Liddon and Wood went on pilgrimage to Horsemonger Lane jail. A Jesuit preacher at Oxford used the imprisonment as proof of the Church of England's lack of spiritual liberty.[38] Membership of the evangelical Church Association, which had financed the prosecution, fell off. The Public Worship Act was reaping the wrong crop.

Tooth tried to retain control of his church from jail by appointing a clergyman to take charge in his absence. The police now saw their duty and were able to keep him out of St. James's without resorting to force.[39] The bishop of Rochester's nominee secured entry and conducted divine worship as the law prescribed. With the law thus vindicated, the prosecution was satisfied and applied to Penzance for Tooth's release from jail, less than a month after his incarceration. The request was granted. Yet the inhibition would remain in effect until Tooth agreed to obey Penzance's original monition.

At the local yearly vestry meeting of Tooth's parish an aggressively Protestant churchwarden was elected, an indication of the opinion of the majority within the territorial parish as distinct from the congregation which had attended Tooth's services. The new churchwarden took the keys to the church. Tooth broke in through a window of the church early one Sunday morning in May and opened the doors to three hundred of his faithful supporters. He proceeded to celebrate Holy Communion dressed in what *The Times*' reporter described as 'a richly-wrought chasuble of white material, with coloured orphreys'.[40] Before the bishop's current nominee arrived to conduct the eleven o'clock service legally, Tooth was gone. Soon afterwards the new churchwarden, determined to cleanse the church of popery, destroyed the altar in the Lady Chapel and pulled down the crucifix in the centre of the church.

At this juncture the problem fell into Tait's lap. For the bishop of Rochester was translated to the new see of St. Albans, and pending the consecration of a new bishop of Rochester the provincial archbishop had to take over. Tait's first step was to bring Tooth in for an interview to try and discover what authority Tooth would defer to. Tooth ruled out Penzance's court, the Judicial Committee, and the diocesan bishop—now Tait—to whom he had taken an oath of canonical obedience at his ordination. Yet he seemed willing to follow the dictates of Convocation. Tait therefore referred him to Convocation's resolutions of 1867 against departure from long-sanctioned ceremonial without the consent of the diocesan bishop. After retiring to consider this point, Tooth replied that the resolutions did not amount to proper synodical acts.[41] After another attempt to persuade Tooth by letter, Tait gave up: 'it is, I fear, needless for me to reason further with you.'[42]

All that could be done now, excluding further imprisonment, was to wait for the three years till Tooth would be deprived of his benefice. Suddenly the whole case collapsed. The procedural rules drawn up under the Public Worship Act stipulated that each case must be tried either in the cities of London or Westminster or in the diocese of the accused cleric. It dawned on the English Church Union's lawyers that Lambeth Palace where Tooth's case had been heard, though just across the Thames from Westminster, was in the county of Surrey and the diocese of Canterbury. The proceedings might therefore be invalid. In the autumn of 1877 the E.C.U. lawyers applied to the court of Queen's Bench to restrain further proceedings, and it agreed to do so.

Adding insult to injury, two of the judges of Queen's Bench including the Lord Chief Justice stated in the course of their judgment that Penzance's court as created under the Public Worship Act was an entirely new jurisdiction not intrinsically related to the old ecclesiastical court of Arches;[43] this although

Penzance was also dean of Arches and had heard the case ostensibly as such. Ritualists were delighted. This pronouncement bore out their claim that Penzance's court was purely a creation of Parliament without a tincture of the ecclesiastical authority of the court it had superseded. Tait only demeaned himself and did not enhance the prestige of the Public Worship court when he had his chaplain send a memorandum to *The Times* in an attempt to refute the Lord Chief Justice's remark.[44]

Lord Penzance had already compromised his claim to possess an ecclesiastical jurisdiction by the manner in which he became dean of Arches on the resignation of the previous dean in 1875. He declined to go through the formalities hitherto necessary for appointment as dean: the taking of oaths as required by the Church's canons, subscription to the Thirty-nine Articles, acceptance of letters patent from the archbishop, and confirmation by the dean and chapter of Canterbury cathedral. He insisted that his appointment as dean was simply the automatic, statutory consequence of his position as judge under the Public Worship Act; he would do nothing which might seem to question the validity of his position and rights by Parliamentary statute.[45] Thus, as High Churchmen interpreted it, he admitted himself to be an Act-of-Parliament judge, not an ecclesiastical one at all. His disregard of ecclesiastical sensitivities here was an indication of his general lack of familiarity with ecclesiastical law. This corpus of law was a formidable maze which had largely escaped the knife which nineteenth century English legal reformers had wielded everywhere else. It left Penzance at the mercy of the experts with whose aid the English Church Union helped prosecuted ritualists.

Fresh proceedings could have been instituted against Tooth. He prevented this by resigning his benefice. The letter in which he announced this to Tait[46] was a song of triumph particularly over the assessment by Queen's Bench of Penzance's court. Tooth was even entitled to sue his prosecutors and Lord Penzance for false imprisonment, but with condescending charity declined to do so. He claimed that his health was broken. He lived until 1931, directing an orphanage, a nunnery and a home for drunkards.[47] His parish did not survive so peacefully. When another though less extreme High Churchman took over as vicar, a riot broke out inside the church,[48] and bitterness persisted for the rest of the decade.

Subsequent Prosecutions

The Tooth case proved to be the crisis in the fortunes of the Public Worship Act. Confronted by tough resistance, its machinery had cut too deeply and then fallen apart. Though Tooth had not won a martyr's crown in everyone's eyes, and though it was widely assumed among the public that ritualists took advantage of legal niceties simply in order to preserve their 'fat' benefices, his incarceration angered high churchmen and discredited his Protestant prosecutors, while his subsequent escape from the courts gave new heart to ritualists and humiliated those who had meant to restrain them. *The Times* was already disgusted by the collapse over a legal technicality of the only other prosecution under the Act which had approached serious proportions. The bishop of London had consented to the prosecution of the Rev. Pelham Dale, incumbent of a largely deserted parish in the City of London, and Dale had been inhibited. Then the bishop was found to have a remote proprietary interest in the patronage to the benefice and for that reason to be ineligible under the Act to proceed as he had. 'The least that could have been expected, after Parliament had gone somewhat out of its way to furnish the Bishops with these additional powers,' *The Times* commented, 'would be that they should be effectually employed, and that they should not be thrown away by mere negligence in their application.'[49]

Fearful of the possible course and consequences of further litigation, the bishops began to exercise their veto almost indiscriminately. As soon as Tooth escaped, Tait accepted an extra-legal settlement arranged by the bishop of Lichfield for a parish in Wolverhampton whereby the ritualistic incumbent was permitted to continue his practices, provided that he conduct other services in a strictly lawful manner at convenient times for any parishioners who so desired.[50] Seven of the eight suits initiated in 1878 were vetoed.

The suits which did proceed were retarded or collapsed over further technicalities. The hope of the Public Worship Act's creators that it would expedite and cheapen litigation were dashed. No ritualist defendant or Protestant complainant with spine would submit to arbitration by the diocesan bishop. The Act allowed trial in the local diocese in order to reduce travel costs, but it proved cheaper to bring witnesses to London than to send lawyers to the provinces. Prosecutors had to lavish great care on their representations, with the result that litigation was as expensive as ever.[51] For proceedings turned into a game of snakes and ladders in which the least error threw the complainants back to the starting position. Civil courts such as Queen's Bench intervened at the slightest provocation. The Act had been passed to defend the majesty of the law, but lawyers turned it into a mockery.

Even the one feature of the Act which redeemed it for High Churchmen and was pointed to by Tait as proof of the Act's moderation lost its unique charm. The bishops' right of veto over the commencement of suits was a power which Tait believed they lacked under the 1840 Church Discipline Act, the statute governing all litigation about clerical offences until the Public Worship Act introduced its alternative procedure. Then in 1879 Canon Carter, a venerable Tractarian incumbent who had introduced many ritualistic practices into his parish in the diocese of Oxford, was prosecuted under the Church Discipline Act precisely in order to obviate the veto. But the bishop, Mackarness, claimed a veto here too. Though he disapproved both of Carter's ritualism, which had driven many of his parishioners away from his church, and of his refusal to submit to episcopal direction, the bishop did not want any suit instigated by the Church Association as this one was to go on.[52] The prosecution challenged the validity of the veto and induced Queen's Bench to force the bishop to withdraw it. Mackarness appealed to the House of Lords in its judicial capacity, and it decided in his favour.

The fervent gratitude which Tait won from high churchmen in another episode only illustrated, as far as he was concerned, the excited state of ecclesiastical opinion under the impact of the Act. The Rev. R. W. Enraght, incumbent of a Birmingham parish, was prosecuted for, among other things, using wafer bread. Warned by the failure of the prosecution in the Ridsdale case to prove that Ridsdale had actually used wafer bread, Enraght's prosecutors induced a person who took communion at his church to bring away to them the consecrated wafer which Enraght gave him for the purpose of communion. The prosecutors marked it with the date on which it was received and submitted it as an exhibit to the court, which duly stamped it. The court was not informed that the wafer had been consecrated.[53] When this became known, it was not only High Churchmen who were scandalized.

Protest meetings were held throughout the country, and Tait was besieged by 231 petitions to end the sacrilege.

To do so was not easy, though Tait censured the communicant's action as soon as he heard of it.[54] The Church Association which had inspired the prosecution was reluctant to surrender the exhibit.[55] Penzance was not certain of his power to order its removal.[56] Furthermore two wafers had been deposited with the court, only one of which was consecrated, and to tell them apart was difficult. At length, in December, the prosecution agreed to apply for release of the consecrated wafer. They wanted Tait to summon Enraght to swallow it in his presence.[57] If Enraght obtained the wafer independently, he would have turned its reception into a public service. Tait had the wafer spirited away from the court to the chapel of his country residence and there he reverently consumed it,[58] due announcement being made in the press. Wood lauded him for his conduct. Tait's registrar took a different view: 'What Doctors can preserve the Primate's health,—if he can be occasionally *forced* to eat wretched Wafer bread, kept in a Pill box for *five months or more*!!!'[59]

The prosecutions under the Public Worship Act left an unsavoury taste in other ways. Mackonochie, who was in trouble with the courts again from 1874 on, found himself on one occasion standing side by side as a fellow culprit with a clergyman charged with adultery.[60] Moreover, the complainants whom the Church Association induced to come forward were rarely estimable characters. Ridsdale claimed that none of the complainants in his case had ever attended his church or, for as long as he had known Folkestone, any other.[61] One of them announced his willingness to withdraw from the case if he were given £200, and another, a publican, agreed to do the same.[62] The Public Worship Act presupposed that all residents of a parish who called themselves Churchmen were entitled to lodge a complaint about the services in the parish church. To confine eligibility to those who attended the church regularly, as ritualists demanded, would be to ignore the fact that ritualistic worship often drove churchmen away. However, the pews they deserted were as often filled by others, perhaps from beyond the parish's boundaries, whose religious desires ritualism satisfied. Men of tolerant charity hesitated to drag a conscientious clergyman backed by a devoted congregation before the courts. The kind of man who would agree to prosecute lessened the moral weight of parishioners' rights which the Act was intended to protect.

In short, the Act was a fiasco. It was bound to be so because it relied ultimately on force either in the form of inhibition and deprivation or through imprisonment. As ever in a contest with determined religious conviction, force backfired on those who employed it. In this case force was particularly dangerous because employed, not by the State against the Church, but within the Church by one of its parties supported by the State against another. The Act was meant to prevent a widening of this internal division and of the division between Church and country by restraining ritualism. Instead the Act brought out the tenacity of ritualism, won new sympathy for its advocates, deprived its opponents of popular favour, and allowed them to be frustrated through the bishops' vetoes and the Act's own intricacies.

The popular Protestantism which had given rise to the Act was far from dead. In embarrassment it turned its primary attack away from the ritualists' conduct of public worship to another of their practices. In June 1877, the earl of Redesdale informed the House of Lords of a published manual entitled *The Priest in Absolution* for use by clergymen of the established Church in hearing confessions.[63] It had in fact been written for and cautiously circulated by the Society of the Holy Cross to which Mackonochie, Carter and Tooth among others belonged. The subsequent controversy only accentuated the division of 1874 between popular opinion in Church and country on the one hand and extreme high churchmen on the other. The public and the bishops reacted to the book even more strongly than they had to enriched ceremonial,* for the book not only awakened Protestant aversion to priestly claims of power to absolve sinners. It also suggested questions for clerical confessors to ask penitents, even children, about their conduct including any sexual transgressions, an outrageous invasion of privacy if not worse in most Victorians' eyes.† Undeterred by

---

* See e.g., *The Times'* leader, 25 June 1877, 'nothing less than a conspiracy against public morals'; and Tait, 'if any man were to put such questions to my wife and daughter I would turn him out of the house', quoted in the Rev. Henry Nihill to Tait, 3 July 1877, Tait papers, Vol. 233.

† *The Priest in Absolution*, part II (privately printed, n.d.), pp. 115 and 144. The controversy over this book merits study for the light it sheds on Victorian moral preconceptions. Lewis Carroll appealed to all who remembered their days of youthful innocence to recall the principle that sinful thoughts should be kept at arm's length,

obloquy, Tractarians closed ranks with ritualists on this issue without the misgivings they felt about ritualistic worship; both of the extreme High Church groups regarded sacramental confession as an indispensable means through which the clergy could discover the depth and extent of sin and counteract it.

Negotiations Towards a Truce

1877, the year of the Ridsdale judgment, Tooth's imprisonment and eventual escape from the courts, and Redesdale's denunciation of *The Priest in Absolution*, exposed most of the rocks on which the barque of the Church of England could break up. It was driven hard toward them by the waves of internal controversy. Both Evangelicals and ritualists organized satellite pressure groups among their working-class adherents, the Working Men's Protestant League against the Church of England Working Men's Society. A Reformed Episcopal Church, recently formed by secession from the Church of England's counterpart in the United States, attempted to extend the schism to England by winning over Evangelicals unhappy about the established Church's failure to check ritualism.[64]

Bishop Ellicott thought that only war in the Middle East could divert Churchmen's attention enough to prevent the impending split.[65] Instead Disraeli's foreign policy accentuated the Church's division.[66] Liddon, Mackonochie, Wood, Denison and Pusey, to name only the best known High Church leaders, agitated on behalf of the Bulgarian Christians being butchered by Turkey whom Britain was supporting against Russia. High Churchmen felt an affinity for the Orthodox Churches of the Balkans and saw

---

banished to 'the realm of shadows and dreams' (Lewis Carroll to ed., *Pall Mall Gazette*, 14 July 1877). In defending sacramental confession, Pusey cited the following statistics given him by the chaplain of a large Anglican school (Pusey to Tait, 17 July 1877, Tait papers, Vol. 97, f. 219).

	before confession	after confession
boys who had sinned in some way with others	66	4
boys who had sinned by themselves	24	28
boys innocent	10	68
	100	100

their oppression by the infidel Porte as parallel to ritualists' suppression by an indifferent State at home. Tait and most Evangelical and Broad Churchmen, on the other hand, accepted the patriotic line of support for Turkey against Britain's enemy Russia. Every new controversy, whatever its subject, seemed to provide grist for the mills of dissension within the Church. Its comprehensive unity, necessary for survival as the established Church, seemed in danger.

Archbishop Tait rose to this challenge, the gravest he ever faced, with true magnificence. In some disputes, over the Athanasian Creed for one, he had underestimated the strength of extreme high churchmanship and the old traditionary orthodoxy. On other issues, education for example, he had underestimated the power of secularism. The challenge to the Church's unity he recognized fully and in good time. Ecclesiastical comprehensiveness, after all, was an essential ingredient of his ideal of a national Church. As bishop of London he had accepted all extremes among his clergy, however much he might dislike their particular bent, so long as they would work for their parishioners' Christian well-being. His intolerance of ritualism as archbishop until now had been an aberration. Even in this he had not lost sight of his goal. The Public Worship Act had been intended to preserve the existing breadth and unity of the Church against a movement which threatened to stretch it to the breaking point. The Act had not narrowed the Church's ceremonial rules, only enabled the courts to enforce them. The Act's consequences, however, proved the folly and the danger of repression by force. While never admitting his error, Tait responded to the events of 1877 with a sustained attempt to restore peace.

His first stratagem was humour. Invited by the dean and chapter of St. Paul's cathedral, a hotbed of high churchmanship, to a dinner in January 1877, he spoke to them on the theme, 'He is not such a bad fellow after all when you come to know him'.[67] He applied it to one of their members, Canon Gregory, who was at the time the centre of a fight over elementary board schools in London. The archbishop made them laugh and went away hoping that they might apply the text to himself and others with whom they differed.

Then he tried argument. He took the occasion of a published letter which Canon Carter addressed to him, outlining the reasons for high church discontent, to issue a lengthy reply.[68] In it he defended the Judicial Committee as supreme ecclesiastical appeal court, warned Carter that any attempt by extreme High Churchmen to tailor the constitution of the Church to their own liking could backfire, criticized the direction in which their theology and practice was moving, and pointed out that an 'overwhelming Protestant majority . . . constitutes the very backbone of the English Church'.[69]

In August and again in December he convened large meetings of clergymen of all shades of opinion for united prayer and discussion of their differences in a way meant to evoke mutual understanding and deprecate intolerance.[70] Carter, Ryle and Lightfoot, as representing the three main divisions within the Church, High, Low and Broad, supported the project. Liddon, however, unable to bring himself to trust the archbishop whom he had so recently loathed, stayed aloof; and Ryle and the *Record* had strong reservations.[71]

In October, between these two meetings, Tait took to the rostrum by presiding over the annual Church Congress as bishop of the host diocese. The Congress could have been used to air the Church's dissensions by those who attended, and this was expected. Tait preached, encouraged, cautioned and pleaded before his audience to avoid it. His opening sermon and inaugural address were on the theme of unity. 'A compromise', he said, 'may be a concealment, or repression of the truth, and for that I have not one word to say; but a compromise also may be an equitable recognition of the various phases of the one unchanging truth as it presents itself to various minds.'[72]

Throughout the Congress his resounding note was one of confidence in the Church's prospects. Everyone had been impressed by recently published official statistics of the number of Anglican churches built or restored since 1840, 8,871 at a cost of over £25½ million largely from private donors; and these figures ignored the churches on which less than £500 had been spent.[73] In no previous age had the Church of England been more active. Why doubt that it could move on from strength to strength? Its very internal dissensions could be ascribed to its vigour; all three of its schools were alive. Their fights could, of course, be differently interpreted, as signs of feverish excitement such as preceded final decay, insistence on one's own panaceas for fear that unless they were adopted the Church would prove obsolete. Or one could accept the Liberationists' diagnosis: that the Church's quarrels proved it to be an artificial creation held together only by establishment. Tait preached the first view because he believed it and also to counteract the prophets of doom within as well as outside the Church. 'Some think', he said,

that I never speak without an undue exaggeration of the brightness of the prospects of the Church over which I am called in God's providence to preside. But they are bright. Look abroad. What other country in the world would you change Churches with? Look at home; which of the denominations would you prefer? Look back. What age are you prepared to say it would have been more satisfactory to have lived in? For my part, I thank God and take courage. . . .[74]

The Church's Nonconformist opponents reacted sourly. 'If he is the best captain, who, having to steer his vessel through a narrow and tortuous channel, resolves simply to ignore its hidden rocks and shallow places, and persists in asserting that it will be brought triumphantly into port,' said the *English Independent*, 'then we may believe that the Primate is the fittest ruler for the Anglican Church in a time of trouble and difficulty like the present.'[75] But Churchmen at the Congress and outside responded to his plea for unity with a warmth which surprised themselves and heartened him. He had managed to draw out the large amount of fellow feeling which held Churchmen together, forgotten in the glare of the year's events.[76]

This feeling was not a creation of the archbishop's. Ritualism had destroyed uniformity in public worship as a bond of unity within the Church, but not the prayer book. It was still followed in all congregations however they truncated or embellished it. Probably more important, the Church of England was bound together by its history. Each school looked back with pride to great moments in it, Evangelicals to the Reformation and the Evangelical revival of the eighteenth century, High Churchmen to the Caroline divines of the seventeenth, Broad Churchmen to a steady tradition of scholarship and, more intermittently, of attempted comprehensiveness. They were also united by the Church's national position and responsibilities which all, even Tractarians, valued. Undoubtedly the Church's endowments buttressed its cohesion, but by themselves they could not have sustained it. Each school contemplated the possible break-up of this unity as disastrous. They used the threat of secession, like the threat of opting for disestablishment, as a club with which to beat each other into submission, a threat whose hollowness became more obvious each time it was uttered and not carried out. They were starting to think of themselves, somewhat as English political parties had begun to do at least fifty years earlier,* as 'loyal opposition' to each other.

As a result, the Reformed Episcopal Church made virtually no inroads among frustrated Evangelicals. Apart from their general loyalty to the established Church, Evangelicals were impressed, though reluctantly, by ritualist missions like Mackonochie's in the London slums. At the end of 1877, Shaftesbury confided to his diary that ritualists were showing more Christian zeal than his own school.[77] As for the High Church camp, they showered Tait with explanations of their discontent and possible terms for a truce. Canon Trevor, an old fashioned high churchman, wrote to say that he was trying to refute the new extremists of his school by argument but that his attempts were vitiated by the introduction of force through prosecutions into the debate.[78] In the letter to the archbishop which Canon Carter had published he outlined the constitutional reforms he thought necessary. And realizing that they might not be generally acceptable, he insisted only on acceptance of his group's cardinal tenets and practices as admissible within the Church.[79]

Most of the extreme High Church's eirenicons concentrated on the conduct of public worship. Pusey hoped that young ritualists would reduce their demands to, and that the bishops would tolerate, a few central practices including vestments.[80] Wood repeatedly proposed to Tait that ritualists be allowed to do as they wished at early celebrations of the Holy Communion so long as they agreed—and he was sure they would—to celebrate at midday without lights or vestments for any parishioners who so requested.[81] However, any such truce would involve toleration of what the courts had declared illegal. During a visit to the archbishop's country residence early in 1879, Carter returned to this point, and in a memorandum developed a scheme for reconstitution of the ecclesiastical courts including the supreme court which

* The phrase 'His Majesty's opposition' was first used by Hobhouse in the Commons in 1826.

would leave the determination of spiritual points at issue to representative clergy and bishops.[82]

1877 was the year of ecclesiastical crises and the archbishop's
first initiatives towards a truce; 1878 was a year of personal tragedy
for the archbishop which surrounded him with waves of sympathy
and deepened his desire for peace. He had one son, Craufurd, who
had survived the scarlet fever epidemic which killed five of Tait's
daughters in 1856. (One daughter also survived it, and two others
were born after it.) A quiet, unassuming but able young man now
twenty-eight, he had just come back from the United States where
he served as his father's emissary to the American bishops in
preparation for the forthcoming Lambeth Conference of the
international Anglican episcopate. In February Craufurd was
engaged to the daughter of the bishop of Ripon, and took charge
of a London parish. But already he was an invalid, suffering from
a bladder infection caught in the United States. He died at the end
of May. The iron which had entered his father's heart over the
previous calamity was melted and turned gold.

> O dear Companion of my age
> Wise councellor (sic) beyond thy years
> Firm friend—true son—Thy failing sire
> Reft of thy help is filled with fears
> Fears for the remnant of my life
> Fears.*

Almost immediately the overseas bishops began to arrive for
the conference for which his son had helped to prepare. The
archbishop carried himself through the receptions and assemblies
hospitable, in command, but always on the verge of tears. He did
not forget the problems of his Church. After Tooth's imprisonment Wood had appealed on the question of regulating ceremonial
to the Lambeth Conference, then a year away.[83] Tait won the
conference's agreement that no departure from long customary
ceremonial should be made contrary to the request of the diocesan
bishop; that excessive diversities in public worship endangered
the union between Churches of the Anglican Communion; and
that 'order and obedience, even at the sacrifice of personal pre-
ferences and tastes, lie at the foundation of Christian unity, and
are even essential to the successful maintenance of the Faith.'[84]

* Tait's diary, 6 September 1878.

This amounted to endorsement of the view Tait had adopted and not abandoned. Yet he was also becoming conscious that the fault for the unrest lay partly with the personal irritation which he shared at trivial ceremonial innovations.[85]

In November the archbishop and Mrs. Tait, as weighed down as ever by Craufurd's death, went to Scotland for a brief holiday. Death struck again. Mrs. Tait was a great strength to her husband. Surprisingly enough she was in sympathy with the principles of the Oxford Movement. Before her marriage, when she heard that one of the Oxford tutors who had protested against Newman's Tract XC, Tait, was a candidate for the headmastership of Rugby, she had hoped that he would not succeed. Marriage did not alter her religious opinions, but then Tait did not usually discuss his ecclesiastical dealings with her.[86] Her part was to foresee all his personal needs, which she did with the most loving attention, and to create the family atmosphere in which he relaxed. Few but kin and intimate friends were invited in to see this close-knit Victorian family, reading aloud, riding, taking holidays in Scotland or abroad together, united by the loss of the five little girls and by the threat of the paralytic strokes which had repeatedly nearly carried its father off.

Craufurd's death was too much for Mrs. Tait. In Scotland she suffered a bilious attack and a week later, on Advent Sunday, she died. Almost instantly the archbishop became an old man. And to his fellow churchmen whatever their school he became a man apart, beyond calumny, elevated by his acquaintance with death, to Victorians the supreme mystery. In the summer of 1879 he began to encounter signs of popularity for the first time. One young man, evidently a ritualist, even knelt down and kissed the hem of Tait's robe, to his astonished embarrassment.[87] This new veneration of him was confirmed by the response to the publication that autumn of a memoir of his wife and son which he prepared.[88] The story of the scarlet fever epidemic was recalled in the haunting words of Mrs. Tait's diary.

Her death also confirmed him in his endeavour to think freshly about the strain created by ritualism. He took note of parallels with the history of Methodism a century before.[89] It too had been the product of irregular zeal; it too had aroused arguments about the limits of obedience to bishops; and now all Churchmen deplored its departure from their ranks. In October the archbishop attended Holy Communion in a chapel where the clergyman wore eucharistic vestments, and Tait called it ritualism 'in a mild form'.[90] He would not now follow the crusty line of the bishops of George III. Nevertheless, with inter-school tolerance in earliest infancy and with the gulf between the courts' rulings and ritualistic practice as wide as ever except for the eastward position, real peace or even a recognized truce was still distant.

Chapter Ten

CONCILIATING THE NONCONFORMISTS

It is an awkward thing for a Bishop to do justice to Dissenters.
Jowett to Tait, 10 Nov. 1854

Archdeacon Purey-Cust: The speech of Archdeacon Fearon is one of expediency and of sympathy with Dissenters, but there is another side to that point which ought not to be overlooked, and that is sympathy for ourselves. ('Hear, hear.')
Chronical of Convocation, 15 Feb. 1878

APART from the establishment itself, only one of the old Nonconformist grievances remained after the abolition of university religious tests in 1871. Every member of a parish, whether a Churchman or not, possessed the civil right to burial in the parish churchyard; but the right was limited by the ecclesiastical requirement that the burial service be conducted according to the prayer book and by the local Anglican incumbent. This privilege of the Church of England was anomalous since it did not apply in Ireland when the Church was established there or to the Church of Scotland. Yet until the 1830s it provoked only sporadic expressions of resentment. Most English Dissenters acquiesced in this as in their other disabilities, and incumbents commonly exercised their power leniently, for example by ignoring the prayer book's stipulation that the unbaptized should not receive religious burial.

Then the new self-assurance of Dissent, coupled with the Oxford Movement's treatment of the differences between Church and Dissent as essentials, fanned the smouldering discontent into flame. Dissenters demanded burial in parish churchyards by their own ministers and with their own services; incumbents began to scrutinize the religious credentials of those presented to them for burial more rigorously. Anglican clergymen tried to belittle the resulting discontent both by questioning its existence and by claiming that those who protested were political Dissenters in contrast to the truly devout, religious Nonconformists who appreciated the prayer book service; but the old distinction between Dissenters, those who objected to their disabilities and the Church of England's establishment, and Nonconformists, those who respected the position of the established Church but separated themselves from it on conscientious religious grounds, was evaporating.

The burials controversy was both eased and exacerbated by the Acts of the 1840s and '50s which closed overcrowded burial grounds for sanitary reasons and authorized the creation of new ones in which part would be left unconsecrated for other than Anglican burials. The legislation was used mainly in urban areas, not in the countryside where the churchyard remained the only burying place. Many Nonconformists whose kin had already been interred in the churchyard wanted to be buried beside them. And the opening of unconsecrated burial grounds gave Anglican clergymen an excuse for harshness about admission to parish churchyards. Bishop Phillpotts insisted on the erection of a wall dividing the consecrated from unconsecrated ground in new cemeteries, and was stopped only by the courts.[1]

Bills to open churchyards to Dissenters were introduced throughout the 1860s by Sir Morton Peto, a wealthy Baptist. Since his denomination did not believe in infant baptism, it suffered more than most from the Anglican insistence on baptism as a prerequisite to religious burial. When he left Parliament in 1868, the banner passed to Osborne Morgan, the son of a Welsh vicar. Morgan never withdrew from the Church of England, but his knowledge of its age-old neglect of Wales and the consequent strength of Nonconformity there had turned him into a fervent advocate of this reform and indeed of total disestablishment. Morgan's bills secured second reading, by large majorities in the Commons every year from 1870 to '73; and it was another cause of Nonconformists' disenchantment with Gladstone's Liberal government that it did not press the bills on the Lords. The Conservative High Churchman Lord Beauchamp carried bills through his House in 1871 and '72 to allow silent burial for those whose relatives might prefer it to the prayer book's service. To Nonconformists, however, this gesture was little better than an insult. In the general election of 1874 full admission of Nonconformists to churchyards was a plank in most Liberal candidates' platforms.

Paradoxically, the Conservatives' victory in that election made settlement of the burials controversy more urgent because of its relation to the over-arching question of disestablishment. If Nonconformists were admitted to churchyards, steam might be taken out of the demand for disestablishment towards which the Liberal party now began to move. For two years Liberals, taken aback by the extent of their defeat and deprived of a leader by Gladstone's retirement, looked round for a rallying cry. The two issues in the Liberal air were a further extension of the franchise and disestablishment.[2] Disestablishment was less attractive than ever to moderate Liberals in the immediate light of the election. Within a few months, however, the subject became highly topical in Scotland because the Church Patronage Act of 1874 provoked Scottish Nonconformists by terminating lay patronage in the established Church. This was salt in the wounds of the tens of thousands who had borne all the costs of secession from the Church in 1843 when the demand for a similar reform was refused.* If disestablishment became practical politics in Scotland, it was certain to be extended to England.

Taking advantage of their opportunity, the Liberation Society organized 2,600 public meetings in Britain between 1874 and '77, and circulated from five to six million leaflets.[3] Working independently of the Society but with the same object in view, two prominent English Congregationalist ministers, R. W. Dale and Guinness Rogers, stumped the country in 1875 and 1876.[4] The hand of Joseph Chamberlain, who was planning the Radical campaign within the Liberal party on a platform of disestablishment and a broader franchise, was strengthened by his entry into Parliament in 1876 and, much more, by the creation of his National Liberal Federation, England's first modern political machine, in 1877. Gladstone too seemed to be toying with disestablishment. The Public Worship Regulation Bill had shaken him so much that over the really minor issue of Holt's amendment he had threatened to abandon defence of the English establishment.† Selborne was apprehensive over Gladstone's failure to discourage the efforts of the Liberal Whip, W. P. Adam, when Adam declared himself for disestablishment in Scotland late in 1874.[5] Suddenly in

---

* For a full account and explanation of the disruption of 1843 and the Act of 1874 see J. H. S. Burleigh, *A Church History of Scotland* (London, 1960), pp. 334–69 and pp. 375–6. † *Supra*, 189–90.

1876 the advanced Liberals' search for a crusading issue was diverted and answered by the Bulgarian atrocities which Disraeli's pro-Turkish foreign policy seemed to facilitate. Then talk about the possibility of disestablishment was taken up by more restrained Liberals such as Lord Hartington,[6] perhaps in order to draw the party's attention away from the government's foreign policy which they were inclined to accept.

The resurrection of disestablishment as a political cry after the setback it suffered by the rout of the Liberals in 1874 made defenders of establishment anxious to allay subordinate grounds for discontent. The Conservative party appeared about ready for a settlement of the burials controversy. In 1875 Morgan's Burials Bill was defeated by only fourteen votes in the House of Commons which had a usual Conservative majority of fifty. This inclined the cabinet to the belief that resistance would not be practicable for much longer, and Cross informed Archbishop Tait of this tentative opinion.[7] Tait followed the lead more fully than at least some of the cabinet reckoned on.

The Archbishop and Nonconformity

Like his seventeenth-century predecessor, Tillotson, to whose policies for befriending the Nonconformists he harked back, Tait had been born and brought up in a non-Anglican Protestant household, and unlike most converts he looked on his religious heritage with thankfulness and veneration. The roots of his faith went back to his Scottish Presbyterian childhood, particularly to his nurse Betty Morton who cared for him almost as a mother after his own mother died, who went with him to Whitworth while his club feet were straightened out, who even acted as his school days tutor hearing him recite his Latin lesson though she could judge his performance only by the sound of the words. Her simple, stern piety kindled a response in the prematurely serious boy.[8] Though he abandoned strict Calvinism in his teens and on going up to Oxford joined the Church of England, he could not believe what his Tractarian contemporaries taught: that the faith of his Protestant countrymen was gravely defective, and that their Church was no true Church at all. His mentor as an Anglican was Thomas Arnold who pleaded for broadening of the national Church to embrace Nonconformity.

Accordingly, in an age notorious for its vituperative denominational warfare, Archbishop Tait was distinguished by his cultivation of good relations with English Nonconformists. Critics dubbed him 'the Presbyterian archbishop'. His social sympathies extended even more widely. He entertained the Roman Catholic priests around Addington, his official country residence; and he was on such cordial terms with Sir Moses Montefiore, a Jewish patriarch who lived near Tait's private home on the Isle of Thanet, that Montefiore contributed to the orphanage Mrs. Tait founded in the neighbourhood and attended the consecration of its chapel, though from his carriage. Nevertheless, Tait had little hope or even desire for serious co-operation with Roman Catholics. In his view their Church stood off, behind 'so sharp a line of arrogant exclusiveness, built on a superstructure of false doctrine',[9] and accentuated by the declaration of papal infallibility at the Vatican Council of 1870. Nonconformity on the other hand was united with the Church of England by 'our common Protestantism'[10] to which Tait unqualifiedly adhered. In contrast to the Oxford Movement, he emphasized the doctrines which Church and Dissent agreed upon.

He also urged his clergy to participate in what facilities there were for joint action with Nonconformists, for instance the Bible Society which circulated the Scriptures without explanatory comment.[11] And he fostered new opportunities for co-operation. Knowing that he would respond favourably, in 1876 a group of Nonconformist ministers asked him to help convene a conference of ministers from various English Protestant denominations on the problems posed by the advance of irreligious thought.[12] Tait discussed the proposal with several of his episcopal colleagues, some of whom were far from enthusiastic. The bishop of Rochester blamed Nonconformists for impeding the Church's work in elementary education, so germane to the suggested topic for discussion. The High Church pair Selwyn and Wordsworth urged that the Nonconformist ministers discountenance attacks on the Church of England's privileges and property, and Selwyn wanted the meeting to be called a 'Catholic' conference. On the other side, some of the Dissenting ministers who supported the proposal were nervous about it.[13] Late in July Tait and six bishops met for the conference with twenty-two English Nonconformist ministers and two from the Church of Scotland. The discussion was frank

and searching. Though nothing concrete was achieved, interdenominational understanding was fostered. In 1881 the archbishop was joined by representative churchmen of all schools and
leading Nonconformists in issuing an invitation to the public to
observe a special day of prayer for the religious life of the country.

Many Evangelicals and Broad Churchmen would have been
happy to go farther. Bishop Ellicott wanted to conciliate Nonconformists even at the price of alienating Tractarians like Pusey
and Liddon.[14] After all, Evangelicals had much more in common
religiously with Nonconformists than with those two. Dean
Stanley, the broadest of the broad, liked to gloss over denominational divisions by thinking of Dissenters as 'Nonconforming
members of the Church of England'. The archbishop, however,
was not enamoured by the prospect of a Church based on narrower
doctrinal beliefs such as Ellicott would have preferred. Tait also
recognized, as Stanley was reluctant to do, that conscientious
Nonconformists did not want to belong to a Church which was to
them repellently hierarchical and tolerated or taught heinous false-
hoods.[15]

Tait's desire for amity with the Nonconformists was, in fact,
rather shallow. At best he wanted co-operation between Church
and Dissent against the common enemy, secularism. Often his
motive was merely to lessen Nonconformist hostility toward the
Church of England and so to preserve its establishment. The ideal
of reunion was in his eyes dangerous for a Church already strained
by its wide internal divisions, and impractical, to be dismissed to a
utopian future. He refused even to concern himself over the
responsibility of past generations of Churchmen for the birth and
growth of Dissent.[16] His nearest approximation to reunion was to
make the Church of England more attractive to Nonconformists
in the hope that some would join it. His Act of Uniformity
Amendment Act,* which allowed for the preaching of a sermon
unaccompanied by the whole of one of the prayer book's services,
was intended partly toward this end, as was his attempt to curb
ritualism. He urged the Church of England not to confine its
attention to its devoted supporters but to welcome the fringe of
men who hung loosely to it in order to strengthen their allegiance.[17]
These were timid gestures. And Tait even gloried in some of the
more invidious distinctions between Nonconformist ministers and

* *Supra,* 106–9.

their Anglican counterparts, as for instance the difference in their social standing.

Consequently, he dealt with some interdenominational enterprises less sympathetically than some churchmen would have liked. Lord Cairns asked him to endorse the crusade which the American revivalists, Moody and Sankey, conducted in England in 1875. To Cairns' disappointment, Tait qualified his approval by expressing doubts about the way those who stayed behind for personal guidance after each public session of the crusade were handled.[18] 'I cannot but fear from what I have heard', he wrote, 'that the counsel given at these Meetings must often be crude and founded upon no knowledge of the real circumstances and state of mind of those to whom it is addressed'. He also questioned the evangelists' implication that instantaneous conversion was almost universally necessary. However, he concluded,

looking to the vastness of the field that lies before us, and the overwhelming difficulty of contending with the mass of positive sin and careless indifference which resists on all sides the progress of the Gospel, I for my part rejoice that, whether regularly or irregularly, whether according to the Divine, Scriptural, and perfect way, or imperfectly, with certain admixtures of human error, Christ is preached and sleeping consciences are aroused.

R. W. Dale retorted angrily at this complacency and arrogance.[19]

The archbishop responded more sympathetically to another even more irregular movement, the Salvation Army, founded in 1878. For however bizarre its methods, it concentrated on the teeming lanes and alleys scarcely touched by other denominations or by the Moody and Sankey mission. The Salvation Army also attempted to steer clear of theological controversy by ignoring all doctrines on which Protestants were divided. Tait made a nominal donation of £5 toward the Army's purchase of the Eagle Tavern, the Grecian Theatre and adjoining premises to redeem what was then a notorious den of iniquity in east London. He spoke favourably of the Army in the House of Lords,[20] and he explored the possibility of bringing the Army under the aegis of the established Church. The Army's enthusiastic eccentricities, shocking in their novelty, and, more significant, its own insistence on a free hand, made union impossible, though relations between the two became amicable.[21]

Towards Nonconformists who wished to join in the public

services of the Church of England Tait was decidedly generous. Many Nonconformists had taken communion intermittently in the local parish church during the seventeenth and eighteenth centuries, sometimes as what was called a 'healing practice' but more often to qualify themselves for public office. This motive was removed with the repeal of the Test and Corporation Acts in 1828. The practice survived, though less frequent, as an expression of vestigial loyalty to the Church. In 1870 when a notorious instance of it occurred, the archbishop had to do battle to preserve the custom. In a rare moment of tolerance, Convocation had just authorized the appointment of a committee of scholars to be selected irrespective of their denomination to revise the King James translation of the Bible. The eventual committee contained several Nonconformists including a Unitarian minister, Dr. Vance Smith, but no Roman Catholics since Newman declined the invitation to serve.* Dean Stanley invited the committee to Westminster Abbey for a preparatory service of Holy Communion before its first meeting in June. All including Vance Smith attended and received the communion.

High churchmen were scandalized, particularly by the communion of the Unitarian. On behalf of the English Church Union C. L. Wood told Tait that for non-Churchmen to receive communion was a grave dishonour to Christ, an ostentatious abandonment by the Church of its last shreds of discipline, and an implied admission that doctrines so fundamental as that of the Trinity, which Vance Smith as a Unitarian denied, were matters of indifference.[22] Tait too was surprised, but pleasantly so, that Vance Smith should have been willing 'to join in the solemn doctrinal statements contained in our Communion Service'.[23] It seemed to vindicate the archbishop's confidence in the fruitfulness of interdenominational cooperation. 'I shall not be surprised', he told Wood, 'if Unitarians, as well as others, are greatly benefited by being associated in this attempt faithfully to interpret the written Word of God, undertaken, as the service to which you allude shows it to be, in a spirit of earnest prayer for Divine guidance.' Wood was softened but not satisfied. He wrote back to say that while he did not ask for any who presented themselves for communion to be repelled, he did object to the issuing of an invitation to Nonconformists including a Unitarian to communicate.[24]

* Pusey also refused.

Vance Smith then undercut Tait's defence of the revisers' communion by informing *The Times* that he had not recited the Nicene Creed,[25] which was part of the Holy Communion service. He justified his behaviour partly on the principle that every Englishman was *ipso facto* a member of the established Church. This argument was embarrassing to Tait who always maintained as one of the virtues of the Church that its clergy had a responsibility for the Christian well-being of all residents in their parishes whether they attended the parish church or not. Vance Smith's statement recharged the batteries of the high church. Wood threatened secession.[26] Several memorials, one with over fifteen hundred signatures, protesting about 'the Westminster scandal' were sent to Tait. The newspapers of the differing Church parties were full of the debate.

Tait felt obliged to issue another letter amplifying his letter to Wood.[27] This time he qualified his defence of the service by confessing his inability to 'understand the frame of mind which would lead a teacher of religion at once to protest against the Nicene Creed, and at the same time to join in a solemn Service, of which that Creed and its doctrines form, from the beginning to the end of the Service, so prominent a part.' Nor would he condone anyone inviting such a person to take communion. On the other hand he held that the invitation had been to the revising committee generally, not to each member personally. He deplored the fact that the religious faith of an individual should have become the subject of acrimonious controversy in the press. He also quoted from a letter Vance Smith had sent him in which Smith said that he did not deny the divinity of Christ as he found it declared in the New Testament;* which proved, Tait argued, how difficult it was to define the exact degree of divergence between the Church of England and Unitarians.

Subsequently Tait's stand was again compromised, this time by Stanley, who informed the archbishop, though not the public, that Vance Smith had given advance notice of his intention to take communion.[28] Had this become public knowledge, Tait would have had difficulty in preventing Convocation from recommending new restrictive regulations on communion. As it was,

---

* Later Vance Smith drew a distinction between the 'divinity' of Christ which he believed and the 'deity' of Christ which he denied. Letter to ed., *Guardian*, 24 Aug. 1870.

the Lower House passed a resolution expressing deep regret over the offence caused by reception at Holy Communion of a person who publicly denied the Nicene Creed.[29]

The Burials Bill of 1877

Relief of the Nonconformists' grievance over burials was a policy exactly in line with Archbishop Tait's general attitude toward Dissent. He adopted the policy in a conservative spirit, to preserve the establishment by removing a festering source of Nonconformist ill-feeling towards the Church. Yet the outcry over the revisers' communion provided only a faint foretaste of the opposition he would encounter from his clergy. In that instance he defended the practice of Nonconformists willing to participate in the Communion service of the Church of England, a practice endorsed by some historic Anglican authorities. Now he would be attempting to admit Nonconformist services conducted by Nonconformist ministers into hitherto purely Anglican churchyards, for which there was no precedent.

On no issue were clergymen of the Church of England more united than in their opposition to this policy. Eventually fifteen thousand of them, almost three out of every four, signed a protest against it. High Churchmen not particularly keen on the establishment opposed the proposal for doctrinal reasons: that it would open consecrated soil to heretics and abandon baptism as a prerequisite to religious burial. Others reacted against it as an invasion of their ministerial preserves and of their proprietary rights over churchyards, but above all as the most alarming step to date toward disestablishment. In 1868, at Nonconformists' insistence, compulsory church rates had been abolished, with the result that Nonconformists no longer had to pay for the upkeep of the parish church and churchyard. For them to insist now on unfettered admission to the churchyard seemed either inconsistent or proof of steady malevolence. The malevolence of the Liberation Society, which fostered the agitation for both reforms, was avowed and undisguised. Nationalization of churchyards, the Society said, was only a step toward nationalization of the churches. Both, according to Liberationist propaganda, were originally intended for the use of the whole nation, and to the nation they must be restored.

Tait was not dismayed by the intentions of the Liberation Society for he knew that it did not speak for all Nonconformists. The Dissenting M.P. Samuel Morley had recently said that, once the burials controversy was settled, disestablishment should be deferred until members of the Church of England recognized its wisdom.[30] Furthermore, like all Whig politicians Tait banked on the fact that protest movements often lost impetus and so failed to achieve their ultimate objectives when their subordinate, day-to-day grievances were removed. In 1875 therefore, soon after the Burials Bill's near success in the Commons and after his discussion with Cross, Tait decided to seek a settlement of this issue.

Since the Conservative party seemed ready for concession, Tait's first task was to try to win some support from the clergy, and he developed his case both in conferences with his own diocesan clergy and through his public addresses. Reminding his auditors of the angry English reaction when, for example, Italians refused Christian burial to a non-Catholic Englishman who happened to die in their country, Tait maintained that Nonconformists' grievance was valid.[31] He gained information from other European ambassadors in London to prove that English law on burials was less charitable than in many continental states. Yet he asked for conciliation from both sides. To Nonconformists he pointed out that no bill as yet published dealt adequately with the practical problems involved,[32] in particular with the possibility of provocative conduct at the graveside. 'What we have to propose', he told Churchmen, 'is such a measure of concession as will satisfy the people at large and if it does not quite content our opponents yet at least withdraw from them public sympathy (*sic*)'.[33]

Clerical response was worse than discouraging. Its most unyielding spokesmen were High Church, in particular Bishop Wordsworth. Churchyards, Wordsworth said, were consecrated to the service of God according to the discipline and doctrine of the primitive Church, and to allow heretical services in them was simply sacrilege. Better disestablishment, than voluntarily to surrender God's acre. Steeped in the stories of the martyrs under the Roman Empire, he had longed for an occasion to take a similar stand, and he seemed to have found it. He delighted to recall the words of St. Ambrose when ordered by the Emperor Valentinian to surrender some churches in Milan to Arians: 'If you want my property, seize it; if you wish for my body, here it is'. Wordsworth was only sorry that he was unlikely to be asked for his life.[34]

He repudiated the imputation that he was being uncharitable to Nonconformity. Indeed, he was anxious for reunion with Methodism, which was very strong in his diocese.[35] But he would not countenance any lowering of the Church's teaching for this purpose; and he made his eirenical endeavours ridiculous by treading on Methodist self-respect. In 1874 the daughter of a Methodist minister in his diocese died and was interred in the parish churchyard. Her father proposed to erect a gravestone which would describe the girl as the daughter of 'the Rev. H. Keet, Wesleyan Minister'. The vicar of the parish refused to allow the insertion of the words 'Rev.' and 'Wesleyan Minister'. Keet appealed to Wordsworth, who replied magisterially that the vicar was acting within his legal rights. Keet then wrote to Archbishop Tait. Tait abstained from giving an opinion on the legal question but deplored the vicar's objection, and added that he would be surprised if the diocesan bishop did not take the same view as his own. Keet told Wordsworth of Tait's reaction. Wordsworth still upheld the vicar, saying that to apply the term Reverend to what he called Wesleyan 'preachers' would be to compromise the Church of England's insistence on episcopal ordination.[36]

Most clerical opponents of appeasing the Nonconformist grievance over burials realized that Parliament would do so eventually, but this did not weaken their resolve to fight. Nevertheless, the clergy too had a grievance about the existing law. Apart from the three categories—suicides and those who died excommunicate or unbaptized—to whom the prayer book denied its burial service, clergymen were legally obliged to read the service over all brought to them, even those who died in a state of notorious, unrepented sin. On one occasion when a reprobate was thrown out of a Cambridge tavern and died in a ditch, the local incumbent felt unable in good conscience to read the service with its words of assurance of salvation over the body. As a result he was fined by the courts and suspended from his benefice for six months.[37] If Tait could induce Parliament to deal with this grievance together with the Nonconformist one, clerical opposition to the second might be restrained.

The controversy reached its crisis in 1877. The first move was inauspicious. Acting on behalf of the government the duke of

Richmond introduced a Bill, avowedly for sanitary reasons, to consolidate previous Burials Acts and to provide for new cemeteries where existing ones were overcrowded. The Bill's one concession to Nonconformists lay almost hidden, in the seventy-fourth of its eighty-eight clauses, which offered silent burial for those whose relatives and friends might prefer that to the prayer book service. Tait had already pointed out the inadequacy of offering Dissenters what was at present meted out to suicides.[38] But mean-spirited though the Bill was, Tait recognized that it might be all the government's supporters would allow it to propose. He hoped that they would appreciate the necessity of accepting more charitable amendments in committee. Toward this end he supported the Bill's second reading against Liberal opposition.[39]

Once the second reading was passed, however, the government lost even the modicum of courage it had shown. Although Disraeli agreed with the archbishop's desire for concession,[40] two members of his cabinet, Salisbury and especially Gathorne Hardy, both High Churchmen, did not. Since they were standing loyally by their chief in the strained argument within the cabinet on the Eastern question which was of all-consuming importance, Disraeli could not afford to offend them. He told Tait privately to go ahead.[41] But the government intimated its intention of withdrawing clause 74. Tait responded by becoming virtually the leader of the opposition on the subject of burials. He had more confidence in his policy than ever. For he had received encouraging evidence of Nonconformist support for his efforts; the evangelical *Record* and the occasionally Liberal though high church *Guardian* were favourable; and so seemed the House of Lords in spite of its preponderance of Conservatives. Moreover, he wanted the controversy completely settled before another general election.[42]

Working in collaboration with Tait, the archbishop of York attempted to couple relief of the clergy's grievance with relief for the Nonconformists. In committee he moved an amendment to permit a clergyman to refuse to read the prayer book service in cases where his bishop agreed that its use would give rise to scandal among the parishioners. Unable to see the relation between this and the Nonconformist agitation, the government opposed the amendment.[43] This proposal also aroused lay fears that clergymen would be setting themselves up as judges of dead men's spiritual condition, and therefore was easily defeated. The loss of this olive branch to the clergy did not weaken Tait's determination now to do full justice to Dissenters.

Lord Harrowby, who was also in harness with Tait, proposed to allow any Christian and orderly religious service or silent burial in the churchyard to any person with a civil right to be buried there. This would concede all that Osborne Morgan demanded. Only a year before Tait had opposed a similar motion by Lord Granville,[44] but by now had come to see that until it was accepted, there could be no peace. It was a courageous decision. Only two other bishops, Mackarness and Temple, both Liberals, supported it. Because Gathorne Hardy would never stomach it, the government put its whips to work to secure defeat of the amendment. However, the government's usual support was divided; Harrowby himself was a Conservative with a son, Lord Sandon, in Disraeli's Ministry. The result was a tie, 102 to 102, and so by the rules of the House the amendment was lost.[45] Politically this vote was the watershed. When in the House of Lords, in a heavily attended division, and with its whips at work, the Conservative government could secure no more than a tie, and when on such an issue the archbishop of Canterbury voted against the government, some concession at least as generous as Harrowby's was certain to become law eventually. Tait was delighted at his political coup, and amused to see Disraeli (now earl of Beaconsfield) 'sitting quietly through the debate without saying a word and voting with his colleagues while hoping that they would be beaten.'[46]

Harrowby brought his amendment forward again at the report stage. This time he won by 127 votes to 111. The duke of Richmond immediately called for adjournment to consult his colleagues.[47] Most of the cabinet were prepared to give in to some extent, but Gathorne Hardy threatened resignation if they did.[48] As a result, they withdrew the whole Bill. To this Tait did not object, assuming that a similar bill would be introduced again next session. For the meanwhile he urged calmness on the public, particularly on the clergy.[49]

Clerical reaction was insistent and massive. Though a few clergymen announced their support for the archbishop, it was now that fifteen thousand of them signed a protest drawn up by the Church Defence Institution against his policy.[50] Wordsworth warned that if the nation profaned churchyards, it must expect severe retribution from God. He even played on Protestant aversion to popish ceremonies which Harrowby's amendment would admit at the graveside on Anglican soil.[51] The Lower House of Convocation declared that the amendment would be detrimental to the Church's spiritual character and a breach of trust.[52] Reaction was not confined to clergymen, thirty thousand laymen signed the Church Defence Institution's protest. On the other hand most bishops, more sensitive to political realities, began to fall in with Tait.[53]

The opposition was quite sufficient to confirm the cabinet in its wish to avoid the question, and Tait's expectations for the Parliamentary session of 1878 were disappointed. In 1879 a Conservative backbencher, A. G. Marten, slipped a little measure innocuously entitled the Public Health Act (1875) Amendment (Interments) Bill through the Commons. Osborne Morgan did not notice until the Bill was about to go to the Lords that by its reference to existing Acts of Parliament it made the creation of new cemeteries extremely easy and so might indirectly meet the Nonconformist demand. Though this Bill passed the Lords, the awakened Liberal opposition there helped to ensure that Nonconformists would not forget their grievance.

Simultaneously Convocation recommended not only relief of the clerical grievance but also provision for some sort of religious burial service to be conducted by the clergy for those at present denied it by the prayer book, particularly for the unbaptized.[54] A general election was around the corner, the Conservatives seemed to be losing popular favour, and therefore the need for some gesture by the Church to appease the rising Liberals and their Nonconformist supporters was urgent. The details of Convocation's proposals were included in its reply to the Letters of Business on revision of the rubrics. However, Nonconformists would not be satisfied with any arrangement which left the burial of their dead to the local Anglican incumbent.

The General Election and the Burials Act of 1880

Encouraged by a couple of byelection successes, Disraeli appealed to the electorate with unexpected abruptness in March 1880. To his chagrin, the five per cent swing to the Conservatives in 1874 compared to 1868 was exactly reversed. The Liberal party won 353 seats, a majority of fifty-four over the total of the opposition which was divided between Conservatives (238) and Irish nationalists (61).[55] These results seemed more serious than an oscillation of the pendulum; 1874 now looked like a temporary aberration in the normal voting habits of the electorate as extended under the 1867 Reform Act. A vista of many years of Liberal rule opened up.

The Liberals seemed certain to be less sympathetic than ever to the established Church. The Liberation Society and its allies had thrown their support unreservedly behind Liberal candidates in the election campaign rather than insist on prior commitment to disestablishment, and by this moderation won increased sympathy within the party.[56] Eighty-three English Nonconformists* and from eight to fifteen Scottish Nonconformists were elected as Liberals, whereas in 1868 the figures had been respectively fifty-three and from seven to eight, in 1874 forty-four and from five to nine.[57] At least thirty-seven other M.P.s in the new House of Commons and, including ministers below cabinet rank, eighteen members of the new government had expressed themselves in favour of complete disestablishment.[58] Almost half of the victorious Liberal M.P.s favoured some step in that direction.[59] Chamberlain joined the cabinet with the power-house of the National Liberal Federation at his control. To Archbishop Tait the political atmosphere seemed 'electric'.[60]

Prominent among the legislative measures proposed in the Queen's speech to the new Parliament was a Burials Bill. But Tait's fear that the Bill might be intolerably radical was already assuaged. For the government had decided to introduce the Bill first in the Lords; it was therefore placed initially in the custody, not of Osborne Morgan the new Advocate General, but of Selborne as Lord Chancellor; and Selborne had asked Tait for suggestions.[61] The selection of Selborne for this assignment was an indication of the predominant Whiggery of the government belying the Radical bark of many of its supporters. No member of the government was better disposed toward the Church than Selborne, a nearly obsessive defender of the union of Church and

---

* 24 Congregationalists, 21 Unitarians, 11 Quakers, 10 Wesleyan Methodists, 8 Baptists, 4 Presbyterians, 3 Calvinistic Methodists, 1 Primitive Methodist, and 2 of unspecified Nonconformist denomination, a total of 84 of whom I was a Conservative.

State. Though determined to appease the Nonconformists, privately he belittled their agitation by blaming it on activist leaders.[62]

In replying to Selborne, Tait stood by the principle of Lord Harrowby's amendment,[63] but raised two other points: the need to provide punishment for and so to prevent disorderly conduct at the graveside, and relief of the clerical grievance in having to read the burial service over scandalous evil-livers. The second point could, he said, be dealt with by accepting Convocation's recommendations on burials in its recent report on revision of the rubrics. Selborne pointed out that the first would have to apply to obstructive incumbents as well as to those admitted into the churchyard.[64] With this extension, the Bill he introduced[65] followed Tait's suggestions.

It permitted anyone with the civil right to interment in the parish churchyard to be buried as his relatives, friends or legal representatives requested, either silently or with a Christian* and orderly service conducted by whomsoever they wished. Any person would be guilty of a misdemeanour who behaved indecently or obstructed the burial, or delivered an address not part of the religious service, or attempted in the churchyard to bring Christianity or the belief or worship of any Christian denomination into contempt. After referring to the two Convocations' reports on the rubrics, the Bill relieved the clergy from all existing civil and religious penalties for acting in accordance with the recommendations of either Convocation as appended to the Bill. In this appendix the prohibitions on the use of the prayer book service were extended to cover those who died in the commission of any grievous crime, but the prohibition against suicides was softened to exclude those who had been found to be insane; in all prohibited cases, the clergyman was permitted at the request of those in charge of the burial to use portions of the Bible and prayer book as approved by the bishop; a further optional shortened service was outlined; and silent burial by the clergy was allowed if those in charge of the burial agreed.

The Bill angered both Radical Dissenters and diehard clergymen. Radical Dissenters particularly deplored the Bill's violation of the principle of religious equality in refusing to tolerate non-Christian funerals in churchyards. From the other side, Words-

---

* Selborne later inserted a clause defining a Christian service as one used by any denomination or person professing to be Christian.

worth called the Bill 'an Act for burial of the Church of England'. Archdeacon Denison saw its treatment of the Church's property rights as the dawn of communism. One especially wild incumbent described Nonconformist ministers who would be admitted into churchyards as 'the company of Korah, the ministers of the many-headed monster which, at home, poisons so many spiritual influences, and abroad renders our missionary work all but futile.'[66]

But Conservative politicians and the Lower House of Convocation accepted that the game was up. The Lower House appreciated that the Bill was framed to balance concession to Nonconformity with removal of the clerical grievance, and though they passed a general resolution of protest against the Bill, they intended the protest to be calm and formal.[67] The Conservative leaders who met to work out their tactics decided against last ditch resistance. Even Gathorne Hardy recognized that the Bill might be the best they could secure, and Beresford Hope, the most High Church of Conservative backbenchers, knew now that unless this particular agitation were appeased, worse might befall the Church.[68] Nevertheless, Disraeli would not dispirit his followers by easy capitulation, and he asked Wordsworth to spearhead the opposition to the Bill in the House of Lords.[69]

As soon as Wordsworth concluded his speech moving the rejection of the Bill, Tait rose to support it. Striking to the heart of Wordsworth's case, namely his insistence on the exclusiveness of the teaching and discipline of the Church of England, Tait said that Wordsworth had never perfectly mastered

what I conceive to be the glory of the Church of England, that it is a National Church, wide as the nation, ready to embrace all in the nation who are anxious to join it, and not making narrow sectarian distinctions between those who adhere very rigidly to one or another set of opinions.[70]

The Bill, Tait continued, would not only strengthen the establishment against Liberationist attacks but would also remove a serious cause of disunity between Churchmen and Dissenters and encourage brotherly relations between the two. He carried nine bishops with him against five on Wordsworth's side, and the Bill was passed by 126 votes to 101.

Thereafter in dealing with amendments Tait, unlike a majority of the bishops, voted steadily on the government's side. In particular he opposed Lord Mount Edgcumbe's amendment prohibiting Nonconformist services in churchyards where other unconsecrated burial grounds were available. The amendment passed, the opposition's one success in the Lords. Just after the Bill was sent down to the Commons, Tait demonstrated his determination to see an adequate measure passed even more markedly by attending a meeting of the Church Defence Institution which was hotly opposed to it. He stood up to a lot of abuse there including a remark that he ought to be shot, then thanked the audience for their advice, and presented his own case.[71]

The government's Radical supporters in the Commons were sufficiently dissatisfied with the Bill to be prepared to bring on a collision with the Lords[72] and so to delay legislation for a year. Prolonged agitation, they hoped, would enable them to force through a more extreme measure and one which would not relieve the clergy of their grievance. Mount Edgcumbe's amendment was of course thrown out with the government's ready consent. Morgan had difficulty in retaining the restriction on services permissible in churchyards to Christian ones. The Radicals on their own, however, were not sufficiently strong to deflect the government from its course. But Radicals found some Conservative support for their opposition to the Convocation clause and appendix which, by permitting clergymen to act in accordance with Convocation's recommended revision of the burial rubrics, eased the obligation on the clergy to read the prayer book service over all but those proscribed in the prayer book.

Gladstone was determined to treat Convocation with respect and to keep faith with Tait.[73] However, the Convocation clause was unpopular even among members of Convocation, and was also disliked by M.P.s for the universities of Oxford and Cambridge, whom Gladstone treated, anachronistically, as representatives of the clergy.[74] The clause provided an instance of what the Lower House of Convocation had feared might happen when it reported the results of its general revision of the rubrics to the Crown: the government had extracted the recommendations dealing with burials and ignored the rest.[75] To Beresford Hope, the member for Cambridge University, the Bill's reference to Convocation was a bribe to implicate it in the passage of a measure of which it disapproved. Spencer Walpole, the other member for Cambridge, and Sir J. R. Mowbray for Oxford disliked the amount of official recognition which the clause and the appendix would give Convocation.[76]

A Wesleyan Methodist M.P., H. H. Fowler of Wolverhampton, presented an acceptable solution. He proposed to replace the reference to Convocation and the appendix with a less detailed clause to the same effect. It would permit the clergy, either where the prayer book service could not be used or at the request of those in charge of the burial, to conduct such a service as the bishop might sanction. With Tait's consent, Morgan accepted the amendment, and it was passed.[77] When the Bill with the Commons' amendments returned to the Lords, Disraeli and the archbishop of York put up a fight for restoration of Mount Edgcumbe's clause. As Disraeli was not prepared to create a clash between the two Houses on this issue, the Commons' amendments were accepted by a comfortable majority.[78]

In contrast to the reception of the Act disestablishing the Irish Church once it was finally passed, the now enacted Burials Bill was not accepted with generally quiet resignation by the Church of England. There were flickering indications that it would meet with resistance similar to that the Public Worship Regulation Act had encountered. One incumbent warned Tait that his congregation would deter the intrusion of Dissenting preachers with pitchforks.[79] Another wrote to his parish clerk, 'Please remember to have the Church locked, and even the Tower Door locked, and no bell to be rung, and if the parties do not finish the Service before three o'clock, they will be guilty of a misdemeanour. You cannot attend the funeral as parish clerk, . . . but you should attend to protect the Church and Grave-yard. . . . My fees and your charges you must ask for just the same, and they must be paid you.'[80] One unusually sensitive layman claimed that he had been driven to the Church of Rome by Archbishop Tait's conduct over the Bill.[81]

The irreconcilable bishops, Wordsworth, Ellicott, Magee and Woodford, decided not to consecrate any more churchyards or parts of cemeteries. They refused even to attend a meeting of bishops called by Tait to discuss the administration of the Act.[82] Wordsworth drew up a form for his clergy to consecrate separately each grave to be used for an Anglican burial, and encouraged the creation of private cemeteries exclusively for Anglicans.[83] The Rev. J. Hall of the parish of Shirland refused as a peril to his soul to enter the burial of a Nonconformist in his parish register as required by the Act. Eventually, after charges were levied against him and he refused to pay, he was threatened with imprisonment. He refused a dispensation from his religious scruples which Tait offered him on the model of the one Ridsdale accepted,[84] but he seems to have escaped the martyrdom he courted.

Such defiance was, however, exceptional and was never embraced by any school within the Church. Unlike the Public Worship Act, the Burials Act was viewed by the vast majority of churchmen, not as a religious measure imposed by improper authority, but as a political concession which, however religiously distasteful, was legitimate. On the whole the Act went into operation smoothly. This may have been partly because comparatively few Nonconformists took advantage of the Act's provisions,[85] apparently bearing out the clergy's claim that the grievance was not widely felt.

Still, it would have given Liberationist Radicals a nasty weapon during a few years particularly difficult for the establishment. The agricultural depression which began in 1878 led in 1881 to agitation among hop farmers in Kent and Sussex with Liberationist encouragement against clerical tithe owners,[86] an ominous straw in the wind since the Liberals intended to democratize the rural franchise very soon. Tait felt obliged to speak out against the Liberation Society and on behalf of the Church Defence Institution more than ever before.[87] At the same time, discontent among both High Churchmen and Evangelicals about the treatment ritualism was receiving kept talk of disestablishment alive in Anglican circles.

The Burials Act of 1880 turned out to be the most successful political measure to which Archbishop Tait was a party. The respectful appreciation which his conduct won from Nonconformists[88] helped ease tension between Church and Dissent. Much more remarkable, this Act was the last major political victory of militant Dissent in England. Although Nonconformist influence over the Liberal party was never greater than in the following two or three decades, it expressed itself largely by heightening the tendency of the party to think of politics in moral terms. Now that the last of its old disabilities had been removed, Dissent could not convince public opinion, and therefore could not convince Gladstone and his successors in the Liberal leadership, to push on and disestablish the Church of England. Even on the practical issue on which English Nonconformists continued to feel most strongly, the persistence of denominational, mainly Anglican elementary schools as a large part of the national network, they failed to impose their wishes on the country. The disestablishment in 1914 of the Church of England in Wales, where it had little more support than in Ireland, was more a Welsh than an English Nonconformist achievement. Tait's statesmanship helped, therefore, to preserve the establishment of his Church. Whether he could also ensure it enough room for action to sustain its vitality within this union was another matter.

Chapter Eleven

PUSHED ASIDE

May the Lord guide his Church and our country in the somewhat anxious times which seem to threaten the return of Gladstone to the head of affairs with a majority so reckless of all but
politics as to have elected Bradlaugh.

Tait's diary, 18 April 1880

Now that Stanley and Tait are gone, I am the last of the Erastians.

Sir William Harcourt

IN July 1880 while Parliament was still debating the Burials Bill,
Archbishop Tait received word that the Church Association intended to apply to Lord Penzance for imprisonment of three convicted ritualists who had ignored sentences of suspension given
against them: Pelham Dale who had eluded imprisonment in 1877
but later been charged afresh, Enraght of wafer fame, and S. F.
Green from Manchester.[1] Masked by the comparative calm which
had descended over ritual disputes after Tooth's escape, a few suits
had been allowed by the bishops of some dioceses to go ahead and
now, suddenly and simultaneously, reached the stage which
threatened to revive the storm. It would strike just when the
clergy were agitated by the imposition of the Burials Act.

The prospect was all the more distressing to Tait because he
had been moving toward a resolution of the ritual controversy.
Seeing that High Churchmen were impressed by the anxiety of
most bishops after 1877 to avoid court action and to settle disputes independently, Tait had sounded a few ritualists out in the
Spring of 1880 on the possibility of reverting to the original conception of his Public Worship Regulation Bill: arbitration of
ritual disputes by the bishop in his spiritual capacity without
reference to statute law. Ritualists' reaction had been very cautious
particularly about those dioceses governed by the minority of
bishops who showed little desire to conciliate,[2] but at least hopeful discussions had been initiated.

Moreover, the problem of ritualism showed signs of working itself out in practice and informally on a congregational basis, each congregation worshipping as it wished and tolerating without approving of conduct elsewhere. Though Tait strongly disapproved of this[3] as ignoring each church's responsibility to keep the wishes of all residents of its territorial parish in mind, the tendency toward congregationalism in worship seemed unexceptionable in towns with several parish churches in reach of all inhabitants and among which they could pick and choose according to personal predilection. The tendency also allowed the extent of the ritual problem to be seen in calm proportion. Of the roughly five hundred Anglican churches available to Londoners for example, only seventeen were thoroughly ritualist in 1880,[4] surely not cause enough to justify those who found ritualism repugnant in pushing their opposition to extremes. Unofficial acceptance of ritualism on this scale would take the wind of martyrdom out of its sails and so retard, perhaps even stop its advance.

Tait pleaded with the officers of the Church Association to refrain from demanding imprisonment. The ministers in question were, he said, earnest, hard working parish clergy, and the effect of their imprisonment on the Church would be grave. The Church Association held its ground,[5] angry at its previous frustration in the courts and by bishops' vetoes, and determined to show up the timidity of moderate evangelicalism and the vacillation of public opinion both of which were disconcerted by a ritualist's imprisonment. The Church Association too recognized that this was an inappropriate punishment but hoped that its repeated imposition would bring about an amendment of the law to replace imprisonment with summary deprivation. Unsuccessful with the Church Association, Tait tried to induce Dale, the first victim on its agenda, to leave his parish in the custody of a nominee of his bishop,[6] but again without avail. Then Tait urged Penzance to reject the petition for Dale's imprisonment; but relations between the archbishop and his judge had deteriorated badly, Tait being concerned less with vindication of the law than with the peace of the Church, Penzance being convinced that 'an impotent or half-hearted display of the law, is worse surely than no recourse to the law at all'.[7] He declared himself unable to turn the Church Association's request down unless it were objectionable on purely legal grounds which it was not.[8]

So at the end of October Dale found himself in Holloway jail. Fifty churches promptly offered up public prayer for him, and in many of them sermons were preached on his martyrdom.[9] Tait publicly censured the Church Association's procedure,[10] and the bishops in private conclave unanimously agreed with him.[11] But they could not agree on how else to deal with a clergyman who defied the courts.

The next imprisonment, Enraght's, was the least defensible. Penzance waited almost a month before dealing with this case in the hope that Dale's fate would bring Enraght to a better mind.[12] But Enraght had already come to a mind quite satisfactory to his ecclesiastical superiors though not to Penzance. When the complaint about Enraght's conduct of worship first reached his bishop, Philpott of Worcester, Philpott requested Enraght to desist from the practices which seemed of main importance. Enraght refused with the result that Philpott allowed the case to proceed to the courts. In July 1879 as soon as Convocation recommended a revised ornaments rubric which stipulated that vestments should not be used contrary to the monition of the diocesan bishop, Enraght did as Philpott had originally requested.[13] By now it was too late for Philpott to veto the suit, but both he and Tait urged the complainants and the Church Association which was financing their action to withdraw the suit.[14] Philpott's orders to Enraght had not dealt, though, with all the detailed accusations brought against him, and the Church Association would be satisfied with nothing less.[15] The case went ahead.

Penzance condemned Enraght on sixteen counts, some so trivial that Philpott, though an Evangelical, deemed them 'unworthy of attention in matters of complaint still more unworthy of solemn monition from a judge'.[16] Some were practices Enraght claimed never to have used. He refused to obey the decision, and lost even that willingness to obey the bishop he had had. Toward the end of November Penzance agreed to the Church Association's request for Enraght's imprisonment, and he entered Warwick jail. Feeling ran high. The bishop of Rochester's carriage windows were smashed by irate High Churchmen.[17] Worse did not develop only because both imprisonments were expected to end quickly and did. Dale was released on bail on Christmas eve. In January the folly of his incarceration and Enraght's was counteracted by the frivolity of the law, and their punishment was invalidated on the procedural ground that the writs involved were not opened in the presence of justices of Queen's Bench.[18]

These arrests and the passions they revived had a decisive effect on Archbishop Tait. Following as they did hard on the heels of his successful attempt to see the burials controversy settled, they brought his attention sharply back to the Church's internal discord. As soon as Enraght was imprisoned, Tait initiated a many-sided bid for peace. He was nearly sixty-eight; and feeling that he might not live very much longer, he was determined to put the Church's house in order for his successor. Peace became his all-consuming objective. To attain it he poured out all his dwindling energies to within days of his death.

To be securely achieved, peace had to be fought for on three fronts. First, the scandal of the imprisonments must be removed. Tait urged the Church Association to ask for the imprisoned men's release and the imprisoned men to comply with the court's orders governing their conduct of worship.[19] What he could not accomplish by direct persuasion lawyers did on a technicality. Secondly he needed to revive and extend the discussions in search of a settlement of the ritual controversy which were broken off by the autumn imprisonments. Finally, no settlement would commend itself to High Churchmen unless it enhanced the role of Convocation; nor was any settlement likely to be sufficiently authoritative to secure from Parliament whatever legislation it might entail unless Convocation had accepted it. All this implied some adjustment of relations between Convocation and Parliament in favour of Convocation.

The archbishop began his campaign in mid-December 1880 with a speech at Westbere[20] in which he presented churchmen with 'the absolute necessity, if you are dissatisfied with the present state of matters, of gravely and calmly considering the side issues raised in this controversy about ritual', specifically the constitution of the courts, the powers of Convocation, and the authority of the bishops. None of those discontented with the present state of affairs had, he said, come forward with a practicable alternative likely to command general support among clergy and laity. Calmly ask yourself exactly what it is you want, he pleaded; Convocation could consider any definite proposals when its meetings resumed in February.

His request sent clergymen scurrying to their desks or into conference. His letter box was flooded with replies, and many more filled the correspondence columns of ecclesiastical newspapers. Two responses overshadowed the rest. One indicated the extent and direction of High Church discontent, a memorial written, predictably, by Dean Church and eventually signed by nearly four thousand of the clergy.[21] The inevitable counter-memorial was signed by only three hundred.[22] Church's memorial asked first for tolerance: tolerant forbearance from the bishops in dealing with ritual disputes; recognized tolerance within the Church of wide diversities in ceremonial as 'alone consistent with the interests of true religion, and the well-being of the English Church at the present time'. Yet tolerance, the memorial held, would not provide more than a temporary and superficial solution. Lasting peace could be secured only after the system of ecclesiastical courts had been thoroughly reconstructed to command the conscientious obedience of those of the clergy who regarded the present network as an encroachment by the State on the rights of the Church.

This memorial was highly generalized, far from the definite proposals Tait had called for, but was in line with the practical advice he received in the second important communication which his Westbere speech elicited, a letter from J. G. Talbot,[23] one of the M.P.s for the university of Oxford. Talbot suggested asking the cabinet for a royal commission—that refuge of all politicians with vexing problems—on the whole subject of ecclesiastical judicature. 'I can't help thinking it would do much to soothe wounded feelings and relieve distress.'

Tait had been worried about the cabinet as soon as it took office. Gladstone's appointment of one Roman Catholic to represent the Crown as viceroy of India, and of another to the office of Lord Chamberlain,* an office which usually handled some ecclesiastical matters, struck the archbishop as ominous. In August he went the unusual length of voting against a purely political measure of the government's, its Irish Compensation for Disturbance Bill, because he thought it lenient when what Ireland needed was a show of resolute strength. Nevertheless, because of his stand on the Burials Bill his relations with the two members of the cabinet who dominated its ecclesiastical policy, Gladstone

* Lord Ripon and Lord Kenmare respectively.

and Selborne, were fairly good at the moment. He turned to Gladstone with new appreciation in December after reading Disraeli's last novel, *Endymion*, for it left Tait 'with a painful feeling that the writer considers all political life as mere play and gambling.'[24]

Tait had initiated discussions with Gladstone and Selborne on the ritual problem even before Talbot made his suggestion and with a more substantial proposal than Talbot's. The day before his Westbere speech Tait asked them about enacting Convocation's revision of the rubrics.[25] Trifling though the revision was for the most part, it would make the rubrics reflect in some measure the considered judgment of the contemporary Church rather than simply leave the existing sixteenth- and seventeenth-century rubrics to be interpreted by the courts. Moreover the revised ornaments rubric would rule out eucharistic vestments when used against the order of the diocesan bishop. Tait also referred to the fact that Convocation had coupled its report on the rubrics with the Draft Bill which would introduce a new procedure for enacting any revision. The procedure would not only increase the role of Convocation but also curtail disturbing debate in Parliament.

Gladstone's response[26] was sympathetic but very cautious. While assuring the archbishop that the government wished well to every pacific effort by the leaders of the Church, he expressed doubts firstly as to whether Parliament could find time to debate important ecclesiastical legislation, and secondly as to whether Parliament would in any case stomach the Draft Bill. As Beresford Hope put it later: 'Parliament does not desire to legislate upon ecclesiastical matters at all. But when it is driven to legislate there appears to be a ridiculous jealousy of what it thinks over-influence on the part of the Church.'[27] Gladstone told Selborne that, 'If there is any man alive who could procure the adoption of such a plan it is the Archbishop'.[28] It certainly could not be done by the cabinet.

Selborne was completely hostile. The Draft Bill was in his opinion of a piece with 'the pretensions of a large body of the Clergy to reject Parliamentary legislation in Ecclesiastical matters as not binding on their consciences, and to carry that principle to the length of organized disobedience to law'.[29] Nothing was more offensive to Selborne than this. He had drifted far from the

High Churchmanship of his youth and imbibed the prejudices of his profession as barrister and judge until the law replaced the Church as the fixed star in his firmament. Like his fellow judge Penzance, Selborne was almost as erastian as Sir William Harcourt, insistent that the established Church remain subordinate to State-made law and State-made courts.[30] He recognized the straitjacket in which the Church was placed by its dependence for legislation on Parliament,[31] but could see no alternative compatible with establishment except greater use of Convocation within existing procedure. Since this alternative had been followed slowly under Tait during the 1870s, there was no need in Selborne's opinion for such a constitutional readjustment of relations between Convocation and Parliament as the Draft Bill involved.

The mounting pressures on Parliament's time induced all three men to agree to shelve the Draft Bill. From the outset the new Parliament had bogged down, despite its massive Liberal majority, in unproductive but highly charged debate. Much of the 1880 session was lost disputing the right of the recently elected member for Northampton, Charles Bradlaugh, to take his seat because as a conscientious, indeed notorious atheist he had tried to avoid swearing the required oath. Domestic legislation to satisfy the government's Radical supporters fell behind. At the best of times Radicals resented any expenditure of Parliamentary time on legislation for the established Church. Even when Disraeli was in power they had managed to make ecclesiastical legislation difficult. Now when their numbers had increased and action on their demands had been deferred, it would be unthinkable for the government to burden itself with a controversial measure such as the Draft Bill. Even some Conservatives, perhaps many of them, would oppose it as evidence of a High Church premier truckling to Convocation.

Ireland compounded these difficulties. It drove news of Church scandals such as the imprisonments off the main pages of the press and out of men's minds. There would never be another session of Parliament like 1874. Irish nationalist M.P.s under their new leader Charles Stewart Parnell were obstreperous in Parliament. During the autumn, in reply to the Lords' rejection of the Irish Compensation for Disturbance Bill which would have helped tenants evicted for non-payment of rent, Parnell and the Irish Land League fomented unrest in the Irish countryside. The tenantry scarcely needed inciting since the agricultural depression had made their always tenuous position desperate. Arson, cattle maiming, the boycott, assaults on persons and finally murder reduced Ireland to near anarchy. The cabinet, torn between members anxious chiefly to repress the violence and members who wanted chiefly to remedy the tenants' cause for discontent, decided to do both. Remedial legislation trenching on the rights of landlords would shock the landed interest on both sides in Parliament; repressive legislation would provoke Irish nationalist M.P.s. The session ahead was certain to be extraordinarily busy and tumultuous.

Tait could appreciate the impossibility of securing ecclesiastical legislation at the moment. Characteristically he was one of the very few bishops who took an active interest in Irish affairs. Worried and preoccupied though he was by the distress of the Church, he recognized that the situation in Ireland was more grave.[32] He therefore abandoned the Draft Bill with good grace. For the same reason he gave up a related proposal[33] which he had made to Gladstone and Selborne: reform of the composition of the Lower House of the Convocation of Canterbury. At present eighty-seven of its 157 members sat *ex officio* as deans or archdeacons appointed by the Crown or the bishops, another twenty-three represented cathedral chapters composed of royal or episcopal nominees, and only forty-six represented the parochial clergy. The many clergymen working in educational institutions had no spokesmen at all, save the provost of Eton who sat *ex officio*. If the proportion of parochial representatives could be increased, Convocation would be better able to claim that it expressed the will of the clergy and so to enhance its legislative position. Selborne insisted, however, that because the Act of Union between England and Scotland safeguarded the governments of their respective established Churches, any change in Convocation would require another Act of Parliament.[34] Again the need for legislation as well as a threat to Convocation's independence.

Tait fell back upon Talbot's suggestion of a royal commission on the ecclesiastical courts. The advantages of the proposal were manifold. To be put into effect it required only the consent of the cabinet and, if thought desirable, a simple address from one House of Parliament. Royal commissions composed of representatives of Church and State were the traditional way to work out solutions for problems affecting their union. It was a royal commission which had revised the prayer book in 1661 and another which had tackled the rubrics in 1867. The commission's report could lead naturally to a bill embodying its recommendations, a bill to which the government could be expected to give serious consideration because of its source.

Tait, however, may not have expected or even strongly desired eventual legislative action on the ecclesiastical courts. Primarily what he wanted through the appointment of the commission was immediate peace, in particular the replacement of public, inflamed debate by a practical examination within closed doors of the grounds for discontent. Once a commission was at work, moderates of all schools would discourage agitation both because something was being done and because agitation would make the commission's search for a generally acceptable solution hopeless. Tait was also confident that many grievances would prove upon investigation to be illusory and many current schemes for reform to be impracticable. The commission would thus diffuse 'sound education'[35] even if it did not come up with a solution to the controversy over ceremonial and the courts; and in the meantime peace.

Furthermore, appointment of a commission could be made to seem a perfectly neutral resort because the Church Association as well as High Churchmen were dissatisfied with the present state of affairs. The Church Association was annoyed by the intricate procedure in ecclesiastical litigation, with the need to resort to imprisonment to gain prompt obedience to court orders, and with the bishops' power of veto. In reality, however, the commission was sure to concern itself mainly with High Church grievances since High Churchmen were comparatively united and insistent in voicing their discontent, whereas Evangelicals were divided and demoralized. The commission was therefore a disguised avenue of retreat and escape for Archbishop Tait. It enabled him to throw the Public Worship Regulation Act and the policy for which it stood, repression of ritualism through the courts, into the melting pot without admitting their failure* and without having any alternative to propose.

---

* The farthest he went in this direction was in a letter to Disraeli (1 Feb. 1881): 'I may confess that the Act of 1874 has not worked smoothly.' Beaconsfield papers, B/XII/F/19.

After taking a short time to consider Tait's proposal, Gladstone promised him the government's co-operation.[36] Apart from obviating contentious ecclesiastical legislation for the moment, a royal commission might lead to genuine toleration of the very High Church which Gladstone desired. He was pleasantly surprised that the archbishop should wish to talk with and conciliate them. 'When I think of the days of the Public Worship Regulation Act', Gladstone told Pusey, 'I can hardly believe him to be the same man.'[37]

Tait sustained Gladstone's pleasure by writing to Disraeli and Salisbury to secure their agreement, thus preventing serious Parliamentary controversy. Disraeli replied[38] that a commission might do some good, though only if proposed to Parliament by Tait and not the government; any initiative of the government would be interpreted as a step toward disestablishment. Disraeli was reluctant to give his mind to ecclesiastical problems at all; 'I have many other difficult things to consider'. It was his last comment on Church affairs. Salisbury also agreed to the commission,[39] but with characteristic penetration stripped away any illusions which might be attached to its creation. Because commissioners would be selected to represent the full spectrum of Anglican opinion they were unlikely to agree on an adequate remedy. Even if they did, Parliament would in all probability either refuse to touch the question or act against the high church. In a word, the commission would mean only delay and whatever benefits delay could confer. 'It will not cure the evil: and the same causes which have brought on the present crisis, will still exist, to bring it on again.'

Salisbury went on to express his hope that the issuing of a commission would be accompanied by an attempt by the bishops to smooth over local disputes rather than allow them to go before the courts for settlement. This was precisely what Tait intended since otherwise the pacifying effect of the commission would be lost. In an unprecedented statement, almost a speech from the throne, to both houses of the Convocation of Canterbury before they moved into their separate chambers, the archbishop placed responsibility for settlement of ritual disputes squarely on the bishops,[40] thereby implying that they would veto all new litigation at least until the commission had reported.* Almost all the bishops

* Tait felt obliged to deny this implication in the Lords (*Hansard*, 3rd series, CCLXIV (1881), 1504), but nonetheless it was generally recognized.

in both provinces were willing to follow this policy. Even Ryle, the new bishop of Liverpool and the most determined Evangelical on the bench, agreed to prevent proceedings threatened by the Church Association against a ritualist in his diocese, J. Bell Cox.[41]

The one dissident was Thomson, the archbishop of York. On holiday in Biarritz, he had not been present for the annual new year's meeting of the English episcopate which had discussed Tait's proposals. Thomson was full of gloom about ecclesiastical affairs despite his pleasant surroundings. Parliament would disestablish the Scottish Church before the next election he predicted,[42] and afterwards if ritual disorders in England persisted would tackle the English Church. Once disestablished, the Church would split. These forbodings did not arouse him to make any new preventive proposals or to welcome anyone else's. 'No court that could be devised would satisfy the ritualist; unless it would shew that he could get off', Thomson told Tait. 'Remember the triumph of poor Sam [Wilberforce] when he heard that the bishops were turned out of the Privy Council. But the Ridsdale case soon made the new court, for which the rit[ualist]s had striven, as unpopular as the old.' A royal commission on the courts combined with a moratorium on ritual litigation would only serve to take the heat off ritualists and so give them time to entrench themselves. The archbishop of York urged Tait to hold to the policy of the Public Worship Regulation Act. Tait mollified him by promising to present Parliament with the case for a commission in such a way as to dispel the impression that he was retreating from his stance of 1874.[43] Thomson fell into line though with persistent reservations.

Tait's motion in the House of Lords for appointment of the commission 'to inquire into the constitution and working of the Ecclesiastical Courts, as created or modified under the Reformation Statutes of the twenty-fourth and twenty-fifth years of King Henry the Eighth and any subsequent Acts' was accepted with little debate,[44] the only protest coming from the most fanatically Protestant of the peers, Lord Oranmore and Browne, an Irishman. Gladstone then selected the commissioners in close consultation with Tait. The men who agreed to serve formed a representative, well qualified group: both archbishops, six bishops including Benson of Truro who was to be Tait's successor, a battery of lawyers including Penzance and the Lord Chief Justice, distinguished laymen such as Cross, and assorted clergymen most notably William Stubbs, regius professor of modern history at Oxford, whose scholarly researches for the commission into the history of ecclesiastical judicature were to be of permanent value: twenty-five in all. They asked Tait to serve as chairman, and set to work at the end of May interrogating witnesses and examining written submissions.

The Green Case

Calm had begun to descend in February when the public first heard of the projected commission and pause in litigation. Before the commission met, tempers were rekindled. On 19 March 1880 the third of the ritualists who had been on the Church Association's books for imprisonment since the previous summer, Sidney Fairthorne Green, went to jail.

Green's history[45] was a perfect paradigm of the ritual controversy. A zealous and able priest, he served in a slum, Miles Platting, one of the most densely populated, poorest and dirtiest suburbs of Manchester. His predecessor was an Evangelical who attracted a large congregation drawn from all over Manchester. Green quickly dispersed that congregation but replaced it with another, also drawn from all over Manchester.[46] Though always a ritualist, he had been willing to restrain his practice in the early 1870s when the bishop of Manchester, James Fraser, so ordered; but Green became intransigent in the middle of the decade when faced by Archbishop Tait's policy of repression and the Public Worship Regulation Act.

In 1878 320 people calling themselves parishioners sent a petition to Bishop Fraser complaining of Green's practices. The petition was a rough piece of work, obviously put together by poorly educated men; Fraser doubted the validity of some signatures but felt unable to dismiss the petitioners without giving them a fuller opportunity of presenting their case. The Church Association then took up the case and knocked the petition into shape as a formal complaint by three parishioners under the Public Worship Act. Though Fraser disliked the Church Association's intervention, he did not consider that as sufficient reason to veto proceedings on the complaint. He asked Green, in the light of the recent Lambeth Conference's resolutions on ceremonial, to regulate his

275

conduct of worship as his bishop advised. Green refused, saying that to give up the mixed chalice, the one of his practices to which most exception was taken, would be to 'deny my Lord and imperil my own salvation'.[47]

Fraser might still have used his veto, justifying his action perhaps on the grounds that litigation on ceremonial had proved contrary to the best interests of the Church. He allowed the suit to go before the courts because, as he explained,

> when the excesses are just in those points which have been most signally declared to be illegal, and the Bishop's counsel and entreaty alike are disregarded, I am at a loss to know, unless absolute anarchy is to prevail, how a Bishop is to act except to take the course marked out for him by the law. If I do not like the law, I am justified in using every effort to get it repealed: but as long as it is the law, I am bound by all the obligations of a good citizen and a loyal Churchman to obey it. I may save my conscience, by protesting while I obey, but I must obey.[48]

The real victim of the suit was Bishop Fraser. He had been a very tolerant Broad Churchman, admired throughout the Church for his robust common sense, blunt speech, and involvement in the life of his industrial diocese. The prosecution of Green undermined Fraser's well-earned popularity and turned him into a hard disciple of the rule of law.

In 1879 Penzance issued Green with a monition which he disregarded, then pronounced a sentence of suspension which was similarly ineffective. Now Green was in Lancaster jail, and no technical slip could be discovered to release him. The Church Association had at last mastered its craft. It pressed its legal victory to the point of outrage. In order to recover its costs which Green had been condemned to pay—costs which included the hire of informers—the prosecution secured an order for the sale of his household furniture.* His wife and children were obliged to leave home.

Hopes for peace suffered a setback as the ecclesiastical temperature shot up. It did not reach boiling point partly because imprisonment was generally recognized to be an anomaly which the courts commission would straighten out and partly because of the farce to which Green's imprisonment gave rise. For over a year and a half he held on to his mantle of martyrdom, foiling attempts

---

* In extenuation of the Church Association's conduct, it should be noted that legally Green's effects had to be sold before his living could be sequestered.

by nearly all the great officers of Church and State—the prime minister, the Lord Chancellor, the Home Secretary, both archbishops—and many lesser lights to get him out of jail. Since the Public Worship Regulation Act had not contemplated imprisonment, it made no provision for a prisoner's release. The Act's inadequacies became ridiculously obvious.

Still, Green's imprisonment could have been stopped at any moment either by himself or by the prosecution. Green had only to intimate willingness to obey Penzance's court, but said that for him to do so would be no better than for an early Christian to burn incense to the gods of the Roman empire.[49] The prosecution had only to apply to the court for Green's release, and they might have done so if Bishop Fraser had agreed to prevent further violations of the law at Miles Platting. Fraser could have installed a replacement for Green (such as had led to Tooth's release), or he could have closed the church. He refused to do the first for fear of a violent protest by Green's congregation, and the second for fear of bearing out ritualists' claims that the alternative to ritualism was empty pews.[50] Accordingly Green remained behind bars. Parnell, whose agitation in Ireland seemed an infinitely more serious offence against law and order, went to jail seven months later than Green and was released six months earlier.

Early in August 1881 Lord Beauchamp presented Parliament with a Bill* providing for automatic release after six months imprisonment of anyone committed to jail for contempt of an ecclesiastical court. Archbishop Tait and, more grudgingly, Lord Selborne supported the Bill and in modified form† it passed the Lords. Gladstone did not, however, throw the government's support behind it in the Commons because it provoked considerable opposition from Protestant opinion and from lawyers concerned for the majesty of law and because it did not even satisfy all high churchmen.[51] The Commons did not find time for the Bill till an evening at the end of the session. Then just as Beresford Hope began to present the Bill, W. E. Forster, the Chief Secretary for Ireland, drew attention to the fact that less than forty M.P.s were present, and the House was automatically adjourned.[52]

* Called the Ecclesiastical Courts Regulation Bill. *Hansard*, 3rd series, CCLXIV (1881), 1346–58.

† Now called the Discharge of Contumacious Prisoners Bill, it integrated the proposed change more thoroughly into the procedure prescribed under the Church Discipline and Public Worship Regulation Acts.

In September Gladstone asked Harcourt about the possibility of releasing Green on medical grounds. Harcourt wrote to the prison commissioners implying that he would be glad of an excuse to free Green. Their reply drew a cry of mock despair from Harcourt to Gladstone: 'What is one to do with a martyr who gains 9 lb. in weight in his bondage?' High Churchmen were showering Green with edible tokens of their esteem.[53] Many of the clergy urged the bishops collectively to petition the Crown for Green's release. The government's law officers blocked this resort by insisting that it would be tantamount to a claim by the Crown to set the law aside,[54] the very power of dispensation which James II had used to aid his fellow papists, thus bringing on the Glorious Revolution.

In order to divert the bishops from such extra-legal action, Selborne pressed Tait in the first few months of 1882 to try again for legislation to release Green.[55] As a result the archbishop of York devised a bill to be in effect for three years by which time the courts commission would have recommended some permanent and general settlement of the problem of ritualism and the courts. Until then any person committed to jail for contempt of an ecclesiastical court could be released if the provincial archbishop informed the court that the imprisonment was causing scandal.[56] In other words an Act was to be passed treating the legitimate consequences of another Act still on the statute books as scandalous. Both Convocations and all but two of the bishops, Liverpool and Norwich who were Evangelicals, endorsed the bill, as did Selborne.[57] The Lords passed it in May with very little debate, Lord Oranmore and Browne alone opposing it.

But again failure in the Commons. This session of Parliament like the last was clogged with contentious debate, on Bradlaugh, Egypt and Ireland, and on amendment of the Commons' rules to overcome the tactics which Parnell had introduced in 1881 of sustained obstruction of the business of the House. None of the domestic legislation promised in the Queen's speech at the beginning of the session to appease the Radicals was enacted. Meanwhile, the Bill for Green's release aroused strong opposition among members of the Church Association.[58] In mid-July when Archbishop Thomson's Bill seemed unable even to gain a hearing in the Commons, Tait urged Gladstone to give it the necessary facilities; but the government was unable to add to its legislative burdens.[59] The Bill finally came up for debate late on the second last day of the session. Dillwyn, a Liberationist, proposed adjournment; the Attorney General announced his personal opposition as a lawyer. Then abruptly the House was again counted out since less than forty members were present.[60] Gladstone had obtained promises from another twenty Liberals to be in their places when the Bill came on for debate, but they arrived just after the count.[61] The hope to free Green by legislation evaporated.

Another key to his cell was at hand. Under the Public Worship Regulation Act, if a clergyman refused obedience to the courts for three years after a sentence of suspension was pronounced against him, he would automatically be deprived of his benefice. Accordingly Green ceased to be incumbent of Miles Platting on 16 August 1882. Tait, in bed from the exhaustion which would lead to his death, wrote immediately urging Gladstone to try by executive action to release Green from what now seemed the superabundant punishment of prison.[62] However, technically Green was in jail not because he had conducted worship illegally but because he showed contempt of court in ignoring Penzance's orders. In strict law Green might not be entitled to his freedom until he purged himself of this contempt by indicating willingness to submit to the court. There was also much doubt as to whether he would respect deprivation of his benefice any more than his previous suspension. Gladstone wrote back that although he and his colleagues were anxious to see Green out, the way was still impeded by legal difficulties.[63] The letter found Tait in a serious decline, and further action was deferred.

A few weeks before, the archbishop had delivered what proved to be his last address in the House of Lords.[64] It was directed against the duke of Argyll's attempt in connection with the Bradlaugh affair to allow members of either House of Parliament to make an affirmation before admission to Parliament rather than take the existing oath. Through its reference to God the oath was the last faint theological restriction on membership in the legislature. Very High Churchmen were not greatly interested in this controversy because they considered the supposedly Christian character of Parliament to be already a fiction. After all, John Stuart Mill had been an M.P. Liddon thought that Bradlaugh's admission might even benefit the Church by making Parliament's unfitness to handle ecclesiastical business obvious.[65] Some of the Liberal bishops also tended to accept the necessity of admitting Bradlaugh as one of the few steps remaining to be taken toward the creation of a State which was open to all citizens regardless of their religious beliefs although it recognized one denomination as the State Church. Tait, however, fought to the end to keep the State religious just as he strove to keep the Church national and established. The attempt to alter the oath was defeated in the Lords on this occasion by a vote of over two to one. Yet the archbishop knew that his speech, which was delivered without his former force, had not won the victory. As he left the chamber he whispered to his chaplain, 'They didn't listen to me. It is the first time for twenty years. My work is done.'[66]

The comment was a telling one not only for the aged archbishop but for his Church. Parliament would not listen now to either. The House of Commons was pushing Church affairs aside. All of the ecclesiastical legislation which was attempted in 1881 and 1882 met a fate similar to that of the bills for Green's release. The most important attempt came as a result of the royal commission on cathedrals which Disraeli had appointed and Gladstone renewed. It recommended the formation of a committee of the privy council with power to examine, approve or amend, and so give force of law to what new statutes the royal commission might propose for each cathedral.[67] These powers went beyond those of the usual statutory commission such as the recent university commissions whose recommendations could be turned down by either House of Parliament. Nevertheless, Gladstone gave his approval to the proposal. Tait as chairman of the royal commission presented the necessary Bill to Parliament in June 1882, and the Lords passed it.[68] It was held up in the Commons until near the end of the session and then met with another count out.[69]

Legislative paralysis was turning out to be the alternative to disestablishment. Opposed to home rule for itself, the Church fell under what amounted to a boycott. In the autumn of 1881 Captain Boycott, an Irish landlord who had taken over the land of an evicted tenant, met with a new punishment inspired by Parnell: Boycott was shunned by the surrounding Irish citizenry and was thus deprived of essential services. So M.P.s who belonged to the

Liberation Society cut off essential legislative services from the Church of England whose establishment deprived them of religious equality. Their opposition in the Commons was enough to achieve this whenever, as was usual, ecclesiastical bills did not command support among virtually all Churchmen.

The prime cause of the legislative paralysis of the Church was not, however, the hostility of a minority pressure group, nor was it the Church's internal divisions. All Churchmen but the stiffest supporters of the Church Association and the most rigorous legalists seemed to accept the wisdom of Thomson's Bill for Green's release. It and all the other ecclesiastical bills foundered because the government and the House of Commons were preoccupied with urgent purely political issues: anarchy in Ireland, backlash in Afghanistan, Egypt and South Africa after Disraeli's imperialistic thrusts, economic depression, and Radical demands for far-reaching reform at home. However distressed the established Church, its problems seemed less than important in such a context. And whatever inclination politicians might have to enact Church bills was diminished by embarrassment at the quixotry of the Public Worship Regulation Act.

The government treated the Church's legislative requests like those of any major but private interest and refused to sponsor though it might support them. Therefore when ecclesiastical bills reached the Commons they had to be placed in the custody of a private member—generally a Conservative was chosen—who then had to compete for debating time against a welter of other private members with bills of their own. If he was lucky and gained a hearing, it came generally at the end of the session. By that time M.P.s, tired by long months and late nights of debate on the major legislation and issues of the session, were leaving for the country; hence the count outs. Attachment to the Church was too weak to hold even forty members in their seats.

In 1868 when Tait became archbishop, Irish disestablishment topped the Parliamentary agenda while English disestablishment seemed certain and not far distant. In 1882 when he spoke in Parliament for the last time, English disestablishment was no closer and was less likely. Yet this was not a flattering achievement. The survival of the establishment was the result not only of Radical Nonconformists' inability to force their will on the country, but also of a general decline of popular and political interest in questions of Church and State. Disestablishment would have been a backhanded compliment to the Church. Instead Parliament began to ignore it as much as possible. This development was all the more significant because it occurred during the time when in Archbishop Tait the Church had a spokesman more respected in Parliament than any other prelate at least since the seventeenth century. He himself never came to doubt the wisdom of establishment. When Archbishop Trench of the disestablished Irish Church failed to make reference to the troubled condition of Ireland in his Charge of 1881, Tait noted the omission as possibly another indication that disestablishment withdrew a Church from concern for the social and political life of the community.[70] Yet even Tait had been obliged to rely more and more on Convocation. Apparently England's way of becoming a secular society was not to break Church from State but rather to push Church affairs aside.

Tait slept so much in the last two weeks of August 1882 that his doctors feared that death was on its way. Instead the rest gave Tait enough energy to reflect from his bed on the recent history of the Church of England and to bandage two of the sores distracting the Church.

First, using a recently published volume of reminiscences of Oxford and the Oxford Movement as his springboard, the archbishop published an article[71] in which he pronounced his verdict on men and movements in his time. He wrote with astonishing candour for a man still in high office—he called Gladstone 'at one time at least . . . the great lay high-priest of the Oxford School'[72]—but he sensed that in spite of revived strength his day of power and responsibility was almost over. The bulk of the article consisted of an indictment of the Oxford Movement and praise of Thomas Arnold and his following. He accused the first of promoting scepticism in Oxford and the country at large by trying 'to stiffen the great national Church after an alien and antiquated model'.[73] Stanley's *Life of Arnold* and the last two volumes of Arnold's sermons on the other hand 'set forth that view of a comprehensive, loving, yet zealous Christian teaching which approved itself to the consciences and seeks to be embodied in the lives of the vast majority of intelligent persons throughout the kingdom'.[74]

By any standard Tait's judgment was too severe on the one and too favourable toward the other. He never understood that the Oxford Movement and ritualism expressed the strongest purely religious impulse in the mid-nineteenth century Church. Pure religion unrelated to and often at odds with the mundane but exciting growth of Victorian thought, industry, politics and power had little attraction for the archbishop. On the other hand, the very determination with which he adhered to his own ideal of a national Church in a Christian country sometimes suggested that he knew that its prospects were fading. 'When I despair—', he wrote in his diary in 1881, 'the cause of a liberal National Church may be said to be gone.'[75] The postscript he added, 'Unless when I die God finds as He very likely will—a better instrument', was more pious than confident.

The bite of his final review of the Church was not in his analysis of the past but of the present. He recognized that the controversies of his lifetime would not be the controversies of the future: 'the Church and the world', he said, 'seem entering on totally new phases.'[76] This remark attracted great attention and all commentators endorsed it. Neither they nor the archbishop knew quite what these new phases were. One change which he expected was the waning of the Oxford Movement's influence,[77] whereas in fact it was embracing an expanding circle of the clergy.

But another change all could see. Roughly from 1830 to 1880 England had been occupied with religious debate more than most countries and more than at most times in its own history. Although symptomatic of theological unsettlement and doubt as much as of faith, the debate had been between rival faiths and degrees of faith. By 1882 the debate was subsiding to the discomfiture of faith: 'the age', the archbishop knew, 'has become sceptical.'[78] Superficially he was inclined to blame the Oxford Movement for this. Yet his leniency toward ritualism in recent years had been dictated partly by his realization that in the battle against scepticism the Church needed all its forces.

Apart from reviewing the past Tait used his Indian summer to extract and keep ritualists from jail in order to clear the decks for the report of the courts commission. In October Selborne and he put pressure on Bishop Fraser to apply to Lord Penzance for Green's release in view of his deprivation.[79] Selborne argued that Penzance could then summon all parties to the suit to attend before him and could tell the prosecution, who would probably bow to his request, that they should agree to the release. With their consent it would be fully legal.

Fraser hesitated because Green's supporters, the English Church Union and Sir Percival Heywood who had given him the benefice, had declared their refusal to respect his deprivation, and therefore in all probability Green would refuse too. Finally, with grave misgivings, Fraser did what might have freed Green many months before: he appointed a temporary replacement to look after Miles Platting: and simultaneously he applied for Green's release.[80] Penzance, implying surprise that this had not been requested in August, promptly agreed on the ground that imprisonment became unnecessary the moment Green was deprived of his benefice.[81] Early in November, almost twenty months after Green had entered Lancaster jail, he left it. The trouble was not over. Heywood as patron nominated the Rev. H. Cowgill, Green's curate, to succeed him. Since Cowgill would perpetuate the practices for which Green had been condemned, Fraser refused to institute him. Heywood sued the bishop, and the case dragged on till 1884 when Heywood lost. Nevertheless, once Green was free the sequel was anti-climactic and had few repercussions.

By November Tait's health was again in decline. Yet he was anxious to dispose of the last ritual case still before the courts. Mackonochie had been in trouble with them continually since 1867. After his temporary suspension in 1870 he had ignored or eluded judicial censure. In 1882 the courts closed in around him, and deprivation seemed imminent. This might rock high churchmen even more than Green's long imprisonment, for Mackonochie was the patriarch of slum ritualism. As soon as Green was freed, Tait dictated an appeal to Mackonochie to resign his benefice in the interests of peace and of setting 'men's minds free for the pressing duties which devolve upon the Church in the face of prevailing sin and unbelief'.[82] Mackonochie was not, however, to do all the conceding. Tait's letter represented a surrender on his part since it revealed how anxious he was to end the crusade of the 1870s against ritualism and to keep ecclesiastical controversies out of the courts. This was what the High Church opposition to him had sought throughout his primacy.

It was hard if not impossible for Mackonochie to resist the appeal because it came from a man on his death-bed, a fact of which Tait made use. Furthermore, Mackonochie and Tait had retained strong personal respect for each other from the days of Tait's London episcopate. Yet the whole, highly effective strategy of thoroughgoing ritualists since 1870 had been one of unyielding resistance to all authority, force or argument. Mackonochie pleaded for time to consider the request.[83] After ten days during which Tait's condition continued to deteriorate, Randall Davidson as his chaplain stepped up the pressure. He wrote to Mackonochie that 'among the very few matters concerning the outside world which at present find a recurring place in [the archbishop's] thoughts' was Mackonochie's response to his request; every morning the archbishop asked if a letter from him had arrived.[84] Mackonochie replied by asking for assurance that his bishop, the bishop of London, would help him find other work in the diocese.[85] The Society of the Holy Cross met in emergency session to advise Mackonochie, and the general feeling was against his resignation.[86] But next day, without waiting for Davidson's reassurance, Mackonochie sent Tait his agreement.[87] Tait had secured the temporary pacification of the Church which he had sought for the last two years.

Mackonochie sensed that any benefit which the Church derived from his agreement would be at high cost to himself. 'I am contented,' he told Tait, 'if so it be, to give up my peace for the Church's.' It was to be. Mackonochie's action was greeted with admiration from all but extreme Evangelicals and shed a becoming light on ritualists generally. Thus he helped secure them a recognized place within the established Church. Even *The Times* expressed willingness now to tolerate ritualism though not high church doctrine.[88] But Mackonochie lost his own peace. His resignation took the form of an exchange of livings with the Rev. Robert Suckling of St. Peter's, London Docks, but this did not free Mackonochie as Tait thought it would from further prosecution.[89] Subsequently Mackonochie's mind began to fail him. In 1887 he lost himself in a winter storm in the Highlands and died.

Tait died on 1 December 1882, one week after receiving word of Mackonochie's agreement, fourteen years after becoming primate. It was Advent Sunday, the same Sunday on which his wife had died four years earlier. He had no wish to survive once strength to work was gone. In another three weeks he would have been seventy, old for someone with a damaged heart.

Few archbishops of Canterbury have received as high and wide acclaim at death as he. *The Times* gave him credit for the 'vastly strengthened' hold of the Church on the nation 'since the time when men were predicting its downfall in 1870'.[90] *The Times* also played down his responsibility for the Public Worship Regulation Act: 'Tait has stood at the helm in troublous times;' it said, 'he has steered the ship past many a storm, and he leaves it in comparatively tranquil waters.' Whether or not the Church of England was the nation's Church, he was recognized as the nation's archbishop and was offered burial in Westminster Abbey.* A lament on his passing was preached in a Jewish synagogue in Liverpool.[91] His correspondence with Mackonochie, which reached the papers just after his death, won genuine praise from his stiffest opponents during life, the High Church. His most lasting tribute was the change he effected in his office. For over a century before he became primate the see of Canterbury had been bestowed on safe and retiring men. Even Tait's appointment had been regarded by many, and momentarily by himself, as honourable retirement after his exertions in London which seemed to have shattered his health. When he died, all the papers insisted that an extremely able successor must be found.

The praise which was heaped upon Tait was, however, open to ominous interpretation. What *The Times* described as the strength of the Church's hold on the nation was in fact the comparative indifference of Parliament to ecclesiastical affairs and questions of Church and State. What it described as the 'tranquil waters' in which the Church found itself were in fact backwaters. For example, the elementary schools over which it retained control were mainly in rural areas and not in the van of educational advance. At higher levels of intellectual discussion the Church was on the defensive and spoke with hesitancy and confusion.

What made the appointment of an able replacement for Tait mandatory was the continuing strain over ceremonial and the courts. Tait's success in regard to Green and Mackonochie had

---

* which, after consultation with the Queen, his family declined. He was buried, as he had wished, in Addington churchyard beside the country residence of the archbishops of Canterbury.

merely dealt with scandals. Lasting pacification depended on the ability of the royal commission on ecclesiastical courts to discover a generally acceptable way to relax the underlying tension. Then Parliament would have to be persuaded to enact whatever legislation about the judiciary was required. Failure was likely both in the commission and in Parliament. The witnesses whom the commission heard revealed again the unbridgeable gulf between the extremes of high and low church. Militant evangelicals argued that the Public Worship Regulation Act was too favourable towards ritualists, that enforcement of the law should be easier, quicker and cheaper, and that the bishops' power of veto should be abolished.[92] Mackonochie, on the other hand, maintained that there should be no exercise of the royal supremacy in spiritual matters, that all jurisdiction in the Christian Church had been uncertain since its original union with the State under the emperor Constantine, that no valid ecclesiastical court had existed in England since the Reformation, and that the present bishops' injunctions had no authority because they were influenced by civil courts.[93]

Nevertheless, encouraged by the weak resistance of moderate evangelical witnesses to moderate high church demands,[94] the commission was working on a settlement when its deliberations were suspended by Tait's illness. The prospect of his death threw the commission into uncertainty;[95] no other man was likely to be able to secure Parliament's approval to a solution based on concessions to the High Church. After his passing, however, the commission held its ground and produced a report the principles of which had been endorsed by the dead archbishop, so his chaplain and the new archbishop claimed.[96] Even in death Tait was regarded as the Church's most effective voice in Parliament.

The report[97] recommended revitalization of purely ecclesiastical diocesan courts in which the role of the bishop would be greatly enhanced, and re-establishment of the ecclesiastical character of the provincial judge. The court of final appeal, representing the royal supremacy, would be a purely lay tribunal. It was 'not in any sense to determine what is the doctrine or ritual of the Church, but to decide whether the impugned opinions or practices are in conflict with the authoritative formularies of the Church in such a sense as to require correction or punishment',[98] a useful though fuzzy distinction. Imprisonment for refusal to obey a court order was replaced by suspension until the order was obeyed or by deprivation in the case of a beneficed clergyman who disobeyed an initial sentence of suspension. These main recommendations and the other subordinate ones were almost exactly what moderate High Churchmen had demanded in the 1870s. The report represented an attempt to uphold something of the authority of the law by tailoring the courts to High Church wishes: increasing the ecclesiastical character of the lower courts, and reducing the ecclesiastical authority of the supreme court which acted perforce in the name of the Crown.

There is no evidence to doubt that Archbishop Tait approved of this tactical retreat. Like all his manoeuvres to settle the ritual controversy, it was not likely to succeed. Penzance, still championing royal supremacy and law as Tait had done until 1877, refused to sign the report, and the archbishop of York signed reluctantly.[99] Over half the commissioners signed with qualifications,[100] some like Thomson of York in favour of a more rigorous respect for law, some for more respect for the Church's spiritual autonomy. Even moderate High Churchmen were not entirely satisfied. Dean Church and Gladstone regarded the commission's report as a useful contribution to the education of the Church but not as adequate in its exact recommendations.[101] With so much disagreement the report had no hope of producing legislation. Furthermore, Benson, the new archbishop of Canterbury, was out of his element in Parliament and came to be treated by some political leaders such as Balfour with contempt.[102] In the absence of any generally respected court to decide ritual disputes, trouble continued to erupt. Enraght was inhibited from serving in his parish by his bishop in 1883;[103] Bishop Ryle permitted proceedings under the Public Worship Regulation Act which led to the imprisonment of J. Bell Cox in 1887; in the 1890s ritualism entered a still more advanced stage provoking Protestant sentiment anew.

Still, the royal commission of 1881 and its report in 1883 marked a turning point for the Church of England. The one sustained effort to repress ritualism in order to keep the Church in harmony with popular tastes and prejudices was abandoned. Ritualists' policy of civil disobedience and its consequence of imprisonment had both embarrassed evangelicals and cemented an alliance with the moderate High Church, thus posing a threat to the unity of the Church if the attempt to crush ritualism was kept up. Archbishop

Tait was therefore obliged to subordinate his concern for national opinion and devote himself to mending his ecclesiastical fences. Forays against ritualism after his death were sporadic and half-hearted.

Tait's death marked the end of a generation in Church and State. Dean Stanley, Disraeli and Edward Miall died in 1881, Pusey before Tait in 1882; Shaftesbury who died in 1885 knew that he had lived beyond his age; Gladstone was revered as a figure from the past before he died in 1898. Their generation had not been just one in a continuing story. It was the last age in which bishops and the leaders of schools of thought within the Church were figures of national importance. It marked the last serious attempt to make the Church of England the Church of the English. The heights of the Church of England's mid-Victorian strength and security sloped away to inconsequential lowlands.

References and Notes

INTRODUCTION

1. Census of Great Britain, 1851. Religious Worship. England and Wales. Report and Tables, Parl. Papers, 1852–3, LXXXIX, 158.
2. *Ibid.*, 159.
3. *Quarterly Review*, CXXXVII, 273 (July 1874), 147.
4. *Catharine and Craufurd Tait, Wife and Son of Archibald Campbell Archbishop of Canterbury:* A memoir (London: Macmillan and Co., 1879).
5. Davidson and Benham, *Tait*, I, v–vi.
6. J. B. Hope Simpson, *Rugby since Arnold* (London, 1967), 13.
7. Disraeli to the Queen, 4 Nov. 1868, in G. E. Buckle, ed., *The Letters of Queen Victoria*, second series (London, 1926), I, 550.
8. Disraeli to Derby, 12 Nov. 1868, Monypenny and Buckle, *Disraeli*, V, 69.
9. *Op. cit.*, V, 70.

CHAPTER ONE

The Disestablishment of the Irish Church, 1868–1869

1. Robert Blake, *Disraeli*, 496 and 498.
2. Census of Ireland for 1861, Parl. Papers, 1863, LIX, 6.
3. Even Conservative defenders of the Irish Church admitted this, and during the election campaign. See J. R. Page, *The Question for the Electors* (London, 1868), 34, and G. A. Denison, *The Charge of the Archdeacon of Taunton* (London, 1868), 12.
4. Edward Miall declared at Manchester in 1859: 'The Irish Church will be the first victim. The English Establishment will follow'. Quoted in B. J. Mason, *The Rise of Combative Dissent, 1832–1859* (Southampton M.A. thesis, 1958), 161.
5. The Rev. H. Allon to Gladstone, 5 May 1868, Gladstone Papers, Add. MSS. 44,095, ff. 310–11; and H. J. Hanham, *The General Election of* 1868 (Cambridge Ph.D. dissertation no. 2491, 1953), chapt. II, 9.

References

6. *Speeches of the Right Honourable William Ewart Gladstone, M.P., in South-west Lancashire, October, 1868* (Liverpool, [1868]), 53 and 68.
7. Gladstone's memorandum to the Queen on the government's Irish Church policy, 13 Jan. 1869, copy, Gladstone papers, Add. MSS. 44,757, ff. 95–6.
8. G. F. A. Best, *Shaftesbury*, 61–2.
9. G. A. Denison, *The Churches of England and Ireland, One Church by Identity of Divine Trust* (London, 1868), 10; *Chronicle of Convocation*, 1869, p. 56.
10. *Chronicle of Convocation*, 1868, pp. 1552 and 1556; and Denison, *op. cit.*, 11 and 21.
11. Denison, *op. cit.*, 36.
12. Birks, *Church and State* (London, 1869), 410.
13. E. M. Goulburn, *John William Burgon*, II, 35. Cf. Denison, *op. cit.*, 24.
14. *Chronicle of Convocation*, 1868, p. 1489.
15. *Church and State Defence Society:* Address to the Crown, a letter from Denison to the ed. of *John Bull*, 15 July 1868; and the *Liberator*, 1 Jan. 1869.
16. Hanham, *op. cit.*, chapt. II, 23–4.
17. See A. T. Lee, *The Irish Church Question*, Eight short papers (London, 1868); and J. R. Page, *op. cit.*
18. A. T. Lee, *op. cit.*, papers III and IV.
19. See *Hansard*, 3rd series, CXCII (1868), 2122–9, and *Speeches Delivered at the Great Meeting Held in St. James's Hall . . . May 6, 1868, in support of the United Church of England and Ireland* (London, 1868), 16–19.
20. *Hansard*, 3rd series, CXCII (1868), 2128–9.
21. See Sir Joseph Napier to Tait, 1868, Tait papers, vol. 85, f. 190.
22. F. M. Sadler's speech, *Chronicle of Convocation*, 1868, p. 1516.
23. VII (Jan.–Apr. 1868), 54–65.
24. Between 14 Aug. and 25 Sept.
25. R. K. Pugh, *The Political Life of Bishop Wilberforce* (Gladstone Memorial Exhibition essay, 1955, Jesus Coll., Oxford), 27.
26. J. T. Coleridge, *A Memoir of the Rev. John Keble* (Oxford, 1869), II, 522 and 529.
27. Disraeli to the Queen, 19 Aug. 1868, in G. E. Buckle, ed., *The Letters of Queen Victoria*, 2nd series, I, 534. See also Robt. Blake, *Disraeli*, 506–11.
28. Quoted in Dean Lake to Tait, 15 Aug. 1874, Tait papers, vol. 93, f. 294.
29. Conservatives 274, Liberals 384. H. J. Hanham, *Elections and Party Management* (London, 1959), 217.

References

30. Morley, *Gladstone*, II, 259.
31. Four of the victorious Liberals in Wales were Nonconformists. J. F. Glaser, *Nonconformity and Liberalism, 1868–1885* (Harvard Ph.D. dissertation, 1949), 488.
32. John Vincent, *The Formation of the Liberal Party, 1857–1868* (London, 1966), 69.
33. Arthur Miall, *Life of Edward Miall*, 263.
34. *Chronicle of Convocation*, 1870, pp. 94–5.
35. Wm. Benham, ed., *Catharine and Craufurd Tait* (London, 1879), 100.
36. *Hansard*, 3rd series, CXCVIII (1869), 419.
37. *Hansard*, 3rd series, CXCVI (1869), 1708–9 and 1713.
38. Tait to the archbishop of Armagh, 1 Feb. 1869, Tait papers, vol. 87, ff. 50–1.
39. Denison, *Notes of My Life, 1805–78* (Oxford, 2nd ed., 1878), 339.
40. J. C. MacDonnell, *Life of Archbishop Magee*, I, 218–19.
41. The Queen to Tait, 15 Feb. 1869, Tait papers, vol. 87, ff. 70–2.
42. Minutes of Bishops' meeting, 9 Feb. 1869, Tait papers, vol. 163, M. 102.
43. Tait to the Queen, 22 Feb. 1869, copy, Gladstone papers, Add. MSS. 44,330, ff. 61–2.
44. *Chronicle of Convocation*, 1869, pp. 104–8.
45. Tait to the Queen, 22 Feb. 1869, Royal Archives, D 25/47.
46. For a full account of Derby's fight against Irish disestablishment, see W. D. Jones, *Lord Derby and Victorian Conservatism* (Oxford, 1956), 337–49.
47. Denison, *The Charge of the Archdeacon of Taunton* (London, 1869), 7.
48. Tait to Earl Grey, 4 Mar. 1869, copy, Tait papers, vol. 87, ff. 82–3.
49. A. T. Lee, *The Irish Church Bill* (London, [1869]); and J. D. Massingham, *Mr. Gladstone's Irish Church Bill* (London, 1869).
50. Tait's memorandum on his visit to Disraeli, 10 Apr. 1869, Tait papers, vol. 75, ff. 269–77.
51. Arthur Miall, *Life of Edward Miall*, 302–3.
52. Tait to Cairns, 4 June 1869, rough draft, Tait papers, vol. 87, ff. 124–5.
53. Notes on the meeting, Ascension Day 1869, Tait papers, vol. 163, M. 102.
54. Ellicott to Disraeli, 30 Apr., 6 May and 3 June 1869, Beaconsfield papers, B/XXI/E/183–5.
55. Tait to the Queen, 6 June 1869, copy, Gladstone papers, Add. MSS. 44,330, f. 88; and Tait to Disraeli, 8 June 1869, copy, Tait papers, vol. 87, f. 138.

56. Tait to Gladstone, 3 June 1869, Gladstone papers, Add. MSS. 44,330, ff. 79–82.
57. Gladstone to Tait, 3 June 1869, copy, Gladstone papers, Add. MSS. 44,330, ff. 83–4.
58. Tait to Gladstone, 4 June 1869, Gladstone papers, Add. MSS. 44,330, ff. 85–6.
59. Tait to the Queen, 7 June 1869, copy, Tait papers, vol. 87, ff. 136–7.
60. E.g. Sir Walter Farquhar to Tait, 13 June 1869, Tait papers, vol. 86, ff. 167–70.
61. A. R. Ashwell and R. G. Wilberforce, *Life of Bishop Wilberforce*, III, 288.
62. W. D. Jones, *op. cit.*, 348.
63. *Hansard*, 3rd series, CXCVII (1869), 729–30 and 1077–8.
64. *Hansard*, 3rd series, CXCVII (1869), 1128 and 1514–17.
65. Tait to the Queen, 8 July 1869, copy, Gladstone papers, Add. MSS. 44,330, ff. 91–3.
66. *Hansard*, 3rd series, CXCVII (1869), 1516–17.
67. G. M. Trevelyan, *Life of Bright*, 403.
68. Gladstone to the Queen, 12 July 1869, in G. E. Buckle, ed., *op. cit.*, I, 617–18; and the Queen to Tait, 11 July 1869, copy, Gladstone papers, Add. MSS. 44,330, f. 94.
69. For descriptions of this and the subsequent events see Morley's *Gladstone*, II, 273–8, and Tait's diary, 25 July 1869.

CHAPTER TWO

Theological Paralysis

1. For an account of the importance of Colenso's work, hitherto usually ridiculed, see Peter Hinchliff, *John William Colenso*, chapt. 5.
2. *Infra*, 149.
3. A. P. Stanley, *The Athanasian Creed* (London, 1871), 89.
4. *Ibid.*, 78.
5. E. S. Ffoulkes, *The Athanasian Creed* (London, 1872), 273–4.
6. E. H. Coleridge, *Life and Correspondence of John Duke Lord Coleridge*, II, 215–16.
7. Thomas Hughes, *James Fraser, Second Bishop of Manchester*, 204.
8. Shaftesbury to Tait, 4 July 1872, Tait papers, vol. 91, f. 166.
9. Stanley, *op. cit.*, 52–3.
10. Parl. Papers 1870, XIX, 501.
11. *Ibid.*, 612.

12. Parl. Papers 1870, XIX, 468ff.
13. *Ibid.*, 468; Tait, *The Present Position of the Church of England* (London, 3rd ed., 1873), 64.
14. C. W. Sandford to ed., in the *Times*, 3 Feb. 1870.
15. Tait to the bishop of London, 27 Dec. 1870, in the *Times*, 11 Jan. 1871.
16. Morley, *Gladstone*, II, 516.
17. Tract XXII was a plea to this end.
18. Gladstone to Tait, 23 Jan. 1871, copy, Gladstone papers, Add. MSS. 44,330, ff. 175–6; *Chronicle of Convocation*, 1874, p. 115.
19. D. C. Lathbury, ed., *Correspondence on Church and Religion of William Ewart Gladstone* (London, 1910), II, 409.
20. *The Law Reports:* Privy Council Appeals, III, 1869–71, pp. 360–1 and 407; and Tait's notes on the Voysey case, 1st book, Tait papers, miscellanea and P. C. appeals.
21. J. W. Burgon, *The Athanasian Creed to be Retained in its Integrity: and Why* (Oxford and London, 1872), 47.
22. J. A. Froude, *Thomas Carlyle . . . 1834–1881*, II, 263.
23. Liddon to Tait, 2 Jan. 1872, Tait papers, vol. 91, f. 85.
24. Liddon to Tait, 30 Dec. 1871, Tait papers, *loc. cit.*, f. 81.
25. J. W. Burgon, *op. cit.*, 9.
26. Liddon to Stanley, 10 Mar. 1864, in R. E. Prothero and G. G. Bradley, *The Life and Correspondence of Arthur Penrhyn Stanley*, II, 168.
27. J. W. Burgon, *op. cit.*, 12–13.
28. Denison to Miss Phillimore, 9 Mar. 1878, in L. E. Denison, ed., *Fifty Years at East Brent* (London, 1902), 202.
29. E. H. Coleridge, *op. cit.*, II, 119.
30. G. F. A. Best, *Shaftesbury*, 66–7.
31. Pusey to Tait, 28 Oct. 1872, Tait papers, *loc. cit.*, f. 209.
32. Thirlwall to Tait, 16 Jan. 1872, Tait papers, *loc. cit.*, f. 101.
33. Burgon, *op. cit.*, 6.
34. J. D. Chambers to Tait, 31 July 1872, Tait papers, vol. 91.
35. Tait to Thomas Chambers, 23 May 1871, copy, Tait papers, *loc. cit.*, ff. 22–3.
36. Tait's speech to the archdeacons and rural deans of the diocese of Canterbury, *Guardian*, 11 Oct. 1871.
37. Pusey to Wilberforce, 19 Oct. 1871, in Liddon, *Life of Pusey*, IV, 233–4; and A. R. Ashwell and R. G. Wilberforce, *Life of Samuel Wilberforce*, III, 390.
38. Mozley, *Lectures and Other Theological Papers* (London, 1883), 190 and 194–6.
39. *Chronicle of Convocation*, 1873, p. 354.

40. Stanley to Tait, 22 Nov. 1873, Tait papers, vol. 92, ff. 288–9.
41. Stanley, *The Athanasian Creed*, 86.
42. *Chronicle of Convocation*, 1872, p. 359.
43. Stanley, *The Athanasian Creed*, 87.
44. *Chronicle of Convocation*, 1872, p. 363.
45. *Ibid.*, p. 599.
46. Liddon, *Life of Pusey*, IV, 238.
47. Liddon to Tait, 23 Dec. 1871, and 3 Jan. 1872, Tait papers, vol. 91, ff. 61–2 and 86.
48. J. O. Johnston, *Life of Liddon*, 167.
49. Pusey to Tait, Oct. 1872, Tait papers, *loc. cit.*, ff. 203–4.
50. *Chronicle of Convocation*, 1872, pp. 342–3.
51. Parl. Papers 1870, XIX, 617.
52. *Authorized Report of the Meetings in Defence of the Athanasian Creed . . . on January 31, 1873* (London, 1873).
53. Tait, *The Present Position of the Church of England*, 68.
54. Lightfoot to Tait, 28 Dec. 1871, Tait papers, *loc. cit.*, f. 67.
55. *Chronicle of Convocation*, 1872, p. 96.
56. *Ibid.*, 459–60.
57. *Infra*, 106–9.
58. Denison to Tait, in the *Times*, 7 Aug. 1872.
59. Tait, *The Present Position of the Church of England*, 65–6.
60. *Chronicle of Convocation*, 1872, p. 576.
61. *Chronicle of Convocation*, 1873, p. 308.
62. *Ibid.*, p. 405.
63. See Bishop Magee to Tait, 19 July 1879, Tait papers, vol. 99, ff. 144–6.
64. 16 and 28 Nov. 1877.
65. Shaftesbury to Tait, 3 Dec. 1877, Tait papers, vol. 231, ff. 271–3.
66. SPCK, Minutes of the General Meeting, 3 May and 14 June 1870, LI, 218 and 241; Minutes of the Standing Committee, 27 June 1870, XVIII, 158–61.
67. SPCK, Christian Evidence Committee Minutes, 6ff.
68. SPCK, Minutes of the General Meeting, 14 Apr. 1874, LIII, 34–5; *Report of the SPCK*, 1874, Catalogue G, class II.
69. SPCK, Minutes of the General Meeting, 5 May 1874, LIII, 49.
70. SPCK, Christian Evidence Committee Minutes, 16 Nov. 1871.
71. Maitland, *The Argument from Prophecy* (London, 1877), 14.
72. pp. 3–4, 6–7 and 200.
73. p. 8.
74. pp. 120–2.
75. pp. 193–4.
76. pp. 199–200.

77. pp. 191–2.
78. Maitland to Tait, 24 Jan. 1878, Tait papers, vol. 239.
79. Shaftesbury's diary, 8 Dec. 1877.
80. 2 Jan. 1878.
81. 11 Jan. 1878.
82. Tait to Maitland, 30 Jan. 1878, copy, Tait papers, *loc. cit.*, ff. 361–8.
83. Shaftesbury's diary, 10 Feb. 1878.
84. Ellicott to Tait, 31 Oct. 1878, copy, and Ellicott to Maxwell Spooner, 11 Jan. 1879, Tait papers, *loc. cit.*, ff. 383 and 1878 Home 230.
85. Ellicott to Spooner, 11 Jan. 1879, *loc. cit.*
86. G. G. Stokes to R. T. Davidson, 9 Dec. 1880, Tait papers, 1881 Home 199.
87. Goodwin to Tait, 8 July 1878, copy, Tait papers, vol. 239, ff. 375–9.
88. SPCK, Minutes of the General Meeting, 4 Feb. 1879, LV, 193.
89. *The Argument from Prophecy*, 2nd ed. (London, 1878), iv and 190–1.
90. SPCK, Minutes of the General Meeting, 4 Mar. 1879, LV, 206.
91. SPCK, Minutes of the Standing Committee, 28 Jan. 1878, XXIV, 482–3 and 25 Mar. 1878, XXV, 51–2; Christian Evidence Committee Minutes, 7 Mar. 1878; Minutes of the General Meeting, 4 June and 1 Oct. 1878, LV, 89 and 123.
92. SPCK, *Report for 1880*, 19.
93. SPCK, *Report for 1878*, 34, and *Report for 1879*, 28.
94. See *infra*, chapt. 7.
95. Tait's diary, 12 Dec. 1874.
96. Goldwyn Smith to Tait, 15 June 1874, Tait papers, vol. 94, f. 239.
97. Gladstone to the duke of Argyll, 28 Dec. 1872, in Morley, *Gladstone*, II, 524.
98. A. W. Benn, *History of English Rationalism in the Nineteenth Century* (London, 1906), II, 387.
99. Green to Tait, 25 Apr. 1877, Tait papers, vol. 97, ff. 126–7.
100. See 'Some current fallacies respecting supernatural religion', *Macmillan's Magazine*, XXXI, 182 (Dec. 1874), 89–98.
101. *Some Thoughts on the Duties of the Established Church of England as a National Church* (London, 1876), chapters 2 and 3.
102. *The Church of the Future* (London, 1880), chapters 2 to 5.
103. Tait's diary, 16 Apr. 1876.
104. *Some Thoughts on the Duties of the Established Church of England as a National Church*, 28.
105. 'Some current fallacies respecting supernatural religion', 94.

106. *Some Thoughts* . . ., 22.
107. Wace to Tait, 10 Jan. 1875, Tait papers, vol. 94, f. 28.
108. *Some Thoughts* . . ., 17.
109. *Ibid.*, 43.
110. Davidson and Benham, *Tait*, I, 341.
111. *Some Thought* . . ., 25.
112. *Ibids.*, 31–2.
113. *Fallacies of Unbelief* (London, 1876), 18.
114. *Some Thoughts.* . . , 32.
115. *Fallacies of Unbelief*, loc. cit.
116. See Tait, *Some Thoughts* . . ., 30.
117. *Fallacies of Unbelief*, 6.
118. *Some Thoughts* . . ., 33.
119. Tait's sermon before the League of St. Martin, in *The Christian World Pulpit*, 8 Mar. 1882.
120. 'Some current fallacies . . .', 95; *Fallacies of Unbelief*, 11–13.
121. Tait to the synod of Greece, *Guardian*, 5 Oct. 1870.
122. *The Church of the Future*, 116.
123. *Ibid.*, 155–6.
124. See Tait, *Harmony of Revelation and the Sciences* (Edinburgh, 1864), 19.
125. Tait's diary, 29 Aug. 1880.
126. *Fallacies of Unbelief*, 9–10.
127. Tait, preface to *Some Modern Religious Difficulties: Six sermons, preached by the request of the Christian Evidence Society* (London, [1876]), xiii.
128. *Fallacies of Unbelief*, 14.
129. 28 Sept. 1876, in Tait papers, vol. 96, ff. 209–209a.
130. Manning to Tait, 2 Oct. 1876, Tait papers, vol. 96, f. 214.
131. E. W. Olivès to Tait, 30 Sept. 1876, Tait papers, vol. 96, ff. 204–208a.
132. T. L. Henly, *Christianity, as set forth by His Grace the Archbishop of Canterbury* . . . (London, 1877).
133. W. R. Brown to R. T. Davidson, 3 Jan. 1881, Tait papers, 1881 Home 199.
134. Minutes of the Conference on the Relations between Science and Religion, 7 Jan. 1881, Tait papers, *loc. cit.*
135. Farrar to Tait, 13 Dec. 1880, Tait papers, *loc. cit.*
136. G. G. Stokes to Tait, 9 Dec. 1880, Tait papers, *loc. cit.*
137. Arnold to Fontanès, 25 Mar. 1881, in G. W. E. Russell, ed., *Letters of Matthew Arnold 1848–1888* (London, 1895), II, 191.
138. *Hansard*, 3rd series, CCXX (1874), 1431.

CHAPTER THREE

No Longer England's Schoolmaster

1. Denison, *The Tempter's Cup* (Oxford and London, 1875), 50.
2. For the best short description of these schools and their reform, see David Owen, *English Philanthropy, 1660–1960* (Harvard University Press, 1965), Chapt. 9.
3. Report of the Schools Inquiry [Taunton] Commission, Parl. Papers 1867–8, XXVIII, pt. 1, p. 139.
4. 32 and 33 Vict. c. 56, clauses 15, 17 and 18.
5. L. T. Hobhouse and J. L. Hammond, *Lord Hobhouse*, 46.
6. *Hansard*, 3rd series, CCVII (1871), 878.
7. Tait's speech at the annual prize day of the Whitgift Middle-Class School, *Croydon Advertizer and East Surrey Reporter*, 16 Aug. 1873.
8. Editorial, 26 Apr. 1871.
9. Lord Salisbury's speech, *Hansard*, 3rd series, CCXVI (1873), 77.
10. *Supra*, 23.
11. *National Church*, Jan. 1873.
12. Lord Salisbury's draft of what may have been a circular letter to the bishops, 24 Feb. 1873, Salisbury papers, C/5/68–9; and Salisbury to Tait, 7 Mar. 1873, Tait papers, vol. 92, ff. 63–5.
13. *National Church*, July 1873.
14. A. T. Lee to Salisbury, 24 July 1873, Salisbury papers, Class M; and *National Church*, Aug. 1873.
15. D. C. Richmond to Tait, 18 Mar., and Tait to the charity commissioners, 5 Apr. 1878, copy, Tait papers, vol. 236, C48.
16. Tait to the charity commissioners, 30 Jan. 1879, copy, Tait papers, 1881 separate packet 3. See also the memorandum from the archbishop to the commissioners, 28 Feb. 1881, copy, Tait papers, *loc. cit.*
17. D. C. Richmond to Tait, 2 July 1881, Tait papers, *loc. cit.*
18. David Owen, *op. cit.*, 262ff.
19. For the best account of what was accomplished in this field by the Church up to 1870, see H. J. Burgess, *Enterprise in Education* (London, 1958).
20. Alfred Blomfield, ed., *A Memoir of Charles James Blomfield*, I, 247.
21. Quoted in C. K. F. Brown, *The Church's Part in Education, 1833–1941* (London, 1942), 15. I have not been able to find this quotation's original source.

22. Marjorie Cruickshank, *Church and State in English Education, 1870 to the present day* (London, 1963), 17. This book is the source of much of the information used below.
23. H. J. Burgess, *op. cit.*, 210.
24. *Ibid.*, 132.
25. *Chronicle of Convocation*, 1870, p. 111.
26. 12 Aug. 1870.
27. *Chronicle of Convocation*, 1870, p. 113.
28. Denison, *The Three Policies* (London, 2nd ed., 1871), 34.
29. The Rev. J. D. Massingham's speech, *National Church*, June 1870.
30. *National Church*, Aug. 1870.
31. Tait to Gladstone, 29 June 1870, Gladstone papers, Add. MSS. 44,330, ff. 157–8.
32. See Tait's speech at the opening of Archbishop Sumner's Memorial Schools, in the *Times*, 18 Oct. 1871.
33. Tait to the Rev. W. Rogers, 3 Apr. 1866, in Davidson and Benham, *Tait*, I, 532.
34. H. J. Burgess, *op. cit.*, 212.
35. Tait, *The Present Position of the Church of England*, 11.
36. Marjorie Cruickshank, *op. cit.*, 51–2.
37. *Hansard*, 3rd series, CCXXXI (1876), 792–7.
38. Duke of Richmond's speech, *Hansard*, 3rd series, CCXXXI (1876), 945–6, and Tait's diary, 13 Aug. 1876.
39. Tait to Canon Jenkins, 2 Feb. 1875, copy, Tait papers, vol. 209, J92, and Tait to W. Gibson, 7 May 1875, copy, vol. 208, H75.
40. Tait, *Some Thoughts on the Duties of the Established Church of England as a National Church*, 92–3.
41. Tait's speech to the Canterbury Diocesan Education Society, 1877, Tait papers, vol. of news clippings, 1877–80, f. 124.
42. Tait to the annual meeting of the National Society, in the *Guardian*, 29 May 1878.
43. Marjorie Cruickshank, *op. cit.*, 47.
44. Canon Norris' speech, *Chronicle of Convocation*, 1881, p. 442.
45. W. H. G. Armytage, *A. J. Mundella, 1825–1897*, 217 and 219.
46. Tait to the annual meeting of the National Society, in the *Times*, 23 June 1881.
47. *Chronicle of Convocation*, 1881, p. 435.
48. p. 437.
49. Reported in the *Times*, 1 Dec. 1881.
50. J. Duncan to Tait, 15 Jan. 1882, Tait papers, 1882 Home 62.
51. Tait to the annual meeting of the Church Defence Institution, in the *National Church*, Aug. 1882.
52. Davidson and Benham, *Tait*, I, 55 and 69–70.

53. Davidson and Benham, *Tait*, I, 157ff.
54. W. R. Ward, *Victorian Oxford* (London, 1965), 161. This book is the source of much of the following information.
55. A. P. Stanley's draft of a statement to be published if a memorial was issued against the commission, Tait papers, vol. 78, f. 196.
56. *Ibid.*
57. H. P. Liddon, *Life of Pusey*, IV, 201.
58. First Report from the Select Committee of the House of Lords on University Tests, Parl. Papers 1871, IX, 291.
59. *Ibid.*, 309–10 (answer 802).
60. W. R. Ward, *op. cit.*, 253–4.
61. *Ibid.*, 255.
62. W. R. Ward, *op. cit.*, 257.
63. *Guardian*, 29 Oct. 1873.
64. *Hansard*, 3rd series, CCXXVII (1876), 1666–7.
65. *Ibid.*, 1670.
66. *Ibid.*, 1672.
67. *Ibid.*, 1673.
68. Brian Simon, *Studies in the History of Education, 1780–1870* (London, 1960), 299.
69. *Hansard*, 3rd series, CCXXVIII (1876), 948–54.
70. Jowett to Tait, 27 Mar. 1876, Tait papers, vol. 95, ff. 263–4. See also the protest from Oxford dons against Tait's proposal, Tait papers, vol. 224, ff. 227–8.
71. *Hansard*, 3rd series, CCXXVII (1876), 1671–2.
72. Parl Papers 1881, LVI, pt. II, 102ff.
73. *Ibid.*, 169.
74. The Rev. E. C. Woollcombe to Tait, 10 July 1877, Tait papers, vol. 97, f. 217.
75. Parl. Papers, *loc. cit.*, 154–5.
76. *Ibid.*, 140–2; and Bradley to Tait, 21 Jan. 1881, Tait papers, 1880 Home 182. Jowett sympathized with Bradley's point of view. Jowett to Tait, 27 Dec. 1880, Tait papers, *loc. cit.*
77. Bradley to Tait, 21 Jan. 1881, *loc. cit.*
78. 22 Jan. 1881, copy, Tait papers, *loc. cit.*
79. *Ibid.*
80. For a list, see Owen Chadwick, *The Founding of Cuddesdon* (Oxford U.P., 1954), 126n.
81. Speech in aid of Wycliffe and Ridley Halls, in the *Guardian*, 2 June 1880.
82. *Hansard*, 3rd series, CCLXVII (1882), 168–71.
83. *Hansard*, 3rd series, CCLXVIII (1882), 1792–4, and CCLXIX (1882), 537–8.

84. *Hansard*, 3rd series, CCLXIX (1882), 546.
85. Liddon to Tait, 7 Mar. 1882, Tait papers, 1882 Home 74.
86. Tait, 'Thoughts suggested by Mr. Mozley's Oxford Reminiscences', *Macmillan's Magazine*, XLVI, 276 (Oct. 1882), 418–19.
87. *Hansard*, 3rd series, CCXXVIII (1876), 604–6.
88. See e.g. Tait's speech to the quarterly meeting of the Bishop of London's Fund, in the *Guardian*, 9 Aug. 1871.
89. G. W. Kitchin, *Edward Harold Browne, D.D., Lord Bishop of of Winchester*, 339.
90. See e.g. the report of a speech by Tait in the *Daily News*, 25 Mar. 1876.
91. Printed 'Quotations from National Society's Reading Book Standard V,' Tait papers, 1879 Home 357a.
92. Printed letter from the committee to the Standing Committee of the National Society, 14 Feb. 1879, Tait papers, *loc. cit.*
93. Duncan to Oakley, 10 Mar. 1879, Tait papers, *loc. cit.*
94. Duncan to Davidson, 11 Nov. 1879, Tait papers, *loc. cit.*
95. Robert Collier to Tait, 2 Oct. 1879, and enclosure, Tait papers, *loc. cit.*
96. Henry Broadhurst to Tait, 6 Oct. 1879, Tait papers, *loc. cit.*
97. Oakley to Tait, 23 Oct. 1879, Tait papers, *loc. cit.*
98. Reported in the *Daily Chronicle*, 14 Nov. 1879.
99. The Rev. W. T. M. Webber to Davidson, 13 Nov. 1879, Tait papers, *loc. cit.*
100. Tait to Brownlow, 15 Nov. 1879, copy, Tait papers, *loc. cit.*

CHAPTER FOUR

Reforming the Church under Gladstone

1. T. H. Huxley, *Methods and Results* (London, 1893), 284.
2. *Church Congress Reports*, 1869, p. 487.
3. Cf. Sir Stafford Northcote's speech, *Church Congress Reports*, 1873, p. 173.
4. *Croydon Guardian*, 1 Sept. 1880.
5. *Hansard*, 3rd series, CCX (1872), 229.
6. At roughly the same time, Magee handled his first Charge to the diocese of Peterborough similarly. J. C. MacDonnell, *The Life and Correspondence of William Connor Magee*, I, 278.
7. 7 Nov. 1872.
8. D. C. Lathbury, ed., *Correspondence on Church and Religion of William Ewart Gladstone* (London, 1910), I, 393.

9. Gladstone to Döllinger, 6 Sept. 1872, copy, Gladstone papers, Add. MSS. 44,140, f. 291.
10. See Gladstone to the bishop of Colombo, 5 May 1870, Gladstone papers, Add. MSS. 44,538, f. 141.
11. D. C. Lathbury, ed., *op. cit.*, II, 142.
12. Tait to the synod of Greece, *Guardian*, 5 Oct. 1870.
13. Tait to Bishop Wilberforce, 7 Oct. 1871, Wilberforce papers, Dep. c. 195.
14. Gladstone to Tait, 19 Mar. 1869, Tait papers, vol. 86, ff. 87–8.
15. Tait to Wilberforce, 1 Dec. 1868, Wilberforce papers, *loc. cit.*
16. Tait to Gladstone, 16 and 23 Apr. 1869, Gladstone papers, Add. MSS. 44,330, ff. 63–5 and 69–70; and Gladstone to Tait, 24 Apr. 1869, Tait papers, vol. 86, f. 124.
17. Gladstone to Tait, 3 Aug. 1869, Tait papers, vol. 86, ff. 194–5.
18. Gladstone to Tait, 6 Aug. 1869, Tait papers, vol. 86, f. 196.
19. *Chronicle of Convocation*, 1869, pp. 108 and 110.
20. 5 Oct. 1869, Gladstone papers, Add. MSS. 44,330, ff. 119–24.
21. Gladstone to Tait, 28 Oct. 1869, Tait papers, vol. 89, ff. 307–8.
22. Tait's diary, 3 Nov. 1869.
23. Gladstone to Tait, 3 Nov. 1869, Tait papers, vol. 89, f. 324.
24. *Chronicle of Convocation*, 1873, pp. 16–17 and 72–3.
25. For a statement of some of these criticisms, see Canon Gregory's speech, *Chronicle of Convocation*, 1870, pp. 242–3.
26. *Supra*, 42.
27. Tait to Gladstone, 7 Feb. 1870, Gladstone papers, Add. MSS. 44,330, f. 151.
28. Tait's address to the clergy of the rural deanery of West Dartford, *Guardian*, 8 Sept. 1869.
29. Jebb's speech, *Chronicle of Convocation*, 1870, pp. 250ff.
30. *Chronicle of Convocation*, 1870, pp. 276 and 312.
31. Bishop Wordsworth, for example, said that the reference in the lectionary Bill to Convocation's agreement would relieve the consciences of clergymen. *Hansard*, 3rd series, CCII (1870), 1610.
32. Gregory's speech, *Chronicle of Convocation*, 1870, p. 246.
33. *Hansard*, 3rd series, CCII (1870), 1604–6, and CCIII (1870), 99.
34. The Lord Chancellor's speech, *Hansard*, 3rd series, CCIV (1871), 1267.
35. Including improvement of the law governing ecclesiastical dilapidations and a reform of the ecclesiastical courts.
36. 19 Nov. 1870, Gladstone papers, Add. MSS. 44,330, ff. 166–7.
37. 27 Dec. 1870, in the *Times*, 11 Jan. 1871.

38. Tait to the bishop of London, 14 Jan. 1871, copy, Tait papers, vol. 91, f. 8. Tait had copies of this letter sent to Gladstone, the Lord Chancellor, and the Home Secretary.

39. Gladstone to Tait, 25 Nov. 1870, copy, Tait papers, vol. 88, f. 188.

40. Gladstone to Tait, 5 Feb. 1871, Tait papers, vol. 89, f. 299.

41. Gladstone to Tait, 10 Jan. 1871, Tait papers, vol. 89, f. 101.

42. The Lord Chancellor's speech, *Hansard*, 3rd series, CCIV (1871), 1267; Gladstone to Tait, 6 June 1871, copy, Gladstone papers, Add. MSS. 44,540, f. 48.

43. Gladstone to Tait, 21 Apr. and 10 May 1871, Tait papers, vol. 89, ff. 186 and 196–8; Gladstone's speech, *Hansard*, 3rd series, CCVII (1871), 959.

44. *Hansard*, 3rd series, CCV (1871), 1455–63.

45. Gladstone to Tait, 24 June 1871, Tait papers, vol. 89, ff. 222–3.

46. Tait to Gladstone, two letters of 24 and one of 25 June 1871, Gladstone papers, Add. MSS. 44,330, ff. 193–200.

47. *Chronicle of Convocation*, 1870, p. 246.

48. *Chronicle of Convocation*, 1871, p. 455.

49. See Gregory's speech, *Church Congress Reports*, 1871, p. 118.

50. *Hansard*, 3rd series, CCIV (1871), 1969–71.

51. *Hansard*, 3rd series, CCVII (1871), 1202–3; Tait's diary, 10 July 1871.

52. See the *Guardian*'s editorial, 14 Feb. 1872.

53. Davidson and Benham, *Tait*, I, 486.

54. See his speech on ecclesiastical legislation, in the *Times*, 10 Oct. 1871.

55. Tait's speech, in the *Times*, 10 Oct. 1871.

56. Tait to Gladstone, 22 Jan. 1872, Gladstone papers, Add. MSS. 44,331, ff. 7–9.

57. Tait to Wilberforce, 7 Oct. 1871, Wilberforce papers, Dep. c. 195.40. See also Tait to Gladstone, 1 Nov. 1871, copy, Tait papers, vol. 89, ff. 296–7.

58. Gladstone to Tait, 5 Nov. 1871, Tait papers, vol. 89, f. 299.

59. Tait to Wilberforce, 12 Dec. 1871, Wilberforce papers, *loc. cit.*; Tait to Gladstone, 22 Jan. 1872, *loc. cit.*, ff. 9–10; Wilberforce to Tait, 12 Mar. 1872, Tait papers, vol. 184, ff. 134–9.

60. *Infra*, 212ff.

61. Tait to Gladstone, 29 Jan. 1872, copy, and Gladstone to Tait, 30 Jan. 1872, Tait papers, vol. 184, ff. 105 and 108–9. For a copy of the Letters, see the *Chronicle of Convocation*, 1872, appendix.

62. *Chronicle of Convocation*, 1872, pp. 28, 36–7, and 237–8.

63. Tait to the archbishop of York, 13 Mar. and 3 Apr. 1872, copies, Tait papers, vol. 184, ff. 140–3 and 176–83.

64. *Chronicle of Convocation*, 1872, pp. 71–2 and 227.
65. *Church Congress Reports*, 1869, p. 487.
66. The *Guardian*'s editorial, 3 Jan. 1872.
67. Tait to Gladstone, 22 Jan. 1872, *loc. cit.*, ff. 6–7.
68. Gladstone to Tait, 8 and 9 Mar. 1872, Tait papers, vol. 90, ff. 82 and 84.
69. *Hansard*, 3rd series, CCX (1872), 229.
70. Gladstone to Tait, 14 May 1872, and Tait to Gladstone, 24 May 1872, copy, Tait papers, vol. 90, ff. 117–20.
71. *Chronicle of Convocation*, 1872, p. 583.
72. *Supra*, 50.
73. See the *Daily Telegraph*'s editorial, 9 Feb. 1872.
74. Printed circular from Tait to the clergy of Canterbury diocese, 20 Feb. 1882, Tait papers, vol. of news clippings, 1181–3, f. 228.
75. R. C. D. Jasper, *Prayer Book Revision in England 1800–1900* (London, 1954), 117.
76. The *Guardian*, however, asserted that 'in general the Archbishop is warranted in his endeavour to adapt the institutions and machinery of the Church to the wants of the times' (3 Jan. 1872).
77. The objection of Lord Beauchamp, Beresford Hope, and Gregory. Fourth Report of the Commissioners Appointed to Inquire into the Rubrics, Parl. Papers 1870, xix, 469–70.

CHAPTER FIVE

Ritualism and the Courts

1. Forster to Tait, 14 July 1874, Tait papers, vol. 93, f. 236.
2. Wilberforce papers, Dep. c. 195.40.
3. Michael Reynolds, *Martyr of Ritualism*, chapters 13 and 14; L. E. Elliott-Binns, *The Development of English Theology in the later nineteenth century* (London, 1952), 122.
4. Newman to Manning, 1 Sept. 1839, in E. S. Purcell, *Life of Cardinal Manning*, I, 233.
5. See F. T. Palgrave, 'A plain view of ritualism', *Macmillan's Magazine*, XVII, 98 (Dec. 1867), 116.
6. *Manchester Courier*, 15 Jan. 1873.
7. *Some Thoughts on the Duties of the Established Church of England as a National Church*, 57.
8. *Chronicle of Convocation*, 1875, p. 324.
9. Davidson and Benham, *Tait*, I, 501.
10. *Ibid.*, 500–1.

11. *The Work of Our National Church*, 10.
12. Gladstone, *The Church of England and Ritualism* (London, 1875), 24.
13. *A Charge to the Clergy of the Diocese of London* (London, 1866), 8–9.
14. *Church Association Monthly Intelligencer*, 1 July 1869.
15. *Some Thoughts on the Duties of the Established Church of England as a National Church*, 56.
16. *The Present Position of the Church of England*, 45. Cf. the archbishops' reply to the Church Association's memorial, *Times*, 21 June 1873.
17. *Hansard*, 3rd series, CCVI (1871), 1761.
18. *The Present Position of the Church of England*, 37.
19. C. A. Bury, *The Church Association* (London, 1873), 19.
20. Rev. R. Cornall to Disraeli, 12 Aug. 1874, Beaconsfield papers, B/XII/F/76.
21. See J. O. Serjeant and others to Tait and the bishop of London, 28 Feb. 1881, Tait papers, 1881 Home 240.
22. E. M. Goulburn, *John William Burgon*, II, 84–6.
23. A. R. Ashwell and R. G. Wilberforce, *Life of Samuel Wilberforce*, III, 298–9.
24. J. T. Coleridge, *Memoir of Keble*, II, 540.
25. Liddon, *Life of Pusey*, IV, 216; Denison, *The Church of England in 1869* (London, 1869), 30–1.
26. Liddon, *op. cit.*, IV, 271.
27. See *Life and Letters of William John Butler, late Dean of Lincoln*, 210.
28. Keble to J. T. Coleridge, 11 Dec. 1855, in Coleridge, *Memoir of Keble*, II, 425.
29. R. E. Prothero and G. G. Bradley, *Life of Dean Stanley*, II, 378.
30. John Hassard to Tait, 14 Apr. 1873, Tait papers, 1873 Home.
31. *The Three Policies* (London, 2nd ed., 1871), 27.
32. Parl. Papers 1883, XXIV, 261–2.
33. See the preface he wrote in G. C. Brodrick and W. H. Fremantle, ed., *A Collection of the Judgements of the Judicial Committee of the Privy Council in Ecclesiastical Cases relating to Doctrine and Discipline* (London, 1865), xi.
34. *Hansard*, 3rd series, CCXV (1873), 1469–72.
35. *The Law Reports*, Privy Council appeals, III, 1869–71, pp. 381–408.
36. *Op. cit.*, IV, 1871–3, p. 404.
37. Michael Reynolds, *Martyr of Ritualism*, 156.
38. *Hansard*, 3rd series, CCIX (1872), 630.
39. Michael Reynolds, *op. cit.*, 173.
40. Archbishop Thomson, 'The Ritual of the English Church', *Quarterly Review*, CXXXVII, 274 (Oct. 1874), 565.

41. E.g. Beresford Hope, *Hansard*, 3rd series, CCXIII (1872), 198–203.
42. News clipping dated Jan. 1869, Pusey House no. 5782.
43. *Chronicle of Convocation*, 1869, p. 326.
44. Michael Reynolds, *op. cit.*, 174–5.
45. Robert Gregory, *Autobiography*, 110.
46. English Church Union Annual Report, June 1872, Pusey House news clipping no. 5804.
47. J. O. Johnston, *Life of Liddon*, 145–6.
48. Gregory, *op. cit.*, 108–10.
49. Tooth to the bishop of Rochester, 31 May 1871, copy, Tait papers, vol. 176, T 142.
50. Liddon, *Life of Pusey*, IV, 225.
51. In the *Times*, 13 Apr. 1871.
52. *Ibid.*
53. See Salisbury's speech, *Hansard*, 3rd series, CCXV (1873), 1465–6.
54. See the speeches of Wilberforce and Tait, *Hansard*, 3rd series, CCVII (1871), 392, and CCXV (1873), 1469 and 1481.
55. Herbert Paul, *A History of Modern England* (London, 1904–6), III, 194.
56. *Hansard*, 3rd series, CCVII (1871), 1212.
57. Salisbury's speech, *Hansard*, 3rd series, CCVII (1871), 389, and Beresford Hope's speech, *Church Congress Reports*, 1871, p. 141.
58. Report of a Church Association paper, July 1873, Tait papers, vol. of news clippings, 1868–77, f. 107.
59. See Lord Harrowby's speech, *Hansard*, 3rd series, CCVII (1871), 1212.
60. Gladstone to Tait, 4 July 1873, Tait papers, vol. 92, ff. 176–7; *Hansard*, 3rd series, CCXVI (1873), 1793.
61. W. E. Gladstone, *Remarks on the Royal Supremacy as it is defined by Reason, History, and the Constitution* (London, 1850).
62. *Hansard*, loc. cit., 1794.
63. Tait to Gladstone, 5 July 1873, Gladstone papers, Add. MSS. 44,331, ff. 105–8; Tait to Gathorne Hardy, 7 July 1873, copy, Tait papers, vol. 92, ff. 186–7; Tait to Disraeli, 7 July 1873, Beaconsfield papers, B/XXX/T/13; Tait's diary, 13 July 1873.
64. *Church Association Monthly Intelligencer*, 1 June 1873.
65. *Chronicle of Convocation*, 1873, p. 387.
66. Edwin Hodder, *The Life and Work of the Seventh Earl of Shaftesbury*, III, 336–7.
67. In the *Times*, 21 June 1873.
68. Papers entitled 'Remedial legislation in Church matters' and 'Remedies proposed' by the Church Association, Tait papers, 1874 PWRA.

References

69. Church of England Laymen's Defence Association, *An Apology for the Laity* (London, 1873), 12–14.
70. 21 June 1873.

CHAPTER SIX

The Tenacity of the Establishment

1. *The Church and Law*, 44.
2. *Some Thoughts on the Duties of the Established Church of England as a National Church*, 103–4.
3. *Op. cit.*, 105.
4. Tait at the annual meeting of the Church Defence Institution, Tait papers, vol. of news clippings, 1881–3, f. 34.
5. *National Church*, 1 April 1870.
6. Salisbury to the Rev. J. S. Pickles, Salisbury papers, C/5, Secretary's Note-book, 1868–80, f. 15; *Hansard*, 3rd series, CXCV (1869), 1338.
7. *Hansard*, 3rd series, CCVI (1871), 474.
8. Address to the clergy of the rural deanery of West Dartford, *Guardian*, 8 Sept. 1869.
9. 9 May 1871.
10. *Hansard*, 3rd series, CCVI (1871), 539.
11. Miall, *The British Churches in relation to the British People* (London, 1849), 384.
12. *Op. cit.*, 382.
13. *Op. cit.*, 384–5.
14. *Op. cit.*, 387–8, Cf. *Hansard*, 3rd series, CCVI (1871), 493–4.
15. Denison, *The Church of England in 1869*, 23.
16. Miall, *op. cit.*, 368 and 376–7.
17. W. G. Addison, *Religious Equality in Modern England, 1714–1914* (London, 1944), 92.
18. *Hansard*, 3rd series, CCXII (1872), 539; address to the annual meeting of the British Anti-State Church Association, May 1849, in B. J. Mason, *The Rise of Combative Dissent, 1832–1859* (Southampton M.A. thesis, 1958), 168.
19. *Hansard*, 3rd series, CCVI (1871), 545–6.
20. See Edwin Hodder, *Life of Samuel Morley*, 279–80.
21. *Hansard*, 3rd series, CCXXI (1874), 39.
22. *Hansard*, 3rd series, CCVI (1871), 507–20.
23. *Hansard*, 3rd series, CCVI (1871), 505–6.
24. *National Church*, Dec. 1872.

25. See *supra*, 131. However, to spend State funds on education in denominational schools was a different matter.
26. *Hansard*, 3rd series, CCI (1870), 1291–9.
27. *Hansard*, 3rd series, CCVI (1871), 559–71, and CCXVI (1873), 37–49.
28. *Hansard*, 3rd series, CCXVI (1873), 43.
29. *Ibid.*, 49.
30. *Ibid.*, 47–8.
31. See Fraser's Charge, in the *National Church*, Jan. 1873.
32. By Gilbert Venables (London, 1872).
33. *National Church*, April 1872.
34. *National Church*, May 1872.
35. *National Church*, Feb. 1873.
36. *National Church*, Jan. 1874.
37. *The Work of our National Church*, 7.
38. *Church Congress Reports*, 1873, pp. 168–9.
39. Sir George Leveson Gower, *Years of Content, 1858–1886*, 164–5.
40. Morley, *Gladstone*, II, 431.
41. Tait's diary, 26 Aug. 1869; Tait to Gladstone, 7 Oct. 1869, Gladstone papers, Add. MSS. 44,330, f. 125; E. G. Sandford, *The Exeter Episcopate of Archbishop Temple, 1869–85* (London, 1907), 23–4. Except where otherwise noted, the ensuing narrative is based on Sandford's book.
42. *Chronicle of Convocation*, 1864, pp. 1683 and 1830.
43. Liddon, *Life of Pusey*, IV, 207.
44. E. G. Sandford, *op. cit.*, 25; Wilberforce to Tait, 22 Oct. 1869, Tait papers, Private correspondence 1869–71.
45. Dated November 1869, Tait papers, vol. 166, ff. 5–27.
46. 29 Dec. 1869.
47. In the *Times*, 22 Nov. 1869.
48. D. C. Lathbury, ed., *Correspondence on Church and Religion of William Ewart Gladstone*, I, 208.
49. See Sir Robert Phillimore, *The Ecclesiastical Law of the Church of England* (London, 2nd ed., 1895), I, 48.
50. *Chronicle of Convocation*, 1870, pp. 42–3.
51. Jackson to an archdeacon, 18 Dec. 1869, Tait papers, vol. 166, f. 64.
52. Albert Grey and W. H. Fremantle, ed., *Church Reform*, 218; E. M. Goulburn, *The Existing Mode of Electing Bishops* (Oxford and London, 1870); *National Church*, March 1870.
53. Tait to Wilberforce, 8 June 1870, copy, Tait papers, vol. 88, f. 99.
54. *Chronicle of Convocation*, 1870, appendix.
55. Tait papers, 1871 Home 112.

56. Stanley, *Essays Chiefly on Questions of Church and State* (London, 1870), 350.
57. *Chronicle of Convocation*, 1874, p. 165.
58. F. Bennett, *The Story of W. J. E. Bennett*, 246–7.
59. *Church Review*, 17 Dec. 1870.
60. Letter to ed., *Times*, 16 Jan. 1869.
61. Liddon, *Life of Pusey*, IV, 223–4.
62. J. O. Johnston, *Life of Liddon*, 130.
63. See Desmond Bowen, 'Anglo-Catholicism in Victorian England', *Canadian Journal of Theology*, XII, 1 (Jan. 1966), 45.
64. E.g. Pusey's *The Royal Supremacy not an arbitrary authority but limited by the laws of the Church of which kings are members* (London, 1850).
65. Owen Chadwick, *The Victorian Church*, part I, 232–5.
66. See J. O. Johnston, *op. cit.*, 129.
67. J. P. F. Davidson to the ed., *Guardian*, 10 June 1868. See *supra*, 97–8.
68. A. E. Gathorne-Hardy, *Gathorne Hardy, first Earl of Cranbrook*, I, 311.
69. H. J. Hanham, *Elections and Party Management*, 121.
70. J. L. Garvin and Julian Amery, *Life of Joseph Chamberlain*, I, 146.

CHAPTER SEVEN

The Public Worship Regulation Act, 1874

1. Robert Blake, *Disraeli*, 543 and 550.
2. *Hansard*, 3rd series, CCXVII (1873), 278.
3. T. R. Andrews to Tait, 12 Jan. 1874, Tait papers, Vol. 197, ff. 119–22.
4. The Queen to Tait, 15 Jan. 1874, in G. E. Buckle, ed., *The Letters of Queen Victoria*, 2nd series, II, 300; Tait's diary, 11 Jan. 1874.
5. Minutes, Tait papers, 1874 PWRA.
6. Tait to the Queen, 16 Jan., and the Queen to Gladstone, 20 Jan. 1874, copy, G. E. Buckle, ed., *op. cit.*, II, 300–2.
7. Gladstone to the Queen, 21 Jan. 1874, G. E. Buckle, ed., *op. cit.*, II, 303–5.
8. G. E. Buckle, ed., *op. cit.*, II, 306–10.
9. *Ibid.*, 306.
10. Tait, *Some Thoughts on the Duties of the Established Church of England as a National Church*, 57. In this Charge, Tait's first after the passing of the bill, he recounted the events which had led the bishops to propose it.

11. Dated 24 Feb. 1874, Beaconsfield papers, B/XII/F/3.
12. The Queen to Tait, 15 Jan. 1874, and Tait to Victoria, 16 Jan. 1874, G. E. Buckle, ed., *op. cit.*, II, 300–1.
13. The bishop of Winchester to Tait, 18 Jan. 1874, Tait papers, 1874 PWRA.
14. 23 Feb. 1874, Beaconsfield papers, B/XII/F/2.
15. Disraeli to Lady Bradford, 26 Mar.1874, Marquis of Zetland, ed., *The Letters of Disraeli to Lady Bradford and Lady Chesterfield*, I, 63.
16. Disraeli to Salisbury, 22 Feb. 1874, Monypenny and Buckle, *Disraeli*, V, 293.
17. Disraeli to Beauchamp, 7 June 1874, copy, Beaconsfield papers, B/XII/F/45b; Disraeli to the Queen, 7 June 1874, Royal Archives, D4/58.
18. Monypenny and Buckle, *Disraeli*, V, 293.
19. Derby to Disraeli, 3 Mar. 1874, Beaconsfield papers, B/XII/F/34.
20. Monypenny and Buckle, *Disraeli*, V, 317.
21. Salisbury to Ellicott, 25 Feb. 1874, Tait papers, 1874 PWRA.
22. Tait to Delane, 6 Mar. 1874, copy, Tait papers, 1874 PWRA.
23. 10 March.
24. In *Times* on 19, 24 and 30 March.
25. Liddon, *Life of Pusey*, IV, 273–4.
26. In E. F. Russell, ed., *Alexander Heriot Mackonochie*, 222–6.
27. On 19 March, the same day Pusey's first letter was published. Pusey's letter was written on 13 March. Liddon, *Pusey*, IV, 275. Delane therefore had time to show it to Tait so that the letter and the editorial reply could be published at the same time. See Brunel to Tait, 19 Mar. 1874, Tait papers, 1874 PWRA.
28. The bishop of Peterborough to Tait, 19 Mar. 1874, Tait papers, 1874 PWRA; *Times*, 1 Apr. 1874.
29. Lake to Tait, 21 Mar. 1874, Tait papers, *loc. cit.*
30. The bishop of Peterborough to Tait, 13 March 1874, Tait papers, *loc. cit.*
31 Tait papers, *loc. cit.*
32. 21 Mar. 1874, Tait papers, *loc. cit.*
33. 23 Mar. 1874, Tait papers, *loc. cit.*
34. Shaftesbury to Tait, 27 Mar. 1874, Tait papers, *loc. cit.*
35. 10 Mar. 1874, Tait papers, *loc. cit.*
36. Tait to Disraeli, 11 Mar. 1874, copy, Tait papers, *loc. cit.*
37. Beaconsfield papers, B/XII/F/20.
38. Cairns to Disraeli, 25 Mar. 1874, Beaconsfield papers, B/XII/F/21a.
39. Tait to the Queen, 17 Mar. 1874, Royal Archives, D4/16.

40. The dean of Windsor to Tait, 19 Mar. 1874, Tait papers, vol. 93, ff. 150–1.
41. The Queen to Disraeli, 20 Mar. 1874, copy, Royal Archives, D4/21.
42. Disraeli to the Queen, 21 and 24 Mar. 1874, Royal Archives, D4/23a and 27.
43. 1 Apr. 1874, Tait papers, 1874 PWRA.
44. Tait to Disraeli, 2 and 4 Apr. 1874, Beaconsfield papers, B/XII/ F/7–8; Tait to the bishops, 7 Apr. 1874, copy, Tait papers, *loc. cit.*
45. Disraeli to Tait, 13 Apr. 1874, Tait papers, *loc. cit.*
46. Disraeli to the Queen, 18 Apr. 1874, Royal Archives, D4/35.
47. Tait's diary, 25 Apr. 1875.
48. Disraeli to the Queen, 18 Apr. 1874, *loc. cit.*
49. Beaconsfield papers, B/XII/F/87.
50. *Hansard*, 3rd series, CCXVIII (1874), 786–98.
51. *Ibid.*, 804–5.
52. *Chronicle of Convocation*, 1874, pp. 36–7.
53. *Ibid.*, pp. 125ff.
54. *Ibid.*, p. 211.
55. *Ibid.*, pp. 212 and 228.
56. *Ibid.*, appendix.
57. *Hansard*, 3rd series, CCXIX (1874), 65.
58. *Ibid.*, 55.
59. Augustus Arthur to Tait, 4 May 1874, Tait papers, 1874 PWRA.
60. Close to Tait, 7 May 1874, Tait papers, Vol. 93, ff. 169–70.
61. See e.g. J. H. Stephenton to Tait, 12 May, and A. Oates to Tait, 15 May, 1874 Tait papers, 1874 PWRA.
62. J. C. Whish to Tait, 3 June 1874, Tait papers, *loc. cit.*
63. See *Chronicle of Convocation*, 1874, p. 160; and E. V. Bligh to Tait, 30 May 1874, Tait papers, *loc. cit.*
64. Stanley's words, *Chronicle of Convocation*, 1874, pp. 163–4.
65. Bligh to Tait, 10 June 1874, Tait papers, *loc. cit.*
66. *Chronicle of Convocation*, 1874, pp. 42–3; Wordsworth, *A Plea for Toleration by Law, in Certain Ritual Matters* (Lincoln, 1874).
67. Carter to Tait, 3 May 1874, Tait papers, *loc. cit.*
68. John Martin to Tait, 2 May 1874, and L. R. Natpy to Tait, 6 May 1874, Tait papers, *loc. cit.*
69. *Hansard*, 3rd series, CCXIX (1874), 938.
70. Selborne, *Memorials*, part II (London, 1898), Vol. I, 343.
71. Thomson, 'The Ritual of the English Church', *Quarterly Review*, CXXXVII, 274 (Oct. 1874), 569; Selborne, *op. cit.*, part II, Vol. I, 344–5; Temple to Tait, 13 May 1874, and Jackson to Tait, 25 May 1874, Tait papers, *loc. cit.*

72. Edwin Hodder, *Life of Shaftesbury*, III, 346–7; and Tait's diary, 7 June 1874. See also Cairns' speech, *Hansard*, CCXIX (1874), 1148.
73. *Hansard*, 3rd series, CCXVIII (1874), 1664–6.
74. *Ibid.*, CCXIX (1874), 945.
75. *Ibid.*, 959.
76. *Ibid.*, CCXX (1874), 142.
77. *Ibid.*, CCXIX (1874), 1143.
78. *Ibid.*, 1143–8. Shaftesbury voted against his own proposal.
79. Disraeli to the Queen, 5 June 1874, Royal Archives, D4/56.
80. Bishop Charles R. Alford to Tait, 6 June 1874, Tait papers, 1874 PWRA.
81. *Hansard*, 3rd series, CCXIX (1874), 938.
82. The bishop of Peterborough to Tait, 13 June 1874, Tait papers, *loc. cit.*
83. Memorandum handed to the bishop of Peterborough, dated 10 June 1874, Tait papers, *loc. cit.*
84. *Hansard*, 3rd series, CCXIX (1874), 944–5.
85. *Ibid.*, CCXX (1874), 152.
86. *Church Times*, 19 June 1874.
87. *Pall Mall Gazette*, 18 June 1874.
88. *Hansard*, 3rd series, CCXX (1874), 407.
89. Carnarvon's speech, *ibid.*, 401.
90 *Hansard*, 3rd series, CCXX (1874), 399.
91. *Ibid.*, 407.
92. 1 July 1874.
93. 23 June 1874, Royal Archives, D4/78.
94. *Chronicle of Convocation*, 1874, pp. 317ff.
95. *Ibid.*, pp. 464–5.
96. Tait to Disraeli, 8 July 1874, Beaconsfield papers, B/XII/F/16.
97. Lord Granville to the Queen, 16 July 1874, and General Ponsonby to the Queen, 17 July 1874, Royal Archives, D5/14–15.
98. Morley, *Gladstone*, II, 498.
99. Granville to the Queen, 16 July 1874, Royal Archives, D5/14.
100. See D. C. Lathbury, ed., *Correspondence on Church and Religion of William Ewart Gladstone*, I, 398 and II, 310.
101. *Hansard*, 3rd series, CCXX (1874), 1372–92.
102. *Ibid.*, 1414–23.
103. *Ibid.*, 1423–31.
104. *Ibid.*, 1438.
105. Hart Dyke to Disraeli, 10 July 1874, Beaconsfield papers, B/XII/F/61.
106. The Queen to Disraeli, 10 July 1874, copy, Royal Archives, D5/2.

107. Disraeli to the Queen, 11 July 1874, G. E. Buckle, ed., *op. cit.*, II, 342.
108. Disraeli to the Queen, 12 July 1874, Royal Archives, D5/9.
109. *Hansard*, 3rd series, CCXX (1874), 1523-7.
110. *Ibid.*, CCXXI (1874), 38-44 and 67-75.
111. *Ibid.*, 61-2.
112. A. E. Gathorne-Hardy, *op. cit.*, I, 341.
113. *Hansard*, 3rd series, CCXXI (1874), 76-82.
114. Tait's diary, 19 July 1874.
115. *Hansard*, 3rd series, CCXXI (1874), 118-9.
116. Thirlwall to Tait, 18 July 1874, Tait papers, Vol. 93, f. 240.
117. Tait's diary, *loc. cit.*
118. *Ibid.*
119. For example, Beresford Hope's amendment to make bishops and archbishops liable to prosecution under the Bill was defeated 173 to 65. *Hansard*, 3rd series, CCXXI (1874), 900-5.
120. In the *Times*, 20 July 1874.
121. *Hansard*, 3rd series, CCXXI (1874), 626.
122. Tait and Thomson to Disraeli, 3 Aug. 1874, Beaconsfield papers, B/XII/F/69a.
123. 8 Aug. 1874.
124. 103 to 37. *Hansard*, 3rd series, CCXXI (1874), 888.
125. Disraeli to Tait, 3 Aug. 1874, Tait papers, Vol. 93, f. 262.
126. Tait to Thirlwall, 19 Aug. 1874, Tait papers, Vol. 93, ff. 300-1.
127. Tait related the events of this crisis in his diary and in a letter to the dean of Wells copied in the diary, Vol. LIV, 3-18.
128. Gladstone to his wife, 4 Aug. 1874, in D. C. Lathbury, ed., *op. cit.*, I, 393-4.
129. The bishop of Winchester to Tait, 13 Aug. 1874, Tait papers, Vol. 93, f. 292.
130. The bishop of Winchester to Tait, 10 July and 5 Aug. 1874, Tait papers, Vol. 93, ff. 230-3 and 271.
131. *Hansard*, 3rd series, CCXXI (1874), 1237.
132. Gladstone to his wife, 3 Aug. 1874, *loc. cit.*, 394.
133. The bishop of Rochester to Tait, 7 Aug. 1874, Tait papers, Vol. 93, f. 276.
134. Disraeli to Lady Chesterfield, 5 Aug. 1874, in the Marquis of Zetland, ed., *op. cit.*, I, 121-2.
135. The duke of Richmond to Tait, 5 Aug. 1874, Tait papers, Vol. 93, f. 274.
136. *Hansard*, 3rd series, CCXXI (1874), 1253.
137. *Ibid.*, 1341-54.
138. *Ibid.*, 1358-9.

139. *Hansard*, 3rd series, CCXXI (1874), 1360–6.
140. Disraeli to Salisbury and Salisbury to Disraeli, copy, 5 Aug. 1874, Salisbury papers.
141. W. C. Lake to Tait, 2 Aug. 1874, Tait papers, Vol. 93, ff. 257–8.
142. Tait to the Queen, 5 Aug. 1874, Royal Archives, D5/41.
143. Cf. Tait's speech on first presenting the Bill, *Hansard*, 3rd series, CCXVIII (1874), 791.
144. Delane to Tait, 9 Aug., Wellesley to Tait, 11 Aug., and Jowett to Tait, 13 Aug. 1874, Tait papers, vol. 93, ff. 278, 286 and 291.
145. *Hansard*, 3rd series, CCXXI (1874), 79.
146. See *The Press and St. James's Chronicle*, 8 Aug. 1874.

CHAPTER EIGHT

Reforming the Church Under Disraeli, 1875–1879

1. CXXXVII, 273 (July 1874), 281–2.
2. Disraeli to Tait, 8 Apr. 1874, Tait papers, Vol. 93, f. 36.
3. Gorst to Disraeli, 29 July 1874, Beaconsfield papers, B/XII/F/67.
4. Beaconsfield papers, B/XII/F/81a.
5. *Loc. cit.*, B/XII/F/86.
6. Rev. W. G. Cookesley to Disraeli, 7 Aug. 1874, *loc. cit.*, B/XII/F/74.
7. S. Maccoby, *English Radicalism 1853–1886* (London, 1938), 196.
8. D. C. Lathbury, ed., *op. cit.*, I, 395.
9. Russell to Tait, 25 Jan. 1875, Tait papers, Vol. 94, f. 58.
10. Monypenny and Buckle, *Disraeli*, VI, 97.
11. R. T. Shannon, *Gladstone and the Bulgarian Agitation 1876* (London, 1963), 65.
12. Analysis of rural deans' returns, Tait papers, Vol. 211, ff. 101–2.
13. Shaftesbury to Tait, 9 Dec. 1874, Tait papers, Vol. 93, f. 331. See also the bishop of London to Tait, 17 Dec. 1874, Tait papers, *loc. cit.*, f. 337.
14. Ecclesiastical Fees Redistribution Bill, Parl. Papers, 1875, II, 19–26.
15. Tait's diary, 25 Apr. 1875; Disraeli to Tait, 17 June 1875, Tait papers, Vol. 94, f. 242.
16. Parl. Papers, 1875, II, 27–32.
17. Tait to Disraeli, 9 July 1875, Beaconsfield papers, B/XII/F/17.
18. Ecclesiastical Offices and Fees Bill (as brought from the House of Lords to the House of Commons), Parl. Papers, 1876, II, 181–212.
19. Tait to J. B. Lee, 25 Jan. 1876, copy, Tait papers, vol. 220, f. 26.

20. J. B. Lee to J. M. Davenport, 17 Jan. 1876, Tait papers, *loc. cit.*, f. 15.
21. Tait papers, *loc. cit.*, f. 35.
22. Report of the Committee on the Ecclesiastical Offices and Fees Bill, 23 Nov. 1876, *Chronicle of Convocation*, 1877, appendix.
23. W. H. Stephenson, C. I. Herries and A. West to the bishops, 2 June 1876, copy, Tait papers, 1877 Home 36.
24. G. T. Townsend to Tait, 14 Mar. 1876, Tait papers, vol. 220, f. 73.
25. Tait to Cross, 4 Dec. 1876, copy, Tait papers, vol. 229, ff. 31–2.
26. Disraeli to Tait, 21 Dec. 1876, Tait papers, *loc. cit.*, f. 34.
27. Resolution of a general meeting of registrars and secretaries, 18 Apr. 1877, Tait papers, *loc. cit.*, f. 40.
28. Parl. Papers, 1877, II, 83.
29. Penzance to Tait, 29 July 1876, Tait papers, vol. 221, ff. 198–9.
30. See the *Saturday Review*, 14 Apr. 1877.
31. Penzance to Tait, 2 Feb. 1879, Tait papers, vol. 99, ff. 42–5.
32. *Chronicle of Convocation*, 1878, pp. 47–8.
33. Benson to Cross, 1 Jan. 1882 [1883], Cross papers, Add. MSS. 51,273, f. 126.
34. Monypenny and Buckle, *Disraeli*, V, 368.
35. *Times'* editorial, 31 May 1877.
36. *Hansard*, 3rd series, CCXXI (1874), 1239.
37. CXXXVII, 273 (July 1874), 281–2.
38. The bishop of Winchester to Tait, 27 and 31 Oct., and 21 Nov. 1874, Tait papers, vol. 93, ff. 98–104 and 114–16.
39. The bishop of Winchester to Tait, 21 Nov. 1874, *loc. cit.*, f. 120.
40. The bishop of Winchester to Tait, 14 Jan. 1875, Tait papers, vol. 93, ff. 9–12; Cross's speech, *Hansard*, 3rd series, CCXXII (1875), 1773–4.
41. The bishop of Rochester to Tait, 6 Oct. 1876, Tait papers, vol. 96, f. 224.
42. Tait to Cross, 9 Dec. 1875, Cross papers, Add. MSS. 51,271, f. 104.
43. See Beresford Hope to Tait, 5 Mar. 1875, Tait papers, vol. 94, ff. 115–16.
44. Cross to Tait, 22 Dec. 1875, Tait papers, vol. 216, ff. 388–9.
45. *Ibid*.
46. Tait to Archdeacon Earle, 14 Feb. 1876, copy, Tait papers, vol. 217, ff. 203–6.
47. Cross to Tait, 4 Aug. 1876, Tait papers, vol. 232, ff. 188–9; the bishop of Exeter to Cross, 13 Sept. 1876, Cross papers, Add. MSS. 51,271, f. 152.

48. Cross to Tait, 13 Mar. 1876, Tait papers, vol. 216, f. 381. Originally the Cornish see was to be created under this bill.
49. *Hansard*, 3rd series, CXCV (1869), 1330–1.
50. Tait to Lyttelton, 13 Mar. 1875, copy, Tait papers, vol. 94, ff. 137–8.
51. Harcourt to Tait, 25 Feb. 1875, Tait papers, vol. 94, f. 99.
52. *Hansard*, 3rd series, CCXXIV (1875), 1077–81.
53. Cross to Tait, 13 Mar. 1876, *loc. cit.*, ff. 381–2.
54. The bishop of London to Tait, n.d., Tait papers, vol. 96, f. 176.
55. The bishop of Lincoln to Tait, 4 Apr. 1876, Tait papers, vol. 217, ff. 214–15.
56. The bishop of Lincoln to Cross, 25 Jan. 1878, Cross papers, Add. MSS. 51,271, ff. 219–20.
57. Tait to Cross, 29 Nov. 1876, Cross papers, Add. MSS. 51,271, f. 172.
58. *Hansard*, 3rd series, CCXXXIV (1877), 180–1.
59. *Guardian*, 20 Mar. 1878.
60. Editorial, 20 Mar. 1878.
61. *Leeds Mercury*, 31 May 1877.
62. Northcote to Tait, 4 July 1878, Tait papers, vol. 98, f. 87.
63. Cross, *A Political History* (privately printed, 1903), 61.
64. Cross to Tait, 11 Feb. 1879, Tait papers, vol. 247, ff. 238–9.
65. Cross, *op. cit.*, 60–1.
66. Minutes of the bishops' meeting, 22 Jan. 1875, Tait papers, memoranda of bishops' meetings, 1871–9.
67. This estimate is based on the figures for 1830 when 7,268 of the 11,342 livings in England and Wales had private patrons. *Extraordinary Black Book* (1831), 41.
68. *Hansard*, 3rd series, CCXXII (1875), 832–5.
69. Tait, *Some Thoughts on the Duties of the Established Church of England as a National Church*, 12.
70. *Hansard*, 3rd series, CCXLVI (1879), 386–8.
71. Shaftesbury to Montagu Corry, 11 July 1874, Beaconsfield papers, B/XII/F/54.
72. *Hansard*, 3rd series, CCXX (1874), 1421.
73. *Hansard*, 3rd series, CCXXI (1874), 1165.
74. *Times*, 7 Nov. 1877.
75. *Chronicle of Convocation*, 1879, p. 353.
76. *Ibid.*, 393.
77. Michael Reynolds, *Martyr of Ritualism*, 210.
78. Liddon, *Life of Pusey*, IV, 289.
79. *Supra*, 107.

80. For a description of the Bill, see the Report of the committee of the Lower House on Matters Parliamentary, *Chronicle of Convocation*, 1874, appendix.
81. CXXXVII, 273 (July 1874), 277–80.
82. *Chronicle of Convocation*, 1878, p. 95.
83. See *Chronicle of Convocation*, 1874, p. 420.
84. *Hansard*, 3rd series, CCXX (1874), 413.
85. *Supra*, 102ff.
86. In the *Guardian*, 4 Apr. 1877.
87. *Times*, 6 Apr. 1877.
88. 5 April 1877.
89. Tait papers, vol. of news clippings, 1877–80, f. 47.
90. *Church Congress Reports*, 1877, p. 291.
91. *Ibid.*, 283–4.
92. *Ibid.*, 595–7.
93. 17 Oct. 1877.
94. Editorial, 12 Oct. 1877. Cf. editorial on 5 Apr. 1877.
95. *Chronicle of Convocation*, 1878, pp. 91–110.
96. *Ibid.*, 127–8.
97. Copy in *Chronicle of Convocation*, 1878, appendix.
98. *Chronicle of Convocation*, 1879, pp. 318 and 321–2.
99. *Ibid.*, 203.
100. *Ibid.*, 323–4.
101. *Chronicle of Convocation*, 1879, pp. 436–7 and 442–3.
102. *Church Times*, 1 Aug. 1879.

CHAPTER NINE

The Failure to Put Down Ritualism

1. CXXXVII, 273 (July 1874), 274–5.
2. Speech at the annual meeting of the Canterbury Diocesan Church Building Association, 12 Aug. 1874, in *Times*, 13 Aug. 1874.
3. Address to a diocesan conference of laity and clergy, Tait papers, vol. of news clippings, f. 201.
4. 1875, p. 324.
5. G. B. Roberts, *The History of the English Church Union, 1859–1894* (London, 1895), 404.
6. Pusey to the Association of the Catholic Union for Prayer, *Times*, 17 Sept. 1874.
7. Liddon, *Life of Pusey*, IV, 279–80.
8. *Times*, 8 Mar. 1875.

9. The bishop of Salisbury to his archdeacon, 8 Mar. 1875, printed copy, Tait papers, vol. of news clippings, 1868–77, f. 205; the bishop of Durham to ed., *Times*, 11 Mar. 1875.
10. The archbishop of York to Tait, 16 Feb. 1875, Tait papers, vol. 210, ff. 185–6.
11. The bishop of Gloucester and Bristol to Tait, 10 Feb. 1875, Tait papers, *loc. cit.*, f. 139.
12. The bishop of Lichfield to Tait, 12 Feb. 1875, Tait papers, *loc. cit.*, f. 142.
13. B. A. Smith, *Dean Church*, 184.
14. *Times*, 17 Sept. 1874.
15. Ridsdale's address to his congregation, 25 Sept. 1875, Tait papers, vol. 211, f. 117.
16. Ridsdale to Tait, 3 Jan. 1876, Tait papers, vol. 217, f. 281.
17. B. Shaw to Tait, 27 Apr. 1875, and Dr. Deane to Tait, 3 May 1875, Tait papers, vol. 211, ff. 218–23.
18. *Chronicle of Convocation*, 1876, pp. 93–101; Tait's diary, 13 Aug. 1876.
19. The bishop of Lincoln to Craufurd Tait, 20 Sept. 1876, Tait papers, vol. 215, f. 62.
20. Tait to Cairns, 5 Oct. 1876, copy, Tait papers, *loc. cit.*, f. 113.
21. Pusey to Tait, 1 Nov. 1876, Tait papers, vol. 221, ff. 303–4.
22. Tait to Pusey, 4 Nov. 1876, copy, Tait papers, *loc. cit.*, ff. 310–13.
23. Tait's diary, 28 Jan. 1877.
24. Stanley to Tait, 21 Jan. 1877, Tait papers, vol. 97, ff. 4–5.
25. Pusey to Tait, 15 Mar. 1877, Tait papers, vol. 97, ff. 24–5. Pusey also wrote to Selborne, one of the law lords hearing the case, on the same day with similar purpose. Selborne, *Memorials*, part II, vol. I, 383–4.
26. Sir Fitzroy Kelly to the Rev. P. C. Ellis, in *Times*, 29 Oct. 1877; Sir Robert Phillimore, *The Ecclesiastical Law of the Church of England* (London, 2nd ed., 1895), II, 976.
27. *Chronicle of Convocation*, 1877, p. 192.
28. Tait to Ridsdale, 7 June 1877, copy, Tait papers, vol. 231, f. 164.
29. *Chronicle of Convocation*, 1878, p. 111.
30. Editorial, 27 Mar. 1878.
31. D.C.L. to ed., *Pall Mall Gazette*, 28 Nov. 1877.
32. The bishop of Rochester to Tait, 1 Jan. 1877, Tait papers, vol. 97, ff. 181–2.
33. *Globe*, 13 Jan. 1877.
34. The bishop of Lincoln to Canon Hole, in *Guardian*, 17 Jan. 1877.
35. 53 Geo. III, c. 127.
36. Penzance to Tait, 1 Jan. 1877, Tait papers, vol. 96, f. 136.

37. J. G. Lockhart, *Charles Lindley Viscount Halifax*, I, 207–13.
38. Pusey to Tait, Easter Eve 1877, Tait papers, vol. 97, f. 73.
39. *Guardian*, 24 Jan. 1877.
40. 14 May 1877.
41. Tooth to Tait, 30 June 1877, in *Times*, 16 July 1877.
42. Tait to Tooth, 9 July 1877, *loc. cit.*
43. *Times*, 20 Nov. 1877.
44. 27 Nov. 1877.
45. Penzance to Tait, 13 Nov. 1875, Tait papers, vol. 233, f. 84.
46. Tooth to Tait, 21 Nov. 1877, Tait papers, vol. 232, ff. 100–3.
47. Michael Reynolds, *Martyr of Ritualism*, 203 and 205.
48. *Guardian*, 5 Dec. 1877.
49. 14 July 1877.
50. The bishop of Lichfield to the Rev. C. Bodington, 8 Nov. 1877, Tait papers, vol. of news clippings, 1877–80, f. 105; Statement of the archbishop of Canterbury why proceedings should not be taken on the representation against the Rev. C. Bodington, 19 Nov. 1877, Tait papers, vol. 228, ff. 109–10.
51. Report of the Commissioners appointed to inquire into the Constitution and Working of the Ecclesiastical Courts, Parl. Papers, 1883, XXIV, 48.
52. The bishop of Oxford to Tait, 24 Apr. 1878, Tait papers, vol. 98, ff. 64–5; J. F. M. Carter, *Life and Work of the Rev. T. T. Carter*, 52 and 56.
53. Penzance to Tait, 15 Nov. 1879, Tait papers, vol. 245, ff. 247–8.
54. R. T. Davidson to C. Powell, 4 Nov. 1879, copy, Tait papers, *loc. cit.*, ff. 216–17.
55. J. B. Lee to Tait, 5 Dec. 1879, Tait papers, *loc. cit.*, f. 321.
56. Penzance to Tait, 15 Nov. 1879, Tait papers, *loc. cit.*, f. 249.
57. J. B. Lee to Tait, 24 Nov. 1879, Tait papers, *loc. cit.*, ff. 301–2.
58. Tait to the bishop of Worcester, 12 Dec. 1879, copy, Tait papers, *loc. cit.*, f. 340.
59. Lee to R. T. Davidson, 18 Dec. 1879, Tait papers, *loc. cit.*, f. 389.
60. Mackonochie to Tait, 20 May 1875, Tait papers, vol. 209, f. 207.
61. Ridsdale to C. L. Wood, 19 Dec. 1881, Tait papers, 1882 separate packets A2.
62. J. G. Lockhart, *Charles Lindley Viscount Halifax*, I, 226.
63. *Hansard*, 3rd series, CCXXXIV (1877), 1741–5.
64. G. R. Balleine, *A History of the Evangelical Party in the Church of England* (London, 1951), 185; three printed sheets and a printed letter by the Reformed Episcopal Church congregation in Southend, Essex, Tait papers, vol. 231, ff. 149–53.

65. The bishop of Winchester to Tait, 2 Apr. 1877, Tait papers, vol. 97, f. 75.
66. R. T. Shannon, *Gladstone and the Bulgarian Agitation 1876*, 171ff.
67. Tait's diary, 28 Jan. 1877.
68. *The Church and Law* (London, 1877).
69. p. 15.
70. Tait's diary, 12 Aug. and 9 Dec. 1877.
71. *Record*, 12 Dec. 1877; Ryle to ed., *Record*, 14 Dec. 1877.
72. *Church Congress Reports*, 1877, p. 18.
73. Parl. Papers, 1876, LVIII, 553–658.
74. *Church Congress Reports*, 1877, pp. 20–1.
75. 18 Oct. 1877.
76. *Times'* editorial, 13 Oct., Tait's diary, 14 Oct., and the *Church Times*, 19 Oct. 1877.
77. 8 Dec. 1877.
78. Trevor to Tait, 14 Nov. 1877, Tait papers, vol. 233, ff. 154–5.
79. T. T. Carter, *Constitutional Order* (London, 1877), 40–3.
80. Liddon, *Life of Pusey*, IV, 290.
81. Memorandum by Wood, 13 Apr. 1878, and Wood to Tait, 9 Nov. 1878, Tait papers, vol. 241, ff. 181–2 and 202–3; Wood to Tait, 19 May 1878, Tait papers, vol. 98, ff. 83a–e.
82. Suggestions toward the peace of the Church, n.d. [? 20 Jan. 1879], Tait papers, 1878 Home 289.
83. J. G. Lockhart, *Charles Lindley Viscount Halifax*, I, 207.
84. *Conference of Bishops of the Anglican Communion*, holden at Lambeth Palace, July 1878: Letter from the bishops . . . (London, 1878), 18 and 40.
85. See Tait's diary, 6 Oct. 1878.
86. Davidson and Benham, *Tait*, II, 554.
87. Tait's diary, 27 July 1879.
88. *Catharine and Craufurd Tait*, ed. Wm. Benham (London, 1879).
89. Tait's diary, 22 Dec. 1878.
90. Diary, 12 Oct. 1879.

CHAPTER TEN

Conciliating the Nonconformists

1. W. G. Addison, *Religious Equality in Modern England 1714–1914* (London, 1944), 117.
2. Selborne, *Memorials*, part II, vol. I, 364–5.
3. R. Tudur, *Congregationalism in England 1662–1962* (London, 1962), 277.

4. A. W. W. Dale, *The Life of R. W. Dale of Birmingham*, 378.
5. Selborne, *op. cit.*, part I, vol. I, 359.
6. *Times*, 7 Nov. 1877.
7. Rough outline of Tait's speech to the archdeacons and rural deans of his diocese, Sept. 1875, Tait papers, vol. 211, f. 182.
8. Davidson and Benham, *Tait*, I, 13–18 and 22.
9. Tait, *The Church of the Future*, 8.
10. Tait's speech at the Mansion House, *Times*, 18 June 1874.
11. Tait, *Some Thoughts on the Duties of the Established Church of England as a National Church*, 107.
12. Memorandum dated 8 June 1876, Tait papers, vol. 216, f. 348.
13. The bishop of Rochester to Tait, 12 July 1876; the bishop of Lichfield to Tait, 4 July 1876; the bishop of Lincoln to Tait, 7 July 1876; Dr. John Stoughton to Tait, 15 May 1876, Tait papers, *loc. cit.*, ff. 334 and 359–64.
14. The bishop of Gloucester and Bristol to Tait, 26 Sept. 1870, Tait papers, vol. 88, ff. 155–6.
15. Tait, *The Church of the Future*, 14.
16. Tait, *Some Thoughts on the Duties of the Established Church of England as a National Church*, 101–2.
17. Speech to a group of clergy, *Times*, 24 Sept. 1869.
18. Tait to Cairns, 18 May 1875, in *Record*, 24 May 1875.
19. Dale, *The Day of Salvation* (London, 1875).
20. *Hansard*, 3rd series, CCLXIX (1882), 823.
21. Tait to the Rev. R. P. Pelly, 17 Jan. 1882, copy, and G. S. Railton to R. T. Davidson, 10 Aug. 1882, Tait papers, 1882 separate packets A 3. Cf. Richard Collier, *The General next to God*, 103.
22. Wood to Tait, 29 June 1870, Tait papers, vol. 168, f. 221.
23. Tait to Wood, 2 July 1870, copy, Tait papers, *loc. cit.*, f. 224.
24. Wood to Tait, 8 July 1870, Tait papers, *loc. cit.*, f. 225.
25. *Times*, 11 July 1870.
26. Wood to Sandford, 15 July 1870, Tait papers, *loc. cit.*, f. 236.
27. Tait to Canon Carter, 11 Aug. 1870, copy, Tait papers, *loc. cit.*, ff. 277–84.
28. Stanley to Sandford, 15 Aug. 1870, Tait papers, *loc. cit.*, f. 296.
29. *Chronicle of Convocation*, 1871, pp. 276–80.
30. Edwin Hodder, *Life of Samuel Morley*, 351–2.
31. Rough outline of Tait's speech to the archdeacons and rural deans of his diocese, Sept. 1875, Tait papers, vol. 211, f. 182.
32. Tait's opening address to the Canterbury diocesan conference, in *Times*, 19 Jan. 1876.
33. Rough outline of Tait's speech to the archdeacons and rural deans of his diocese, Sept. 1875, *loc. cit.*, f. 183.

34. J. H. Overton and Elizabeth Wordsworth, *Christopher Words-worth*, 267–9.
35. *Ibid.*, 242ff.
36. *Times*, 11 Aug. 1874; J. H. Overton and Elizabeth Wordsworth, *op. cit.*, 243–5.
37. W. G. Addison, *op. cit.*, 118.
38. Rough outline of Tait's speech to the archdeacons and rural deans of his diocese, Sept. 1875, *loc. cit.*
39. *Hansard*, 3rd series, CCXXXIII (1877), 1893–9.
40. Tait's diary, 13 May 1877.
41. Tait's diary, 20 May 1877.
42. D. Fraser to Tait, 26 Apr. 1877, Tait papers, vol. 244, f. 225; Lord Harrowby to Tait, 10 May 1877, and the bishop of Glouces-ter and Bristol to Tait, 2 Apr. 1877, Tait papers, vol. 97, ff. 80 and 153–4; *Hansard*, 3rd series, CCXXXIV (1877), 1045.
43. Richmond's speech, *Hansard*, 3rd series, CCXXXIV (1877), 1076–7.
44. *Hansard*, 3rd series, CCXXIX (1876), 616–26; Tait's diary, 21 May 1876.
45. *Hansard*, 3rd series, CCXXXIV (1877), 1081–92; Monypenny and Buckle, *Disraeli*, VI, 162–3.
46. Tait's diary, 20 May 1877.
47. *Hansard*, 3rd series, CCXXXIV (1877), 1928–34.
48. Monypenny and Buckle, *Disraeli*, VI, 163; A. E. Gathorne-Hardy, *Gathorne Hardy, first Earl of Cranbrook*, II, 23.
49. *Hansard*, 3rd series, CCXXXV (1877), 181–3.
50. W. A. Scott Robertson to Craufurd Tait, 12 June 1877, and accompanying memorial, Tait papers, vol. 244, ff. 252–5. *Chronicle of Convocation*, 1878, p. 5.
51. Speech to the Lincoln diocesan conference, 5 Oct. 1877, Tait papers, vol. of news clippings, 1877–80, f. 48.
52. *Chronicle of Convocation*, 1878, p. 144.
53. See e.g. the bishop of Winchester's speech at his diocesan con-ference, *Daily Express*, 2 July 1877.
54. *Chronicle of Convocation*, 1879, pp. 268–9 and 364–70.
55. H. J. Hanham, *Elections and Party Management*, 193 and 232.
56. H. J. Hanham, *op. cit.*, 124.
57. J. F. Glaser, *Nonconformity and Liberalism, 1868–1885* (Harvard University doctoral dissertation, 1949), 484–5.
58. *Nonconformist*, 29 Apr., and editorial in the *Morning Post*, 4 May 1880.
59. Hanham, *loc. cit.*
60. Diary, 6 June 1880.

61. Selborne to Tait, 7 May 1880, Tait papers, 1880 separate packets.
62. Selborne, *Memorials*, part II, vol. I, 481–2.
63. Tait to Selborne, 10 May 1880, copy, Tait papers, *loc. cit.*
64. Selborne to Tait, 12 May 1880, Tait papers, *loc. cit.*
65. Tait papers, *loc. cit.*
66. *Hansard*, 3rd series, CCLII (1880), 1018; *Chronicle of Convocation*, 1880, p. 213; *Correspondence on 'The Burials Bill' between the Lord Archbishop of Canterbury . . . and the Rev. F. C. Hingeston-Randolph* (London, 1880), 7.
67. *Chronicle of Convocation*, 1880, pp. 86–104 and 208.
68. A. E. Gathorne-Hardy, *op. cit.*, II, 142–3; *Church Congress Reports*, 1880, p. 528.
69. Wordsworth to Disraeli, 31 May 1880, Beaconsfield papers, B/XXI/W/519.
70. *Hansard*, 3rd series, CCLII (1880), 1023.
71. Tait's diary, 27 June 1880.
72. Morgan to Tait, 30 Aug. 1880, Tait papers, vol. 100, f. 68.
73. D. C. Lathbury, ed., *op. cit.*, I, 173–4.
74. *Ibid.*, 174.
75. See C. R. Knight's speech, *Chronicle of Convocation*, 1880, p. 211.
76. *Church Congress Reports*, 1880, p. 528; *Hansard*, 3rd series, CCLVI (1880), 574–5; Selborne to Tait, 26 Aug. 1880, Tait papers, 1880 separate packets.
77. *Hansard*, 3rd series, CCLVI (1880), 572–94.
78. Selborne to Tait, 1st letter of 1 Sept. 1880, Tait papers, 1880 separate packets; Robert Blake, *Disraeli*, 727 and 731; *Hansard*, 3rd series, CCLVI (1880), 1162–6.
79. F. W. Doxat to Tait, 6 Sept. 1880, Tait papers, *loc. cit.*
80. C. N. Williams to E. Davis, 19 Oct. 1880, quoted in a poster entitled 'A Modern Illustration of a Christian Spirit', Tait papers, *loc. cit.*
81. F. Strickland to Tait, 4 Sept. 1880, Tait papers, *loc. cit.*
82. Tait's diary, 12 Dec. 1880.
83. The bishop of Lincoln to C. F. Bonner, St. Luke's Day 1880, printed, Tait papers, *loc cit.*
84. *Chronicle of Convocation*, 1881, p. 374; Hall to Tait, 25 July 1881, Tait papers, 1881 Home 100.
85. Selborne, *op. cit.*, part I, vol. I, 487.
86. S. Maccoby, *English Radicalism 1853–1886* (London, 1938), 275.
87. Tait's diary, 3 Apr. 1881, and his speech at the annual meeting of the Church Defence Institution, in the *National Church*, Aug. 1882.
88. Samuel Morley's speech at the meeting in support of a memorial to Tait, *Times*, 27 Jan. 1883.

CHAPTER ELEVEN

Pushed Aside

1. Percy Talbot to Tait, 29 July 1880, Tait papers, 1880 Separate packets.
2. Scott Holland to R. T. Davidson, 9 Apr. 1880, and Davidson to Holland, 17 Apr. 1880, copy, Tait papers, *loc. cit.*
3. See his speech at the Canterbury Diocesan Conference, 16 July 1879, in the *Kentish Gazette*, 22 July 1879.
4. Tait's diary, 12 Dec. 1880.
5. Percy Talbot to Tait, 29 July 1880, and T. R. Andrews to Tait, 3 Aug. 1880, Tait papers, *loc. cit.*
6. Statement prepared for Dale's signature, Tait papers, *loc. cit.*
7. Penzance to Tait, 18 Dec. 1880, Tait papers, 1880 Home 144.
8. Penzance to Tait, 23 Oct. 1880, Tait papers, 1880 Home 183.
9. *Church Review*, 5 Nov. 1880, p. 549.
10. Tait to H. A. Brown, in the *Times*, 13 Nov. 1880.
11. Tait's diary, 12 Dec. 1880.
12. Tait to the bishop of Worcester, 30 Oct. 1880, copy, Tait papers, 1880 Home 96.
13. Enraght, *My Prosecution under the Public Worship Regulation Act* (Birmingham, 1883), 14.
14. *Ibid.*, 15; Tait to J. Anderson, 14 Feb. 1880, copy, and to T. Andrews, 21 Feb. 1880, copy, Tait papers, 1881 separate packets 1.
15. Andrews to Tait, 26 Feb. 1880, Tait papers, *loc. cit.*
16. Philpott to Tait, 2 Nov. 1880, Tait papers, 1880 Home 96.
17. Tait's diary, 12 Dec. 1880.
18. Tait papers, vol. of news clippings, 1881–3, f. 1.
19. Richard Nugent to Tait, 13 Jan. 1881, Tait papers, 1880 Home 177; R. T. Davidson to the Rev. T. L. Taylor, 12 Jan. 1881, copy, Tait papers, 1880 Home 95.
20. *Times*, 18 Dec. 1880.
21. Printed copy, 10 Jan. 1881, Tait papers, 1880 separate packets 4.
22. Newspaper copy of address dated 31 Jan. 1881, Tait papers, *loc. cit.*
23. Talbot to Davidson, 31 Dec. 1880, Tait papers, 1880 separate packets.
24. Tait's diary, 12 Dec. 1880.
25. Memorandum on Ritual Difficulties, and Tait to Gladstone, 16 Dec. 1880, copy, Tait papers, vol. 100, ff. 177–80.

26. Gladstone to Tait, 18 Dec. 1880, and Gladstone to Selborne, 22 Dec. 1880, Tait papers, vol. 100, ff. 199–200 and 207–9.
27. Report of the Commissioners appointed to inquire into the Constitution and Working of the Ecclesiastical Courts, Parl. Papers, 1883, XXIV, 627.
28. 22 Dec. 1880, Tait papers, *loc. cit.*, f. 208.
29. Selborne to Tait, 18 Dec. 1880, Tait papers, *loc. cit.*, ff. 193–4.
30. Selborne to Tait, 24 Dec. 1880, *loc. cit.*, f. 214.
31. Selborne, *Memorials*, part II, vol. I, 394–5.
32. Tait's diary, 26 Dec. 1880.
33. Draft memorandum for Selborne, 18 Jan. 1881, Tait papers, vol. 100, ff. 80–1.
34. Memorandum on the representation of the clergy in Convocation, 31 Jan. 1881, by Selborne, Tait papers, 1880 separate packets.
35. Tait's diary, 20 Mar. 1881.
36. Gladstone to Tait, 22 Jan. 1881, Tait papers, vol. 100, ff. 253–4.
37. Liddon, *Life of Pusey*, IV, 364.
38. 5 Feb. 1881, Tait papers, vol. 100, ff. 298–9.
39. Salisbury to Tait, 5 Feb. 1881, Tait papers, vol. 100, ff. 300–9.
40. *Chronicle of Convocation*, 1881, p. 6.
41. Canon Gregory to Tait, 28 Feb. 1881, and Tait to Ryle, 1 Mar. 1881, copy, Tait papers, 1881 Home 60; M. L. Loane, *John Charles Ryle*, 50.
42. Thomson to Tait, 5 Feb. 1881, Benson papers (Lambeth Palace), Misc. packets, ecclesiastical courts.
43. Tait to Thomson, 12 Feb. 1881, copy, Tait papers, vol. 101, f. 306.
44. *Hansard*, 3rd series, CCLIX (1881), 378–413.
45. Thomas Hughes, *James Fraser*, 254 ff., is the source of much of the following information.
46. Tait's diary, 26 Feb. 1882.
47. Thomas Hughes, *op. cit.*, 259.
48. *Ibid.*, 260–1.
49. Green to R. T. Davidson, 19 Jan. 1882, Tait papers, 1882 separate packets.
50. Thomas Hughes, *James Fraser*, 263; the bishop of Manchester to Tait, 13 Jan. 1882, Tait papers, 1882 separate packets A2.
51. Sir Wm. Harcourt to Tait, 25 Aug. 1881, and the Rev. Benjamin Harrison to R. T. Davidson, 16 Aug. 1881, Tait papers, 1881 Home 57.
52. *Hansard*, 3rd series, CCLXV (1881), 806–7, and Warton's speech, *Hansard*, 3rd series, CCLXIX (1882), 378.
53. A. G. Gardiner, *Life of Sir William Harcourt*, I, 384–5; Katharine Lake, ed., *Memorials of William Charles Lake*, 252.

54. An Opinion, 1 Dec. 1881, by the Attorney General, the Solicitor General, and S. L. Smith, Tait papers, 1882 separate packets A2.
55. Selborne to Tait, 9 Jan. 1882, Tait papers, 1882 separate packets; Selborne to Tait, 15 Apr. 1882, Tait papers, 1882 separate packets A2.
56. *Chronicle of Convocation*, 1882, pp. 156-7.
57. Minutes of bishops' meeting, 2 May 1882, Benson papers (Lambeth Palace), Notebook of Minutes of Bishops' Meetings, 1881-5; Tait to Salisbury, 12 May 1882, copy, Tait papers, vol. 100, f. 154; *Hansard*, 3rd series, CCLXIX (1882), 812.
58. Resolutions of the Birmingham Working Men's Branch of the Church Association, 8 June 1882, Tait papers, 1882 Home no register number.
59. Tait to Gladstone, 15 July 1882, Gladstone papers, Add. MSS. 44,331, ff. 225-7; Gladstone to Tait, 17 July 1882, Tait papers, 1882 separate packets.
60. *Hansard*, 3rd series, CCLXXIII (1882), 1962-8.
61. Malcolm MacColl to Mrs. Davidson, 7 Oct. 1882, Tait papers, 1882 Home 78.
62. 16 Aug. 1882, copy, Tait papers, 1882 separate packets A2.
63. 17 Aug. 1882, Tait papers, *loc. cit.*
64. *Hansard*, 3rd series, CCLXXI (1882), 1374-7.
65. J. O. Johnston, *Life of Liddon*, 294-5. Cf. W. L. Arnstein, *The Bradlaugh Case* (Oxford, 1965), 161-7.
66. Davidson and Benham, *Tait*, II, 585.
67. Parl. Papers, 1882, XX, 20.
68. *Hansard*, 3rd series, CCLXXI (1882), 4-11.
69. *Hansard*, 3rd series, CCLXXIII (1882), 1918-21.
70. Diary, 1 Jan. 1882.
71. 'Thoughts suggested by Mr. Mozley's Oxford Reminiscences', *Macmillan's Magazine*, XLVI, 276 (Oct. 1882), 417-23.
72. p. 421.
73. p. 419.
74. pp. 422-3.
75. 2 Oct.
76. 'Thoughts suggested by Mr. Mozley's Oxford Reminiscences', 423.
77. Tait, *Religious Knowledge and Religious Training* (London, 1876), 19.
78. 'Thoughts suggested by Mr. Mozley's Oxford Reminiscences', 418.
79. Memorandum by the Lord Chancellor on the Case of the Rev. S. F. Green, 9 Oct. 1882, Tait papers, 1882 separate packets. A

copy of this was sent to Fraser. Also Tait to the bishop of Manchester, 10 Oct. 1882, copy, Tait papers, 1882 separate packets A2.

80. Thomas Hughes, *James Fraser*, 273–4.
81. *Times*, 6 Nov. 1882.
82. Tait to Mackonochie, 10 Nov. 1882, copy, Tait papers, 1882 Home 79.
83. Mackonochie to Tait, 11 Nov. 1882, Tait papers, *loc. cit.*
84. 21 Nov. 1882, copy, Tait papers, *loc. cit.*
85. Mackonochie to Davidson, 22 Nov. 1882, Tait papers, *loc. cit.*
86. Michael Reynolds, *Martyr of Ritualism*, 248.
87. Mackonochie to Tait, 23 Nov. 1882, Tait papers, *loc. cit.*
88. Editorial, 12 Dec. 1882.
89. Michael Reynolds, *op. cit.*, 259ff.
90. Editorial, 4 Dec. 1882.
91. Tait papers, vol. of news clippings, 1881–3, f. 180.
92. Parl. Papers, 1883, XXIV, 218–20.
93. *Ibid.*, 602–5.
94. *Ibid.*, 479–83 and 586–7.
95. The bishop of Truro to Davidson, 18 Oct. 1882, and the bishop of Winchester to the bishop of Truro, 19 Oct. 1882, Benson papers (Lambeth Palace), Misc. packets, ecclesiastical courts.
96. Davidson and Benham, *Tait*, II, 588, footnote 1; *Chronicle of Convocation*, 1884, pp. 37–8.
97. Parl. Papers, 1883, XXIV, 5–60.
98. p. 53.
99. Davidson to Archbishop Benson, 28 July 1883, Benson papers (Lambeth Palace), Misc. packets, ecclesiastical courts.
100. Parl. Papers, 1883, XXIV, 61–7.
101. B. A. Smith, *Dean Church*, 194.
102. Balfour to Sir Richard Webster, 6 Oct. 1896, copy, Benson papers (Trinity College, Cambridge), Various letters, vol. 2.
103. Enraght, *My Prosecution under the Public Worship Regulation Act*, 25–6.

Select Bibliography

This list contains only those sources found particularly helpful. It does not include mention of newspapers, periodicals, novels, or the various official and semi-official law reports.

The place of a book's publication is given only when not London.

Manuscript Sources

Beaconsfield papers, Hughenden Manor
Benson papers, Lambeth Palace and Trinity College, Cambridge
Broadlands Archives, National Register of Archives
Cross papers, British Museum
Gladstone papers, British Museum
Royal Archives, Windsor Castle
Salisbury papers, Christ Church, Oxford
Tait papers, Lambeth Palace
Wilberforce papers, Bodleian Library

Official Records

The Chronicle of Convocation, being a record of the Convocation of
    Canterbury
Church Congress Reports
Hansard's Parliamentary Debates
Parliamentary Papers
SPCK, Minutes of the General Meeting, of the Standing Committee,
and of the Christian Evidence Committee

Contemporary Works

Annual Register
Arnold, Thomas, *Principles of Church Reform*, introd. M. J. Jackson and
    J. Rogan (1962)
Ashwell, A. R., 'The State of the Church', *Quarterly Review*, CXXXVII,
    273 (July 1874), 246–82
Athanasian Creed, *Authorized Report of the Meetings in Defence of the . . .
    on January 31, 1873* (1873)
Bateman, James, *The Church Association* (1880)

Birks, T. R., *Church and State* (1869)

Burgon, J. W., *The Athanasian Creed to be Retained in its Integrity: And Why* (1872)

Bury, C. A., *The Church Association* (1873)

Carter, T. T., *Constitutional Order* (1877)

[Chambers, J. C.], *The Priest in Absolution,* part I (1866), part II (privately printed, n.d.)

Church Defence Institution, *Facts and Comments bearing on Mr. Osborne Morgan's Burials Bill* (n.d.)

—, Tracts, Circulars, etc., 2 vols. (in the British Museum)

—, *The Principles and Objects of the* (n.d.)

Church of England Laymen's Defence Association, *An Apology for the Laity* (1873)

Church, R. W., *Occasional Papers,* 2 vols. (1897)

—, *The Oxford Movement* (1891)

Cross, R. A., first viscount, *A Political History* (privately printed, 1903)

Dale, R. W., *The Day of Salvation* (1875)

Denison, G. A., *The Churches of England and Ireland One Church by Identity of Divine Trust* (1868)

—, *The Church of England in 1869* (1869)

—, *The Episcopate with Two Voices* (1874)

—, *The Synod of Canterbury and 'The Bishop of Exeter'* (1869)

—, *The Three Policies* (1871)

Enraght, R. W., *My Prosecution under the Public Worship Regulation Act* (Birmingham, 1883)

Gladstone, W. E., *The Church of England and Ritualism* (1875)

—, *Speeches of . . . in South-west Lancashire, October, 1868* (Liverpool, n.d.)

Goulburn, E. M., *The Existing Mode of Electing Bishops, and Any Alterations That May Be Made Therein Consistent with the Union of Church and State* (1870)

Grey, Albert, and Fremantle, W. H., ed., *Church Reform* (1888)

Henly, T. L., *Christianity, as Set Forth by His Grace the Archbishop of Canterbury, together with a Few Remarks on the Turkish Atrocities* (1877)

Hingeston-Randolph, F. C., *Correspondence on 'The Burials Bill' between the Lord Archbishop of Canterbury . . ., the Lord Chancellor Selborne . . ., and* (1880)

(Irish Disestablishment) *Speeches Delivered at the Great Meeting Held in St. James's Hall, on . . . May 6, 1868, in support of the United Church of England and Ireland* (1868)

Lee, A. T., *The Aid Given to the Spiritual Work of the Church by Establishment* (1872)

Lee, A. T., *Facts Respecting the Present State of the Church in Ireland* (1868)
—, *The Irish Church Bill* (n.d.)
—, *The Irish Church Question* (1868)
Maitland, Brownlow, *The Argument from Prophecy* (1877)
Massingham, J. D., *Mr. Gladstone's Irish Church Bill* (1869)
Maurice, F. D., 'The Dean of Cork and the Irish Establishment', *Contemporary Review*, VII (Apr. 1868), 586–90.
—, 'The Irish Church Establishment', *Contemporary Review*, VII (Jan. 1868), 54–65.
—, *Social Morality* (1869)
Miall, Edward, *The British Churches in Relation to the British People* (1849)
Mozley, J. B., *Lectures and Other Theological Papers* (1883)
Page, J. R., *The Question for the Electors* (1868)
Palgrave, F. T., 'A Plain View of Ritualism', *Macmillan's Magazine*, XVII, 98 (Dec. 1867), 114–22.
(Purchas judgment) *An alphabetical List of the Signatures to a Remonstrance Addressed to the Archbishops and Bishops of the Church of England on Occasion of the Report of the Judicial Committee of the Privy Council in re Hebbert v. Purchas* (1871)
Pusey House, Oxford, collection of news clippings
Roberts, G. B., *The History of the English Church Union, 1859–1894* (1895)
Rogers, W. L., *A Review of a Paper (written by the Archbishop of Canterbury in 'Good Words' May, 1875) Called 'The Fallacies of Unbelief'* (1875)
Ryle, J. C., *Yes or No! Is the Union of Church and State Worth Preserving?* (n.d.)
Shairp, J. C., *Studies in Poetry and Philosophy* (Edinburgh, 4th ed., 1886)
Skeats, H. S., and Miall, C. S., *History of the Free Churches of England 1688–1891* (1894)
Stanley, A. P., *The Athanasian Creed* (1871)
—, *Essays Chiefly on Questions of Church and State* (1870)
Tait, A. C., 'Cathedral Reform', *Edinburgh Review*, XCVII (Jan. 1853), 152–82
—, *The Church and Law* (1877)
—, *The Church of the Future* (1880)
—, pref. to *A Collection of the Judgements of the Judicial Committee of the Privy Council in Ecclesiastical Cases Relating to Doctrine and Discipline*, ed. G. C. Brodrick and W. H. Fremantle (1865)
—, *Fallacies of Unbelief* (1876)
—, 'Government Education Measures for Poor and Rich', *Edinburgh Review*, XCIX (Jan. 1854), 158–96.
—, *Harmony of Revelation and the Sciences* (Edinburgh, 1864)
—, *The Present Position of the Church of England* (3rd ed., 1873)
—, *Religious Knowledge and Religious Training* (1876)

Tait, A. C., 'Some current fallacies respecting supernatural religion', *Macmillan's Magazine*, XXXI, 182 (Dec. 1874), 89–98.

—, *Some Thoughts on the Duties of the Established Church of England as a National Church* (1876)

—, 'Thoughts suggested by Mr. Mozley's Oxford Reminisences', *Macmillan's Magazine*, XLVI, 276 (Oct. 1882), 417–23.

—, *The Work of Our National Church* (1873)

Thomson, Wm., 'The Ritual of the English Church', *Quarterly Review*, CXXXVII, 274 (Oct. 1874), 542–86.

Wordsworth, Christopher, *A Plea for Toleration by Law, in Certain Ritual Matters* (Lincoln, 1874)

Biographical Works, and Letters

Armytage, W. H. G., *A. J. Mundella, 1825–1897* (1951)

Ashwell, A. R., and Wilberforce, R. G., *Life of the Right Reverend Samue Wilberforce*, 3 vols. (1880–2)

Bell, G. K. A., *Randall Davidson, Archbishop of Canterbury* (2nd ed., 1938)

Benham, Wm., ed., *Catharine and Craufurd Tait* (1879)

Bennett, F., *The Story of W. J. E. Bennett* (1909)

Best, G. F. A., *Shaftesbury* (1964)

Blake, Robert, *Disraeli* (1966)

Blomfield, Alfred, ed., *A Memoir of Charles James Blomfield*, 2 vols. (1863)

Buckle, G. E., ed., *The Letters of Queen Victoria*, 2nd series, 3 vols. (1926, 1928)

—, 3rd series, 3 vols. (1930–2)

Butler, William John, late Dean of Lincoln, *Life and Letters of* (1897)

Cecil, Lady Gwendolen, *Life of Robert, Marquis of Salisbury*, 4 vols. (1921–32)

Church, M. C., ed., *Life and Letters of Dean Church* (1895)

Coleridge, E. H., *Life and Correspondence of John Duke Lord Coleridge, Lord Chief Justice of England*, 2 vols. (1904)

Coleridge, J. T., *A Memoir of the Rev. John Keble*, 2 vols. (2nd ed., 1869)

Collier, Richard, *The General next to God* (1965)

Dale, A. W. W., *The Life of R. W. Dale of Birmingham* (1898)

Dark, Sidney, *Seven Archbishops* (1944)

Davidson, R. T., and Benham, Wm., *Life of Archibald Campbell Tait*, 2 vols. (1891)

Denison, G. A., *Notes of my Life, 1805–78* (1878)

Denison, L. E., ed., *Fifty Years at East Brent* (1902)

Fallows, W. G., *Mandell Creighton and the English Church* (1964)
Froude, J. A., *Thomas Carlyle:* A history of his life in London 1834–1881, 2 vols. (1884)
Gardiner, A. G., *The Life of Sir William Harcourt*, 2 vols. (1923)
Garvin, J. L., and Amery, Julian, *Life of Joseph Chamberlain*, 4 vols. (1932–51)
Gathorne-Hardy, A. E., *Gathorne Hardy, first Earl of Cranbrook*, 2 vols. (1910)
Goulburn, E. M., *John William Burgon, Late Dean of Chichester*, 2 vols. (1892)
Gregory, Robert, *Robert Gregory, 1819–1911* (1912)
Hinchliff, Peter, *John William Colenso* (1964)
Hodder, Edwin, *The Life and Work of the Seventh Earl of Shaftesbury*, 3 vols. (1886)
—, *The Life of Samuel Morley* (3rd ed., 1887)
Hughes, Thomas, *James Fraser, Second Bishop of Manchester* (1887)
Hutchings, W. H., ed., *The Life and Letters of Thomas Thellusson Carter* (1903)
Johnston, J. O., *Life and Letters of Henry Parry Liddon* (1904)
Kirk-Smith, H., *William Thomson, Archbishop of York* (1958)
Kitchin, G. W., *Edward Harold Browne, D.D., Lord Bishop of Winchester* (1895)
Lake, Katharine, ed., *Memorials of William Charles Lake, Dean of Durham* (1901)
Lake, W. C., *The Power of Reality* (Durham, n.d.)
Lathbury, D. C., ed., *Correspondence on Church and Religion of William Ewart Gladstone*, 2 vols. (1910)
Liddon, H. P., *Life of Edward Bouverie Pusey*, 4 vols. (1893–7)
Loane, M. L., *John Charles Ryle, 1816–1900* (1953)
Lockhart, J. G., *Charles Lindley Viscount Halifax*, 2 vols. (1935–6)
Longford, Elizabeth, *Victoria R.I.* (1964)
Lough, A. G., *The Influence of John Mason Neale* (1962)
MacDonnell, J. C., *The Life and Correspondence of William Connor Magee*, 2 vols. (1896)
Mackarness, C. C., *Memorials of the Episcopate of J. F. Mackarness* (Oxford, 1892)
Maurice, Frederick, ed., *The Life of Frederick Denison Maurice Chiefly Told in His Own Letters*, 2 vols. (N.Y., 1884)
Miall, Arthur, *Life of Edward Miall* (1884)
Miall, C. S., *Henry Richard, M.P.* (1889)
Monypenny, W. F., and Buckle, G. E., *The Life of Benjamin Disraeli*, 6 vols. (N.Y., 1916–20)
Morley, John, *The Life of William Ewart Gladstone*, 3 vols. (1903)

Overton, J. H., and Wordsworth, Elizabeth, *Christopher Wordsworth Bishop of Lincoln, 1807–1885* (1888)

Prothero, R. E., and Bradley, G. G., *The Life and Correspondence of Arthur Penrhyn Stanley*, 2 vols. (1893)

Pugh, R. K., *The Political Life of Bishop Wilberforce* (Gladstone Memorial Exhibition essay, Jesus College, Oxford, 1955)

Reynolds, Michael, *Martyr of Ritualism* (1965)

Russell, E. F., ed., *Alexander Heriot Mackonochie:* A memoir by E. A. T[owle] (1890)

Russell, G. W. E., *Portraits of the Seventies* (1916)

Selborne, Roundell Palmer, first earl of, *Memorials*, Part II, Personal and Political, 2 vols. (1898)

Smith, B. A., *Dean Church* (1958)

Sweet, J. B., *A Memoir of the Late Henry Hoare* (1869)

Wace, Henry, 'Archbishop Tait and the Primacy', *Quarterly Review*, CLV, 309 (Jan. 1883), 1–35.

Wake, C. M., *The Biography of Archibald Campbell Tait, Archbishop of Canterbury, and Other Reminiscences*, 2 vols. (typescript in the possession of Mrs. E. H. Colville)

Zetland, Marquis of, ed., *The Letters of Disraeli to Lady Bradford and Lady Chesterfield*, 2 vols. (1929)

Other Secondary Works

Adamson, J. W., *English Education 1789–1902* (Cambridge, 1930)

Addison, W. G., *Religious Equality in Modern England 1714–1914* (1944)

Allen, W. O. B., and MacClure, Edmund, *Two Hundred Years* (1898)

Annan, N. G., *Leslie Stephen* (1951)

Arnstein, W. L., *The Bradlaugh Case* (Oxford, 1965)

Balleine, G. R., *A History of the Evangelical Party in the Church of England* (new ed., 1951)

Baring-Gould, S., *The Church Revival* (1947)

Benn, A. W., *The History of English Rationalism in the Nineteenth Century*, 2 vols. (1906)

Best, G. F. A., *Temporal Pillars* (Cambridge, 1964)

Brose, O. J., *Church and Parliament* (Stanford, 1959)

Brown, C. K. F., *The Church's Part in Education, 1833–1941* (1942)

Burgess, H. J., *Enterprise in Education* (1958)

Burn, W. L., *The Age of Equipoise* (1964)

Butler, Cuthbert, *The Vatican Council, 1869–1870* (1962)

The Canon Law of the Church of England: Being the report of the archbishops' commission on Canon Law (1947)

Select Bibliography

Chadwick, Owen, *The Founding of Cuddesdon* (Oxford, 1954)
—, *The Victorian Church*, part I (1966)
—, *Victorian Miniature* (1960)
Clark, K. M., *The Gothic Revival* (revised ed., 1950)
Clarke, W. K. L., *A History of the S.P.C.K.* (1959)
Cockshut, A. O. J., *Anglican Attitudes* (1959)
Cornish, F. W., *The English Church in the Nineteenth Century*, 2 parts (1910)
Cruickshank, Marjorie, *Church and State in English Education, 1870 to the present day* (1963)
Dicey, A. V., *Lectures on the Relation between Law and Public Opinion in England during the Nineteenth Century* (2nd ed., 1914)
The Ecclesiastical Courts, Principles of Reconstruction: Being the report of the archbishops' commission on ecclesiastical courts (1954)
Ensor, R. C. K., *England 1870–1914* (Oxford, 1936)
Feuchtwanger, E. J., 'The Conservative party under the impact of the second Reform Act', *Victorian Studies*, II, 4 (June 1959), 289–304.
Glaser, J. F., *Nonconformity and Liberalism, 1868–1885* (Ph.D. dissertation, Harvard University, 1949)
Hanham, H. J., *Elections and Party Management* (1959)
—, *The General Election of 1868* (Ph.D. dissertation 2491, University of Cambridge, 1953)
Holdsworth, Wm., *A History of English Law*, ed. A. L. Goodhart and H. G. Hanbury, 16 vols. (1964)
Hope Simpson, J. B., *Rugby since Arnold* (1967)
Inglis, K. S., *Churches and the Working Classes in Victorian England* (1963)
Irvine, Wm., *Apes, Angels and Victorians* (1956)
Jasper, R. C. D., *Prayer Book Revision in England 1800–1900* (1954)
Jones, R. Tudur, *Congregationalism in England, 1662–1962* (1962)
Jones, W. D., *Lord Derby and Victorian Conservatism* (Oxford, 1956)
Kemp, E. W., *Counsel and Consent* (1961)
Kitson Clark, G., *The Making of Victorian England* (1962)
Laski, H. J., *Studies in the Problem of Sovereignty* (New Haven, 1917)
Maccoby, S., *English Radicalism 1853–1886* (1938)
Makower, Felix, *The Constitutional History and Constitution of the Church of England* (1895)
Mason, B. J., *The Rise of Combative Dissent, 1832–1859* (M.A. thesis, University of Southampton, 1958)
Mathieson, W. L., *English Church Reform, 1815–1840* (1923)
Moule, H. C. G., *The Evangelical School in the Church of England* (1901)
Newsome, David, *The Parting of Friends* (1966)
Overton, J. H., *The Church in England*, 2 vols. (1897)

Owen, David, *English Philanthropy 1660–1960* (Cambridge, Mass., 1965)

Paul, Herbert, *A History of Modern England*, 5 vols. (1904–6)

Phillimore, Sir Robert, *The Ecclesiastical Law of the Church of England*, 2 vols. (2nd ed., 1895)

Ramsey, A. M., *F. D. Maurice and the Conflicts of Modern Theology* (Cambridge, 1951)

Reckitt, M. B., *Maurice to Temple* (1947)

Robbins, Wm., *The Ethical Idealism of Matthew Arnold* (1959)

Shannon, R. T., *Gladstone and the Bulgarian Agitation 1876* (1963)

Simon, Brian, *Studies in the History of Education, 1780–1870* (1960)

Stephen, J. F. M. D., *Gladstone and the Anglican Church in England and Ireland, 1868–74* (M.Litt. dissertation b.136, University of Cambridge, 1955)

Thompson, F. M. L., *English Landed Society in the Nineteenth Century* (1963)

Townsend, W. J., Workman, H. B., and Eayrs, Geo., ed., *A New History of Methodism*, 2 vols. (1909)

Trilling, Lionel, *Matthew Arnold* (1963)

Underwood, A. C., *A History of the English Baptists* (1947)

Vidler, A. R., *The Orb and the Cross* (1945)

—, *The Theology of F. D. Maurice* (1948)

Vincent, John, *The Formation of the Liberal Party 1857–1868* (1966)

Wagner, D. O., *The Church of England and Social Reform since 1854* (N.Y., 1930)

Ward, W. R., *Victorian Oxford* (1965)

Wickham, E. R., *Church and People in an Industrial City* (1957)

Wood, H. G., *Frederick Denison Maurice* (Cambridge, 1950)

Index